Augmenting Basic Communication in Natural Contexts

by

Jeanne M. Johnson, Ph.D.
Washington State University

Diane Baumgart, Ph.D.
University of Idaho

Edwin Helmstetter, Ph.D.
Washington State University

and

Chris A. Curry, M.S.
Center for Supportive Education, Washington

with invited contributions by Tom Weddle, M.A.

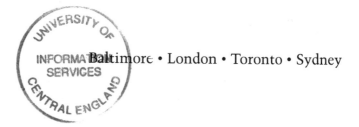

Baltimore • London • Toronto • Sydney

Paul H. Brookes Publishing Co.
Post Office Box 10624
Baltimore, Maryland 21285-0624

Typeset by PRO-IMAGE Corporation, York, Pennsylvania.
Manufactured in the United States of America by
Vail-Ballou Press, Binghamton, New York.

Most of the vignettes in this book, and all of the scenarios involving Mary and her family, tell the stories of real users of communication systems; these stories are related with the permission of the individuals or their families or guardians. Two of the vignettes are composites, reflecting the authors' varied experiences with students. Other examples of children using communication systems provided within the text are fictitious. Any similarity to actual individuals or situations is coincidental, and no implications should be inferred.

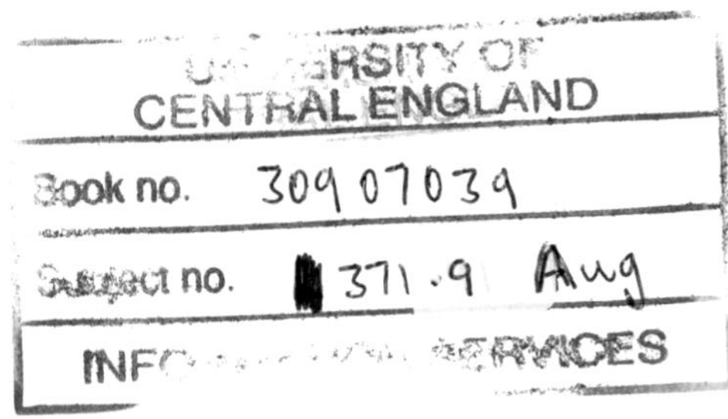

Library of Congress Cataloging-in-Publication Data

Augmenting basic communication in natural contexts / Jeanne M. Johnson
. . . [et al.].
p. cm.
Includes bibliographical references and index.
ISBN 1-55766-243-6
1. Handicapped children—Education—United States—Case studies.
2. Communication in Education—United States—Case studies.
3. Handicapped—Means of communication—United States—Case studies.
I. Johnson, Jeanne, 1951–
LC4031.A85 1996
371.91′0973—dc20 95-39457
CIP

British Library Cataloguing-in-Publication data are available from the British Library.

Contents

Foreword

The team of authors who produced the 1990 text *Augmentative and Alternative Communication Systems for Persons with Moderate and Severe Disabilities* approached the task of updating their book in a precise and thoughtful manner. This book, with its new title and additional author, reworks and adds substantially to its predecessor in a number of important ways that make it much more than a rehash of the original. For example, in the Introduction the authors describe the implications of two recent legal cases for the provision of communication services. They also introduce the challenges posed to communication service delivery by the demands of collaboration and classroom inclusion. These themes are echoed in detail later in Section IV, entitled Mentoring and Collaboration, and in Chapter 18, Lessons Learned; the authors offer a refreshingly honest discussion of the difficulties encountered when trying to implement communication systems in the real world of the general classroom.

Another major change from the original text is the increased emphasis in this book on assessment for augmentative communication. The first three chapters of this new volume replace the one assessment chapter in the previous volume, allowing the authors to provide much more detail about this important issue. In addition, a case history has been added to illustrate the assessment process and strategies as well as to provide continuity throughout Section III on implementation. This section has been expanded from two chapters to three, again allowing the authors to provide more detailed information and to address the issues of teaming and involving classroom teachers in the implementation process. The result is that the reader gains a real sense of how to approach the daunting task of AAC assessment and intervention within the realities of the school setting.

Augmentative and Alternative Communication Systems for Persons with Moderate and Severe Disabilities was distinguished by the inclusion of seven case studies about augmented communicators across the age range, which were paired with discussions of the special challenges presented by preschool-age, elementary-age, and adolescent or adult AAC users. Wisely, the authors chose to retain this feature in the sequel, although the case histories are new. An added bonus (for those of us who hate to be kept in suspense) is that Chapter 18 provides case study updates on the individuals whose stories were featured in the first book; this chapter is written in such a way that readers who missed the earlier volume will also find them useful. The authors use these revisited case histories to discuss what went wrong and what was missing in the original interventions. Readers who often wonder, "Why doesn't it ever go so smoothly when *I* try it?" will find this section straightforward and useful.

The fact is that this is a new book more than it is a revision. The similarities with the earlier version are mainly in the areas where it really counts: The authors' values about communication and people with severe disabilities remain the same. Their inclusive language, emphasis on functionality and natural contexts, and solid grounding in daily educational practice were what made their first book so relevant for teachers, speech-language pathologists, parents, and other members of AAC users' support teams. It is not surprising that, in this new volume, they continue to demonstrate their commitment to these principles. It is clear that the passage of time has been a boon to this writing partnership and has allowed the authors to hone their skills in ways that enhance their ability to both educate and inform.

Pat Mirenda, Ph.D.
CBI Consultants, Ltd.
Vancouver, British Columbia, Canada

Preface

This book is a new version of *Augmentative and Alternative Communication Systems for Persons with Moderate and Severe Disabilities* (Baumgart, Johnson, & Helmstetter, 1990). The volume's new title, *Augmenting Basic Communication in Natural Contexts,* reflects the strong trend throughout the United States toward increasing the inclusion of individuals with disabilities in general education settings and eliminating isolated, special education and pull-out therapy services models. In this new volume, we attempt to show how assessment and implementation can be conducted in natural contexts and how communication becomes more age appropriate when the communication patterns of peers are considered.

This book provides real examples from our many interactions with families, individuals, and school staff. Throughout this book, we refer to Mary and her experiences with augmentative and alternative communication to illustrate techniques, results, and insights. Presented are vignettes about nine individuals with moderate to severe disabilities in the eight chapters of Section V. Two of the vignettes were contributed by Tom Weddle (Education and Behavior Consultation for Home and School, Spokane, Washington). In Chapter 18, we candidly discuss what happened to the individuals featured in the earlier volume.

Commonly accepted terminology from the fields of special education and speech-language pathology are used throughout this book, but one term seems integral to the overall text and so is described here. *Communication system* refers to any mode or means of communicating with an individual. This may involve a behavior form the individual has in combination with a symbol system. It also may involve consistent responses from partners. The *system* can be anything the individual or partner does to transmit thoughts, needs, preferences, or opinions. *Communication system* does not necessarily refer to a device or a homemade communication notebook or board. The *system* involves all means and modalities of communicating: verbal, vocal, and gestural, as well as using external symbols or having a partner interpret behaviors in a particular way so the individual can learn to control the actions of others. We do not believe there are prerequisites to having a communication system; everyone—without exception—communicates.

In a preface, authors typically list what readers will find in each chapter of the volume and suggest that all of the chapters should be read in the order presented. In contrast, we refer readers to the Contents page to learn what the chapters discuss. This is a very personal book and the order in which the chapters are presented reflects what has worked for us, but the chapters *may* be read in a different sequence. For example, a general education teacher might want to begin with Chapter 7. A teacher whose classroom includes a student with behavior problems may first read the latter part of Chapter 1. The vignettes (Chapters 10–17) also might spark special interest and may be read first and in any sequence.

We hope that readers will gain insight into the complexity of communication as well as a strong foothold on how to begin working on communication. Do not assume that someone else knows more than you do or that you should have known something before. In the field of augmentative communication, everyone learns by struggling with first one student or individual and then others. Each individual who needs augmented forms of communication is so very different from others, and so generalizations are difficult. We want you to gain confidence in your own skills and to use common sense to guide your decisions. It is important to remember that we are all learning together.

REFERENCE

Baumgart, D., Johnson, J., & Helmstetter, E. (1990). *Augmentative and alternative communication systems for persons with moderate and severe disabilities.* Baltimore: Paul H. Brookes Publishing Co.

To
Georganna Mitchell Stanton
(1929–1995)
and her family

and

To Carolyn and Tom Maloney, parents of Mary Maloney.
They have given so much to ensure
their daughter's right to be a valued part of her family, school, and community.
Their dream for their daughter has never waivered,
and they have been an example and inspiration
to both parents and professionals.

Introduction

Everything we do with individuals who have moderate to severe disabilities is and has been significantly influenced by court cases. Court cases are not just impersonal tomes that exude dust; they are steeped in family frustrations, injustices resulting in violations of human rights, and family commitments to paving the road for others. The two cases discussed here illustrate where we have been and where we are going in the area of augmenting communication. The two legal cases were selected based on their relevance to *where* and *to whom* communication services are provided. The first case, *Timothy W. v. Rochester* (1989), reaffirms the rights of students with the most severe disabilities to a free appropriate public education (FAPE). The second case, *Oberti v. Clementon Board of Education* (1993), has set legal precedents for inclusion of students with severe disabilities and addresses the opportunities such placement has for communication. Our discussion is based in part on the work of Laski, Gran, and Boyd (1993) regarding the *Timothy W.* case and that of Martin (1993) regarding the *Oberti* case.

The *Timothy W.* case arose when, in 1980, a school district in New Hampshire refused to provide educational services to Timothy, a 13-year-old with multiple disabilities, based on its assessment that his disabilities would prevent him from receiving any benefit from those services. Eventually, the district allowed Timothy to attend a 3-hour "diagnostic/prescriptive" program each day but continued to deny him any "educational" services.

Timothy's family and professionals in the disabilities field continued to assert that Timothy was able to learn and had a right to an educational program under PL 94-142, the Education for All Handicapped Children Act of 1975; the corresponding New Hampshire state law; and Section 504 of PL 93-112, the Rehabilitation Act of 1973. In May of 1984, a complaint was filed against the school district, and in 1989 the court ruled that Timothy had been wrongly denied his right to appropriate public educational services. This decision reaffirmed the "zero student rejection" concept: School districts cannot determine eligibility criteria for services based on the severity of a student's disability or assumptions that he or she will not benefit from services. This case supports the premise of this volume—that all students are eligible for services, including services that enhance existing communication. Exclusion of students because they do not obtain certain scores on tests is in violation of their legal rights.

More than a decade after Timothy's initial exclusion, legal arguments shifted to issues of where and how education is provided. In New Jersey, 5-year-old Raphael Oberti, a student with Down syndrome, initially was to attend a school exclusively for students with disabilities located 45 minutes from his home. His family refused this placement and an alternative was agreed upon. Raphael attended a kindergarten in his neighborhood school in the morning and a special education class in the afternoon. His special needs were addressed in the afternoon class, but few individualized education program goals, curricular modifications, or supplemental supports were provided in his kindergarten.

Raphael had difficulty in the kindergarten class and was considered disruptive. At the end of the school year, school district personnel proposed that he be moved to a special education class for students with mental retardation, which would require Raphael to be bused beyond the boundaries of his local school district. His parents requested that he attend a general classroom in their neighborhood school.

In May of 1993, the U.S. Court of Appeals for the Third District unanimously affirmed a federal district court ruling that Raphael was to be provided with special education services in a general class in his local school. The court noted that PL 101-476, the Individuals with Disabilities Education Act (IDEA) of 1990, contains a presumption in favor of inclusion and outlined two reasons for this. First, the benefits and opportunities for social and communication development and enhancement cannot be achieved in a setting in which typical peers are not present. Second, students without disabilities have a right to the reciprocal benefits of inclusion, including learning to work and communicate with their peers with disabilities. Another issue discussed in the ruling was the obligation of the school district to make curricular modifications for Raphael, including supplementary aids and services to enable him to be educated in the general classroom with peers without disabilities whenever possible. Certainly, for students in need of augmentative communication this would include systems and services for interacting and communicating. The *Oberti* case reaffirms the importance of communication in the education of all children and educators' responsibility to design optimal conditions for communication enhancement.

Together, the *Timothy W.* and *Oberti* cases affirm the right to services for all students. Since that time, a plethora of guidelines, rules, and regulations have emerged in each state, thereby merging these decisions with IDEA. At the heart of the issue, however, are some fundamental beliefs or assumptions. Our assumptions related to these two cases, as well as others, are addressed in Chapter 1.

REFERENCES

Education for All Handicapped Children Act of 1975, PL 94-142. (August 23, 1977). Title 20, U.S.C. 1401 et seq: *U.S. Statutes at Large, 89,* 773–796.

Individuals with Disabilities Education Act (IDEA) of 1990, PL 101-476, (October 30, 1990). Title 20, U.S.C. 1400 et seq: *U.S. Statutes at Large, 104,* 1103–1151.

Laski, F., Gran, J., & Boyd, P. (1993, June). *Right to inclusion and services in regular classroom affirmed by federal appeals court.* Philadelphia: Public Interest Law Center.

Martin, R. (1993). In this issue: Inclusion. *Special Education Update, 3*(1), 1–8.

Rehabilitation Act of 1973, PL 93-112. (September 26, 1973). Title 29, U.S.C. 701 et seq: *U.S. Statutes at Large, 87,* 355–394.

Section I

FOUNDATIONS

In Section I, the foundations for discussion of basic communication are laid. Philosophical assumptions are discussed first. These assumptions permeate every action taken by professionals and family members in setting up and using a communication system. Next, eight factors that affect the success of communication system implementation are described. The assumptions and factors are intertwined to create not only the framework but also the foundation for successful communication systems.

CHAPTER 1

Philosophical Assumptions

People interested in studying communication have witnessed tremendous changes since the 1980s as individuals with disabilities have begun attending their neighborhood schools, learning with their peers without disabilities, and working in community jobs. These events indicate a change in attitude and a willingness to reconstruct notions of disability and how and where learning occurs. These changes also have affected the nature and type of communication systems that individuals may need. This chapter describes assumptions and factors that educators rely upon as they work with school communities and families. Seven assumptions are embedded within the chapters of this book and are critical in the design and selection of communication systems. The relevant factors also affect the success of communication and are described along with examples of their use. A list of additional sources of information is located at the back of this book.

ASSUMPTIONS CONCERNING LANGUAGE AND COMMUNICATION

People's assumptions are one of the first areas to review when selecting any assessment and teaching process. Shelia Tobias (1992) quotes Mary Douglas, a noted anthropologist, on the importance of reviewing assumptions, "We can never improve our understanding unless we examine and reformulate our assumptions" (p. 14). An integral part of professionals' everyday practice is to review and clarify what they assume. The process of reviewing assumptions should aid everyone in both clarifying his or her own "givens" and illuminating why certain strategies are advocated in the design and selection of communication systems.

Assumption #1

A dynamically interacting group of components is necessary for the communication process. Communication requires a message sender and a message receiver, both of whom have a background of experience, a means or system for sending the message, a reason for communicating, and a setting and culture in which the exchange occurs and that tempers the nature and appropriateness of the exchange. In the past, most assessments were directed toward determining the "skills" of the sender and toward the system needed to compensate for any deficits. Although the sender is necessary for the exchange, this focus is not sufficient to describe the complexity of the communication process. All of the components are necessary; one alone is not sufficient to characterize the richness of the communication act. In addition, each component must be considered in relation to the others in order to select appropriate communication systems. Assessment procedures must consider the environmental opportunities for communication; the role, functions, and skills of partners in the communication exchange; the skills of the individual with disabilities, including his or her reasons and capacities for sending and receiving messages; and the available means to do so. Throughout this book, the focus of assessment and implementation involves all components of the communication process as described here. In Chapter 3, these ideas are presented as a model to be considered.

Assumption #2

There is a reciprocal relationship between individuals with disabilities and their communication partners. The means of communication affects the receiver of the message, and the partner's response, in turn, affects the sender. The transactions that occur between partners are the products of their history together and/or understandings of and attitudes toward each other and thus are not attributable to one partner alone. Partners' characteristics are integral to assessment processes as they share the responsibility for the exchange. Individuals with disabilities rarely are observed not communicating. However, there are numerous instances in which the receiver of the intended message (the partner) does not respond. In this case, time and effort should be spent enhancing the responsiveness of partners. Typically, all that is needed for the partners to become successful in the exchange is an awareness that a certain behavior is a communication message. It is important to focus on the beliefs, attitudes, responsiveness, and flexibility of the communication partners within the assessment process in addition to the skills of the individual with a disability.

Assumption #3

A primary goal of communication interactions is building and using shared, rather than dictated, meanings. This shared understanding means that partners must use a personalized approach to determine what a person is saying or wants to say. It cannot be assumed that standard gestures and phrases have the same meaning for all people. For example, for most third-graders, "mashed potatoes" refers to a type of food they eat; but for Sara, "mashed potatoes" indicates an exciting event or situation. This meaning was explained by Sara's teacher as follows:

> A fire drill had interrupted a cooking demonstration at school. Upon returning to the classroom, the teacher realized a stove burner had been left on and the mashed potatoes were burning. Her loud and emphatic shout of "the mashed potatoes!", along with the excitement of the fire drill, evidently impressed Sara, who now shouts "mashed potatoes!" during exciting and/or disruptive events.

The meaning of this utterance cannot be found in a dictionary. It was uniquely co-constructed by Sara and her teacher. Individual sayings and meanings, such as "mashed potatoes!", are the kinds of messages that should be represented in an individual's communication book. Vocabulary listings for specific grades, functional word lists, sight word lists, or spelling lists do not reflect these shared meanings and should not be the basis for selecting communication content.

Assumption #4
All individuals are eligible for communication systems or enhancement of an existing system. Each person communicates in some fashion. It is the task of professionals to identify existing systems, enhance communication exchanges, provide additional opportunities, and/or assign intentions for learning new and practicing existing communication skills. It is inappropriate to exclude an individual for any of the following reasons: 1) exhibiting aggressive behaviors, 2) using communication signals inconsistently, 3) failing to score at predetermined levels on cognitive tests, 4) being judged incapable of independent system use, and/or 5) appearing to lack intentionality. If any of these reasons is given for exclusion, it may indicate that professionals do not have needed supports or adequate preparation.

Assumption #5
Communication systems are selected and designed by collaborative teams that include families as integral team members. Team members will sometimes disagree, but the membership must strive to work collaboratively together. Collaborative teams help to ensure the integrity of the communication system and its long-term maintenance and use. Collaboration is not a skill that most professions have implemented; it requires support and time to move from being a collection of educators and family members to becoming a functioning collaborative team. Scholtes (1988) states that "it is folly to assume that a group assigned to work at a task will simply find a way of working cooperatively" (p. 44). Most teams experience a number of stages that involve feelings of anxiety, jealousy, competition, and defensiveness before a working and cooperative team is formed. The intensity and duration of these feelings vary from team to team, and patience and understanding are required to become a collaborative team. Collaboration is discussed in Section III: Implementation.

Assumption #6
A stated outcome for the use of communication systems is a *positive change in the person's quality of life*. These personalized outcomes must be, in part, outcomes that are valued by the person, the family, and society because they reflect desired outcomes for people without disabilities. This orientation recognizes that friends and supports are valued by society and it requires that team members strive for systems that promote interdependence with a range of various partners. Communication and a person's quality of life have not been enhanced adequately when the partners consist only of personnel paid to be with the person or when the system results in its user being alone and lonely.

Assumption #7
Educational policies and services are based on the associated needs of all students and not on their differences. What has become clearer, as described by Minnow (1990), is that policies and practices that focus on providing special services to a person because of his or her differences have resulted in stigmatization that has lasting negative impact. Instead, the authors propose, based on the model of communication described in Assumption #1, the policy analysis of Minnow (1990),

and the service implications described by Baumgart and Giangreco (1996), that communication services become grounded in the *associated needs* of people to communicate with each other. Refocusing on these associated needs can assist professionals to reject the idea that the person with a disability has communication deficits and instead to highlight the need to look at people as communication partners who need services to enhance their communication with each other. Using this principle, a communication device might be provided to a student with disabilities while partners receive assistance to use and respond to this system during interactions. The associated needs perspective is a reminder that both partners need to learn to communicate with each other and that both partners, not just the one with disabilities, may need services in order for this to occur.

FACTORS TO CONSIDER

Prior to selecting communication systems, there are numerous factors that should be systematically considered. Too often, in the rush to select and design systems, critical factors are overlooked and the resulting system may actually limit, rather than enhance, communication. There are numerous examples in which the best intentions in design and selection did not produce the anticipated positive outcomes. In one instance in which sign language was selected as the system for use and expansion, school personnel actually reprimanded a junior high school student, Katie, for verbalizing "Hi" and redirected her to sign. In another example, a communication system that was quite successful was left behind when the student moved to the middle school. To avoid unforeseen limitations and delays in communication, the factors described below should be reviewed before and during the selection and design of systems. Often, their relevance becomes clearer as the system is used and evaluated.

There are at least eight factors that should be reviewed in the design and selection of communication systems. Because of the importance of these factors, each one is described and examples of their relevance to communication are given.

Factor #1: Environments

The factor relating to environments is discussed first to emphasize its importance in the communication process and because, of all the factors, it is the one most likely to be overlooked. The environment or context in which a person learns, works, recreates, and lives must offer opportunities for communication and interactions with a variety of people, including peers without disabilities. Typical routines and activities within the environment offer repeated opportunities for a person to learn to anticipate events and to respond to needs or changes within these events. Environments that offer opportunities to communicate are so germane to the communication process that this factor should be assessed prior to the other communication factors and enriched as needed to allow for maximizing communication.

The environment naturally provides a means for "generalizing" skills in the most functional manner possible. It is difficult to imagine a student with learning disabilities receiving extensive instruction in selecting and purchasing a beverage in a simulated school store who could then go to a community store and perform this activity with no difficulty and/or instructional support. Typically, students experience difficulties with generalization when people, settings, cues, materials, and contexts are different. In addition, natural environments (e.g., places used in and out of schools by chronological-age peers) offer reasons for communication and opportunities for interacting in a variety of ways that simply cannot be re-created in simulated or segregated places.

For these reasons, optimal assessment and instruction to enhance communication must occur within natural environments and routines within the person's daily schedule. Scheduling a time interval in which to "teach language, communication, or social skills" is justified only when this instruction is in addition to that already provided within naturally occurring routines and interactions with peers without disabilities. It is sometimes necessary and desirable to practice skills that are difficult to perform or to role-play interactions in order to become more proficient. These interactions, along with other instructional practices, can enhance communication but must be coordinated within a systematic instructional plan of teaching during routines embedded in natural environments.

Factor #2: Chronological Age–Appropriateness

Consideration of this factor should result in using materials and activities typical of environments for most people of the same chronological age. Thus, if 10-year-olds have access to certain places in the school and use materials specific to this age group, then the person being considered for a communication system should have these same options. The system and vocabulary selected, as well as the activities, should be consistent with those of this age group. The school library, for example, may have picturebooks of baby animals, preschool toys, transportation systems, and endangered wildlife species. It is likely that the first two types of books are checked out by children who are much younger than 10 while the others are often checked out by 10-year-olds. Thus, only the latter two are age-appropriate for a 10-year-old with disabilities. In addition, the times, activities, and areas used in the library should be consistent with those of other 10-year-olds typically in fifth- or sixth-grade classes. The mental ages of people with disabilities can and will come into consideration when deciding how to instruct (e.g., how to ensure consequences are salient), but not in the process of determining the places, objects, ages of peers, or activities in which communication and instruction will occur. Communication and the messages sent can reflect chronological age if, and only if, the curricula and related materials and goals, objectives, and settings reflect this philosophy.

Factor #3: Activities that are Functional and Purposeful

Communication systems should be designed to be used within functional and purposeful activities. The system should allow the user to have more control and input than would be possible without the system. A functional, purposeful activity is one in which, if the person with disabilities does not perform some actions, another person would be required to perform these same actions. In addition, the activity must be meaningful to the person involved or its purposefulness taught as a requisite skill.

Sometimes the function of objects or events is confused with functionality and purposefulness. For example, doors and safety signs are often considered functional objects. However, walking down a hallway and pointing to doors and signing DOOR is not a functional activity in and of itself, but opening a door or requesting assistance to open a door to go somewhere else is a functional activity. Likewise, pointing to community safety signs repeatedly on a worksheet or in a community location is not a functional activity just because these signs *might* be functional to know sometime in the future.

Within the routines of the day, choices and preferences are often determined for people with disabilities because they lack the means to state their choice or because others have become accustomed to doing this for them. Too often this results in lack of opportunities to make choices. It is critical for functional activities to be used for communication instruction and for the person to be allowed to state his or her choices, preferences, and other messages during these events.

Factor #4: Interactions

Germane to all communication and language systems is the need to have listeners and partners who respond to messages. In addition, it is critical that these interactions occur with a variety of partners, including peers without disabilities within the same chronological-age range. Limiting interactions to involve only personnel paid to care for or instruct a person or only classmates with disabilities also limits the messages and the nature and reasons for interacting. Data collected on the interactions between students and teachers reveal that the majority of messages sent by teachers are requests and commands that require little reciprocal communication. If the goal is to increase communication, then a range of interactions with a variety of partners must be included.

Factor #5: Social Significance

Although we have all witnessed changes in the attitudes toward and beliefs about people with disabilities, certain stereotypes seem to remain. Considering the social significance of the actions and the impact of communication can help to ensure that the perception of the person using a system is enhanced. Social significance plays an important role not only in the selection of referents for a system, but also in the manner in which it is transported, the assistance provided to use the system, and the interactions in which it is used. For example, compare the following two systems, both designed to enhance the communication of Talie, a teenager with visual impairments and moderate mental disabilities.

The first system was a white band of fabric about 4 inches in width that was tied around Talie's waist. Attached to the band were her communication symbols that included a school lunch ticket, a pink toy glass, a pink doll shoe, and a pink toy cassette tape player representing, respectively, a request for an additional school lunch, a beverage during break at work, a walk for her leisure time, and music. The second system was a black cloth waist purse that was attached with a Velcro adhesive closure. The miniatures were attached to cards with typed requests and consisted of a school lunch ticket, a miniature tan coffee mug, a doll-size Nike hiking shoe, and a tape cassette, representing the same requests as above. The latter system used items that enhance the social standing and savvy of the user. When using the pink toy glass to order a beverage at the breakroom cafeteria, a teacher or job coach must translate the message to the order clerk, which does little to enhance the perceived social standing of the user. It seems obvious that the second system used representations that are not only chronologically age appropriate, but also were designed to be used by the system user to interact with familiar and unfamiliar people in a way that can enhance the perceived social standing of the user.

In some cases, especially with adolescents and adults, social significance may be more consequential than cognitive ability or developmental readiness in the selection of the symbol representative and its use. Thus, in spite of the fact that an actual object may be more readily understood by an adult in requesting Rollerblades, the social significance factor would suggest that a photograph or line drawing and words might be a better choice.

Factor #6: Preferences
It is critical that communication systems reflect the unique preferences, likes, and dislikes of the user. Inevitably, adults, including teachers and parents, have vocabulary that they want included on a communication system. Usually these include a symbol for bathroom, drink, some independent leisure activity, and expressions of feelings. Although some or all of these may eventually be included, control over the system content should be afforded the person using the system. A communication system is not the same thing as a pictured or otherwise represented schedule. In addition, a communication system should not be what others want a person to say. Initial symbols should represent messages that an individual is already expressing in some way. This allows a person to "say" what is on his or her mind and what he or she is motivated to say, to learn a minimum of new skills, and to be more readily understood. The response when the message is "no" to a task is to honor the preference of the person. In each case, the partner should respond to the person as if he or she were "heard" and respected. Eventually the environment should be changed and/or a new form of behavior introduced to express the same message with the same power for communicating. For example, imagine having to communicate a best friend's feelings and thoughts for a day. It is very frustrating! Many people would just give up. Many students do give up because their messages are not heard or respected.

Another tendency is to design a schedule of what is to happen during the day and view this as a communication system. Representations of some kind can be used to communicate what is to occur next, but this should not be viewed as a communication system for the person. If people think about their own days, the ideas they want to express are most likely not represented on their calendars or in their appointment books. Again, communication is a complex interaction, and the system must take into account the complexity and preferences of the sender.

Factor #7: Requisites
The process of communicating typically involves skills in addition to those needed to send a message. For instance, pointing to a symbol may send the message, but if the symbols are contained in a notebook, a young child may need to learn to open and hold the book open. The process of communicating and interacting with others is so important that it should remain the focus of instruction. Other skills (e.g., opening and holding a book open to point to a symbol) should be taught concurrently or adaptations used so that a lack of skills does not interfere with opportunities to interact immediately and communicate. Perhaps, for this young child, one page, rather than a notebook, would be a better initial system. Skills or abilities should not be deemed prerequisites to communication and taught prior to communication or before opportunities for interacting are enhanced. It may be necessary to practice requisite skills in an instructional environment, but their performance should not be required prior to interacting with partners in a variety of natural settings. For example, a student may need assistance in holding on to her or his communication photographs. The photograph-holding and reaching skills can be practiced in the classroom, but the student should be given assistance to hold the photograph of her or his preference in the school library simultaneously as she or

he requests a large picturebook of cats from the librarian. The exact instructional procedure and associated goals and objectives for sending messages will vary considerably from person to person, but the requirement that certain skills be in the person's repertoire prior to obtaining or using a system should not differ. In addition, instruction should not detract from the interaction and communication.

Factor #8: Pluralism

For many, the assessment and selection process is directed toward finding one system and getting it in use. In reality, no one uses just one communication system. The goal should be to enhance many systems and monitor how successful this cluster of systems is in engaging others.

Although a 6-year-old may be learning to use a picture system, a smile and a hand gesture to greet others in school hallways remain highly functional and reinforcing. The picture system may work like a charm to request a picturebook of cats from the school librarian but it may become cumbersome and reduce communication at lunch. A picture system may be unnecessary, however, when pointing to the actual milk carton effectively communicates the request.

Communication systems vary for everyone as the situation and the audience vary. Students with disabilities face these same challenges and typically need to draw upon a plurality of systems for communication, not just one. For example, to request a beverage at a restaurant while out with friends, John uses a word and picture communication system that states the type and size of beverage requested along with a "no ice, please" preference. At a picnic with family members a gesture toward the juice container communicates "please, may I have some juice" and is most likely the most convenient and effective way to send the message with these familiar peers. Thus, John, like many people, has at least two forms to send requests for a drink. John can be successful in the communication interaction even though he may not be fully cognizant of the symbolic representations on his card. He has learned to use the picture and word cards to send his message. Although it is preferable to select a primary communication system and one that, one hopes, matches the cognitive abilities of the user, one system does not always meet the existing myriad of communication needs between partners. When designing and selecting communication systems, remember that large discrepancies in cognitive abilities between the sender and the audience typically require that more than one system be available.

Section II

ASSESSMENT

In Section II, the steps in establishing a communication system are presented. In Chapter 2, existing communication skills are examined briefly so that work on improving communication can begin immediately. Next, emergency issues in relation to problem behaviors are addressed. In Chapter 3, assessment of the environment is discussed in keeping with the assumption that the strengths and weaknesses in communication are synergistic, involving the individual, partners, and setting. Chapter 4 then provides a focus on skills specific to the individual who needs extensive or pervasive supports in communication.

CHAPTER 2

Getting Started

This chapter describes initial steps in the assessment process that lead to immediate results. Two key points are addressed. The first emphasizes that, because the individual already is communicating, communication partners can immediately begin to improve communication. Specifically, an immediate focus is to improve consistency within the communication system. It is not necessary to complete a full assessment before beginning.

The second key point addresses emergency issues. If the individual has problem behaviors, these behaviors need to be examined before continuing the assessment. Methods for identifying causes and antecedents to problem behaviors and ideas for making changes that subvert the behaviors are presented. In either case, communication partners should **start now**.

KEY POINT #1: COMMUNICATING NOW

Sometimes educators become so methodical and linear about the assessment process that they lose their perspective of the whole. A holistic view of communication includes two maxims:

1. All behavior has the potential to communicate.
2. Communication is ongoing from birth.

These two maxims mean that even during the assessment process, the individual will be communicating in the course of daily events in a manner that has developed over time. The individual will not wait to communicate until our assessment is "finished." Why, then, should we wait to work on improving communicative competence until all data are gathered?

In short, work on communication can begin immediately. Just as communication is ongoing, assessment is also ongoing. *Assessment data* might already have been obtained in the form of *retrospective observations*; that is, as one considers the ways in which a person typically communicates, patterns of behavior that have been observed over time can be isolated. This is more than just opinion. Opinion has to do with why people think a person is behaving a certain way. Retrospective observations are anchored in behaviors that can be described first and interpreted second. Accumulated memories of these behaviors are legitimate. Combined with the retrospective observations of a few other members of the collaborative team, common behaviors can be sorted out quickly from seldom occurring acts. A team member can also, if willing, confirm or reject his or her opinion regarding why the person is behaving in a particular way. The following question will help the collaborative team begin to work on communication: "*What is one behavior or signal that the individual is trying to use with at least one partner in at least one setting or routine?*" The individual might be using the signal in a preplanned fashion, fully aware of the effect it will have on the partner. Or, the individual might be unaware of the effect of the signal. In this case, the partner has been *assigning meaning* to the signal.

The immediate goal is *consistency*, more specifically, consistency of partners' behavior. The existing partner may need to increase consistency or other partners may need to learn to "read" this signal and respond consistently.

It may be surprising to suggest that team members should *not* focus on the quality of the individual's signal as a first step. As addressed in Chapter 1, communication occurs in a social context. If a partner is not consistent in *identifying* and *responding to* a signal, the individual will become confused and may change, decrease, stop, or escalate use of the signal, as can happen with problem behaviors (see Key Point #2). Inconsistency in identifying and responding to a signal leads to confusion for everyone. Focusing on partner consistency empowers the individual who has disabilities with considerable success and facilitates changing the attitudes of partners such that they think of this individual as a *legitimate* communicator.

Goal of Consistency

To reach the goal of consistency, partners should be able to identify and discriminate use of the signal. Partners have difficulty responding consistently when the signal is subtle, very fast or very slow, inconsistent in its form, and/or infrequent, as is often the case with the signals of people with disabilities.

The best way to capture the signal in its usual context is to videotape the interaction in which it is used successfully. If a video camera is not available, pairs of team members should do live observations together. The following sequence is suggested:

- View the videotape or conduct live observations with team members.
- Have the partner in the videotape identify the signal for the team. If the observation is live, team members can watch the partner interacting with the individual for cues that a signal has just occurred.
- Discuss the interpretation or assigned meaning of the signal given, the setting or routine, and the partner.
- Discuss the way the partner responded to reflect this interpretation and how consistent was the response. If the first partner is consistent, designate another partner to respond in the same way. If the first partner is not consistent, use videotapes and modeling to demonstrate consistency.
- Teach the second partner to identify the signal on the tape and in actual daily situations.

- Help the second partner respond consistently by videotaping and/or discussing each interaction.
- Designate other partners and follow the same procedures.

As an example of these points and others addressed throughout this book, the experiences of Mary, a child with disabilities, are presented. A photograph of Mary is shown below. Three of this book's four authors have worked with Mary's family for 5 years. Her family has granted permission for their successes and frustrations to be shared in the hope that others will benefit. This first scenario describes how Mary's family and school staff were able to work together using a videotape that the family had made prior to Mary's enrollment in school.

Mary

Mary was a 5-year-old with communication behaviors that were difficult to interpret. She was enrolled in kindergarten and received support from a special educator. While the collaborative team at her school was trying to assess and "set up" her program, it was clear she needed immediate attention. She was described as "disruptive" in the classroom. Because Mary did not speak, the teacher and aides had difficultly interpreting her signals.

Fortunately, the family had a videotape of Mary in two home contexts: mealtime and play. Mary's mother and father were very concerned about communication development and establishing an emotional basis for interactions. They felt a videotape might be the best way for the school staff to develop a positive perspective on Mary's abilities so that this affective relationship could be established. They also believed that the etiology of Mary's condition, Rett syndrome, might mislead the school staff to underestimate her abilities.

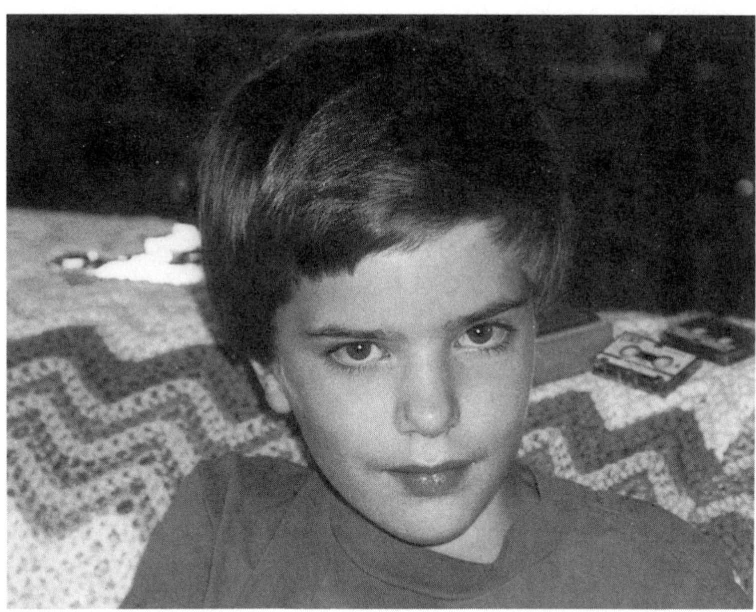

The family brought the videotape to a meeting at school. On the videotape, Mary's signals were not as clear to school staff members as were partners' responses to her signals. The consistent interpretation of requests and protests or rejections by Mary's mother clearly met Mary's needs, as evidenced by Mary's acceptance of the desired item or cessation of the signal. Mary's mother narrated the videotape, pointing out signals, interpreting meanings, and relating communication attempts to Mary's feelings.

By the end of the videotape, most of the school staff could at least identify Mary's signal for rejection (turning her head away or fussing) and her mother's response (removing the item). The staff members immediately decided to honor this signal whenever possible in Mary's current routine and asked for a copy of the videotape to use for training new partners.

Once teams start working on communication consistency, the need for more information will drive remaining assessment efforts, as detailed in Chapters 3 and 4. The time taken to further assess communication will be better spent because teams will have acknowledged some of what is already known and will be able to customize assessment. There may be unexpected benefits as well. The individual may have a wider community of partners than was originally thought, or this person may have a signal of which team members were unaware. Also, what is thought to be nonfunctional behavior actually may have meaning and purpose.

Throughout this process, it is important for teams to remain flexible in their opinions. As Konrad Lorenz said, "Any scientist worth his [sic] salt should take pleasure in discarding a favorite hypothesis before breakfast" (cited in Wolf, 1983). Before breakfast! This next scenario of Mary illustrates how the videotape provided some unexpected benefits.

Mary

An unanticipated outcome of viewing the videotape was that the staff immediately saw that Mary's mother was providing her with choices during meals, something they had not tried at school. It was decided that Mary's aide, to whom she was becoming attached, would provide at least one choice during lunch and snack times and would respond to Mary's signals in the way shown in the videotape.

It was also decided that if Mary showed fussing or turning her head away in other situations, the signal would be interpreted as a rejection. The team quickly decided in which instances the rejection signal would be honored (e.g., choice of activity) and when it would not be honored (e.g., getting on the bus to go home) but would be acknowledged (e.g., "I know you don't want to go on the bus"). This was done ***before*** *all the assessment data had been collected by team members.*

In Chapter 3, more specific guidelines are provided for beginning a detailed assessment. Forms for assessing communication behaviors and strategies for interacting with the individual during the assessment also are included. At this point, the team should at least consider one behavior in one setting with one partner to begin working on the next steps.

For teams that include an individual with behavior problems who needs immediate attention, Key Point #2 is important. If immediate attention to the problem behavior is not needed, then in-depth assessment can begin as addressed in Chapter 3.

KEY POINT #2: EMERGENCY ISSUES: DEALING WITH SERIOUS PROBLEM BEHAVIORS

Some individuals who need extensive or pervasive supports exhibit behaviors that are so problematic that resolving them takes priority over everything else. These individuals, for example, might be self-injurious, hit, bite, or be aggressive in other ways toward people or the environment (e.g., destroy teaching materials), be disruptive (e.g., have a tantrum, scream), or display unusual oral behavior (e.g., eat inedible items, regurgitate food). In the past, such behaviors were reduced by using positive reinforcement and punishment procedures. Punitive methods, including some extremely negative ones, were justified if it was believed that they would be effective. Little consideration was directed toward reasons for the behavior or the function of the behavior from the individual's perspective.

What Is Wrong with Past Approaches to Problem Behavior?

Many have expressed concern about traditional approaches to behavior problems (Guess, Turnbull, Helmstetter, & Knowlton, 1987; Helmstetter & Durand, 1991). These methods fail to improve the quality of the individual's life or to empower the person to make choices, communicate, and otherwise control his or her environment. Unless the methods are implemented systematically across time, places, and people, outcomes are sometimes short-lived and evident only with the specific people and places associated with the intervention. Also, punitive approaches sometimes produce negative side effects such as aggression, self-injury, and emotional responses (e.g., fear, crying). The following scenario involving Mary describes her problem behaviors.

Mary

Mary was very active at kindergarten. She was continually on the move, walking about the room, often picking up items from desks and shelves as she roamed. She also engaged in almost constant finger twisting and tapping or rubbing her hand against her head or hip. Mary had no formal communication system, although she appeared to touch or look at items she wanted and fussed or cried during certain activities, particularly during transitions that involved leaving the classroom. Her learning objectives included learning when to be quiet, tolerating physical assistance, using a napkin, carrying her lunch tray, assisting with dressing, cooperating during toothbrushing, toilet training, and engaging in an independent leisure activity. One of her goals for the coming year was enrollment in a general first- and second-grade–combined classroom. It was feared, however, that she would disrupt the classroom because she frequently left her seat and moved about the room. When pursued, Mary would go faster to elude the individual. Past attempts to address this included let-

ting her get up whenever she wanted, positioning the teaching assistant so as to block Mary's exit from her seat, and reinforcing her for staying in her seat. None of these approaches had been successful.

What Alternatives to Traditional Approaches Do Educators Have?
Concern over past approaches with problem behavior has resulted in a wealth of new research and practices focused on more positive, respectful, empowering, and effective practices with problem behavior. Some of these new developments are described in this chapter. For more information, see the Suggested Readings section at the back of this book.

Generally, positive approaches to behavior problems consider a broad, holistic perspective of individuals and the contexts in which they live, and these approaches attempt to interpret behavior from the individual's point of view. The remainder of this chapter is an overview of one approach to addressing problem behavior.

OVERVIEW OF THE FUNCTIONAL ANALYSIS OF PROBLEM BEHAVIOR

Generally, problem behaviors should not be treated in isolation; instead, they should be considered within the context of the individual's overall communication development. As stated previously, however, problem behaviors often overshadow other needs and must be addressed first.

Understanding problem behavior from the individual's perspective and then using this information to plan an effective intervention is extremely difficult. If children and youth are unable to discuss their behavior adequately, then educators must find other reliable ways to identify the conditions or events associated with problem behavior. Given the multitude of events occurring at any particular moment, possible influences of past events (e.g., something troubling having happened on the way to school), and the individual's physiological and psychological status, this is not an easy task. Further complicating the picture is the fact that problem behaviors may be used for many different purposes (e.g., protesting, requesting), or different behaviors might be used for the same purpose (e.g., the individual may be self-injurious, have tantrums, or engage in a repetitive movement in order to escape an activity).

The complexity of this undertaking necessitates the use of a systematic process (also referred to as a *functional analysis*) to identify the factors associated with the behavior. The process involves the following:

- Assessment of the behavior and the conditions under which it occurs
- Generation of hypotheses about why the behavior occurs
- Testing of the hypotheses

The results are then used to develop and implement an intervention. The following are descriptions of each of these steps and some of the instruments and strategies that might be used.

Assessment Strategies

Structured Interviews Structured interviews can be used with someone knowledgeable about the individual's behavior in order to learn about the behavior and the conditions in which it occurs. Interviews can be broadly based, addressing a range of topics, or focused on obtaining detailed information about a single area, such as communication. An example of a broad-based interview is provided in Appendix A (at the back of this book). It covers many of the factors considered critical to a functional analysis of problem behavior. These factors are briefly described in Table 2.1.

It is possible that a problem behavior is the result of *health problems* (see Table 2.1). Although many health factors are extremely difficult to identify, others may be identified through observation. For example, disruptive behavior associated with activities requiring visual skills may indicate vision problems. It is important to note that individuals respond differently to circumstances—one person might withdraw as a result of pain, but another person might display aggression.

It is important to consider the broader issues surrounding the overall *quality of an individual's life* and how a poor quality of life may relate to problem behaviors. It is also important to note that quality of life factors should be addressed even if they cannot be reliably associated with problem behavior because they are what undergird a quality existence for many people. Examples of ways that quality of life is being addressed include participation in inclusive school and community settings, supporting decision making by individuals with disabilities, and developing educational plans based on an individual's strengths and interests, instead of his or her limitations.

Table 2.1. Factors to consider in a functional analysis of behavior

Health

Health conditions range from diseases and syndromes associated with self-injury to responses to medication, headaches, allergies, and pain.

Quality of Life

Quality of life refers to conditions that people with and without disabilities consider basic to a fulfilling lifestyle, but that are often missing in the lives of individuals with more significant disabilities. This includes having friends of one's own choosing, making choices about daily events (e.g., what to wear or eat) and significant life decisions (e.g., where to live), and being able to pursue one's interests.

Communication

Communication is one of the most important areas to consider when examining problem behavior. All behavior should be considered communicative and the function of behavior from the individual's viewpoint should be understood. Even individuals who have an extensive vocabulary sometimes resort to problem behavior when they are unable to understand something, do not have the vocabulary to express themselves adequately, or are in an emotional situation.

Immediate Setting Events

Immediate setting events are the conditions that occur shortly before, during, or after the problem behavior. These include the physical, social, and curricular/instructional/activity contexts that are most often associated with the occurrence of the problem behavior.

Distant Setting Events

Distant setting events happened in the past but continue to affect behavior after the event ends (e.g., an argument on the way to school, a sleepless night).

Sensory Input

Some behaviors are an attempt to increase the level of arousal or block an overly stimulating environment. For example, a repetitive behavior such as twirling a string might serve to screen out excessive noise in a classroom. Conversely, an understimulated individual might seek sensory input by repeating movements that provide visual, auditory, tactile, or kinesthetic stimulation.

Communication Communication is an extremely important factor to consider in examining behavior problems. As indicated previously, problem behaviors must be regarded within the broader view of overall communication needs, instead of communication training focused only on the problem behaviors. If necessary, however, one could initially focus communication training just on problem behaviors and then expand the communication system to include responses that are not regarded as problem behaviors. The circumstances surrounding problem behaviors are often extremely powerful contexts in which to implement communication training. After all, if an individual is so motivated as to engage in self-injury or aggression, then he or she would be just as motivated to learn an alternative form of communication, as long as that new, appropriate behavior is at least as effective as the self-injury or aggression in fulfilling a communicative function (e.g., to get someone's attention). This approach—the substitution of an alternative communication form for problem behavior—has been highly successful, even with children and youth who have shown little progress after years of effort with other forms of communication training.

Immediate Setting Events Events in the immediate setting are conditions that exist in close proximity to the behavior. They include antecedent events such as a request, the setting (e.g., who is present, physical context, activities), and consequences (e.g., following the behavior a teacher offers to provide assistance to the individual). When recording setting events, factors about the immediate setting that cause the individual to respond with problem behavior should also be identified. For example, if being asked to perform particular tasks is associated with self-injury, what is it about those tasks that causes the child to engage in the problem behavior? Is the task too difficult? Is the child bored with the activity?

Distant Setting Events Sometimes, events in the more distant past affect behavior. Identifying relevant distant setting events is extremely difficult. A suggested approach is to develop a quick checklist of the relevant issues (e.g., sleep, meals, medication). The checklist is completed daily at home and sent with the individual to the school, and vice versa, so that parents and professionals can determine whether there is a relationship between these factors and behavior.

Sensory Input Some behaviors are an attempt to manipulate the amount of sensory input. The environment might be over- or understimulating, and behavior is an attempt to achieve a comfort range of stimulation. Sensory input also may be reinforcing; in which case, the individual will engage in the behavior in order to obtain the stimulation it provides. The behavior will occur regardless of what is happening in the environment.

Information about how the factors described above relate to a particular problem behavior has direct implications for intervention. In many cases, multiple interventions will be possible. For example, if it is determined that a task is too difficult for a student to do independently, then the educator might 1) teach the student how to request help with the task, or 2) alter the setting event by making the task easier (e.g., by breaking it into smaller steps). Or, if an individual becomes disruptive when the daily routine is disrupted, then interventions might consist of 1) altering the setting to be one that is highly predictable and consistent, or 2) preparing a daily picture schedule to which the student might refer in order to predict the next activity. When developing interventions, priority should be given to quality of life factors (e.g., making choices, having friends) and communication training because these approaches place the individual in control of his or her environment.

Other Methods of Assessing Problem Behavior

A contrast to the broad-based interview provided in Appendix A is the Communication Interview Checklist (Schuler, Peck, Willard, & Theimer, 1989). This checklist (Figure 2.1) is designed to gather information about communicative means, functions, and contexts. Listed along the top of the checklist are various means of communication, including both problem behaviors (e.g., aggression) and appropriate responses (e.g., nods "yes"). Listed on the left side of the checklist are common communicative functions (e.g., requests for affection/interaction) and examples of common contexts in which the function might be displayed (e.g., common routine is dropped). To complete the checklist, the interviewee should indicate the behavior(s) that might be used to express each communicative function listed. Comments can be added for clarification. For example, if one behavior precedes another in a sequence of escalating problem behavior related to a particular function, this would be noted in the comments. The checklist shows whether more than one behavior serves the same function, if one behavior serves multiple functions, and what behaviors might occur together or in a sequence (e.g., facial expressions, self-injury, vocalizations) to communicate a need.

Rating Scales The Motivation Assessment Scale (MAS) (Durand, 1990; Durand & Crimmins, 1988) is a 16-item rating scale used to assess communicative function of problem behavior. Examples of items include "Would this behavior occur continuously if your child were left alone for long periods of time?" and "Does this behavior occur when any request is made of your child?" Items are scored on a scale of 0 to 6, in which 0 represents "Never" and 6 represents "Always." The MAS items are clustered into four sets in order to obtain a score for each of the four common motivational factors for problem behavior: to obtain a tangible reinforcer, to gain attention, to escape, and to self-stimulate.

Observation An easy-to-use observation system is the *scatter plot* (Touchette, MacDonald, & Langer, 1985). It involves recording the amount of problem behavior in half-hour intervals (or whatever interval length is appropriate) throughout the day, for several days, or until a pattern emerges with regard to when the problem behavior occurs (Figure 2.2). At the end of each half hour, a recorder fills in the box for that time period, leaving it blank if no behaviors occur, placing an "X" or slash mark ("/") if one or two behaviors occur, and completely filling in the box if three or more behaviors occur. The pattern that evolves over days or weeks of recording allows one to see the time periods when problem behaviors occur most frequently. These time periods are then examined for common factors that might be associated with problem behavior (e.g., demands placed on the individual, location, people present). The scatter plot also allows one to see when problem behaviors do not occur. This might be useful when it is impossible to ascertain the factors associated with the problem behavior. In this case, the educator could, for example, modify the periods of the day when problem behaviors most frequently occur to resemble the times when they do not occur (Touchette et al., 1985). If necessary, the eliminated conditions could be reintroduced gradually into the day.

Another observational system is the *anecdotal (or narrative) recording.* While observing the individual in various situations (e.g., school settings, community, alone, with others), record a description of the behavior, the time it occurs, and the events that immediately precede it (i.e., antecedents) and follow it (i.e., consequences). The information can then be analyzed to find consistent relationships between antecedents and the problem behavior. The relationship can involve linguistic antecedents, such as a request for action (e.g., "stand up," a greeting), and

COMMUNICATION INTERVIEW

Cue questions:	Crying	Aggression	Tantrums/self-injury	Passive gaze	Proximity	Pull other's hand	Touching/moving other's face	Grabs/reaches	Enactment	Removes self/walks away	Vocalization/noise	Active gaze	Gives object	Gestures/points	Facial expression	Shakes "no"/nods "yes"	Intonation	Inappropriate echolalia	Appropriate echolalia	One-word speech	One-word signs	Complex speech	Complex signs
1. Requests for affection/interaction: **WHAT IF S WANTS**																							
Adult to sit near?																							
Peer with disability to sit near?																							
Peer without disabilities to sit near?																							
Adult to look at him or her?																							
Adult to interact with him or her?																							
Other:																							
2. Requests for adult action: **WHAT IF S WANTS**																							
Help with dressing?																							
To be read a book?																							
To play ball/a game?																							
To go outside/to store?																							
Other:																							
3. Requests for object, food, or things: **WHAT IF S WANTS**																							
An object out of reach?																							
A door/container opened?																							
A favorite food?																							
Music/radio/television?																							
Keys/toy/book?																							
Other:																							
4. Protest: **WHAT IF S**																							
Common routine is dropped?																							
Favorite toy/food taken away?																							
Taken for ride without desire?																							
Adult terminates interaction?																							
Required to do something he or she does not want to do?																							
Other:																							
5. Declaration/comment: **WHAT IF S WANTS**																							
To show you something?																							
You to look at something?																							
Other?																							

Figure 2.1. Example of a communication interview checklist; S represents person's name. (Adapted from Schuler, A.L., Peck, C.A., Willard, C., & Theimer, K. [1989]. Assessment of communicative means and functions through interview: Assessing the communicative capabilities of individuals with limited language. *Seminars in Speech and Language*, *10*(1), 54; reprinted by permission of Thieme Medical Publishers, Inc.)

SCATTER PLOT

Name: ____

Behavior description: ____

____

Code each time interval according to the number of times the behavior(s) occurred during that interval:

☐ 0 times

⧄ 1–3 times

■ more than 3 times

Date

Time																				
8:00																				
8:30																				
9:00																				
9:30																				
10:00																				
10:30																				
11:00																				
11:30																				
12:00																				
12:30																				
1:00																				
1:30																				
2:00																				
2:30																				
3:00																				
3:30																				
4:00																				
4:30																				
5:00																				

Figure 2.2. Scatter plot for identifying, in half-hour time segments, the frequency of problem behavior. (Adapted from Touchette, P.E., MacDonald, R.F., & Langer, S.N. [1985]. A scatter plot for identifying stimulus control of problem behavior. *Journal of Applied Behavior Analysis*, *18*, 344; reprinted by permission of the Society for the Experimental Analysis of Behavior.)

nonlinguistic events, such as an increase in noise level, instructional materials placed on the desk, or a change in instructor or peer group. Figure 2.3 is an abbreviated example of requests and transition times that seem to be associated with problem behavior. Information is typically collected over a minimum of several days when making an anecdotal record.

An anecdotal recording also should be analyzed for consistent behavior–consequence relationships. For example, when a student has tantrums, does the teacher frequently end the task, turn away, or provide attention? In behavioral terms, these consequences may be reinforcers that maintain or strengthen behavior. From a communication standpoint, these consequences may mean that the behavior is achieving its intended goal (i.e., serving a communicative function). In Figure 2.3, one pattern that is beginning to emerge is that attention is provided frequently as a consequence of Sara's behavior. In addition, she is sometimes provided with assistance with the activity. This latter point may indicate that she does not un-

Anecdotal Recording

Student: Sara **Teacher:** Ben **Observer:** Tammy

Date: 9/21/95 **Begin time:** 8:30 A.M. **End time:** 3:00 P.M.

Locations: Classroom, school playground, bus, store

Behavior: Biting self: bringing teeth into contact with arm or hand; hitting others: swinging arm and making contact with hand or fist

Time	Antecedent	Behavior	Consequence
8:30	On school bus, a peer companion asked her to stand.	Bit herself and hit the peer on the arm.	Peer said, "Come," and assisted her to stand and walk from the bus.
8:35	Standing in the classroom with three other students nearby, Ben asked her, "Go hang your coat."	Bit herself and hit Tom (peer).	Ben stopped her from hitting again and held her hand as they walked to the coat rack.
9:00	Ben puts away instructional materials used for practicing paying for purchases. Todd (another student) gets up and goes to the coat rack. Next activity is going shopping in the community.	Bit herself, then vocalized, "Mum, mum, mum" and hit Marsha (peer) on face.	Ben yelled, "Sara," and ran to Marsha to interrupt the hitting.
		Sara bit herself, again.	Ben turned to her and prompted her to walk to the coat rack.
10:00	At the cashier after paying for groceries at Main Street Grocery, with Ben, he told her, "Time to go."	Bumped into Ben while she bit her hand.	Ben said, "It's o.k., Sara. Let's go outside," and assisted her to walk from the store.

Figure 2.3. Sample anecdotal recording. A typical anecdotal record requires many more observations in different contexts. This abbreviated sample is for illustration purposes only.

derstand what is expected, that the activities are too difficult for her to complete independently, or that she enjoys the social contact. A drawback of anecdotal recording is that it requires continuous observation. In addition, most anecdotal recordings focus on the conditions when the problem behavior occurs, so little is learned about the conditions when the behavior is absent.

Another observational approach involves the use of a *separate index card* for each occurrence of problem behavior (Carr et. al., 1994). The date, time, general context (e.g., recess), interpersonal context (i.e., antecedents), problem behavior description, and social reaction (i.e., consequences) are recorded on each card. A panel of at least three people—two involved in the assessment of the behavior and one who regularly interacts with the individual—examines each index card in order to derive a hypothesis about the purpose of the behavior (e.g., obtain attention, escape the situation). The hypothesis is written on the back of each card. The cards are then grouped by hypothesis category (i.e., purpose). The cards within each hypothesis category are then reviewed in order to identify common themes, resulting in subgroups of cards within each category. For example, a theme within the category of gain attention might be that problem behavior occurs when the student is left to work alone and the teacher is occupied with another student. Each theme has implications for intervention using communication training. First, however, each must be validated or disproved by systematically manipulating the interpersonal contexts and social reactions associated with the behavior and monitoring whether behavior changes as a result of this manipulation. In the previous example, if the theme is validated, then the student might be taught an appropriate way to gain the teacher's attention upon completion of an independent activity, instead of exhibiting problem behavior (Carr et al., 1994). This approach provides a systematic way of organizing complex sets of data in meaningful ways.

Generating Hypotheses About Problem Behavior

Hypotheses about problem behavior should focus on three aspects: 1) the purpose of the behavior from the individual's perspective (e.g., protest), 2) the context in which the behavior occurs (e.g., when asked to change activities), and 3) what it is about the context that precipitates the behavior (e.g., it is a favorite activity, it is a result of the commotion that accompanies transition, it is the result of a lack of understanding of what is to occur next). Throughout the assessment phase, it is important to begin formulating hypotheses that take all three aspects into consideration. There are six hypotheses that frequently arise with individuals who have limited communication (Donnellan, Mirenda, Mesarsos, & Fassbender, 1984; Evans & Meyer, 1985):

1. ***Emotional response*** Problem behavior may be in response to fear, anger, frustration, pain, confusion, or excitement. For example, aggression might erupt from frustration with a difficult activity or boredom with a repetitive job. Although, technically, emotional responses may not represent a purpose or intention, they do inform us about how the individual regards the situation. As such, they provide valuable insight that supports the generation of a hypothesis about the behavior. In the previous example with Sara, in which aggression was related to task difficulty, a hypothesis might be formulated that states, "aggression occurs as soon as she encounters something she doesn't know how to do." If this hypothesis is validated in the hypothesis-testing phase (described later in this chapter), then possible interventions include 1) teaching her to use a signal

to gain assistance, 2) simplifying the activity by breaking it into smaller steps, 3) teaching the parts with which she is having difficulty, 4) altering the teaching method so that assistance is faded more slowly, 5) implementing a reinforcement program surrounding the difficult parts, and 6) eliminating activities she does not know how to do.

2. ***Self-regulation*** Some individuals may exhibit problem behavior in order to increase the level of arousal because the environment is unstimulating. Conversely, problem behavior, such as repetitive vocalization or motor responses, may be aimed at blocking out an overstimulating or stressful environment (e.g., a noisy setting). If it is hypothesized that the behavior is an attempt to screen out a noisy environment, then possible solutions include 1) teaching the individual to signal that he or she wants to leave the setting; 2) changing the noise level; 3) having the individual avoid visits to those settings; and 4) implementing a reinforcement system for remaining in the setting, perhaps beginning with small increments of time and slowly increasing the amount of time tolerated, or beginning with less noisy settings and gradually increasing the noise level that can be tolerated.
3. ***Sensory reinforcement*** Some behaviors produce input that is reinforcing. Examples of such behaviors are the sound created by spinning a coin on a hard surface or the visual stimulation resulting from flicking an object in front of a light. Possible interventions include 1) teaching the individual to request the object or activity to use during an appropriate time of the day, and 2) substituting an appropriate form of stimulation that addresses the same modality (e.g., a tape recording of similar sounds).
4. ***Social or tangible reinforcement*** The purpose of behavior may be to elicit attention or to obtain a desired object. This may be the result of insufficient access to these reinforcers. Intervention could consist of teaching a more appropriate form of requesting social or tangible reinforcement (e.g., approaching a person, vocalizing for attention, pointing or looking at the object). One also might give free access to desirable objects by placing them where the individual can always obtain them.
5. ***Self-entertainment or play*** The individual may engage in problem behavior because he or she knows no other way to play when alone or with others. An intervention might involve teaching appropriate play or social skills.
6. ***Protest or avoidance of a situation*** An individual may want to escape or avoid a situation. It might be, for example, that the individual dislikes large groups. Possible interventions include 1) teaching the individual a signal to indicate that he or she wants to leave the group; 2) making the group situation more rewarding by adding a reinforcement component; 3) using small groups; and 4) reinforcing participation in small groups, then gradually increasing the size of the group.

Mary's next scenario describes how hypotheses about her behavior were tested.

Mary

An anecdotal recording of Mary's behavior of leaving her chair suggested several possible reasons for her behavior. First, an examination of the antecedents of the behavior indicated that she sometimes left her seat when, if everyone was seated, she saw a peer stand and walk away. Sec-

ond, if she had been engaged in an activity for 2–3 minutes, she would often leave her seat, especially if a peer rather than an adult were with her. The difference in her behavior with peers versus adults may have been because adults were more sensitive to her need for change, because her history with adults led her to believe her chances of leaving were less likely to be successful, or because she preferred being pursued by peers.

An analysis of consequences pointed out that she was consistently pursued and her hand was held as she was led back to her desk. Sometimes, she appeared to enjoy the attention or what she may have perceived to be a game of chase. It did not appear to be strictly for attention, however, because she often was being provided with attention at her seat when she would get up and leave. Therefore, it may have been a way to request a social activity (i.e., chase).

Upon examining her behavior, it was found that on approximately half the occasions, she went first to a particular side of the room where there were open and accessible containers of pencils, crayons, and other materials. She would sometimes grab a handful of materials and move them to another area of the shelf. In examining when the behavior did not occur, it appeared that she was less likely to leave her seat when she had a new activity, particularly if it involved using crayons, pencils, or picturebooks, and if her peers were not frequently leaving their seats. Observation failed to identify any behavior that might be used as a signal that she was about to leave her seat, such as looking about the room or turning her body away from the activity.

As a result of the observation, it was hypothesized that one reason she left her seat was to end an activity she did not like or had been engaged in for several minutes. This seemed to be substantiated by the fact that she frequented the area where other materials were located, as if to request a different activity. A second hypothesis was that seeing another student leave his or her seat was interpreted by Mary as a signal as to what she was to do next.

Testing the Hypotheses

To test a hypothesis about problem behavior, only one condition is manipulated at a time and any changes in behavior are noted. For example, if a teacher hypothesizes that a student throws instructional materials because the activity is too difficult, then the teacher should provide assistance with the activity and observe the behavior. If the student does not throw the materials, then this increases the probability that the hypothesis is correct. To be even more certain, the teacher could switch back and forth between providing and not providing assistance, noting any differences in the behavior under the alternating conditions.

As another example, suppose it is hypothesized that a student throws the materials because he or she can attend for only 2 minutes at a time. To test the hypothesis, the time factor should be manipulated. His or her behavior should be monitored during brief (e.g., 1 minute) and increasingly lengthy (e.g., 4 minutes) sessions in the same day. Because behavior varies from day to day, it is advisable to test hypotheses on more than one day.

Intervention

The results of hypothesis testing are used to plan interventions. Some possible interventions were listed in the discussion of the generation of hypotheses. Those and other interventions generally can be grouped in the following categories:

1. ***Provide communication training.*** Perhaps the most powerful intervention is to prepare the individual to communicate in more acceptable ways, in lieu of the problem behavior. For example, the individual could be taught to use a vocalization or gesture, instead of having a tantrum, to request to leave or end an activity. During observations, behaviors should be watched that might precede the problem behavior and these precursors should be considered as the signal. For example, if the individual vocalizes and then progresses to tantrums, the staff should be trained to watch for and respond to the vocalization.

   Comprehension is an equally important form of communication training. Sometimes, behavior is a reaction to misunderstanding expectations or pending change. Consequently, communication about what is expected or what will happen next must be understandable by utilizing gestures or other symbols the individual can comprehend.
2. ***Accommodate the individual.*** Sometimes it is possible to allow the behavior to continue, but the home, work, school, or community context should be changed so that it is more supportive of the individual and his or her behavior. For example, classmates without disabilities could be taught the purposes of the behavior and how to assist the student when the behavior occurs (e.g., treat the behavior as an attention-getting signal by asking the student what he or she wants). As another example, in a work setting an employee who emits loud vocalizations could be allowed to work in a preferred noisy setting, thereby accommodating his vocalizations (e.g., commercial laundry, printing shop).
3. ***Provide equivalent input.*** If the individual gains sensory input from the behavior, an effective alternative might be to provide equivalent sensory input, but in a more appropriate manner. For auditory stimulation, this could be done by providing headphones and a tape recording of preferred sounds. For visual stimulation, a young child might be provided a kaleidoscope to use during play.
4. ***Teach missing skills.*** Missing skills can be taught by example. For example, if difficulty with physical exertion, such as ascending stairs, is associated with aggression, then skills that make the task easier can be taught, such as using the handrail and proper foot placement.
5. ***Alter the factors associated with behavior.*** For example, if self-injury is found to be related to difficulty with an activity, then the activity could be made easier by breaking it into smaller steps or by providing more assistance.
6. ***Help the individual adapt to the situation.*** For example, if an individual is unable to tolerate large groups, then he or she could begin by being exposed to small groups or being seated away from a large group. Over time, the group with which he or she works could be increased in size or he or she could be seated successively closer to a large group.
7. ***Support quality of life.*** Some individuals have less control than they like over their lives. The possibility that individuals with disabilities have preferred teachers, activities, and spaces is often overlooked, and thus decisions are made for them. Therefore, another approach to problem behavior based upon the em-

powerment or quality of life perspective is to support decision making by the person with a disability. This is also a critical issue in general, not only in problem behavior situations. Every opportunity for children and youth to make choices about such things as styles, activities, friends, and so on, should be capitalized upon. In addition, educators should maximize the extent to which they help individuals pursue their strengths and interests, support their participation in settings they prefer, and have meaningful relationships with individuals of their choosing.

ISSUES CONCERNING THE FUNCTIONAL ANALYSIS OF BEHAVIOR

Violent Behavior

In many cases of self-injury or severe aggression, it is possible to identify precursors to the behavior. Sometimes, these precursors may be a communicative signal. For example, a vocalization or lifting of the hand might be used as a signal for attention or to protest an activity. In other cases, however, self-injury or aggression erupts full blown without prior signals. Communication training is still possible in such instances. For example, a known factor that is associated with the behavior could be introduced, and then a protest signal that results in termination or removal of the event could be immediately taught.

In other cases, the behavior may be so explosive that it is unadvisable to conduct communication training at that time. If the conditions associated with the behavior are known, it may be advisable to eliminate the source of the problem. If necessary, the conditions that are eliminated can be reintroduced slowly at a later time. In other cases, the behavior may be so severe and unpredictable, with no known factors associated with it, that the only recourse is to prevent injury to the student or others.

Another issue with violent problem behaviors is that it may be unethical to conduct systematic assessment and hypothesis testing. In such situations, if a communication intervention is to be used, it must be implemented and tested "on the fly."

Total Elimination of Behavior Is Unlikely

The problem behavior may not disappear once the use of an equivalent and more appropriate form of communication has been successfully taught. In many instances, problem behaviors fulfill multiple functions (e.g., get attention, request an object) and operate in various contexts. They also may occur if newly learned communicative alternatives are not acknowledged, and they may be used for new situations that were not evident in the initial assessment.

Response Efficiency

It is critically important that a new communicative response be as efficient and effective as the problem behavior in meeting the individual's needs (Horner & Day, 1991). A new gesture, for example, must require comparable or less effort than the problem behavior and must achieve results at least as quickly as the problem behavior. Otherwise, the individual may choose to use the problem behavior instead of the new form of communication. This means that communication partners must be vigilant in attending to communication attempts using the new behavior, because if attempts are missed, the individual may return to using the problem behavior.

Abuse of Communication

A frequently expressed concern by those involved in teaching a communicative response in lieu of problem behavior is that the individual will abuse this new ability. For example, he or she might request objects or activities at inappropriate times or request to terminate an instructional activity that is important to development. It is, indeed, critical especially in the early stages of teaching the new communicative response that partners respond to all communicative attempts. After the new communicative response is established, individuals usually do *not* abuse their power by "over requesting." If this should occur, an effective response has been to acknowledge the request through words, pictures, or gestures and then to indicate that it cannot be provided at this time but will be honored later. Sometimes it is necessary to indicate what else must be done before the request can be granted. For example, a sequence of objects or pictures might show what remains to be completed. It may be necessary to increase gradually the amount of an activity that must be completed before the request is honored. In planning the initial communication training, an important consideration is whether the request in a particular situation can be fulfilled. If teachers are unable to respond to communicative behavior in certain contexts, then it may be better that these situations are not used for initial training.

The last scenario in this chapter involving Mary relates what happened after the hypotheses were formed and describes the resulting intervention plans.

Mary

It was hypothesized that Mary left her seat 1) as a signal to end the current activity, and 2) because she interpreted another student's behavior of leaving his or her seat as a signal that she should leave hers. The second hypothesis was dropped because further observation indicated inconsistency and that her behavior in earlier observations was coincidental to the behavior of other students. To test the first hypothesis, her teacher sat with her for 20 minutes, not blocking her exit from her seat, and engaged her in activities that changed every 2 minutes. Later the same morning, the teacher did exactly the same thing, except she extended the time for each activity to 4 minutes. This was repeated the next morning. On both days, Mary left her seat more frequently during the 4-minute activities (five times in 20 minutes) than during the 2-minute activities (once per 20-minute period). It also was observed that activities involving manipulation of materials (e.g., playing with pencils or crayons, pushing buttons on a hand-held game, turning book pages) seemed to be preferred and held her interest for slightly longer periods of time.

The results suggested several possible interventions for addressing Mary's out-of-seat behavior. First, a program could be implemented for increasing the amount of time she engaged in an activity. For example, she could be reinforced for engaging in an activity for 2 minutes. After she consistently did this with several activities for 2–3 days, the time would be increased, whereby she would need to engage in an activity for 3 minutes in order to be reinforced. Second, she could be taught a signal to indicate that she wanted to end an activity. Third, she could be taught to signal when she wanted to leave her seat. Fourth, she could be taught to choose activities in which she wanted to engage.

It was decided to use the second and fourth options above. She would be taught a signal (e.g., pushing objects away) to protest an activity or the continuation of an activity. She would return the materials to a shelf, where she would then be taught to choose a second activity. Part of this routine involved assisting her to carry her own materials between her desk and the shelves. At the same time, it met her need to walk. Future plans involved finding groups of activities from which she could choose that were related to what the rest of the students were doing so that her day matched those of her peers to the maximum extent possible. Furthermore, there were times of the day (e.g., during center activities) during which it was appropriate to stand or walk. Emphasis for Mary during these periods would be activities that did not involve so much seat time.

SUMMARY

This chapter addressed two key points. The first point is that communication training can begin immediately; there is no need to wait for a full communication assessment. Instead, a behavior the individual already uses should be selected and the team should determine what the individual is attempting to communicate or assign a meaning to the behavior. Communication partners should be taught to respond consistently to the behavior. Outcomes should be evaluated and this information incorporated into the ongoing assessment process. The second key point this chapter featured was how to address behavior problems. The chapter described a functional analysis process that utilized a variety of assessment strategies in order to determine the potential causes of the problem behavior and the function the behavior fulfilled for the individual. Hypotheses about the causes and functions of the problem behavior were tested, and the results were used to plan interventions.

CHAPTER 3

Assessing the Communication Environment

After the initial steps toward facilitating existing communication have been taken, it is time to reflect in detail on the process of assessment. The question to be addressed is why communication partners are concerned about the individual's communication. Common reasons for wanting to augment communication are that the individual

- Is hard to interpret
- Does not initiate
- Does not have any system for communicating
- Does not seem motivated to communicate
- Has a "system" but does not use it
- Uses inappropriate communication signals
- Seems to have more to say than what she or he is able to communicate presently
- Seems to understand considerably more than she or he can communicate

Each of these common reasons for wanting to augment communication involves only the individual. What about the *partners and environments* with whom or in which this person is trying to communicate? Chapter 1 emphasized the crucial role of the environment in framing the individual's communicative competence. To help envision the ways in which partners and environments affect the quality of communication, the Sociocommunicative Filter Model is discussed next.

SOCIOCOMMUNICATIVE FILTER MODEL

The Sociocommunicative Filter Model (Johnson, 1995) shown in Figure 3.1 illustrates only the basics of the complex event known as communication. The entire event is embedded in the norms of the majority culture and the norms of the culture for the setting (e.g., expected behavior in classrooms), and it is influenced by the immediate context. The *filter* in the center of the model represents the convergence and transaction between the partner and the individual during communicative interaction. Each person brings particular clusters of skills and shared experience to the social moment in which the communication occurs. The resulting quality of communication, however, is not simply additive. These same two people can have very different qualities of interaction even when the identifiable factors are maintained.

The filter represents the influences of the moment, mainly background conditions. They include, but are not limited to, the immediate setting, visual or auditory distractions, the time of day, and the presence of others, as well as the maxims governing conversation; all of these conditions temper the raw contributions of the partner and the individual. The "quality" of communication is what emerges through the filter. It is about this that opinions about the success or failure of the interaction are formed (Nelson, 1992).

The components of the model related to the partner and environment are shown in the top section of the model, which is noted as the *Partner's Domain*. The individual components in the Partner's Domain are embedded in the partner's *community norms, cultural values, individual personality,* and the following:

- **Training** refers to present and past efforts that influence the partner's attitudes, improve the partner's skills, and facilitate the partner's role in team collaboration.
- **Team Collaboration** is the style of collaboration in which this partner is involved, the partner's role on the team, the successes and difficulties encountered in collaboration, and the attitude toward collaboration.
- **Attitude Toward the Individual** refers to the partner's perspective as to whether the individual is communicating, whether the individual can learn to communicate better in the future, and the partner's belief that working on communication is a worthwhile endeavor.
- **Daily Scheduled Interactions** are those predictable events in which this partner interacts with the individual.
- **Partner Interaction Style** refers to the skill with which the partner interacts with the individual and demonstrates consistency, directiveness, responsiveness, and opportunity provision.

WHY NOT USE THE USUAL METHODS OF ASSESSMENT?

It may seem unusual to look at the partner and the environment as the first step in assessment. Many professionals have been trained to assess skills by inspecting the individual's abilities one by one and then formulating conclusions about competence in a particular skill domain. Unfortunately, the results of such an approach to assessment may be misleading because they lack context. For example, a team of educators decides to assess the *teaching competence* of a fourth-grade teacher, Susan. To do so, the team examines Susan's clarity of speech, hearing acuity, knowl-

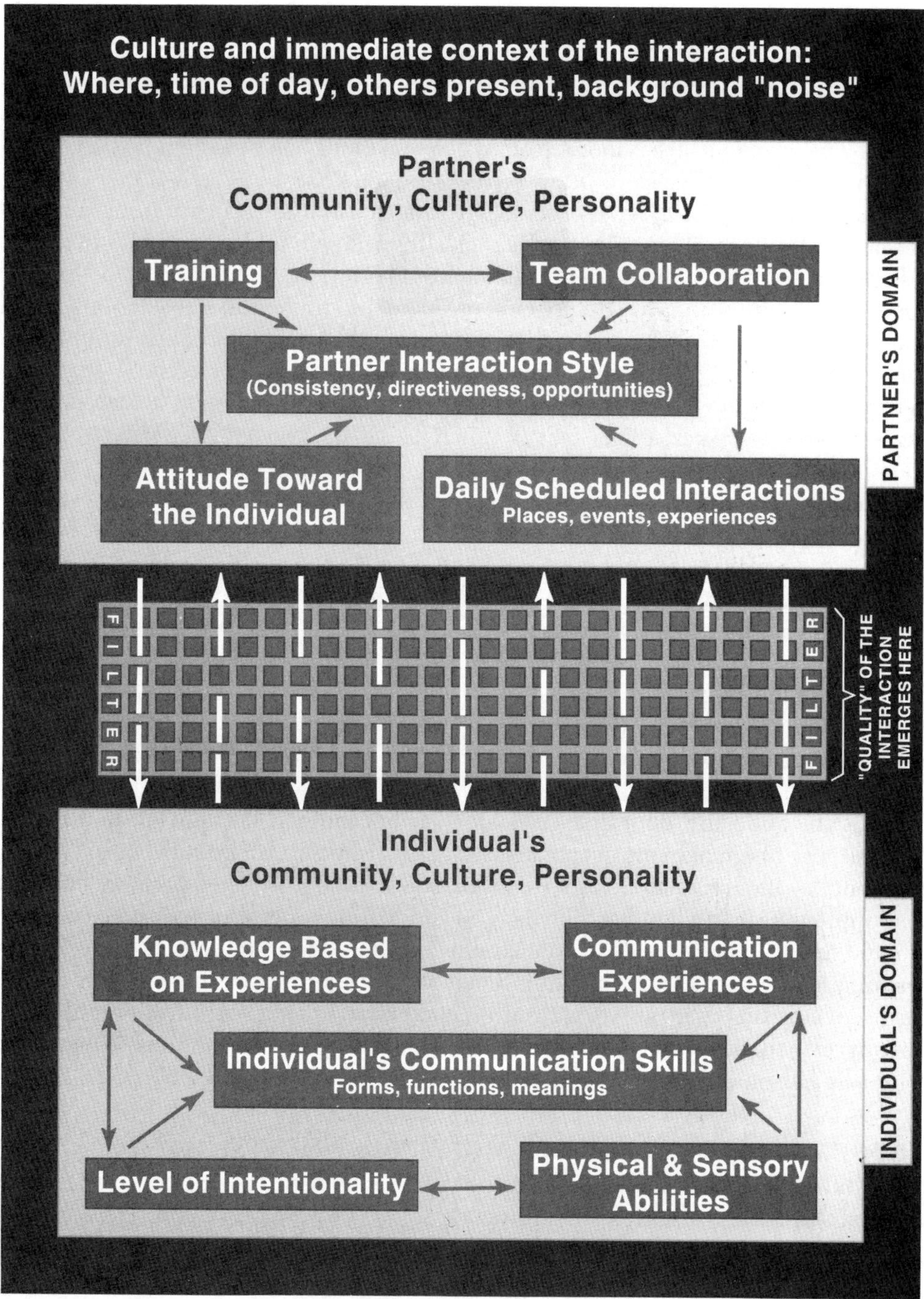

Figure 3.1. The Sociocommunicative Filter Model. (From Johnson, J. [1995]. *The sociocommunicative filter model*. Unpublished manuscript; reprinted by permission.)

edge of key subjects taught in fourth grade, and ability to use a computer. At the end of the assessment process, the team still has no answer as to whether Susan is a competent teacher. In fact, Susan may have serious limitations in one or more of these areas and still be considered a competent, even skilled, teacher in the context of a busy classroom filled with students. How can that be? Such a bottom-up approach to assessment lacks acknowledgment of the synergistic effect of the whole event. The same is even more true when assessing such a complex event as communication.

Many eduators also have been taught that the route to determining an individual's overall competence is to have a meeting wherein all the trained professionals contribute their findings about their particular specialty. This method has proven to be woefully inadequate, as evidenced by the numerous "revelations" each team member has when he or she discovers an ability of which others, in other settings, were aware. The isolated interactions of one partner may mislead that partner to make limited assumptions about the individual. Assessment driven only by expertise-related observations leaves much to be desired when trying to assess something as synergistic as an individual's communicative competence.

Communication is, by definition, a process embedded in context or environment. In fact, in order to interpret the meaning of communication, the context must be known. *Context* refers to where a person is, what the person is doing, to whom that person is talking, how he or she said something, what his or her partners just said, what that person assumes the partner knows, and what the partner assumes that person knows. Bloom (1970) noted that when a child says, for example, "Daddy ball," many interpretations are possible depending on the context. The child might mean "Daddy, help me get the ball" or "That's Daddy's ball" or "Daddy hit the ball." The context determines the interpretation of meaning of these simple utterances. The same is true for augmented communication. For example, if Mary touches the cupboard door and then looks at her mother, it could mean, "I want cookies" or "Mom, help me get cookies" or "This is where we keep cookies." Again, the context, including the shared background of Mary and her partner, helps to determine the meaning of her signals. The context for communication must be considered first. If these aspects of context are considered in relation to the reasons for wanting to augment communication listed at the beginning of this chapter, it may be discovered that there are opportunities and barriers to successful communication already embedded in the environment that affected not only the last interaction with this person but that will affect the very next interaction as well.

STEPS TO ASSESSING PARTNERS AND ENVIRONMENTS

Inspecting the environment for communication opportunities and barriers is, then, the first step. The process is as follows:

1. Assess peer participation patterns.
2. Assess the individual's daily routines.
3. Combine data from schedules (and determine opportunities and barriers).
4. Determine roles of partners in the assessment.
5. Assess interactional styles of partners.
6. Assess partner interactions through self-rating.

Checklists for these steps are provided in Appendix B at the back of this book.

Assessing Peer Participation Patterns

To frame an age-appropriate image of communicative competence, the patterns of peers participating in daily events should be examined as part of the culture of the classroom and the immediate context. This examination is particularly helpful with individuals older than 4 years of age whose developmental levels are much lower than their chronological age because it sharpens the focus on those types of communication that are needed for increased social acceptance by peers. In the Sociocommunicative Filter Model, this examination corresponds to *Daily Scheduled Interactions* as shown in Figure 3.2:

- Observe the activities and events within schedules of peers who are in the same setting (Mirenda & Iacono, 1990).
- Ask the following questions:

  1. In what ways do the peers participate in these daily events?
     - Do they initiate the activity?
     - Do they have responsibilities for certain aspects of the activity?
     - Do they work individually or cooperatively?
  2. What types of communication do the peers use during this activity?
     - Do they give instructions?
     - Do they ask for information, assistance, or particular items?
     - Do they have choices?
     - Do they refuse to participate?

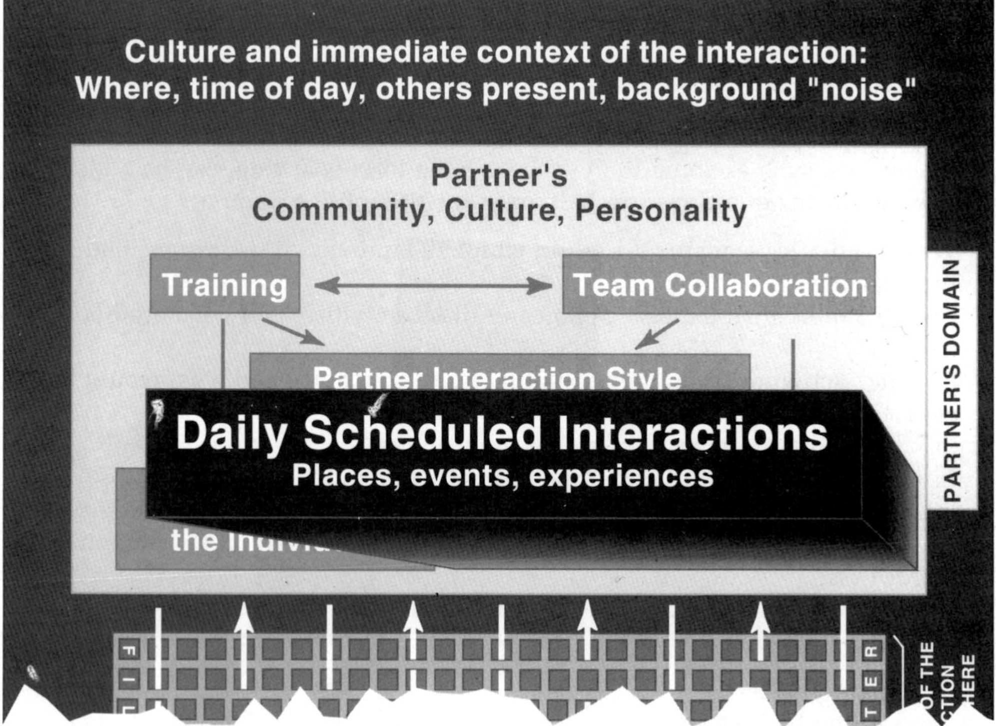

Figure 3.2. Daily scheduled interactions as related to the Sociocommunicative Filter Model. (From Johnson, J. [1995]. *The sociocommunicative filter model*. Unpublished manuscript; reprinted by permission.)

- Do they express their pleasure or displeasure with the activity? (See Appendix B at the back of this book for blank checklist.)

The individual who needs extensive or pervasive supports in the area of communication should be able to participate in similar ways using similar types of communication as much as possible. As described in Chapter 4, this list of peer participation patterns can be used to assess an individual's skills directly.

Assessing the Individual's Daily Routines
To determine further existing social environments that are part of the target individual's routine (see Figure 3.2), communication partners should be asked for a typical outline of what happens when they are with this person. A composite schedule that reflects all of these activities could be made. For example, in Figure 3.3, Mary's daily schedule across major settings and partners is listed. This schedule is expanded, as shown in Figure 3.4, by having less frequent partners, such as the speech-language pathologist or physical therapist, add their schedules. These schedules were a window to Mary's meanings, preferences, expectations, and experiences. They helped to interpret her behavior and determine signals and vocabulary for her communication system.

When schedules are compared, it becomes evident that some activities are repeated in more than one setting with more than one partner; for example, Mary participated in eating and toileting/grooming activities at home, in child care, and at school. The exact sequence of events or the routine within these most common activities can then be detailed by the partner involved. As shown in Figure 3.5 and Figure 3.6, for Mary, the sequence of toileting and washing up was quite different among settings. This lack of consistency may have confused Mary and made her seem disruptive.

At a later date, descriptions of events (e.g., weekend, monthly, and yearly events) that occur less frequently; activities with people who visit occasionally; and special events, such as going to the zoo or going for a boat ride, can be added.

The following questions can help examine these life schedules:

- Which activities seem to go well (in which the individual is involved and showing enjoyment)?
- Does the individual express a choice in these activities, and what are his or her choices?
- In which activities could the individual express a choice and what would be the choices?
- In which activities is the individual independent?
- In which other activities could the individual be independent?
- Is there a rationale for the sequence of behaviors within a specific activity?
- Are there certain activities or settings in which the individual communicates more? Less?
- Are there certain partners with whom the individual communicates more? Less? (See Appendix B at the back of this book for a form useful in addressing these questions.)

Answers to these questions provide not only insight into the individual's perspective, but they also serve as a foundation from which the individual's skills can be examined.

Time	Home	School	Child care
7:00	Wake up, do toileting, wash up, dress, wash up		
7:30	Have breakfast, wash up, get ready for bus		
8:00	Get on bus		
8:30		Arrive, go to classroom, take coat off, have free time	
8:45		Go to morning circle	
9:00		Go to workstation #1	
9:40		Wash up, have snack	
10:00		Do toileting, have recess	
10:20		Return to room, take coat off, go to workstation #2	
10:50		Clean up, choose free time activity	
11:00		Do free time activity	
11:30		Have lunch in lunchroom	
12:00		Go to recess	
12:20		Return to room, take coat off, speech-language pathologist consults	
1:00		Go to workstation #3	
1:30		Clean up, do toileting, go to recess	
1:50		Return to room, take coat off, go to workstation #4	
2:20		Choose free time activity	
2:50		Get ready for bus	
3:00		Get on bus	
3:15			Arrive, take coat off, choose play activities
5:00			Get ready for pick-up, put coat on
5:30	Arrive home, take coat off, have free time		
6:30	Wash up, have dinner		
7:00	Watch television, clean room		
7:30	Groom, dress for bed		
7:45	Read story, go to sleep		

Figure 3.3. A typical weekday schedule for Mary.

Combining Data from Schedules

Insight is achieved when information from peer schedules and the individual's schedules are combined. The following are some examples of what is learned. (See Appendix B at the back of this book.)

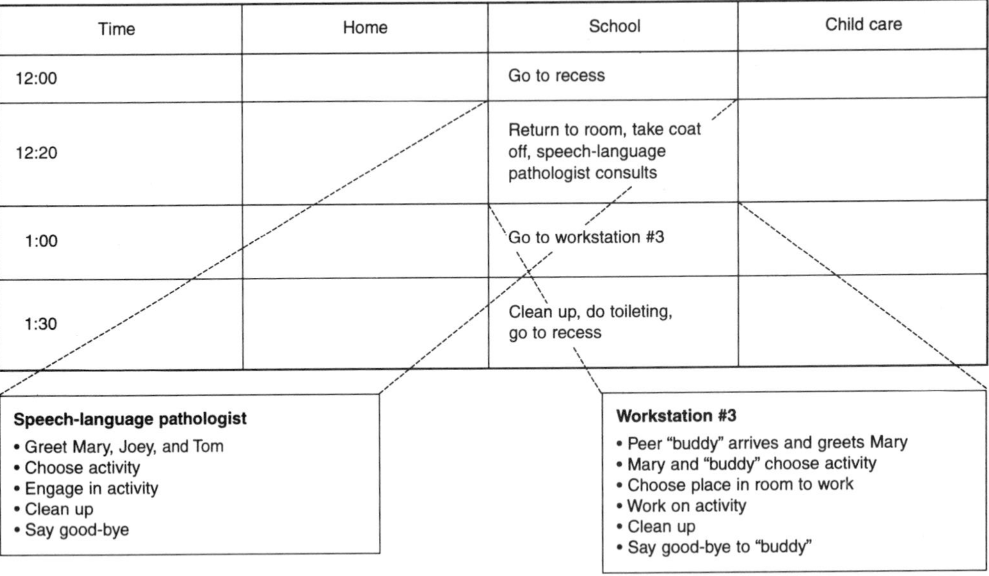

Time
Home
School
Child care
12:00
Go to recess
12:20
Return to room, take coat off, speech-language pathologist consults
1:00
Go to workstation #3
1:30
Clean up, do toileting, go to recess
Speech-language pathologist
• Greet Mary, Joey, and Tom
• Choose activity
• Engage in activity
• Clean up
• Say good-bye
Workstation #3
• Peer "buddy" arrives and greets Mary
• Mary and "buddy" choose activity
• Choose place in room to work
• Work on activity
• Clean up
• Say good-bye to "buddy"

Figure 3.4. Mary's daily schedule, featuring major settings and partners.

- Experiences that are common to this person's life
- Possible meanings conveyed based on these experiences: Meanings include names of things, people, animals, places, and events that the person might want to request or tell about
- The person's preferences for certain activities or people

Activity	Home	School	Child care
Toileting	Shows Mary bathroom picture and says, "Mary, time to potty." Takes Mary's hand and leads her to bathroom. Lets Mary touch toilet paper to turn her around for seating. Pulls down Mary's pants and seats her. When done, lets Mary tear off toilet paper, wipes, pulls Mary to stand. Pulls up Mary's pants.	Says, "Mary, let's go to the bathroom now." Takes Mary's hand and leads or carries her to the bathroom. Prevents Mary from getting into the toilet paper or handtowels while pulling down Mary's pants. Turns Mary around to seat her and helps her sit. When done, wipes, pulls Mary to stand.	Takes Mary's hand and leads her to the bathroom. Lets Mary play with the toilet paper so she won't cry. Pulls down Mary's pants and turns her to sit, then seats her. When done, wipes, and pulls Mary to stand.

Figure 3.5. Specific sequences within a common activity (toileting), from adult's perspective.

Activity	Home	School	Child care
Washing up	Gives Mary a washcloth and says, "Time to wash up." Walks with Mary to bathroom. Lets Mary hold washcloth under warm water. Puts soap on washcloth. Assists Mary in washing face and hands. Lets Mary hold washcloth under warm water. Helps Mary squeeze out and hang up washcloth.	Says, "Time to wash up." Leads Mary by the hand to the classroom sink. Holds Mary's hands under the water and helps her rub the soap. Rinses Mary's hands. Dispenses paper towel and helps Mary dry hands.	

Figure 3.6. Specific sequences within a common activity (washing up), from adult's perspective.

- Specific similarities or differences between this person's daily experiences and those of peers
- Times when opportunities for communicating already exist in this person's daily schedule
- Ways in which communication is inhibited, including:
  - Inconsistency in adult behavior across settings for the same routine
  - Inconsistency in the attitudes of particular partners toward this person (which is discussed further in Section III)
  - Anticipation of all the person's needs
  - Availability of all needed materials
  - Selection of activities that require no communication

To keep the assessment process manageable, two time intervals should be selected from the schedules on which the rest of the partner and environmental assessment will be focused. Two time intervals should be selected: one in which all is going well and one in which things are going poorly. As the next areas of environmental assessment are explored, hypotheses can be formed about why there is such a difference between successes and failures in these two time intervals. Here is what happened with Mary:

Mary

After all of the schedules were compared, the family and school staff decided to examine in more detail Mary's toileting and grooming routines because these were problem areas. The team discovered that Mary was expected to follow a different sequence in each setting. They wondered if this might be the reason Mary objected so strongly to walking into the bathroom. In other words, the team of partners discovered a possible barrier to communication—inconsistency in what was expected.

Schedules: Opportunities Versus Barriers Mirenda and Iacono's (1990) flow chart (Figure 3.7), will help determine the communication opportunities and barriers that exist for the individual. One way to think about opportunities and barriers is to ask whether the individual is seen as a *legitimate communicator* by all partners in all settings. The following are some sample questions to consider:

- Do partners have a preconceived notion of the person's competence even if the individual signals clearly?
- Do partners believe this individual needs to be taken care of or do they believe the person should be able to control what happens to him or her?
- Would the partners be willing to honor a choice that, although allowable, is not what they see as the best choice?
- Do partners see their role as one in which they must follow exact schedules and routines regardless of the individual's desires?
- Can partners be comfortable with the unpredictability and loss of control that comes with allowing choices?

As noted in Figure 3.1 at the beginning of this chapter, attitudes toward and knowledge about individuals who require extensive or pervasive supports in meeting daily living needs may seriously impair any efforts to set up productive communication systems. As Vygotsky (Newman & Holzman, 1993) views communication, the individual's ability to communicate successfully depends on the willingness of the partner to be responsive and flexible enough to allow for the building of "shared meaning" rather than dictated meaning. A give-and-take system is implied wherein the child or individual has as much control over the interaction as does the more competent communication partner. *If the teacher, aide, parent, or specialist believes the individual is not able to communicate, the system will break down.*

Determining Roles of Partners in the Assessment

Once the examination of schedules is accomplished, the partners should determine what role they want to play in the rest of the assessment. This is a good way to establish initial roles and responsibilities (e.g., receiver of information, observer of behavior, informant [regarding background facts], describer of daily life, interpreter of behaviors, validator of opinions, active participant in assessment process, and/or evaluator [Crais, 1993]) for *Team Collaboration*, as seen in Figure 3.8. These roles require varying degrees of assertiveness. Each communication partner who takes part in educational programming should be able to choose which of these roles he or she would like to take initially and then an effort should be made to keep these decisions flexible. By selecting their own roles, partners are afforded the opportunity to participate without coercion and to make positive contributions to the collaboration process.

The next scenario involving Mary illustrates how a mismatch in expectations regarding roles caused difficulties in collaboration.

Mary

Mary's parents initially came to the school to be informants, describers, and interpreters of Mary's behavior. The school staff were uncomfortable with the parents assuming, in particular, the role of interpreters. Although it was not discussed specifically, it was clear that the staff believed interpretation of Mary's behavior belonged to the trained

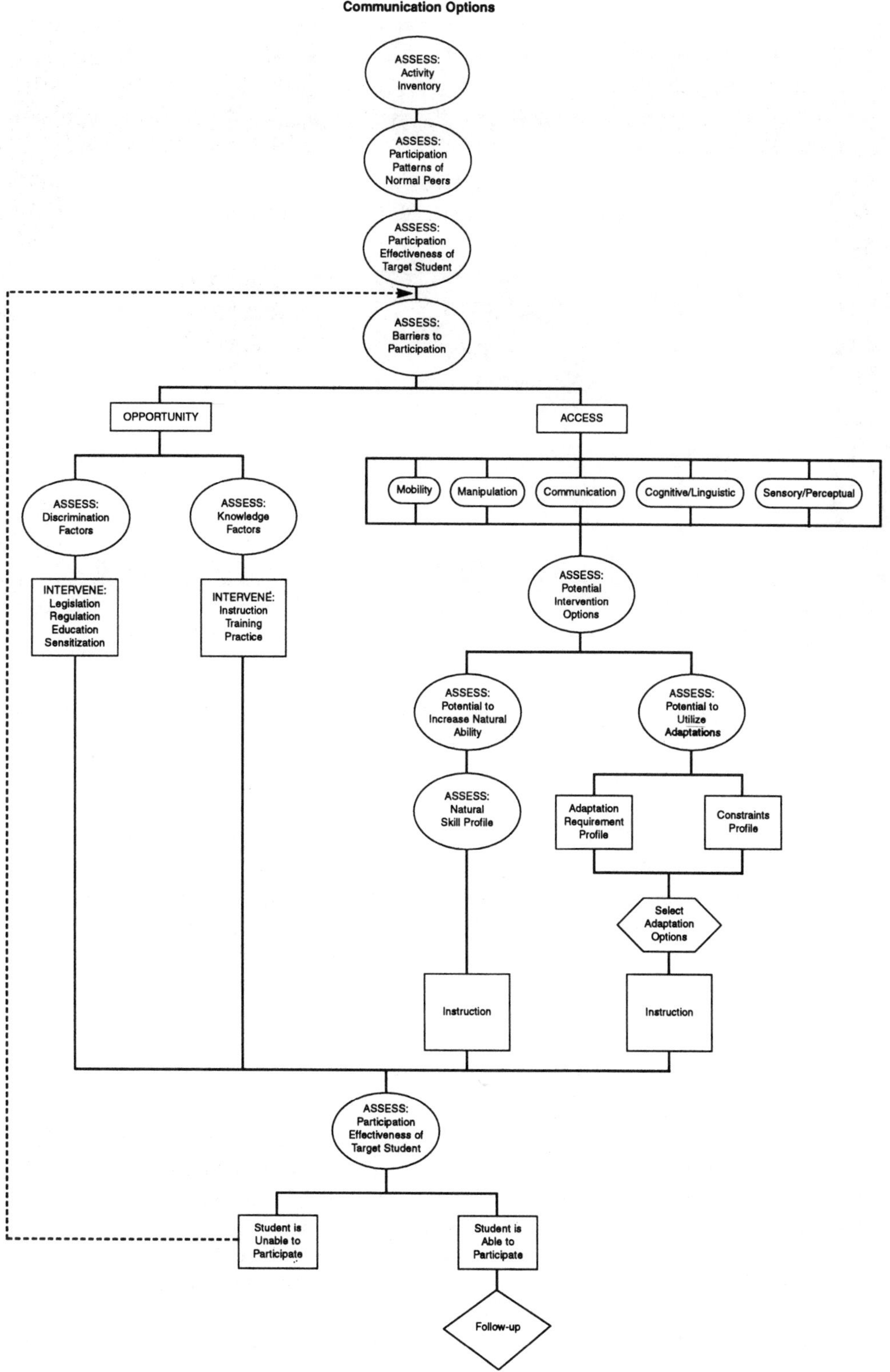

Figure 3.7. Flow chart illustrating communication options. (From Mirenda, P., & Iacono, T. [1990]. Communication options for persons with severe and profound disabilities: State of the art and future directions. *Journal of The Association for Persons with Severe Handicaps, 15*[1], 17; reprinted by permission.)

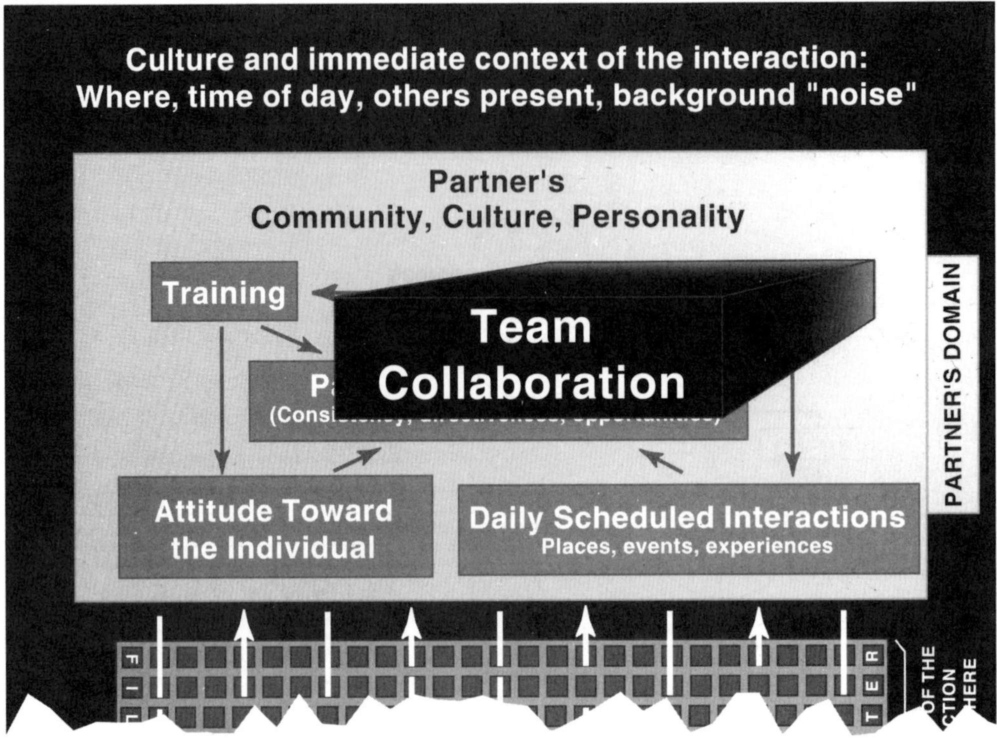

Figure 3.8. Team collaboration as related to the Sociocommunicative Filter Model. (From Johnson, J. [1995]. *The sociocommunicative filter.* Unpublished manuscript; reprinted by permission.)

professionals. This caused much initial friction between the family and the school staff.

After two outside consultants validated the parents' interpretations and demonstrated to the school staff that these parents were exceedingly well informed about the interaction of communication and affective development, the teachers, aides, administrators, and support services staff felt more at ease about listening to the parents' concerns for Mary's educational program. If the whole team had decided initially to allow any and all partners to choose their role in the assessment, these stressful weeks and lingering hard feelings might have been avoided.

Assessing Interactional Styles of Partners

The determination of roles is particularly important to the next step, which is to examine the interactional styles of different partners with this person (see Figure 3.9). A partner's interactional style reflects her or his attitude toward the individual as well as the perception of "what we are supposed to do" when we "teach/work with" individuals who have disabilities with extensive communication needs. This is often based on the type of training this person has had as well as on past experiences with individuals who have multiple disabilities.

Directive Versus Nondirective Styles Much research has focused on the effect of directive, adult-led, or "teaching" styles of interaction versus those of nondirective, child-led, or "nurturing" styles (Duchan, 1983; Mahoney & Powell, 1988; Mir-

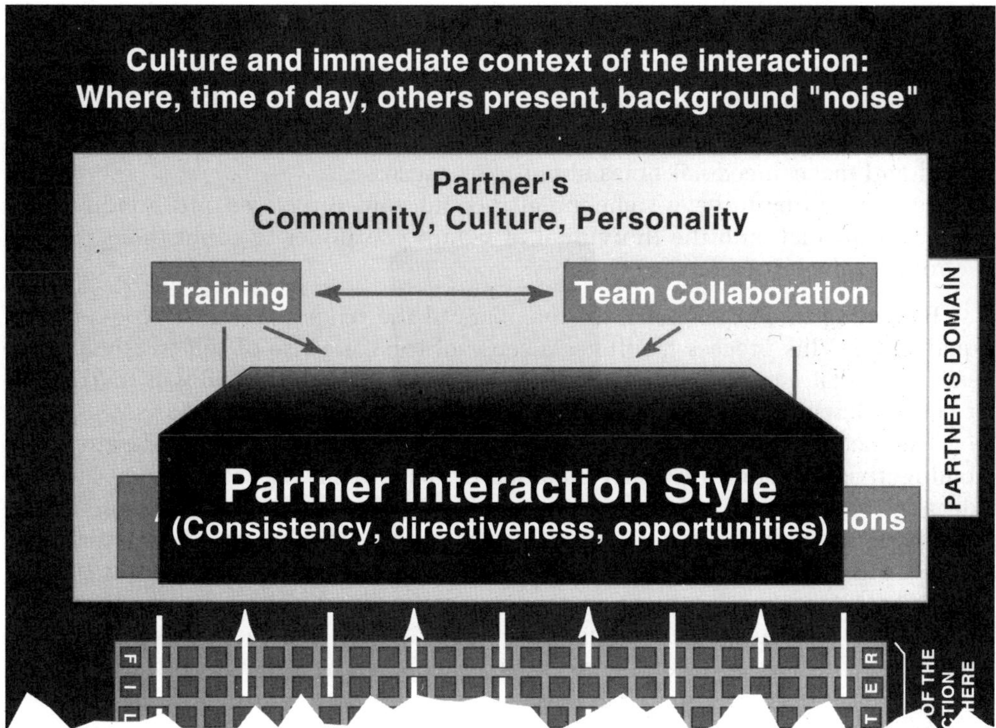

Figure 3.9. Partner interaction style as related to the Sociocommunicative Filter Model. (From Johnson, J. [1995]. *The sociocommunicative filter*. Unpublished manuscript; reprinted by permission.)

enda & Donnellan, 1986; Norris & Hoffman, 1990a). *Directive styles* include more questions, directives (i.e., commands), and imperatives (i.e., demands) from the adult and result in less communication from the child. Directive styles of interaction have been found to be negatively correlated with the rate of language growth (Prizant & Rentschler, 1983). *Nondirective styles* tip the balance toward the student. In nondirective interactions, the adult allows the child to establish the topic of conversation and follows the child's lead in the direction of the topic (Owens, 1995). Adult behaviors such as repeating what the child says or does and expanding slightly the child's utterance are viewed as being nondirective. Both styles can be used effectively in particular situations; however, if communication augmentation is a goal, educators or parents should load the environment with numerous nondirective interactions. This will maximize the opportunities for the individual to initiate and respond legitimately. To do so, educators or parents must examine their own interactional styles and consider the effect they have on the individual's communication.

If members of the team have indicated that they wish to participate in the assessment in any role other than that of a receiver of information, then these questions (see Appendix B at the back of this book) can be asked:

- On what days and at what times do you interact with this individual?
- Are you willing to spend time observing others as they work with the individual?
- Are you willing to make anecdotal, descriptive notes about the successes you observed?

- Are you willing to learn to count directive and nondirective adult behaviors by watching a training videotape and using the definitions in Figure 3.10?
- Are you willing to count directives and nondirectives in one time period of the day when someone else is interacting with the individual?
- Are you willing to have someone else observe you interacting with the individual and make anecdotal notes about your successes?
- Are you willing to have someone else count your directives and nondirectives as you interact with the individual or would you prefer to count them yourself from a videotape?

By asking these questions, all members of the team start to build a sense of equal status. This process facilitates a sense of trust, a sense of self-worth, and the realization that communication involves all the partners. Decisions to participate or not participate should be honored and should remain open to change.

The methods of collecting data and anecdotal notes and counting directive and nondirective behaviors are easily obtained by team members with varying levels of education. Learning to count directives and nondirectives can be accomplished by making a videotape of five 10-minute segments in which five adult–child pairs interact during varying activities. A core group of team members observes the first segment together, pausing the videotape to discuss directive and nondirective adult behaviors as they occur, as defined in Figure 3.6. On the second segment, team members count directives and nondirectives together, again pausing the videotape

Each communication act is tallied on a score sheet according to the following categories:

Directive Communication Act: Adult utterances (sentences), gestures, or other communication acts that serve to introduce a new topic or extend the adult's own topic when the child is focused on (attending to or talking about) something else.

Nondirective Communication Act: Adult gestures and utterances that extend the child's focus of attention or topic. Children indicate their focus of attention by vocalizing while playing with toys or looking at the adult; looking at an object, event, or person; or talking/signing about something. Children extend topics by elaborating and adding new information through gestures, vocalizations, talking, or signing.

Behavioral Regulation Act: Adult acts that are directed toward controlling the child's misbehavior. These may be combined with directive communication acts or examined separately.

Example:
Adult: (Touches ball behind child) "Hey, what's this?" (Directive)
Child: (Touches ball)
Adult: "Yeah, ball." (Nondirective [because child has joined in topic])
Child: (Picks up ball, examines it)
Adult: (Picks up beanbag, shakes it near child's ear) (Directive)
Child: (Ignores adult, picks up toy telephone)
Adult (Picks up second toy telephone) "Hello?" (Nondirective)

The following chart can be expanded for recording:

	Directives	Nondirectives
Gestures	|||| |	|||| |||| ||
Vocal or verbal	|||| |	|||

Figure 3.10. Scoring guidelines: Directive versus nondirective adult communication. (From Johnson, J. [1989]. *A nonintrusive intervention technique for mother–child interactions*. Paper presented at the annual convention of the American Speech-Language-Hearing Association. St. Louis, MO; reprinted by permission.)

for discussion. For the final three segments, team members count directives and nondirectives independently and compare scores at the end of each segment. An agreement level of 90% is desirable and allows for some subjectivity, which is inherent in this type of observation. Then, team members are ready to count behaviors during live observations. Because a "key" will have been established by the core group, the videotape can be used to train new data takers. School psychologists, speech-language pathologists, occupational therapists, and physical therapists will find this method invaluable to their particular specialty interest because they will be able to interpret behaviors ecologically rather than in a context stripped of meaning. Parents, general education teachers, special education teachers, and educational assistants or aides will, in turn, find that their observations strengthen the sense of how partners are influencing the resulting view of the quality of interaction as described in the Sociocommunicative Filter Model.

Other Qualities of Style After the team has determined who the willing communication partners are, assessing their interactions with the individual is a starting point and a focus for the team. The following questions can be asked (see Appendix B at the back of this book):

- Do the partners create the "need" to communicate? In other words, do they wait for the individual to signal? They should provide an example.
- Do the partners set up situations they know will elicit a signal from the individual?
- What is the consistency of response of these partners across settings and routines?
- In what way is this person's "skill" related to consistency? Is more training needed?

If everything the individual needs and wants is available, he or she will not need to signal. If partners automatically interpret the individual's needs based on the time of day or the setting without waiting for the individual to signal, they may be preempting (Halle, 1985) the individual and keeping him or her from signaling. The partner's style influences whether the individual is seen as an active initiator or as a passive responder (Fey, 1986; Norris & Hoffman, 1990b).

Assessing Partner Interactions Through Self-Rating

Another method for examining styles of interaction is to have partners rate themselves on various behaviors (Johnson, 1989); such a rating scale is shown in Figure 3.11. Rating scales have been used in the fields of teaching and psychology to promote self-analysis of particular behaviors (Armstrong & Firth, 1984; Bandura, 1971). The research indicates that people can identify and change their behavior without outside intervention.

Johnson (1989) and Johnson and Harrison (1991) used the scale in Figure 3.11 to see if parents would change to a more nondirective interactional style after viewing a videotape of a play interaction with their child and completing the self-rating. It was found that parents who were highly directive prior to self-rating significantly decreased the number of directives and increased nondirectives immediately following this procedure. In a series of follow-up studies, Giraud-Birney (1991), Marshall (1991), and McLam (1991) found that parents and student speech-language pathologists had learned and maintained a nondirective style of interaction after three sessions in which this "play, watch videotape and self-rate, play again" pro-

SELF-RATING SCALE
FOR YOUNG CHILDREN

Overall, how good are you at talking and playing with this child?

Not very						Very
1	2	3	4	5	6	7

How interested were you in what the child was doing?

Not very						Very
1	2	3	4	5	6	7

How interested was the child in what you were doing?

Not very						Very
1	2	3	4	5	6	7

How often did you communicate with the child?

Not very						Very
1	2	3	4	5	6	7

How often did the child communicate to you?

Not very						Very
1	2	3	4	5	6	7

How often did you talk about the toys or materials?

Not very						Very
1	2	3	4	5	6	7

How often did the child talk about the toys or materials?

Not very						Very
1	2	3	4	5	6	7

How often did you talk about what you or the child was doing?

Not very						Very
1	2	3	4	5	6	7

How often did the child talk about what either of you was doing?

Not very						Very
1	2	3	4	5	6	7

How much did you enjoy playing with the child?

Not very						Very
1	2	3	4	5	6	7

How much did the child enjoy playing with you?

Not very						Very
1	2	3	4	5	6	7

How often did you tell the child what to do?

Not very						Very
1	2	3	4	5	6	7

How often did the child tell you what to do?

Not very						Very
1	2	3	4	5	6	7

Figure 3.11. Self-Rating Scale for Young Children. (From Johnson, J. [1989, November]. *A nonintrusive intervention technique for mother–child interactions.* Paper presented at the annual convention of the American Speech-Language-Hearing Association. St. Louis, MO; reprinted by permission.)

cedure was used; that is, at the beginning of the third session, the parent or clinician used about the same number of nondirectives as he or she had at the end of the second session and maintained this level through at least three more sessions. In all studies, when the number of parent or clinician directives decreased, the number of child communication acts increased. Assessing this area, then, facilitates a self-monitoring process in the search for barriers to communication.

SUMMARY

The process of examining partners and the environment can become quite detailed. The checklists in Appendix B at the back of this book might make this process clearer. Specific steps in examining peer participation patterns, the individual's daily routines, opportunities and barriers, the roles partners want to play in the assessment, and their interactional styles have been outlined. It should be evident whether or not a day for a child with disabilities closely resembles that of peers. After all the partners have reflected on their contribution to both opportunities for and barriers to communication, more opportunities can be added while barriers are removed. Furthermore, these steps in assessment can be used in planning more inclusive communication activities.

It is important to begin with only **two** time intervals. If this is too time consuming, the number can be reduced to one time interval. A complete analysis of even one time interval and the partners involved will afford a wealth of information from which a more efficient system of augmented communication for the individual can be arranged.

CHAPTER 4

Examining the Individual's Skills and Needs

After the individual's schedule, barriers to communication, and partner interaction styles have been learned, the next step is to examine more closely the individual's communication signals in the context of daily routines. Another look at the Sociocommunicative Filter Model, first presented in Chapter 3 and again shown in part in Figure 4.1, may sharpen the focus. This chapter discusses how to assess aspects of the *Individual's Domain*.

THE SOCIOCOMMUNICATIVE FILTER MODEL: THE INDIVIDUAL'S DOMAIN

Just as the partner is influenced by community, culture, and personality, so too is the individual. The individual brings to each interaction his or her own unique combination of these background factors that, again, are embedded in the larger culture and the immediate context of the interaction. Sometimes, the individual's culture has different expectations about what is considered appropriate communication behavior. An individual must not be penalized for showing behavior that is appropriate in his or her home culture (e.g., gaze aversion with adults). Learning about the individual's home culture is necessary for all team members. The immediate context of the interaction includes *where* the individual is communicating, *the time of day* or portion of the individual's daily routine, *others present*—including both familiar and unfamiliar partners, and *background "noise"* such as

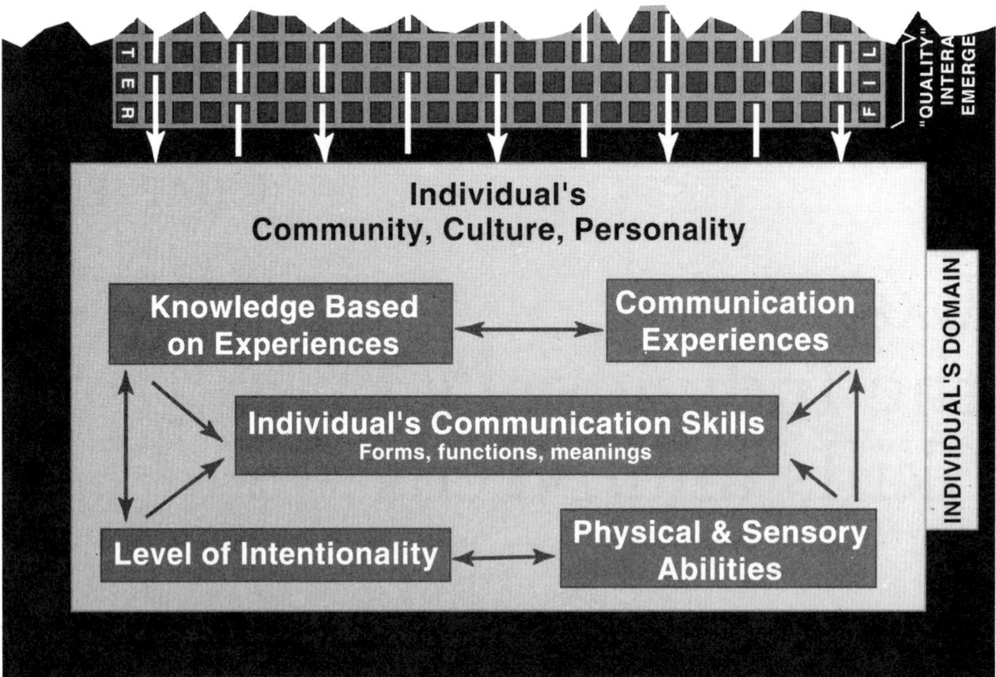

Figure 4.1. The Individual's Domain. (From Johnson, J. [1995]. *The sociocommunicative filter model.* Pullman, WA: unpublished manuscript; reprinted by permission.)

visual or auditory distractions. The following are aspects of the Individual's Domain:

- **Knowledge Based on Experiences** refers to the individual's content for communication. This is reflected, at very young ages, in sensorimotor skills such as object permanence, means–ends skills, and imitation. As the individual gets older, categorical knowledge and vocabulary can be examined.
- **Communication Experiences** refers to the number and quality of experiences the individual has had that relate specifically to communication, including watching others use communication for specific purposes, imitating, being taught to use a specific signal, experimenting with signals, and having successes and disappointments when communicating.
- **Level of Intentionality** refers to the individual's level of awareness that his or her communication signals can have an effect on others. Bates's (1976) paradigm, which describes development of the awareness that one's behaviors have an effect on others, has been expanded by Wetherby and Prizant (1989). They suggest that children progress through the following stages:

  Has no goal awareness →
  Has awareness of goal →
  Formulates simple plan to achieve goal →
  Coordinates a more complex plan to achieve a goal →
  Uses alternative plans to achieve a goal if original attempt was unsuccessful →
  Can preplan strategies to achieve goal and can mentally reflect on successes and failures

Individuals with multiple disabilities may fit anywhere on this continuum. If the individual is in the first or second stage, it would not be expected that he or she would be able to fully use a computerized communication device with speech synthesis to express needs.

- **Physical and Sensory Abilities** refer to an individual's physical and mental health, fine and gross motor skills, hearing, vision, touch, taste, and smell. These abilities obviously affect the modalities available for communication input and output.
- **Individual's Communication Skills** refers to communication forms, their functions, and the meanings they express. These skills are influenced by all of the other components of the model. These skills are the focus of specific assessment efforts.

ASSESSMENT OBJECTIVES

The objectives of analyzing the individual's domain are to determine his or her ability to do the following:

- Comprehend spoken language, signs, and gestures
- Comprehend other symbols or representations of items common to daily activities
- Speak, sign, or gesture intelligibly
- Use aided symbols (Fuller, Lloyd, & Schlosser, 1992), such as pictures and objects
- Combine signals in different modalities (e.g., vocalization plus gesture)
- Chain together individual units of meaning to create larger units of meaning
- Achieve communicative goals, such as requesting, giving information, and protesting or rejecting
- Initiate, extend, and terminate conversations
- "Repair" misunderstandings in conversation

Techniques

To meet the objectives listed above, three nonstandardized assessment techniques are used: direct observation, interview (or "retrospective observation"), and elicitation.

Direct Observation Direct observation can be done in many ways. One common technique is to take *anecdotal notes* on particular interactions whenever there is a free moment. These notes become a diary of the individual's communication successes and failures. This type of recording can be used as an addition to other specific kinds of behavioral observations. An example of anecdotal recording involving Mary follows:

Mary

Mary's diary is kept on the educational assistant's desk. Whenever anyone notices something new or something that did or did not work well, a notation is made in the diary. An excerpt from Mary's diary is as follows:

(date) I was getting Mary's snack ready and I forgot to put her placemat on the table before I set the table. Mary looked at me, walked to the cupboard where the placemats are kept, and reached for the handle on the cupboard door. She

stopped and looked at me again. It took me a minute, but I figured out what she was telling me—she wanted her placemat. She seemed excited that I understood.

A slightly more structured approach delineates the types of observations that need to be made. With all the responsibilities people have, it is sometimes difficult to maintain a focus on the communication behaviors of interest. A checklist or observation guide facilitates the ability to focus. Structured approaches to observation include 1) taking data while watching, otherwise known as *"on-line" recording*; 2) using *time-sampled observations*, in which behaviors and contexts are recorded at noted times; and 3) using *videotapes* for endless analysis ranging from holistic views to minute-by-minute behavioral documentation.

The following are two caveats to the observational process:

1. Never assume that a behavior is nonfunctional because it appears to be repetitive, injurious, or different. What is assumed to be "self-stimulation," for example, may, in fact, be a powerful communication signal to control the actions of others.
2. Consider *all* the individual's behaviors. Everything from a startle, a change in breathing rhythm, or a fleeting gaze on an object to grabbing an object, mouthing it, and saying "eee" can be considered communicative.

For individuals with multiple disabilities, the most challenging assignment might be finding an identifiable behavior that is voluntary, rather than reflexive. "Voluntary" means that the person has some level of control over the movement; however, voluntary movements do not have to be purposeful. Identifying a voluntary movement, purposeful or not, is key to establishing and expanding a communication system. The individual's physical therapist or occupational therapist can tell whether a behavior is an abnormal reflex. A reflex is an "automatic, stereotyped, involuntary response to a specific environmental stimulus" (Bailey & Wolery, 1989, p. 311). Abnormal reflexes occur in individuals with neurological damage and can involve a delay in emergence, persistence of the reflex past the developmental period in which it usually occurs, and hyper- or hypotonicity. The physical therapist and occupational therapist can clarify what partners are seeing, what physical positions cause the reflex, and how to work with the individual to avoid the reflex.

In each of the following sections, ideas are presented about how to characterize communication behaviors in various domains using checklists or charts so that the assessment questions presented at the beginning of this chapter can be answered.

Interview (or "Retrospective Observation") As mentioned in Chapter 2, communication partners should feel confident that recording their observations over time is a valid means of raising hypotheses about communication behaviors. Interviewing is a means by which familiar partners can express their accumulated retrospective observations. As mentioned previously, retrospective observations should be recorded by noting behaviors thought to be communicative and the circumstances in which they usually occur. This is in contrast to direct observation, in which a partner records behaviors as they occur. Team members may disagree about the meaning of the behaviors; however, the recollection of the behavior itself should be considered valid.

Elicitation Eliciting communication behaviors to clarify abilities may be necessary in certain contexts. In the course of a typical day, communication behaviors may not occur frequently or the schedule may not allow for variation in the types of communication behaviors and functions that are used; such limitations may prevent the partner from getting a complete picture of the individual's skills.

A method commonly used to elicit communication behavior is that of *communication temptations* (Wetherby, Cain, Yonclas, & Walker, 1988; Wetherby & Prizant, 1989). A communication temptation, as the name suggests, "tempts" the individual to express him- or herself; a partner may, for example, do something unexpected, such as interrupt a familiar routine, not have needed items readily available, or act in a way the individual does not expect his or her partner to act. Such temptations are used in the context of familiar or easily learned routines. A routine can be anything from singing a favorite song to proceeding sequentially through the steps of grooming.

Communication temptations have a basic structure that is similar and repetitive. The general sequence is as follows:

- Start the routine. If the routine is unfamiliar, demonstrate the whole routine and then start it again.
- Insert the temptation (e.g., pause and look expectantly at the individual, make a needed item inaccessible, pretend to misunderstand).
- Wait for a signal from the individual.
- Prompt with general cues (e.g., "Hmm?" "What?" "What's wrong?") if, after a reasonable period of time, the individual does not respond.
- Prompt with more specific cues (e.g., "Want more?" "Need toothbrush?") if the individual still does not respond.
- Continue the routine regardless of whether a signal was seen.
- Repeat the sequence. If there still is no response, discontinue or finish the routine without inserting a temptation. The individual may not know the routine well enough for the "temptation" to be tempting. Present the routine later in the day or the next day. Some children need more exposure to routines before they will signal.

Examples of temptation routines include the following: For young children, partners may wind up a toy, let it run down, wind it up again, and then wait for the child to signal for "more" when the toy has stopped. If a toy has a knob that is difficult to turn, the child is even more likely to request assistance. Another example is to stop in the midst of a verbal or gestural routine and see if the individual will fill in a turn. For example, if the child is waiting for a drink, the partner may stop before pouring and hold the pitcher at a tilt, looking expectantly at the child. Another example is for the partner to put a needed or desired item in sight, but out of reach, and wait for the individual to signal before giving a cue. Table 4.1 provides other examples.

Examples of temptation routines for older students are a little more involved. For example, when an individual is assisted in drying his or her hair, the routine should be started by turning on the hair dryer, then blowing the hair and combing. The hair dryer should be stopped while the hair is still very wet and then continued when the individual signals. (See Table 4.1 for more examples.)

To avoid providing too many cues, the partner should be very aware of his or her behavior during elicitation activities. The partner should try to respond in a

Table 4.1. Ideas for communication temptations

Set up: Routine	Set up: Materials	First Action	Second Action	Third Action	Fourth Action
Grooming	Toothbrush and preferred and nonpreferred toothpastes	Individual takes toothbrush.	Adult puts nonpreferred toothpaste on toothbrush.	Adult waits for individual to signal.	Adult says, "Oops, wrong toothpaste" and gets out preferred toothpaste.
Grooming	Toothbrush and toothpaste	Adult gives individual toothpaste while holding back, in sight, toothbrush.	Adult waits for a signal from the individual.	When adult sees signal, asks, "Hmm?" or "Oh, need toothbrush? OK."	Adult gives toothbrush to individual.
Leisure time	Tape recorder, favored cassette	Adult starts playing cassette.	After a few moments, when individual is attending to the music, adult pauses the cassette.	Adult waits for signal from individual.	When signal is recognized, adult asks, "More? OK" and resumes tape.
Free play	Wind-up toy	Adults winds up toy just a bit, sets it down, and gives it full attention.	When toy stops, adult looks surprised, looks at individual, and says, "Stop!"	Adult picks up toy again, winds it just a little, and sets it down again, giving it full attention.	When toy stops, adult looks surprised, looks at individual, says "Stop!", and waits. When individual signals, adult asks, "More? OK" and winds it up again.
Music time	None	Adult starts a favorite song with hand motions.	Immediately before a new hand motion, adult stops the song and looks expectantly at the individual.	When individual signals, adult continues the song and hand motions.	

(continued)

Table 4.1. (*continued*)

Set up: Routine	Set up: Materials	First Action	Second Action	Third Action	Fourth Action
Any time	Rocking chair	Adult holds child in lap and begins to rock saying, "Rock, rock, rock," in time with the motion of the chair.	Adult continues to say, "Rock, rock, rock, rock," and then inserts, "Stop!" as he or she stops the chair's movement.	Adult waits for a signal from the individual.	When signal is seen, adult continues to rock and talk rhythmically.
Mealtime	Empty plastic peanut butter jar with lid and a preferred, dry food item that can be broken into pieces	Adult asks, "Want cookie?" and waits for signal.	When individual signals, adult gives a piece of cookie and says, "Cookie, mmm."	When individual has finished eating, adult asks, "Want cookie?" or "Want more?"	When individual signals, adult puts next piece of cookie in the jar and screws the lid on tight. Adult gives the jar to the individual and waits for a signal.
Mealtime	Normal utensils, food, and drink items	In the midst of the meal, the individual gives the adult a cup or plate as a signal for "more."	Adult takes cup/plate, looks at it, and sets it back down in front of the individual and says, "Cup" or "Plate."	Adult waits for some signal from individual.	When individual repeats signal, adult says, "Oh! You want more" and gets more food or drink.

nondirective manner to joint attention to an object, event, or person; that is, when the individual attends to an object, the partner can expand or scaffold the individual's communication behavior by imitating the signal, commenting on what the individual is attending, or treating the signal as a request for the object. *Scaffolding* means "upping the ante" by just one step. The partner also can engage quietly in parallel activity or with occasional verbalizations regarding what the activity is. The partner also can provide choices of objects or activities if the individual's behavior is not focused. Partners should remember to avoid asking questions or giving directions. As mentioned in Chapter 3, these styles of interaction probably will yield a smaller, skewed sample of the individual's communicative abilities.

These temptations will probably elicit the following behaviors: 1) signaling for continuance of activity, 2) signaling for "more" (i.e., quantity), 3) signaling that something is wrong (e.g., broken, missing, defective), 4) signaling a need (i.e., missing materials), or 5) signaling a protest or rejection of the activity or object. In addition, a reflection of the individual's past communication experiences, knowledge for communication, intentionality, and forms of signals will be seen in a more naturalistic context.

Summary of Techniques

To recap, when examining communication, data from observations, interviews, and elicitation activities should be combined to form the basis on which to plan intervention. The result of these efforts will be a rich set of qualitative and quantitative information—much richer than what would have been obtained using standardized tests. All three sources of information are considered valid, particularly because these kinds of data are so specific to the individual.

ASSESSING COMPREHENSION AND SYMBOLIC ABILITIES

When an augmented communication system is set up, as much as possible needs to be known about the individual's knowledge base for communication. Developmental theorists (Bruner, 1975; Moll, 1990; Piaget & Inhelder, 1969; Vygotsky, 1962) generally agree that there is a developmental progression from nonsymbolic to symbolic thinking. As it relates to augmented communication, this belief suggests that it would be unproductive to expect a nonsymbolic thinker to use a complex, computerized, symbolic system of communication. Individuals who have extensive to pervasive communication support needs, however, can be taught to use a basic symbolic system in a concrete manner (Romski & Sevcik, 1988; Romski, Sevcik, & Pate, 1988); that is, an individual could be taught to give a waiter a card with food preferences listed on it even though this individual cannot read. An individual also could be taught to use four or five symbols to request preferred items in a routine activity even though he or she does not fully comprehend the meaning of the symbol. This is more of an ecological approach than a developmental one: The individual is performing an appropriate behavior that yields functional results. Nonetheless, it is necessary to know what the individual comprehends before types of symbols, if any, are chosen to be used in the communication system.

The individual's comprehension of communication is intertwined with the approach selected for augmenting communication. There is a predictable progression in the development of comprehension (Chapman, 1978):

Has reflexive responsive behavior →
Reacts to what is "here and now" →
Retains a sensory-laden, sensory-dependent image of objects, events and people →
Re-presents an object, event, or person when given something concretely related →
Re-presents an object, event, or person when given an arbitrary symbol

Arbitrary means that there is nothing about the symbol that naturally causes one to think of what it represents. For example, there is nothing about a cup that makes one's mouth and lips want to say "k," "uh," and "p" in rapid succession. The relationship between this spoken symbol and its referent (the cup) is arbitrary—(someone made it up!).

Ideally, when augmenting communication, it is necessary to use a system that matches the individual's comprehension level while affording the individual respect for his or her communication signal. The individual and his or her partner probably will comprehend the connotations of the communication act differently; however, they will be able to jointly achieve a communication goal. This happens often in typical development. A young child hears the word "dog" and thinks of "something with four legs," whereas the adult thinks of "canine." The child has a larger category for this word than the adult, yet the two can communicate successfully about the four-legged animal, what it is doing, and that it exists, regardless of the mismatch between the child and the adult.

What happens when an individual's ability to comprehend communicative acts is over- or underestimated? The result is an augmented system with vocabulary or interactional components at too high or too low a level for the individual's interests and abilities. The individual will have a system that he or she just *cannot* (as opposed to *will not*) use in the way that is expected. The individual may appear unmotivated or uninterested in communication. A solid system of communication must be established by providing input at the individual's "right now" level, not where it is hoped he or she will be in a month. Remember, whatever the level of comprehension, all individuals communicate; there are no prerequisites for communicating (Kangas & Lloyd, 1988).

Comprehension

In order to elicit behaviors indicating comprehension of communication, team members need to control the complexity of cues systematically. When people communicate, speech or sign are typically used with an overlay of facial expression, gestures, body orientation, and intonation. This is so natural that it is rarely thought about; yet, if one person imitates another, that person will demonstrate clearly that communication style includes more than just the linguistic units of production.

The main question then is *"What cues or contextual information are necessary for the individual to comprehend communication?"* or *"How contextually embedded is this person's comprehension?"* The less dependence on rich context, the more the person is able to think symbolically. Specifically, does the individual comprehend the following:

- Spoken language without additional cues?
- Signed language without additional cues?
- Gestures without additional cues?
- Intonation without additional cues?
- What to do next without any cues?

Cues refer to other communication signals, such as facial expression or gestures, routines with which the person is familiar, or characteristics of the physical setting. Partners should investigate the kernel that is key to comprehension. It is often assumed that the individual understands one-step directions when, in fact, the person knows the routine so well he or she could perform the action without verbal directions. It also is assumed that the person understands spoken words when, in fact, he or she really only understands pointing, gesturing, and intonation. For example, John and his friend who has a broken leg are sitting in a room with the door open, shivering from the breeze from the doorway. John's friend asks "Nikto barrada klatu?" while looking and pointing at the door. If John had not seen the famous old movie *The Day the Earth Stood Still*, John might assume his friend meant, "Could you close the door?" For that matter, she may as well have said, "Blah, blah, blah, blah?" and John would still have reacted in the same way. (Science fiction buffs know that they should guard the spaceship, not open the door.)

To determine whether the person is receiving cues from the routine, gestures, or from spoken words, elicitation activities can be powerful tools with which to undertake a systematic and thoughtful process. If partners sequentially increase or decrease the complexity of a cue in the context of daily activities, they can determine what aspect of the communication signal the individual comprehends. Beginning with the most symbolic communication behavior, spoken language, partners should follow a sequence in which cues are added to directions until the individual responds, an example is as follows:

Use verbal cues only.
Then use verbal cues + gaze at object of reference.
Then use verbal cues + gaze + gesture toward object of reference.
Then use all cues + touch object.
Then use all cues + hand object to individual.
If the individual responds only when gestures are added, the hypothesis should be tested so that spoken language alone is not being used for comprehension. To do so, partners should start with gesture only → gesture + vocalization → gesture + verbalization.
Document the level at which the person responds.

The next example about Mary illustrates this process.

Mary

There was disagreement among Mary's communication partners as to what they believed Mary understood. Some thought she understood spoken language; whereas others believed Mary needed gestures to understand directions. It was decided to test her level of comprehension during snack time. Mary was standing by the record player in the play area of the room. The aide inquired, "Mary?" and pointed to the snack table. Mary ran to the snack table. Later that day, the aide said, without gesturing or looking at the snack table, "Mary, time for snack." Mary did not move from where she was standing. The aide then looked at Mary and looked at the snack table as she repeated the same sentence. Mary did not move. The aide then added a sweeping point to the snack table as she alternated her gaze between Mary and the snack table and repeated the sentence again. Mary ran to the snack table. During the remainder of the week, the aide alternated her procedure, one day pointing first and one day speaking first. Mary's response to the gesture was consistently appropriate; whereas her response to verbalizations varied widely. Mary seemed to need gestures to comprehend one-step directions.

To test the hypothesis that the individual is relying on cues from the routine or cues from the physical setting in addition to or instead of spoken language or gestures, team members can set up several situations. For example, in the midst of a familiar, much-practiced routine, such as catching the bus, a partner can ask the individual to do something out of the ordinary with an object used in that routine. For example, instead of saying, "put on your coat," the partner could say "hang up your coat." If the individual follows the direction, it can be hypothesized that he or she comprehends more than just the routine. If the individual continues with the routine, either the individual understood just one word and then did what is usually done with that item or the individual does not comprehend words at all. Here is another example about Mary:

Mary

Mary had been learning to set the table. Her partners were not sure if she understood the words "spoon" and "knife." The aide believed that Mary knew the word "spoon" because when asked Mary would add a spoon to the place setting. When we observed this in the context of the routine, however, it was clear that two other powerful cues were present—only the spoon was missing from the setting and an outline of the spoon was on the placemat. The next time, the aide put a blank placemat on the table and asked Mary to "get the spoon" before any other pieces of the place setting were on the mat. Mary did indeed get the spoon.

We then wanted to know if Mary understood "spoon" without the contextual support of the routine and the general physical cues of the snack table. During free time, one day, the aide said, "Mary, get the spoon." Mary ran to the drawer with spoons, took one out, and put it on the table. Mary seemed to have understanding of this word even when it was slightly out of context.

This example of Mary's comprehension highlights another strategy children use to comprehend spoken communication. Chapman (1978) noted that during early stages of comprehension, children use a rule of "do what you usually do with an object" when the name of the object is mentioned in a sentence. Mary put the spoon on the table. Because people are kind caregivers and can anticipate what children can do, children usually are asked to do predictable things with objects; for example, children are asked to "hug the baby," "pet the kitty," or "close the door" when those actions are appropriate. The child may comprehend only the last word in the sentence, but it will appear as if he or she understood the whole sentence. If "tickle the baby," "feed the kitty," or "touch the door" were asked the child may go to the correct object but not perform the right action. This would further isolate the level at which the individual comprehends spoken language.

Mary

Mary's aide thought that Mary's comprehension of the word "spoon" included the whole routine of taking the spoon from the drawer and putting it on the table. The aide tested this by saying to Mary, "wash the spoon" or "show me the spoon." Mary always responded by taking the spoon out of the drawer and putting it on the table. She, therefore, comprehended only the last word of the aide's sentence.

Comprehension of Yes and No Questions

Many educators and parents assume that a comprehension of "yes" and "no" questions is the most basic of communication systems. The partner asks a question and the individual "answers" using a signal for yes and another for no. Partners will say, "If only we could get a clear 'yes–no' signal, we could really expand communication." The symbolic foundation of these terms, however, is quite complex.

In typical development, the word "no" is comprehended early (8–12 months) (Chapman, 1978) and used early (Owens, 1994) to reject or protest. Prior to that time, children express rejections or protests by turning their head or crying. This word most likely appears in children's vocabularies early because it is a powerful signal that has a history of getting a response. The spoken word "yes," however, is more nebulous not only in its development, but also in its function. "Yes" usually serves the purpose of affirming a request or the truth of a statement. When a child is asked, "Do you want cocoa?", knowing the child likes cocoa, the hot drink will be prepared whether or not the child responds. Lack of response serves to affirm the question. The child does not *need* to say "yes." In this sense, "yes" is not as powerful as "no."

When adults communicate with children or others who are perceived as not being competent communicators, they naturally adjust the demands of the conversation to a level that facilitates ongoing interaction with little likelihood of breakdown or misunderstanding. Asking questions that are anticipated to have affirmative answers is part of this pattern. The following exchange was witnessed as a new aide and a 14-year-old student with multiple disabilities were waiting for the school bus at the end of the day:

Adult: "Do you like your new sweater?"
Student: "Yes."
Adult: "Are you feeling happy today?"
Student: "Yes."
Adult: "Are you going home now?"
Student: "Yes."

Saying "yes" kept the conversation going and seemed to please the adult. This pattern can become so ingrained that the individual answers "yes" to any first question with rising intonation, then responds "no" to the repetition of the question (because it did not satisfy the partner), and finally is confused if the question is repeated again, for example:

Adult: "Are you going home now?"
Student: "Yes."
Adult: "Are you going home now?"
Student: "No."
Adult: "*Are* you going home now?"
Student: No response, frowns.

Before assessing an individual's understanding of "yes" versus "no," it should be determined if answering this question is a priority. By definition, the use of "yes–no" systems makes the individual dependent on the partner to ask a question; that is, the individual becomes only a responder, not an initiator of communication. If the partner wants the individual to be an independent initiator, looking at comprehension of particular choices of, for example, food items, activities, or partners, would be more productive than assessing use of "yes" or "no."

There are two methods for assessing comprehension of "yes" versus "no." The first method is to provide choices of preferred and strongly nonpreferred foods or activities. For example, on a random schedule, a partner might ask the individual,

"Want ____?" If the individual answers yes to the preferred items and no to the nonpreferred items, there is evidence of functional comprehension. If the individual answers yes to the nonpreferred items, there is evidence of lack of comprehension.

The second method, which requires a higher level of cognitive functioning, is to have the individual affirm the truth of a proposition by responding to questions such as "Do you walk?", "Do you fly?", "Do dogs eat?", "Do dogs drive?", and so forth. Of course, if the individual can answer such questions, he or she is probably in need of a more sophisticated communication system, which involves speech output and maximum programmability, than those described in this book.

Comprehension of Symbols and Icons An individual's ability to tie meaning to arbitrary symbols or highly representative icons (e.g., pictures) needs to be assessed before the communication system is set up. It is often surprising to learn that the individual does not understand that a photograph or picture of an object is an icon for that object. It is even more surprising to learn that the individual does not know that a miniature cup stands for "cup" and that a miniature car (which is smaller in size than the miniature cup) stands for "car." A rule of thumb is **never assume** an individual's ability to comprehend.

An individual's level of cognitive development will determine whether he or she can use any type of representation for, as an example, food items or objects. Some of the individuals presented in the vignettes later in this book do not understand that a two-dimensional picture represents a three-dimensional object. To understand what is being communicated, they need to see or touch the actual object, another object just like the actual object, or, in some cases, a portion of the actual object.

The ability to assign meaning to any representation other than the object itself can be assessed in the context of a specific daily routine. Various types of representations for items used during the routine must be selected and how many ways to represent each one decided before the routine begins. The following are some examples:

- A color photograph of the object or a catalog picture of the object
- Colored line drawings of the object ranging in size from full size to 1-inch × 1-inch, a size commonly used on communication boards and devices
- Black-and-white line drawings of objects ranging in size
- Written words to represent the object, in various sizes (e.g., capital and small case letters) in case the individual has learned some sight words

Figure 4.2 illustrates a well-worn match-to-sample kit. This is an all-purpose kit, not designed for a specific individual. A kit could be customized to a specified individual.

Some professionals like to include miniatures; however, unless they have visual impairments, individuals who understand miniatures as icons often understand pictures also. For individuals with visual impairments, a hierarchy of tactile icons might include objects and then increasingly smaller portions of the object. For example, for a cup: first, the whole cup; then, half the cup on its side; and then, the cup rim or the cup handle could be used. A suggested form for recording the results of the match-to-sample task is shown in Figure 4.3 and an example of how it was presented to Mary is presented below.

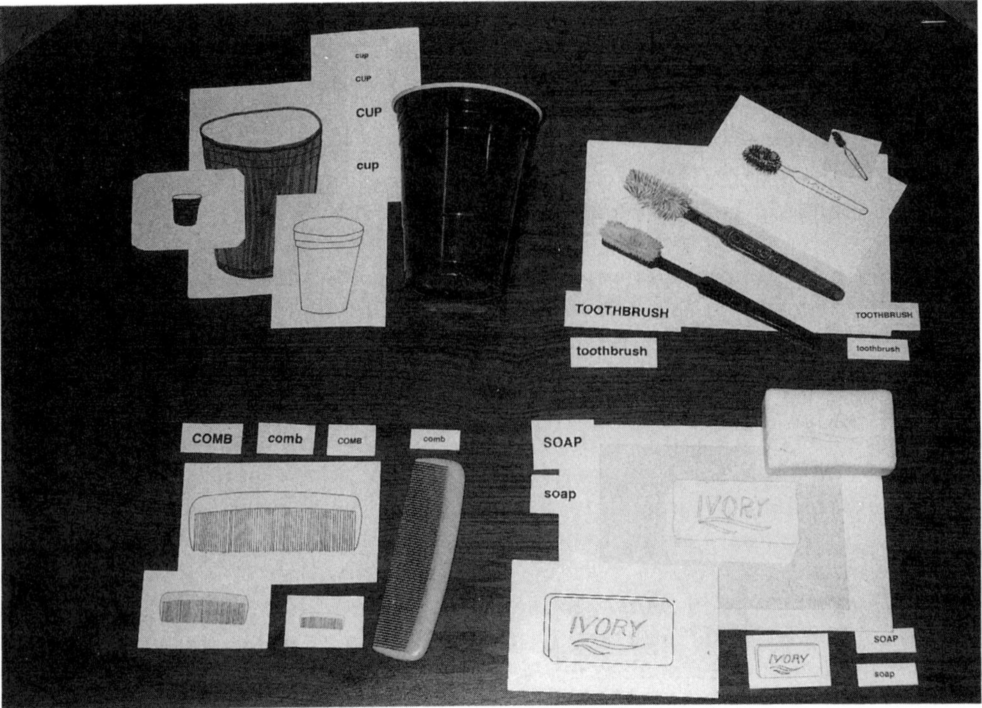

Figure 4.2. A match-to-sample kit with objects and drawings of various sizes.

Mary

A match-to-sample task was planned for Mary during snack time. The aide took photographs, drew pictures, and used large and small pictures from a commercial picture set to represent Mary's current food and drink choices during snack time. Using a photocopier, the hand-drawn pictures were reduced in size, resulting in pictures of three sizes.

During snack time, Mary was seated at the table. Her food and drink choices were displayed on the table in their usual containers. The aide asked Mary what she wanted by holding up the juice pitcher, the milk container, the graham cracker box, and the cookie package and then looking expectantly at Mary. Mary touched the cracker box. The aide took out a piece of cracker and gave it to her. When Mary had finished, the aide asked Mary again what she wanted, but this time, instead of holding up the actual items, the aide set up full-size colored drawings of the items in front of them. Mary looked at the aide and looked away. The aide uncovered the items and Mary touched the cracker box again. The aide tried this procedure with photographs and the commercial pictures. Mary again looked away. It seemed Mary needed the actual item or a representation more suggestive of the item than a picture.

Just by chance, a flattened milk carton was lying on the counter near the aide. Mary had had several pieces of graham cracker and the aide guessed that Mary might be thirsty. The aide held the flattened carton in

MATCH-TO-SAMPLE ASSESSMENT FORM

Item	Cue	Object	Part of object	Photograph	Colored drawn picture	Black and white line drawing	White on black picture	Commercial picture set

Figure 4.3. Match-to-Sample Assessment Form. Prompts include verbal match (V) (e.g., "Where's comb?") and gestural match (G) (e.g., hold up comb, gesture toward an array of objects, look puzzled, and hand comb to individual). For each two-dimensional symbol type, the smallest size successfully identified should be noted. The "object" column should be used to denote that the individual can match object to object. It should be noted whether the matched objects are identical, similar in one regard (e.g., color), or dissimilar but within a category (e.g., a glass and a plastic cup).

front of the real milk carton. Mary touched it. The aide became so excited that by the next day, she had pieces of the containers of each of the food choices ready for Mary. The aide cut off the front of a graham cracker box, the label and cellophane of a cookie package, and the flattened milk carton. She was not sure how to represent the pitcher (she didn't want to destroy a pitcher if she didn't have to). Her final idea was to serve Mary juice from a small juice box and then use the front of the juice box as a symbol. Mary used all of these icons successfully to request more of each item that same day. The aide continued to assess Mary's symbolic abilities with similar results during the following week.

ASSESSING FORMS AND FUNCTIONS OF COMMUNICATION

When asked to describe an individual's communication, most people will focus on the outward behaviors, signals, or forms of communication used when transmitting thoughts. Sometimes people also describe the ways in which these forms are used to achieve communication goals (see Figure 4.4). For those who speak, analysis would focus on orally transmitted forms, including speech sounds; how those forms are combined into words and meaningful parts of words (e.g., "-ly," "-ing"); and how words are combined to express larger meanings. For individuals who have mental retardation requiring extensive to pervasive communication support needs, all behavior potentially can communicate meaning. No behavior should be ruled out as a potential or existing communication signal just because it is inappropriate, nonconventional, self-injurious, or subtle. Before changing behaviors to be more

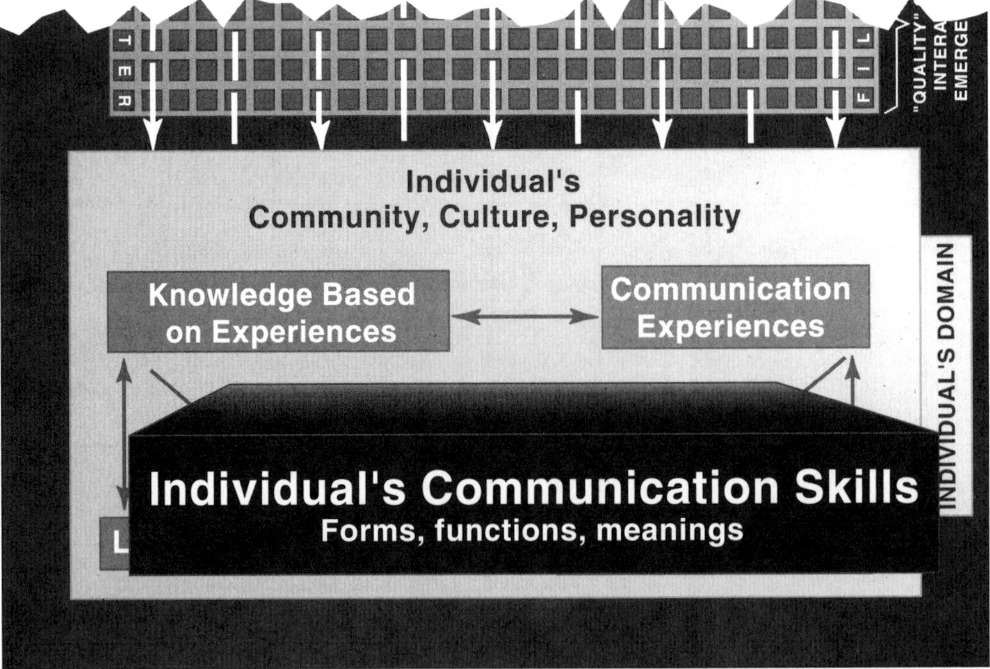

Figure 4.4. Focus on the Individual's Communication Skills. (From Johnson, J. [1995]. *The sociocommunicative filter model.* Pullman, WA: unpublished manuscript; reprinted by permission.)

acceptable, conventional, and clear, the existing forms of communication must be documented.

Observation

The *Form and Use Assessment Sheet* (see Figure 4.5) allows the observer to record contexts and behaviors in one of three situations: 1) on-line, in a random time-sampling manner; 2) retrospectively at the end of a time period, or 3) by videotapes.

To complete a Form and Use Assessment Sheet, partners should use the schedules already gathered and target three or four situations in which more than one partner can take observational data. Partners can take data on different days or at different times during these activities. (An extra benefit of this strategy is the strengthening of team collaboration because all willing partners can participate equally.) Situations should differ according to partner, setting, task, and expectation of passive or active role in communication so that a broad view of the individual's skills is seen. Many of the columns on this form may be filled out just by reflecting on a particular activity and how the individual usually communicates.

The important aspects of the Form and Use Assessment Sheet are as follows:

- ***Context*** is the name of the activity, the physical setting, the preceding event, what others are doing, or what was just said.
- ***Individual's signal*** is any behavior that occurred subsequent to the context, whether the individual is aware of the link or not and whether or not the individual used the behavior purposefully. The signal can include gazing, touching, calming, being excited, whole-body tensing, vocalizing, crying, pointing, biting, striking others, being self-injurious, saying words that are spoken clearly but have a different meaning, imitating words or gestures, or smiling.
- ***Partner's response*** is what the partner did or said when the individual signaled.
- ***Discourse function*** is whether the individual's signal served to initiate, maintain, or terminate the interaction, or to "repair" a misunderstanding.
- ***Pragmatic function*** is a more specific designation of the signal's actual function (regardless of intended function). This relates to what the individual achieved by signaling or how the signal was interpreted:
  - Was he or she able to request an object, action, or person?
  - Was this signal interpreted as a protest or rejection of an action, activity, or object?
  - Was the signal seen as a way of commenting or drawing the partner's attention to something of interest?
  - Did the signal serve as a greeting or as a means of noting the departure of someone or something?

After data have been recorded on the Form and Use Assessment Sheet, the following questions can be asked:

1. Is the individual's communication signal intelligible? If not, what makes the signal hard to understand?
2. Does the individual relate the signal to the preceding context (i.e., contingency)? Does the partner help the individual relate the signal?
3. How consistent is the same signal across several contexts?
4. How many signals serve one particular pragmatic function? (Typically developing children have numerous signals that serve one function.)

FORM AND USE ASSESSMENT SHEET

Individual's Name: ____________________ Date: 1/28/93

Observer: ____________________ Location: ____________________

Context	Partner	Individual's signal	Partner's response	Discourse function	Pragmatic function

Figure 4.5. The Form and Use Assessment Sheet. Discourse functions served by the individual's signal include initiate, maintain/fill in, or terminate conversation; repair a misunderstanding; tell a story; and tell about an event. Pragmatic functions served by the individual's signal include requesting or demanding food, drink, an object, an action, a social routine, attention, clarification, or information; protesting, rejecting, or denying; acknowledging, affirming, or confirming; commenting, labeling, or giving information; greeting, saying good-bye; showing off; or calling someone. (Adapted from Duchan, Hewitt, & Sonnemeier, 1994; Wetherby, Cain, Yonclas, & Walker, 1988.)

5. Do any signals serve more than one function? (Typically developing children use a multitude of signals for one function.)
6. How contingent and appropriate is the partner's response?

An example of a Form and Use Assessment Sheet for Mary is shown in Figure 4.6.

In addition to the Form and Use Assessment Sheet, more structured approaches are available—for example, the Communication Interview (see Figure 2.1 in Chapter 2) by Schuler et al., (1989). The Communication Interview assists team members in establishing typical communication patterns. This observation guide is organized according to the functions of the communication signal, focusing on the earliest developing and most basic of communication functions of regulating the behavior of others, encouraging social interaction, and maintaining joint attention (Wetherby et al., 1988). This chart can be customized by adding more behaviors or functions.

Interview

Familiar communication partners can easily relate how an individual "usually" communicates with them. Partners can identify typical signals used for the various functions noted on the Form and Use Assessment Sheet. Answers do vary depending on a specific partner's experience with the individual and the settings in which the two interact. Just because only one team member, including a parent or aide, says a certain behavior occurred, there is no reason to dismiss this as poor or invalid information.

Partners can interview by asking about specific behaviors or by asking more open-ended questions. To identify specific behaviors of interest, the Communication Interview can be used as a guide. A more open-ended interview format is presented in Figure 4.7. It is appropriate to include any team member in this process. When using an open-ended interview with others, it is productive to use paraphrasing and reflection of perceptions and feelings about those perceptions. This will stimulate further discussion among partners without inserting one partner's bias about the interpretation of the individual's communication behaviors.

Physical and Sensory Abilities

Fine and Gross Motor Skills The occupational therapist, physical therapist, and speech-language pathologist need to work together in assessing the individual's fine and gross motor skills (see Figure 4.8). These professionals need to determine which movements the person can execute voluntarily. This will affect the expectations partners have for vocalizing, pointing, touching, pushing, looking to signal a choice, and positioning of materials. Assuming that speech is not an immediate means of communication for this individual, the three professionals need to decide which part of the body is or can be used for the most consistent, rapid, accurate, and nontiring communication signal that also facilitates fine and gross motor development or stability. This will be a good way to make sure the movement selected for communication does not lead to abnormal postural reflexes or other movements that exacerbate physical abnormalities.

Positioning for Communication In relation to abnormal postural reflexes, it is crucial to have communication between the occupational therapist and physical therapist. Some sitting, standing, or reclining positions exacerbate abnormal reflexes or actually prevent the person from purposefully using his or her head, hands, or arms. Most physical therapists believe that stability of the pelvis is crucial (McEwen & Lloyd, 1990) to inhibiting primitive reflexes, abnormal posture, and abnormal

Individual's Name: Mary
Date: 1/28/93
Observer: Consultant speech-language pathologist
Location: Elementary school

Context	Partner	Individual's signal	Partner's response	Discourse function	Pragmatic function
Morning snack time.	Laura: aide	Touches Laura's cup	"Want some juice? OK?"	Initiation	Request for drink
Laura brings out more juice.		Flaps hands excitedly	"You *really* want juice? OK."	Maintain	Request or confirm
Laura pours juice in Mary's cup.		Drinks juice, sets cup down, reaches for juice	"You want more? OK?"	Maintain	Request
Laura pours more juice.		Drinks some juice, stops, starts to pour remaining juice back into pitcher	"All done? OK. Pour it in the sink."	Maintain	Reject remaining drink
		Jumps up from table, runs to sink, throws her cup in sink, runs off	"Whoa, Mary! Wait. Don't throw." Partner begins to chase Mary, saying, "Mary, come here!"	Terminate	Request for social interaction

Figure 4.6. An example of a completed Form and Use Assessment Sheet for Mary.

I. About what does the individual already want to communicate? How many different things does this person want and need to say?

II. How do you know when the individual wants you to do something, interact, or pay attention to something?
   A. Is there one person with whom the individual is most successful in getting needs met?
      1. What signals is this partner recognizing?
      2. How does the partner interpret the signal?
      3. Can a videotape be made of the individual's signal when he or she is in action with this partner?

III. How do partners know when the individual does *not* want something?
   A. Is there one person with whom the individual is most successful in getting needs met?
      1. What signals is this partner recognizing?
      2. How does the partner interpret the signal?
      3. Can a videotape be made of the individual's signal when he or she is in action with this partner?

IV. What other behaviors does the individual already have that are or could become communication signals?

V. How does the individual express interest or preferences in people or objects of joint reference?
   A. What kinds of things or activities does the person like?
   B. Who are this person's favorite partners?

VI. If the individual wants your attention, how does he or she get it?

VII. When does the individual communicate best?
   A. With whom?
   B. In what settings or activities?
   C. Given what type of responses or cues from partners?

VIII. When does the individual have the most difficulty communicating?
   A. With whom?
   B. In what settings or activities?
   C. Given what type of responses or cues from partners?

IX. Is the individual showing frustration because of communication breakdowns?
   A. How does he or she show frustration?
   B. What is your or the partner's response?
   C. Does showing frustration lead to any tangible outcomes for the individual?

X. Does there seem to be a gap between what the individual understands and what he or she can express?
   A. What evidence do you have that the person understands you?
   B. Does the person understand better with certain people, in certain settings, or within certain common routines?

XI. What communication signals does this person use?
   A. When does he or she use these signals?
   B. What is the result?
   C. How clear are the signals?
   D. Can other people see these signals, or would they have to be trained to recognize them?

XII. What is the most frustrating aspect of communicating with this individual?

Figure 4.7. Sample interview questions for augmenting communication.

(continued)

Figure 4.7. *(continued).*

XIII. Does this person have trouble communicating with peers?
  A. Does this person need to communicate with people who are younger?
  B. Does this person need or want to communicate with pets?
  C. How does this person join in peer group activities?
  D. Does this person try to answer questions? If so, how?

XIV. If an emergency occurred, would this person be able to express what was wrong? Would emergency personnel understand?

XV. Has this person ever used a board, device, switch, or computer for communication or other activities?
  A. Describe how this system was used and how successful it was.
  B. Did/does this system have voice output? If so, does the individual vocalize more or less when he or she hears the voice output? Does he or she attend at all to the voice output?

XVI. In the near future, will this person be learning to read? Will he or she be learning to write?

movements. Both for the assessment process and for communication habilitation, the individual should be comfortably and appropriately positioned for maximum advantage in communication.

Hearing It is surprising, but hearing, as a sensory ability, is often overlooked. Some individuals are exceedingly challenging to assess. Not all schools have their own audiologist. In these cases, the family should be referred to an audiologist who

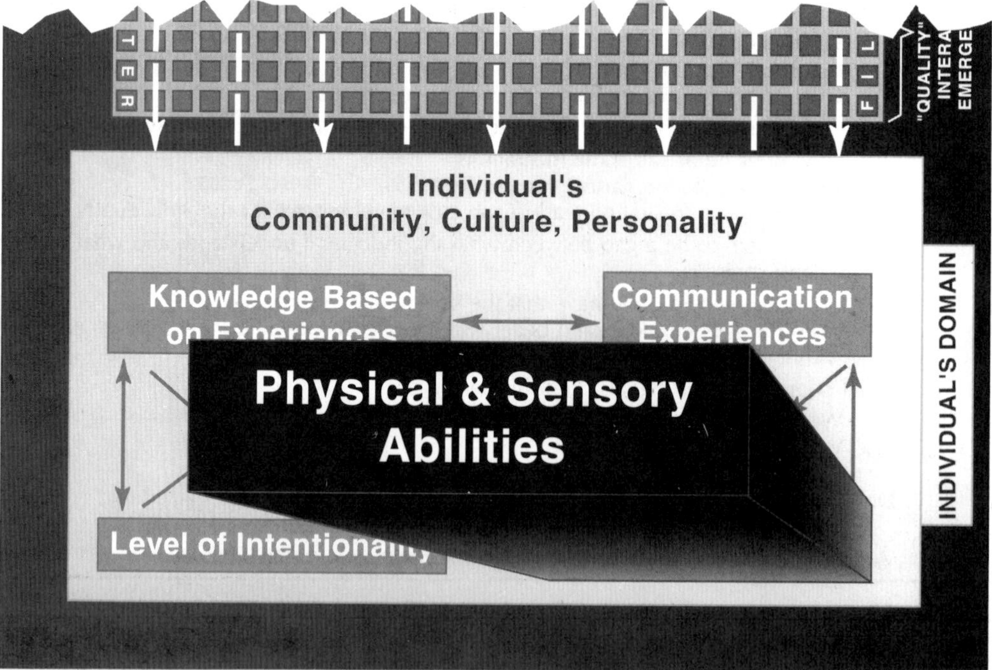

Figure 4.8. Focus on Physical and Sensory Abilities. (From Johnson, J. [1995]. *The sociocommunicative filter model.* Pullman, WA: unpublished manuscript; reprinted by permission.)

is certified by the American Speech-Language-Hearing Association outside of the school system. The audiologist can provide a hearing assessment, which might include electrophysiological measures (e.g., an auditory brainstem response [ABR]) that circumvent the need to condition the individual to respond. Although the interpretation of these kinds of measures may be limited, they provide basic information about the integrity of the auditory system. Parents and educators should not assume that hearing has been checked, and if it has, they should ask which procedures were used and how valid those procedures are. Speech-language pathologists can only do *screening* of hearing. Screening is a quick check of hearing acuity at one level of loudness and for just a few frequencies (tones). It is not uncommon for an individual with a significant hearing loss to pass a screening. If the individual has a documented hearing loss or a history of ear infections or does not seem to be responding as expected, his or her hearing status should be checked.

Visual Field There are a few methods for assessing visual tracking and scanning abilities of people with disabilities. While recognizing that there are other visual functions that are important, such as visual fixation and focusing, this section concentrates on tracking and scanning abilities and their applications to communication systems. These skills are chosen for discussion because they are so critical to the use of alternative and augmentative communication systems. A person with such a system will generally be expected to utilize tracking and scanning in a number of ways, such as searching for a symbol on a communication board (i.e., scanning), watching a person with whom he or she is communicating move across the room, or following a teacher's pointing and other gestures that give direction (i.e., tracking). It should be noted that these assessment procedures are not meant to assess other visual impairments. If the individual has visual impairments, consultation with an ophthalmologist or other vision specialist regarding limitations caused by these problems is suggested. The visual assessment conducted by the teacher or other personnel should provide specific information regarding the visual strengths and limitations of the individual. For instance, if a person has strabismus or uses only peripheral vision, the assessment can help school personnel determine where to place objects and how to maximize abilities.

Visual Tracking Visual tracking is the ability to follow an object or person as it moves through a number of visual planes (Scheuerman, Baumgart, Sipsma, & Brown, 1976). Smooth, consistent tracking is essential because it allows a person to observe the environment efficiently. These observations frequently will be the basis for the events or objects about which an individual will communicate. Also, because people rarely sit still (especially children), tracking allows one to maintain visual contact before, during, and after interactions. Knowing a person's limitations in visually following people or objects (e.g., speed of movement, optimum location in the visual field) allows one to design a communication system that takes advantage of the person's visual strengths and does not penalize him or her for visual impairments.

Visual Planes There are several planes on which a person may visually track objects. Generally, these planes are the vertical plane, the horizontal plane, and the diagonal planes. For each plane, there are at least two directions that the objects may move in the visual field. The typical point of reference for movement in the visual field is called *midpoint*. This is the point directly in front of the person's face at eye level. In the vertical plane, objects may move from the top of the visual field to the bottom, above eye level to below eye level, and in the reverse direction. In the horizontal plane, objects may move from left to right or from right to left. In the more complex diagonal planes, objects may move from the upper right visual field location to the lower left (or the reverse) and, similarly, from the upper left to the lower right (or the reverse). In addition, objects may move in random directions where there is no apparent pattern of movement. The visual assessment forms in Figure 4.9 clearly specify these planes and movements.

Musselwhite and St. Louis (1982) list several considerations for assessing visual tracking. Specifically, they note that the size, shape, and color of the objects used;

VISUAL TRACKING DATA SHEET

Name:__________ **Date:**__________

Observer:__________ **Materials Used:**__________

Instructions: Using objects that the individual will readily watch, begin at the appropriate reference point (indicated by the letters and boxes) and move the object along the designated visual plane. Watch the individual's eyes during tracking and indicate whether the tracking was continuous or interrupted. Also record if there were any indications of nystagmus or strabismus.

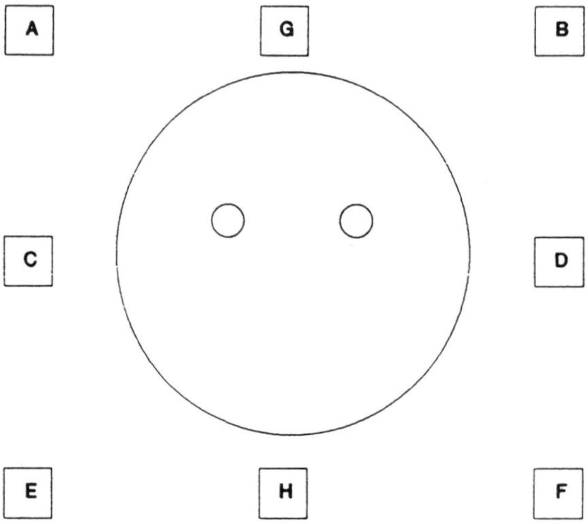

A G B

C D

E H F

Horizontal, above eye level: (A to B and B to A) _____ Continuous _____ Interrupted

Horizontal, at eye level: (C to D and D to C) _____ Continuous _____ Interrupted

Horizontal, below eye level: (E to F and F to E) _____ Continuous _____ Interrupted

Vertical (at midline): (G to H and H to G) _____ Continuous _____ Interrupted

Diagonal: (A to F and F to A) _____ Continuous _____ Interrupted

Diagonal: (B to E and E to B) _____ Continuous _____ Interrupted

Nystagmus (bouncing eyes): _____ Right _____ Left _____ Both

Strabismus (eyes turn in/out): _____ Right _____ Left _____ Both

Comments:

Figure 4.9. Visual Tracking Data Sheet. (From Baumgart, D., Johnson, J., & Helmstetter, E. [1990]. *Augmentative and alternative communication systems for persons with moderate to severe disabilities* [p. 238]. Baltimore: Paul H. Brookes Publishing Co.; reprinted by permission.)

the visual field location; the distance of the objects from the person; the cue(s) used; the speed and path of the objects; and the barriers for shielding objects all can affect the ability to track efficiently. They suggest systematically manipulating each of these variables to test their effect on the individual's tracking. In addition, lighting in the room, foreground–background contrast, and the presence of other visually distracting items in the visual field can affect tracking ability. These latter factors are especially important with people with visual impairments.

Procedure Several early childhood assessment instruments contain visual tracking items that might be helpful in assessing tracking (e.g., Bayley Scales of Infant Development [Bayley, 1969]). For example, there are several items on the Bayley Scales that assess an infant's ability to visually follow a light, a red ring, or a ball. Also, Erhardt (1986) has developed an instrument for assessing the visual functions of infants and young children. These instruments are, however, developmentally based and their use with older individuals with disabilities is not addressed. Furthermore, they were not designed to gather information with respect to functional communication systems. Visual tracking can easily be assessed through more informal methods by having the individual watch an object as it moves through the visual planes. It is important that the person be comfortably positioned, preferably sitting, if there are no apparent motor difficulties. When individuals with disabilities have motor or muscle imbalances, such as cerebral palsy, a physical or occupational therapist must be consulted about correct positioning because it affects head control. Both motor or muscle balance and head control are critical to smooth tracking. People with poor head control may have to be placed in seemingly unusual positions for assessment, such as lying on the floor or sitting on the lap of another person to assess their "best" abilities. A comfortable and stable head position is important.

For individuals with suspected visual problems, brightly colored objects with distinct shapes and edges will help them visually locate the items. Also, variations in room lighting or a contrasting background and foreground can assist the individual in visually locating and tracking objects. For example, lighted objects (e.g., a small pen flashlight, a glow-in-the-dark toy) in a darkened room have been observed to produce tracking and head control in a person previously believed to have neither skill.

Visual tracking can be assessed in an informal manner in many natural daily activities. There are several instances when situations can be structured for such an assessment. For example, Joshua, a young adult with severe physical impairments and mental retardation, required an assistant to feed him due to the lack of functional hand use. The assistant incorporated several mealtime activities to assess Joshua's visual tracking abilities. For instance, once the assistant had seated Joshua at the table she told him to watch her as she set the table, moving slowly from left to right and right to left along the table, opposite where he was sitting. The assistant also placed the ketchup bottle on the end of the table and, when Joshua needed the ketchup, she had the people on the opposite side of the table pass the ketchup bottle to him as she prompted Joshua to watch.

Visual tracking can also be assessed in a more formal manner by using a repeated trials format. Begin by showing the person a preferred object, one that he or she will watch as it is moved. Position the object at eye level to either the left or right side of the person, approximately 12–18 inches away from the nose. If necessary, shake or tap the item to get the person's attention. Then slowly (e.g., 3–4 inches per second) move the object horizontally across the person's field of vision, carefully monitoring his or her eye movements. Repeat this procedure for horizontal tracking, both 6–8 inches above and below eye level, and for vertical and diagonal tracking. A form to facilitate data collection on visual tracking using either of the above methods is provided in Figure 4.9.

While assessing tracking abilities, note whether the person's eyes move in a smooth, continuous motion, or whether they move in a jerky, interrupted fashion. Eye movements in a jerky up and down or side to side direction or eye(s) turning in or out may be noted in some individuals. These movements can be indicative of nystagmus (i.e., oscillating movement of the eyeballs) or strabismus (i.e., eyes that turn in or out. These conditions may require the objects to be moved at slower speeds than would normally be used. Other factors to consider are whether the eyes move together when tracking, where the person begins the tracking (e.g., at the periphery of the visual field, at midline), and if the individual appears to tire as the session progresses. For example, people with only peripheral vision will not be able to "see," scan, or track objects in their central field of vision. It is important to determine where their peripheral field of vision begins and ends to determine placement of items accurately.

Use of the Results The results from the visual tracking assessment are helpful in selecting an appropriate communication system. The assessment allows documentation of the individual's tracking skills: which directions the person can track, consistency of eye gaze during tracking, the preferred or "best" visual field, and potential inhibitors to smooth tracking (e.g., erratic eye movements, poor head mobility). With some people, smooth visual tracking may be observed in only one plane, in one quadrant, or in scattered portions of their visual field. For example, one former student did not track objects vertically and could not smoothly track past midline in either the horizontal or diagonal planes. The assessment results indicated that the area in which he could most easily track and visually observe and/or scan objects was in the upper left visual field, approximately 18 inches away from his eyes. Subsequently, objects were presented visually to him in that area. Objects placed before him on a table (a typical occurrence) were quite difficult for him to observe.

Knowledge of the above factors helps to determine the most appropriate placement of objects or symbols in the person's visual field, whether or not the symbols or objects may need to be highlighted (e.g., made brighter by adding color, using contrasting foreground and background colors), and whether or not the speed of presentation of visual stimuli (e.g., objects, communication symbols) should be slowed or increased. For example, if the individual has peripheral vision only, communication symbols may have to be placed around the edge of a communication board, or extra time allowed for the person to reposition his or her head to adequately view the necessary symbols or person with whom he or she is communicating.

Visual Scanning Visual scanning is the ability to search for parts of an object or to inspect an array of objects (Scheuerman et al., 1976). Essentially, scanning involves the ability to search for and to voluntarily stop and visually select a component part of the object or one item in a series of objects that is being examined. It is a more complex task than visual tracking and is a critical skill for many alternative and augmentative communication systems. Many systems require the user to scan a series of symbols or words visually and then select (e.g., by looking at, pointing to) the desired symbol. For example, a student who utilized a series of miniature items placed in a row according to the daily classroom routine might use the following sequence of visual skills:

Visually locate set of miniature objects
Scan (from left to right) the set of objects for the item representing the next activity
Visually fixate on and pick up (or point to) the desired object

Typically, scanning follows a left-to-right, top-to-bottom sequence of movement. However, this may not be the most efficient pattern for some people. The author recalls a student with severe cerebral palsy who utilized a right-to-left scan for his communication board. Severe muscle spasticity prevented this student from adequately controlling his head for left-to-right movements, or crossing midline when moving from the right. However, he could scan from right to left, beginning at midline and moving to his left. His communication board was constructed such that all items were placed to the left of midline. Also, the nouns were placed on the right side of the symbol set, with the verbs in the middle and the adjectives and adverbs on the left side. Although this was exactly opposite to the way most systems are arranged, it worked wonderfully for this person.

Procedure Visual scanning can be assessed in a number of different ways. For example, the individual being assessed could be shown a picture with several objects on it and asked to locate specific items on that picture. Another way might be to have a student locate a specific object in the classroom, such as another student or certain classroom materials. It is often difficult to observe a person's eye movements as he or she attempts to scan the larger environment; therefore, scanning is often assessed in a more clinical type of setting. Then, once the person's scanning abilities have been documented in a structured setting, they may be observed in more natural situations.

For a more formal assessment procedure, one should begin by seating the person at a table or large desk, making sure there are few distractions. One person should manipulate the items while a second person observes eye movements and records data. The two observers can then confirm the person's eye movements, if necessary. Other arrangements may be necessary if the individual has unique positioning needs, such as lying on his or her side or standing with supportive equipment. Partners should select at least eight items that the person is familiar with and will want to look at and use after a portion or all of the assessment has been completed. Favorite toys or classroom materials (e.g., books, games) are some items that may work for students. The items should be placed in various positions within the person's visual field (see Figure 4.9 for some possible positions). For instance, one object might be placed slightly to the front and left of the individual, one object directly in front, and another object to the front and right. While placing the objects, partners should observe the individual's eyes and note whether he or she shifts the gaze from item to item in a smooth fashion or looks past the object and then returns to it. They should observe if the individual begins searching for objects at a particular place in his or her visual field. Finally, they should watch for a pattern in the visual search. Some people may begin searching in the upper left of their visual field and move across the field in an up-and-down scanning motion, while others look from left to right or the reverse across their visual field and move from top to bottom. Some people will use no identifiable scanning pattern, and some are able to select the correct item without visibly "looking."

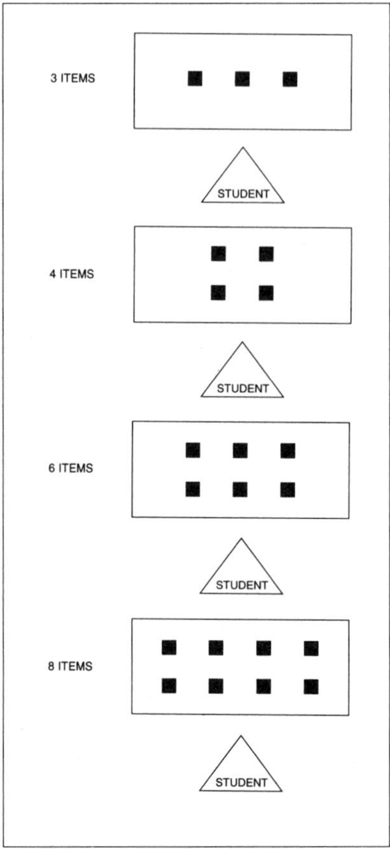

Figure 4.10. Arrangement of items for visual scanning assessments. (From Baumgart, D., Johnson, J., & Helmstetter, E. [1990]. *Augmentative and alternative communication systems for persons with moderate to severe disabilities* [p. 83]. Baltimore: Paul H. Brookes Publishing Co.; reprinted by permission.)

For individuals who may be able to use a communication board, another type of scanning assessment procedure may be useful. For example, items can be arranged in a row or an array in front of the person. Figure 4.10 shows some suggested arrangements of items for scanning three, four, six, or eight items.[1] Then the person should be asked to "find" a specific item. This may be done by having the student pick up the object, point to it, or look at it. For individuals who cannot choose one item from two or more different ones (i.e., discrimination), scanning may be assessed by using two or more objects that are the same. Again, while the person is visually searching the array of objects, his or her eye movements should be monitored. Does he or she first look to one specific area each time? Do his or her eyes wander randomly from item to item or is there a specific pattern in the visual search? What is the pattern? A visual scanning data sheet is provided in Figure 4.11 and lists some of the critical behaviors that should be monitored during the scanning assessment. The procedure should be repeated several times, alternating the

[1]Positioning of the objects and the number of objects used may need to be adjusted depending on the results of the visual tracking assessment and the person's cognitive/discrimination abilities. For example, if the individual only tracks objects on the left side of his or her body, it would not be appropriate to expect the individual to scan on his or her right side.

VISUAL SCANNING CHECKLIST

Name: ______________________ Date: ______________________
Observer: ____

1. Where does the student begin his or her visual search?
   ___ Top left ___ Center ___ Top right
   ___ Bottom left ___ Bottom right
2. What is his or her pattern of scanning?
   ___ Left to right ___ Top to bottom ___ Random pattern
   ___ Right to left ___ Bottom to top ___ No discernible pattern
3. Does the student scan the entire set of materials? ___ Yes ___ No
   If no, which area does he or she not scan? ______________________
4. Does the student maintain his or her attention to scanning task?
   ___ Yes ___ No
   For how long? ______________________
5. Can the student quickly (e.g., less than 10 seconds) locate the requested symbol when presented with:
   3 items ___ Yes ___ No 6 items ___ Yes ___ No
   4 items ___ Yes ___ No 8 items ___ Yes ___ No
   ___ items ___ Yes ___ No
6. How does the student select the appropriate item?
   ___ Maintains gaze ___ Names item ___ Vocalizes
   ___ Points to item ___ Picks up item ___ Shows excitement
   ___ Other (specify) ______________________
7. What type of prompts are helpful in assisting the student to scan?
   ___ Pointing by student ___ Physically turning the student's head
   ___ Pointing by teacher ___ Color cues
   ___ Other (specify) ______________________

Figure 4.11. Visual Scanning Checklist. (From Baumgart, D., Johnson, J., & Helmstetter, E. [1990]. *Augmentative and alternative communication systems for persons with moderate to severe disabilities* [p. 239]. Baltimore: Paul H. Brookes Publishing Co.; reprinted by permission.)

position of the objects each time. Also, the procedure should be repeated using four, six, eight, or more items as appropriate for the individual.

It is useful to confirm a person's scanning skills through natural observation or activities that are structured during the daily routine. This can be accomplished by systematically observing the person's visual scanning skills in several daily activities, such as looking at a book (e.g., does he or she scan the pages or the pictures?), looking at the choices for clothing to wear, or searching a shelf or work area for materials for the next classroom or work activity. An example of a structured natural routine would be to place two coats next to the person's coat on a rack. Then, when it is time to get his or her coat after work, the person must scan across all of the coats on the rack to find his or her own. As with the other methods of scanning assessment, the starting point of the search and the pattern of scanning should be recorded.

Use of the Results Visual scanning skills are critical for using many different communication systems. The results from the scanning assessment will aid in deciding on the appropriate layout and format of the system. In particular, the teacher or therapist will know how to place the system in the visual field to maximize visual contact; the number of objects or symbols the person can efficiently scan and, thus, use in the system; and how to arrange the symbols or objects to match the person's scanning pattern. Finally, by varying the size of the materials used during the scanning assessment, one can determine the most appropriate size of symbols or objects for the individual's system.

Hand Preference Assessment of hand preference is the determination of the dominant hand with which the person reaches for, points to, and/or grasps objects. Prior to age 6 or 7, a child may not have established a dominant hand and may use either equally well. In some cases, physical disabilities may limit or inhibit a person's use of a hand or arm. Hand preference is assessed so that teachers and therapists can design communication systems that allow easy access for the user. One must know the limitations of the pointing and reaching and must know whether or not the individual can reach to and across midline.

Procedure Hand preference should be assessed in both the sitting and standing positions, if possible. For each position, an object should be placed successively at each of the following locations in relation to the front of the individual: left-forward, left-side, forward, middle, right-forward, and right-side (see Figure 4.12, the Data Sheet for Assessing Hand Preference, for specific locations). In the sitting position, the objects should be placed on a table top or desk for easiest access. When standing, the items should be held approximately at the person's chest level. The items should be adjusted as necessary for individual differences in positioning or visual abilities. The person should be allowed to reach for and get the item at each location and the partner should record which hand he or she uses to get it. If necessary, verbal or gestural prompts may be used to facilitate a response. During the assessment, it should be noted whether the person uses the same hand when the item is to the left of midline, at midline, and to the right of midline. Does he or she use the same hand for every reach? Does he or she use the left hand for items placed to the left of midline and the right hand when items are placed to the right of midline?

For some individuals, the hand preference assessment procedure can be completed in 5–10 minutes. For people with motor problems, however, it may take considerably longer. Many times favorite objects can stimulate reflexive movements that will inhibit smooth reach and grasp. Also, changes in muscle tone or the need for frequent repositioning may prolong the assessment and cause frustration or fatigue. In these instances, the assessment can be completed in several sessions throughout several days or even weeks. In addition, some students may not exhibit a strong preference for either hand, even during many trials. There is no need to be alarmed, however, as the student may be ambidextrous or may develop hand dominance at a later date.

Use of the Results The results of the hand preference assessment provide valuable information for designing and constructing a communication system. First, the hand a person is likely to use in manipulating objects (and, subsequently, to use for a communication system) is identified. However, exclusive use of the preferred hand can be beneficial or a hindrance, depending on the system used. For example, one child not only demonstrated a strong right hand preference but had

DATA SHEET FOR ASSESSING HAND PREFERENCE

Date:____________ **Observer:**____________________

Name:____________________ **Time:**____________

Materials used: __________________________

Which hand is used to pick up objects when the object is placed in the following locations in relation to the body? Put an X in the blank which describes the hand used.

Left front **Right front**

Middle

Left side **Right side**

Student is here facing forward

Sitting at table:

Left front:	L hand	___	R hand	___
Left side:	L hand	___	R hand	___
Middle:	L hand	___	R hand	___
Right front:	L hand	___	R hand	___
Right side:	L hand	___	R hand	___

Standing:

Left front:	L hand	___	R hand	___
Left side:	L hand	___	R hand	___
Middle:	L hand	___	R hand	___
Right front:	L hand	___	R hand	___
Right side:	L hand	___	R hand	___

Figure 4.12. Data Sheet for Assessing Hand Preference. (From Baumgart, D., Johnson, J., & Helmstetter, E. [1990]. *Augmentative and alternative communication systems for persons with moderate to severe disabilities* [p. 240]. Baltimore: Paul H. Brookes Publishing Co.; reprinted by permission.)

very weak control and strength in his left hand. He used a communication booklet with line drawings on 2½-inch × 4-inch cards placed in plastic holders in a small binder and had very little difficulty turning the pages with his right hand and using the appropriate cards. However, he became frustrated by the amount of time it took him to use the booklet when eating. Since he was right-handed, he had to put down his spoon, grasp his booklet, and then turn the pages of his booklet to locate the appropriate symbol for his message. But this was not fast enough for him. He tried several alternative methods, such as using his messy spoon to turn the pages, before deciding that anything he wanted to say could wait until he had finished eating.

Second, the hand preference assessment provides information about the person's reaching abilities, specifically his or her ability to cross midline. Although it is not an upper extremity mobility test, it does allow the observer to note those areas that the individual can most easily reach. This is important when considering placement of the communication system and other stimuli for instruction. For example, if the person has a dominant left hand, cannot cross midline while reaching with the left hand, and cannot use his or her right hand at all, materials must be placed on the left side.

Finally, the examiner can observe differences in hand preference in both the sitting and standing positions. Sometimes young children and others with balance and mobility problems use their preferred hand to assist in steadying themselves. If the teacher or therapist is considering a communication system that requires both hands or that must be carried, the person may be unable to use it efficiently in some sitting or standing positions. One solution to this problem is to have the individual sit each time he or she has to use the system. However, the teacher will have to take this into consideration when planning instructional activities, especially those that require extensive movement and communication. Consultation with a physical or occupational therapist is also helpful in these situations.

SUMMARY

This chapter has focused on assessing the individual's domain. By using the methods of direct observation, interview, and elicitation, which are described in this chapter, the team collects information about the individual's comprehension of spoken language and symbols, outward forms of communication (i.e., signals), and the ways in which these forms are used to achieve communication goals. Combined with data from the assessment of the environment, patterns of greater and lesser communication competence (Light, 1989) and reasons for particular communication behaviors should emerge. For example, Roger's requests for his favorite music are better understood when he is with his father or his teacher. Alice's screams of protest occur only when she is making a transition from one activity to the next. The team will use this rich pool of data to design the initial communication system and to make adjustments in Roger's and Alice's existing systems. Assessment is never done. As a communication system is implemented, the team discovers new pieces of information that are lacking and is able to assess for that information using the guidelines presented in preceding chapters of this book.

Section III

IMPLEMENTATION

In Section III, the information collected during the assessment phase is used to develop and expand a communication system. Chapter 5 describes how assessment information is used to develop a written communication plan and how that plan is implemented. Chapter 6 delineates the options for expanding the initial communication system, and Chapter 7 discusses some of the issues educators might face in implementing a communication system in a general education classroom.

CHAPTER 5

Developing and Implementing a Communication Strategy

Teams that have used the strategies described in preceding chapters will have already collected many segments of the assessment information, which will be the foundation for implementing a communication strategy. This chapter addresses how to bring together the various previously collected segments to form a cohesive plan. As noted in Section II, the partners and environments set the stage for communication. Changing the environmental variables is one of the most easily influenced factors and can have a significant impact on the individual's skills. As ways to enhance the existing, or "right now" system, are discussed, partner and environmental factors are combined with individual factors. Thus, the Partner's Domain and the Individual's Domain from the Sociocommunicative Filter Model presented in Chapters 3 and 4 are merged.

DESIGNING AN INITIAL COMMUNICATION STRATEGY

Chapter 4 described the assessment of the individual's skills and needs in terms of the following:

- Behavioral form (e.g., pointing, looking, gesturing)
- Functions (e.g., requesting, protesting, getting attention)
- Use of symbols (e.g., objects, pictures, printed words)
- Comprehension (e.g., understanding the speech or gestures of others)
- Discourse functions (e.g., initiating, maintaining, terminating interactions)

- Sensory functioning
- Gross and fine motor skills and positioning needs
- Hand preference

With this assessment information, the team is ready to begin the process of starting an initial communication system. The following five steps utilize the assessment information to develop an initial communication system:

1. Enhance existing communication forms, functions, symbols, and contexts.
2. Put the various pieces of the plan together.
3. Design a monitoring process.
4. Teach partners to carry out the communication plan.
5. Teach partners to respond to spontaneous communication.

The process is one that strengthens the concept of communication by achieving consistency with *existing* forms and functions in natural contexts and with frequently encountered partners before systematically expanding the system.

Step #1: Enhance Existing Communication Forms, Functions, Symbols, and Contexts

Using the results from the Form and Use Assessment Sheet (see p. 68), one or two existing behavioral forms, pragmatic functions, and discourse functions can be identified. For example, Michael knocks over objects (i.e., behavioral form) in order to protest an activity (i.e., pragmatic function) and terminate the interaction (i.e., discourse function). The team uses this information to enhance the existing forms and pragmatic and discourse functions by asking a series of questions.

Can the forms and functions be used in multiple contexts with multiple partners now and in the near future? Consistent use of these forms will occur if they can be used often and in many different situations across the day. The daily schedule and the specific lists of tasks within routines, which are obtained in the assessment phase, may be helpful in targeting the contexts in which to use the forms and functions across the day.

Does the individual use inappropriate behaviors to communicate? If there are other, conventional behavioral forms that convey the same function as the inappropriate behavior, the team should select the appropriate forms. For example, if a protest is communicated by 1) pushing objects aside, 2) throwing them, and 3) hitting others, then pushing objects aside would be the preferred form. If only one form is available and it is inappropriate, such as hitting others, it may be possible to use the beginning of the behavior (e.g., raising the arm) as the communicative form; this is possible if partners are taught to intervene quickly enough to preempt the continuation of the hitting behavior.

A second alternative is to look for a preceding behavior that can be used as the communication form—a behavior that consistently occurs prior to the problem behavior and signals that the inappropriate behavior will soon occur (e.g., an "unhappy" vocalization). If none of these methods can be used because the inappropriate behavior cannot be preempted or predicted, then the team should identify a substitute behavior that partners can teach the individual to use in protest situations. For example, when the individual begins to protest by hitting, a partner should interrupt the hitting and prompt an alternative movement, such as extending the arm outward or picking up a small object and holding it out to the partner. The alternative should be one that is easily executed by the individual. Following this prompt, the partner states, "You don't want to ___" and immediately separates the individual from the undesirable context. If this approach is infeasible, then it may be best to address the problem behavior in some other way (see Chapter 2). In addition, it may be possible to teach the individual how to protest but in a context that is less volatile and extreme. Once he or she learns to protest in a more conventional way in other situations, an attempt can be made to introduce the use of the conventional form of protest in the more volatile situation.

How stable or consistent are the forms? For example, gaze may be steady one time and brief the next; or an individual may touch and look at novel items, but only touch familiar ones without visually attending to them. Stable forms are more likely to produce consistent responses by partners and should be given priority for the initial communication system. If the only forms displayed are unstable or inconsistent, then the initial communication plan may need to address this in the instructional process. For example, if a youngster's gaze is sometimes steady and sustained but at other times it is a fleeting glance, then the communication plan for responding to the gaze should include a component for reestablishing attention to the requested object. This might be done, for example, by acknowledging the fleeting glance at an object ("Oh, you want the ___") while bringing the object into the youngster's line of vision and enticing further looking by shaking it or manipulating it in some way. Partners also should be aware of factors that contribute to stability and consistency of a behavioral form. Some of these factors are discussed in Chapter 4. For example, physical positioning, body movement, amount of environmental stimulation, and location or position of desired objects are some factors that can influence the speed and accuracy of a response.

Is the individual aware that the signals have a particular effect on partners (i.e., intentionality)? As mentioned in Section II, there is a continuum of intentionality (Wetherby & Prizant, 1989). The first stage of intentionality is characterized by reflexive actions performed with no obvious awareness that others will be affected (e.g., a youngster who does not like to go outside will cry when she realizes she is outside rather than when she is on her way to the door to go outside). This does not mean that because an individual does not appear to be acting intentionally, that we do not use existing forms and the functions we have assigned to them. It does suggest, however, that some children and youth may need repeated experiences with the consequences of their behavioral forms in order to understand that they can be used to affect the behavior of others. As intentionality develops, the individual becomes aware that behavior has an effect on others and begins to plan ahead of time the ways to affect others and to combine behaviors in more complex forms of communication. For example, instead of Joe crying when he is outside, he might begin to cry when he sees the door leading outside; or he might combine behaviors by getting the partner's attention, such as vocalizing and then protesting the upcoming activity of going outside by alternating his gaze between the partner and an area of the room that represents an alternate activity (e.g., looking at the classroom's reading area). The following scenario illustrates how this part of Step #1 of the process for designing an initial communication strategy was completed.

Mary

The information in the completed Form and Use Assessment Sheet for Mary (Figure 4.5) shows that she uses at least two signals to request juice:

1) touching or reaching for the desired cup or pitcher, and 2) waving her hands excitedly. Additional information collected during portions of her classroom, lunch, and recess activities confirms that she does use these two signals for requesting and that the content of the signals also includes preferred books, a tape recorder, audiotapes, a computer, and lunchtime food items.

Information from Figure 4.5 and other contexts also suggests that she makes requests by leaving the situation, in this case to gain social interaction. For example, throughout the day she frequently leaves her seat and walks around the classroom, sometimes increasing her speed and smiling if someone pursues her. In addition to its use to request social interaction, leaving the seat may be her way of requesting a walk, as well as a form of rejection or protest of activities. She protests in others ways as well. Figure 4.6 illustrates that this is evident, as it chronicles instances in which Mary demonstrates that she has had enough juice by pouring it back into the pitcher. In other contexts, she protests by pushing away objects, sitting without interacting with objects, and, as indicated above, by leaving the situation. In terms of discourse functions, she both initiates and maintains interaction through her requests and terminates discourse by her protests.

The team decided to focus on the following signals, all of which could be used across many daily contexts and in interactions with peers: reaching for or touching in order to request objects, leaning forward in her seat in preparation to stand as the request for a walk with a partner, and pushing away to protest an activity or the continuation of an activity. Waving her arms would not be responded to as a request signal because the reaching and touching signals were more appropriate and recognizable and would be easier to shape into a more formal communication system, such as reaching and touching pictures on a communication board. The same reasoning was used in deciding not to respond to her signal of standing up as protest. This signal seemed to have multiple functions, including protesting, requesting social interaction, and requesting to go for a walk. It was decided that the signal would be recognized only as a request to take a walk, which also would involve a social interaction component. The team decided that the existing discourse functions she demonstrated were adequate, and the members were mindful in their planning to provide multiple opportunities for Mary to use the various discourse functions across the day.

Consideration of the communicative forms and functions is intertwined with decisions about the symbol system and contexts in which to support the development of communication. Comprehension of symbols and information about contexts was assessed using the Form and Use Assessment Sheet and the match-to-sample assessment of symbol comprehension described in Chapter 4. The following questions are pertinent to utilizing this information to develop an initial communication system.

Can the symbolic forms be utilized across settings? For example, if a symbol system consists of reaching for actual objects, it may be awkward to have the objects available in certain settings (e.g., on a bus, in a swimming pool). Unless other objects are found to be appropriate to a given setting, that context may not be an appropriate one in which to facilitate communication using those particular forms and functions. This raises an issue, however, about whether different systems are needed for different settings. This includes not only the symbolic forms but also the entire communication system. This is not unreasonable; many people adjust their verbal communication in different contexts and rely on nonverbal communication (e.g., facial expressions, gestures) more in some situations than in others. Similarly, individuals with disabilities may need different systems for different situations. For example, perhaps the individual requests by reaching when in the classroom and at home, but he or she requests by looking at objects when swimming (e.g., diving rings, flotation devices). The implications of this example are that assessment activities should be conducted in multiple environments and that it may be necessary to develop different systems for different settings.

Are the objects and activities represented by the symbols (i.e., the content of communication) age appropriate? It may be more effective to utilize familiar objects and activities; but if some of these objects and activities are age inappropriate (e.g., a baby toy for an 8-year-old), it might be better to limit the selection to age-appropriate stimuli unless these are the only items that motivate the individual (Beukelman, McGinnis, & Morrow, 1992; Fried-Oken & More, 1992).

Are the people represented by the symbols (including people directly pointed to or looked at) same-age peers or people the youngster prefers? The schedule of activities of same-age peers, which was obtained in the assessment phase, may be useful for identifying contexts in which communication can involve peers. The following scenario about Mary illustrates the application of the questions about the utilization of symbolic forms and the appropriateness of symbols and partners.

Mary

In the assessment of Mary's comprehension of symbols and icons (see Chapter 4), we found that she could express herself by reaching for objects and, in some instances, representations of objects, such as the containers in which objects are packaged (e.g., the front of a graham cracker box, label and cellophane of a cookie package, the front of a milk carton or a box of juice). She was, however, unable to utilize photographs or drawn pictures of objects. Her symbol system, then, would consist of representations, whenever possible, and actual items (e.g., the computer, tape recorder, foods at lunch). The content of the symbols represented highly preferred objects and activities. These objects and activities were found in specific contexts and during certain times of the day; therefore, these contexts and times were targeted to provide more structured opportunities to encourage Mary to utilize the various signals to initiate, maintain, and terminate interactions. In the planning process, the team ensured that all of the contexts, partners, activities, and objects utilized were appropriate for same-age peers. They also ensured that, to the maximum extent possible, peers would be involved in the communicative interactions. Figure 5.1 shows the first part of Mary's daily routine and the communication opportunities the team identified during each activity.

Activity (time)	Partner	Description of communication opportunity
8:30 Arrival	Peer	Requests a free-time activity from items placed on her desk (e.g., book, computer disk, audiotape) [initiate interaction]
	Peer	Requests more of activity when a segment ends and partner looks at her expectantly (e.g., end of computer game, song, or story) [maintain interaction]
	Peer	Protests when partner gives her an item she did not select [terminate interaction]
	Peer	Requests walk; partners must be alert to her spontaneous requests for walks, which can be honored during this time [initiate interaction]
8:45 Morning circle	Teacher	No planned opportunities
9:00 Centers	Educational assistant	Requests to choose among computer, reading, and the nonpreferred manipulatives centers [maintain interaction]
	Educational assistant	Requests more of an activity when a segment ends and partner looks at her expectantly (e.g., end of computer game or story) [maintain interaction]
	Peer	Protests when partner gives her an item she does not like (e.g., a manipulative) [terminate interaction]
	Peer	Requests walk; partners must be alert to her spontaneous requests for walks, which can be honored during this time [initiate interaction]
9:40 Snack	Teacher	Requests snack items to eat or drink; partner should place items on table and the snack communication board next to her [initiate interaction]
	Teacher	Requests more of a snack when finished first portion [initiate interaction]
	Teacher	Protests when partner gives her the wrong snack item, one she did not select [terminate interaction]
	Teacher	Requests walk: Partners must be alert to her spontaneous requests for walks, which cannot be honored during this time. The requests should be acknowledged and an explanation should be given as to why she must wait to go for a walk [initiate interaction]

Figure 5.1. Example of scheduling communication opportunities during part of Mary's Tuesday kindergarten schedule. Times are based on the schedule obtained during assessment. (Bracketed notations refer to discourse functions.)

Step #2: Put the Various Pieces of the Plan Together

To help promote consistency in responding to signals, it is helpful to provide a written plan for others to follow. The plan is not meant to inhibit spontaneity, but rather to ensure a minimal level of consistent responding across partners. The plan can specify how to conduct structured interactions as well as when and how to respond to spontaneously occurring signals. Components of the written plan include 1) a description of existing signals, 2) the function of each signal, 3) the symbols the individual uses to communicate expressively, 4) how the partner sets up the communication opportunity, and 5) how the partner responds to the occurrence or nonoccurrence of the signal. It is useful for written plans to be accompanied by a videotape of partners demonstrating the written plan during interactions with the individual. Figure 5.2 is a written plan for how partners should interact with Mary in structured and spontaneous communication situations. (A blank form for writing a plan is provided in Appendix C.)

Step #3: Design a Monitoring Process

As soon as the individual is using one or more signals consistently, it is time to expand the communication system (discussed in more detail in Chapter 6). To determine whether signals are being used consistently, a data collection system should be established that documents communicative behavior during structured interactions as well as the spontaneous use of communicative signals. Data should be collected only as often as needed to obtain a representative picture of performance. Once or twice a week might be sufficient for individuals who progress slowly and whose behavior is consistent. Having observers, such as the speech-language pathologist, collect data during weekly consultative visits is particularly useful because it lessens the burden on the communication partners and provides a fresh perspective on the interactions and how they might be improved. Regularly scheduled team meetings should be arranged in order to review the data and address issues that arise.

Small notepads or file cards make data collection less intrusive, thereby drawing less attention to the individual. Similarly, delaying the recording of data until after the event and during a more private moment is another way to avoid drawing undue attention to the individual with a disability, such as might occur with a more obvious data collection method. Figure 5.3 is a data sheet for collecting information on Mary's communication in structured and spontaneous situations. It was designed to fit on two 3-inch × 5-inch index cards or on one page of a small notebook. The left side of the table monitors communicative behavior in structured situations. For example, in the second column ("Reach/touch to request [initiate]") we see that Mary reached/touched to initiate a request on 9 of the 10 occasions (i.e., 90% of the occasions) in which the symbols were arranged to be within sight or reach. Using a percentage permits us to compare one day or session to another when the number of opportunities to respond varies. For example, if she reached/touched 18 times but there were 20 opportunities for her to do so, then her performance would be comparable to the previous day (18/20 = 90%) even though the total number of initiations doubled. There are many resources on data collection strategies, some of which are listed in Suggested Readings at the end of the book.

Step #4: Teach Partners to Carry out the Communication Plan

While implementing the first three steps, the team agrees upon the signals, symbols, pragmatic and discourse functions, and contexts in which to focus the initial communication training; develops a written plan describing the training process; and designs a data collection procedure. These are all key components in designing a system. If, however, the system is to be successful, all partners must know how to interact with the individual. The use of live demonstrations and videotapes, along with the written plan, is one approach to training. The training content should address the various aspects of the written plan.

Partners must learn to identify the communicative signals. If a signal is difficult to identify, partners may be unable to respond consistently. For example, Donna, a

WRITTEN PLAN

Pragmatic and discourse functions	Symbol system	Procedure
Structured interactions *Requests objects* by reaching for or touching [*initiate* discourse]	**Objects:** Food items, tape recorder or audiotapes, computer disks, computer books, nonpreferred objects **Partial object package:** Front of graham cracker box, label and cellophane of cookie package, front of milk or juice carton	1. Make certain that one or more symbols are within reach or within sight (e.g., on her desk) when she arrives. Wait for her to initiate. 2. If she reaches or touches an object, give it to her while expanding on her communication (e.g.,"You want the ___"). Then help her engage in the activity (e.g., set up the tape recorder, read to her). To provide additional opportunities, stop the activity (e.g., after one song on the tape recorder, after one page of story). Wait for her to initiate reaching/touching as a signal she wants more. 3. If she does not reach or touch, get her attention and repeat the procedure once more. 4. If she responds, carry through as described above. Otherwise, stop and try again later.
Requests objects to make *choice* by reaching for or touching [*maintain* discourse]	Same as above	1. Place two symbols (objects or parts of packages) in front of her. Point to one object/part of package (e.g., audiotape) and ask (e.g., "Tape?"). Repeat with other object/part of package (e.g., "Book?"). 2. If she reaches or touches one of the symbols, give it to her while expanding on her communication (e.g., "You want the ___"). Then help her engage in the activity. 3. If she does not reach or touch, get her attention and repeat the procedure once more. 4. If she responds, carry through as described above. Otherwise, stop and try again later.

Protests by pushing objects away *[terminate* discourse]	Items she does not prefer or want; for example, after she makes a choice, do the activity (e.g., read a story) for a short time and then stop; present something she typically does not want (e.g., manipulative objects such as Lego blocks)	1. Place undesirable items in front of her. 2. If she pushes item away, remove it while saying "No." 3. Provide a choice of desired items, following the plan described above for requesting objects to make a choice. 4. If she does not respond by pushing away the undesirable item, draw her attention to it (e.g., tap or move the object) and ask (e.g., "Lego?"). If she pushes it away, proceed as described above. Otherwise, stop and try again later.
Spontaneously occurring signals *Requests* a walk with a partner *[initiate* discourse]	None	Anytime she leans forward as if to stand, ask, "You want to walk?" Stand up and go with her. After 2 minutes (maximum), return to original activity.
Requests objects by reaching for or touching	Any objects, object packages, or other representations of objects; record new objects or representations so they can be used in future interactions	If she touches or reaches toward an object, give it to her or let her use it while expanding on her communication (e.g., "You want the ___"). Then help her engage in the activity.
Protests by pushing objects away	Same as above	If she pushes an item away, remove it while saying, "No ___."

Figure 5.2. Sample of a written plan for Mary.

	Structured communication opportunities						Spontaneous communication opportunities					
Date	Reach/touch to request [initiate]		Reach/touch to choose [maintain]		Push away to protest		Request walk		Reach/touch to request [initiate]		Push away to protest	
	Content	Times	Content	Times	Content	Times	When	Who	Content	Times	Content	Times
9/12	Audiotape	– + +	Audiotape	+ +	Legos	+ +	8:45 Calendar	MB	Coat to go outside	+	Markers	+
	Drink	+ +	Computer	+ +								
					Food	+ +	9:05 Center	AG				
	Computer	+ +	Book	+ + + + +			1:10 Center	AG				
	Book	+ +			Didn't reject nonpreferred item	– – –	1:20 Center	NH				
			Did not choose	– – – –			2:20 Freetime	CH				
Total	9/10		10/14		5/8		5		1		1	

Figure 5.3. Data sheet for Mary's communication program.

3-year-old with cerebral palsy and visual and hearing impairments, displayed many behaviors that seemed unrelated to the events surrounding her. Each of her partners had a different idea of what was meant by her various behaviors. Consequently, the teacher, speech-language pathologist, and parent chose an existing behavior of slight body tensing as a signal for "more." Other partners remained unable to identify the movement. To ameliorate this confusion, a rocking routine, which is common for 3-year-olds, was chosen as an instructional situation. Donna was held in the adult's lap while he or she sat in a rocking chair. As the chair was moved back and forth, the adult would say, "Rock, rock, rock, rock," in a rhythmic manner. In the midst of this movement, the adult would stop the chair, saying, "Stop," and would wait for a whole body tensing movement from Donna. If Donna moved, the adult said, "More? OK," and resumed rocking. The teacher directly trained the other partners to accept the agreed-upon signal. Data were taken on the number of times these new partners identified Donna's signal within this routine. Videotapes were used to train Donna's other partners who were unable to attend the team meetings. They included frequent partners, such as family members, and less frequent partners, such as her occupational therapist.

Partners must learn how to arrange contexts in order to elicit a communicative response. For example, should the individual be given the wrong item for completing a task in order to elicit a communicative response, or should it be arranged for the necessary item to be missing? Will a nonpreferred item be offered to elicit a protest? Will several food items be placed within reach at lunch in order to permit a choice? Videotapes and live demonstrations of interactions are two ways to help partners understand how to elicit communication.

Partners should understand how to utilize the assessment information about the individual's level of comprehension. If communicating to the individual is part of setting up the context (e.g., requesting that the individual make a choice), it should be at the individual's level of comprehension. Tailoring the request to the individual's level of comprehension may require the partner to point to objects or pictures when speaking to the individual. For example, when arranging the context to elicit a response to indicate a choice, the partner may touch each object while saying its name with a questioning intonation.

The partner's response to a communicative signal should expand upon the individual's signal in order to provide a more advanced communication model. For example, when the youngster chooses by reaching for an object, a verbal response might be, "You want (object name)," accompanied by touching the object.

The data collection system must be reviewed so that partners record reliable data. Having several partners simultaneously record data from videotapes and then discuss their results is sometimes an effective way to clarify the data collection system.

All partners must know how to incorporate special considerations. These considerations may result from sensory or physical needs and may necessitate attending to such factors as lighting, background noise, volume of speech, and appropriate placement of objects and partners so that they can be seen or reached.

Partners must understand the balance between instructionally cued responses and naturally cued initiations or responses. A *cue* is a stimulus that occurs before a particular behavior is performed. It is often assumed that teaching should involve numerous instructional cues. Many researchers challenge this assumption (Falvey, Brown, Lyon, Baumgart, & Schroeder, 1980; Halle, 1985; McDonald, 1985). Many communication cues arise naturally and are not instructional, such as being hungry, needing help, or wanting to avoid a situation. When a high percentage of instructional verbal cues are used, individuals are inadvertently taught to ignore the natural cues and wait for some cue from the instructor. To illustrate, a common teaching method is to hold out a desired object and provide an instructional cue such as, "Sammy, what do you want?" Compare this to how Sammy might respond if the item (e.g., juice) is visible but out of reach and the partner looks expectantly at him. In this situation, Sammy is more likely to initiate communication by reaching for the juice. When the adult cues verbally, he or she needs to be aware that Sammy's chance to initiate has been eliminated. The passivity evidenced in the communication of some individuals with disabilities may result, in part, from overuse of instructional cues.

Step #5: Teach Partners to Respond to Spontaneous Communication

In addition to planned communicative interactions, partners must be prepared to respond to the spontaneous use of identified signals. In some cases, it is possible to respond in the same way one responds in planned situations; however, there may be situations in which it is infeasible to honor the signal. For example, a youngster might request something to eat while on the bus or protest an activity when there is still more work to do. In this situation, the signal can be acknowledged (e.g., "You want to eat," "You want to stop") and the partner may indicate why it is not possible to honor it at this time (e.g., "You can have a snack when we get to school," "We need to finish three more, and then we'll stop").

In addition to knowing how to respond to spontaneous use of targeted signals, partners should know how to respond to all behaviors as potential communicative signals, no matter when or where they occur. This means that training for partners should include the various other communicative functions that might be expressed and how to respond accordingly. Partners should learn to record their observations of potential new signals, functions, and contexts. This is valuable information to use when expanding the communication system.

ADDRESSING COMMUNICATION PARTNER ISSUES

Occasionally issues arise that involve the communication partners, rather than the individual who has a disability. Such issues include attitudinal barriers, conflicting interaction styles, and problems with team collaboration.

Attitudinal Barriers

One of the most important aspects of assessment is the attention given to attitudinal barriers and interaction styles of communication partners. If attitudinal barriers exist, the team must plan ways to address them. For example, a partner may not believe in the individual's ability to communicate. Consequently, the partner may "do things" for the individual—anticipating needs and meeting them—thereby preempting the individual's communication. This attitude must be addressed. One approach is for the team to discuss the philosophy that all behavior is communication. Also, the team should point out how problem behaviors sometimes occur even in individuals who have adequate communication and discuss why this might happen. Examining a videotape of the individual to point out the behaviors that lead to the assignment of meaning to the behavior might be helpful. Readings on the topic might be useful or a trial period might be established during which time the individual helps "test" the hypothesis that a nonconventional behavior is a form of communication.

A second attitudinal barrier is evidenced when a partner is more concerned with following schedules than with providing flexibility to meet an individual's communication needs. Inflexibility surrounding schedules and choice making might be handled by simplifying the schedule of the person with a disability, reducing the number of instructional or other activities, allowing more time to complete tasks, and increasing the emphasis on communication. Later, those aspects of the schedule that were temporarily removed may be reintroduced. Another approach would be to minimize the partner's involvement in the early stages of communicative development until a communication system is established.

A third attitudinal barrier is a partner's discomfort with losing control. Partners sometimes find it difficult to follow the lead of someone who traditionally has been dependent upon them and to provide the individual with an increasing number of choices. It should be pointed out to partners that communication is about controlling one's environment. The reason typically developing children progress from vocalizing and pointing to saying words is that it affords them more control. As mentioned in Section II, there is ample evidence that when communication is controlled by others, individuals with disabilities do not learn to initiate communication (Prizant & Rentschler, 1983).

A fourth attitudinal barrier is the attitude that communication training "is someone else's job," that a team member has "too many things to do already." People communicate all the time, not just during designated portions of the day. Communication training is not tied to a particular discipline or to the particular role or job title of partners. One way to help overcome this attitudinal barrier is to have other partners model how to infuse choices across the day and how to respond to individuals when they do communicate. In addition, administrative support may be necessary in order to decrease the partner's responsibilities while he or she learns the communication system.

Interaction Styles

The assessment phase includes an examination of partners' interaction styles. Two aspects of interaction style are whether the partner is directive or nondirective and if this style is culturally appropriate for the person with a disability. In mainstream American culture, being nondirective is one of many acceptable interaction styles; this style creates multiple opportunities for the individual to initiate and become a more active partner in interactions. A nondirective style also means that partners do not preempt communication by assuming or predicting a need based on the time of day or setting. Instead, they wait for the individual to signal. They also create the need to communicate by arranging situations that will elicit communication. Given the literature on the benefits of a nondirective style to individuals with communication impairments, it is important that this style, if culturally appropriate, be fostered in all communication partners (Prizant & Rentschler, 1983).

Some of the strategies described in the assessment section also can be used as training tools to teach partners to be nondirective. For example, team members can jointly count and discuss directive and nondirective interactions in a videotape or during live observations. Another assessment strategy that can be a training tool is to have communication partners assess their own level of directiveness using a rating scale of interaction style. Also, partners who have directive styles can use the rating scales to record the interaction style of other partners and then discuss their findings. Another training approach is to provide videotaped or live examples of directive and nondirective interactions and then discuss the individual's response to the two styles. It is important to periodically monitor the interaction style of all partners in case some have unintentionally reverted to the more directive form.

If a nondirective style is culturally inappropriate, the communication partners must work with the family to identify culturally appropriate interaction behaviors or the contexts in which it is appropriate for an individual to initiate interactions. These culturally appropriate behaviors and contexts are then incorporated into the plan for facilitating communication.

A second aspect of interaction style is an awareness of how partner behavior, or sequences of behavior, can influence inappropriate behavior. For example, a speech-language pathologist was concerned that her student frequently hit his head with his fist when she worked with him. She videotaped their interaction and completed a Form and Use Assessment Sheet while viewing the videotape. The results clearly showed that her student hit his head when she repeated a request for him to do something. If she asked him once or twice, he did not hit himself; but he typically hit himself during third or fourth requests. She had been unaware that she was repeating her requests so frequently. The assessment process itself provided her with enough motivation to change her style of interaction. Such willingness by all partners to examine interactions continually in order to explain them more fully from a communication viewpoint must become an accepted and expected aspect of their interactions. Any time questions are raised about student communication or behavior, partners should first examine their own behavior in the interaction; systematic examination of videotaped interactions using the Form and Use Assessment Sheet is an effective way to do this.

A third aspect of interaction style is the need to be vigilant in identifying subtle communication signals. It is generally easier for an observer to identify subtle communication signals than it is for the person involved in the interaction to identify them or to use videotapes. It may help frequent partners to be involved occasionally as observers or to examine videotapes. In this way, they can become sensitive to subtle forms of communication and can watch throughout the day for the use of existing signals in other situations and for the occurrence of new signals.

Team Collaboration

The team usually is composed of independent individuals who have all types of experience with augmenting communication, differing views of the individual's communication competence, and varying attitudes toward their roles as team members. It is no wonder that initial meetings of the team are often tense, emotional, and of limited productivity. Rarely does a team meet, agree, and leave the first meeting happy and satisfied. Why then do team members hope for this and feel disappointed when the meeting does not go smoothly? Maybe a different perspective of the team collaboration process is needed.

Fratelli (1993) wrote an excellent article, "Life Stages of a Team." Fratelli describes four stages of team development: *forming*, *storming*, *norming*, and *performing*. During the forming stage, the team is working to establish its goals and ways to work toward them. Team members are excited but also anxious about these goals. In the midst of this, the team is subtly and pervasively establishing the types of

PUPIL EDUCATIONAL TEAM COMMUNICATION (ETC) FORM

Pupil: ______________________

Classroom: ______________________

Date	Concern	Procedure/action	By when	Major responsibility	Disposition/comments	Date
Date of meeting where concern is discussed	Abbreviated version of the concern (i.e., toileting program, behavior on playground)	What will be done in response to the concern (i.e., take to bathroom every hour, reinforce cooperative play with praise and 10 points at end of recess)?	When will the procedure be implemented?	Who will take responsibility for implementing the procedure?	Status of the concern / procedure when reviewed (i.e., accidents reduced to two per week, take to bathroom every 2 hours, continue to reinforce cooperative play but take back to classroom if hits)	Date when concern is reviewed

Figure 5.4. Pupil Educational Team Communication (ETC) Form. (From Lynch, V. [1979]. *Educational Team Communication Form*. Seattle: Experimental Education Unit, Program Development Services, University of Washington; reprinted by permission.)

group behavior deemed acceptable. Usually, the more vocal group members steer the meeting.

The storming stage is just what its name implies. It is a time of unrest, conflict, defensiveness, and questioning. Team members may realize that the initial efforts of the team are taking them in an unexpected direction. Members become territorial about their area of expertise, and there is much tension during the meeting. A good team leader will anticipate this stage and facilitate movement through the stage by acknowledging it as an expected process.

In the norming stage, Fratelli notes that the team members coalesce, thinking collectively rather than individually. The norms for team behavior have been established and all members cooperate in discussions of strategies. This is accompanied by a sense of relief and more camaraderie among team members, with greater balance in the contribution of each.

Finally, during the performing stage, the team members are functioning cohesively to solve problems, make decisions, and reflect on their own interrelationships. Often, a loyalty to the team is formed in the process. All members are considered to be legitimate contributors.

Awareness of the various stages is beneficial in that the team members can cooperate in moving the team through the more difficult early stages to the more productive latter stages. Each time a new team member appears, the process may begin anew.

Team members can periodically assess and discuss their team functioning in greater detail. A Teaming Checklist that might be used for this purpose is provided in Appendix C. To keep better track of team decisions and responsibilities, Lynch (1992) suggests using the Educational Team Communication (ETC) Form shown in Figure 5.4. Instructions for completing each part of the form are included in the figure. The figure includes an example of how the form can be used for a pupil; however, the same headings can be used for team decisions not directly related to an individual. A blank ETC form is provided in Appendix C for pupils and for general team collaboration. This form is used during the course of the meeting to document objectives, time lines, and team member responsibilities. Additional resources on the team process are listed in the Suggested Readings at the end of this book.

SUMMARY

This chapter described the steps in designing an initial communication strategy, including key questions to ask when completing the following steps: 1) enhance existing communication forms, functions, symbols, and contexts; 2) put the various pieces of the plan together; 3) design a monitoring process; 4) teach partners to carry out the communication plan; and 5) teach partners to respond to spontaneous communication. The chapter included a discussion of potential barriers to communication that could arise from partners' attitudes and interaction style. Finally, information was provided about the process of team collaboration.

Chapter 6

Expanding the Communication System

Chapter 5 outlined procedures for starting an initial communication system while relying on existing behavioral forms and functions, contexts, activities, and partners. This chapter builds on the previous one by suggesting means for expanding that system. Such system expansion requires that the individual consistently use initial signals with reliably responsive partners.

METHODS FOR EXPANDING THE SYSTEM

Several options are available for expanding the system. The particular options chosen for a student and the order in which they are implemented depends on the individual's circumstances and the priorities established by the team. Once again, factors from both the Partner's Domain and Individual's Domain from the Sociocommunicative Filter Model (see Chapters 3 and 4) come together in planning a strategy for expanding the communication system. The various options for system expansion are the following:

1. Use the system in new contexts and activities.
2. Introduce new communication partners.
3. Modify the behavioral forms to be more conventional.
4. Select new behavioral forms that serve existing functions.
5. Modify symbolic forms to be more conventional.
6. Add new content.
7. Add new functions to existing behavioral forms.
8. Decrease the level of assistance.

Expansion of the system should be done systematically, with only one or two changes occurring at a time. Communication partners must be trained in how to interact at each successive stage of expansion. Chapter 18 shows how a lack of training and collaboration can result in a swift end to any carefully designed communication system. A list that teams can use to help plan the system expansion is shown in Table 6.1, and an example of a completed list for Mary is provided in Table 6.2 on page 104. The first column of Table 6.1 features the expansion options (e.g., behavioral form) and some areas to consider during expansion (e.g., changing photographs to picture symbols). The other two columns are for describing the existing system and how it might be further developed. In the following sections, each expansion area is discussed in greater detail.

Use the System in New Contexts and Activities

If the frequency of a signal's use is low, the team may want to expand the number of contexts and activities in which it is used. This might involve using parts of the individual's daily routine that were not part of the initial training system or changing the daily routine by adding new contexts and activities. It is important to make the system maximally efficient in as many different contexts and activities as possible. For example, if the signal is recognized consistently during grooming at home, perhaps it could be recognized in a public restroom at a shopping center and in the school restroom.

When selecting new opportunities in which to use the communication system, if the individual has not previously displayed the communicative response in these contexts and activities, the team should be certain that the activities can be arranged to elicit communication. For example, the activities should include stimuli that are highly desirable to the individual, and the team should ensure that the response can be recognized and honored in the new contexts and activities. If interruption or delay of a routine is the instructional strategy, then the activity should be familiar and predictable. The individual must be able to predict what happens next. When the partner delays his or her usual response, the individual should then be able to fill in the missing portion of the routine. For example, if an individual is holding a toothbrush, ready to brush his or her teeth, the toothpaste could be placed in sight but out of reach. The adult could delay the usual routine of getting the toothpaste for the individual until the individual uses his or her request signal.

Similarly, an examination of typical daily activities will reveal situations in which choices could be made available without disrupting the flow of activities. For example, if John were given a choice of each activity in his morning grooming routine, which consists of washing his hands, brushing his teeth, brushing his hair, and shaving, he might not be finished in time to catch the school bus. However, John's mother could ask him which grooming task he wants to do first and then set the order of the remaining tasks herself. Or, his teacher could dedicate a longer time period for grooming as part of a self-help objective. He or she could give John the opportunity to make choices throughout the routine until it is finished.

Mary

The team expanded the contexts and activities in which Mary could use her communication system (Table 6.2). Because she had few opportunities to request non-food-related objects and activities, the team identified a previously unused activity—preparing for dismissal—in which Mary

Table 6.1. Options for expanding an existing communication system

Expansion option	Existing[a]	New[b]
1. Add new contexts/ activities. Frequent (Daily) Infrequent (weekly, monthly)	Describe existing contexts/ activities.	Can new contexts/activities be added using existing partners, functions, and forms? Describe the new contexts/activities.
2. Add partners. Familiar Unfamiliar	List existing partners.	Can new communication partners be added in existing instructional contexts/activities? List the new partners.
3. Modify behavioral forms to be more conventional. Vocal Verbal Gestural Gaze Other	Describe existing forms.	Are more conventional or recognizable behavioral forms needed? Describe the new forms.
4. Select new behavioral forms that serve existing functions.	Describe existing forms and functions.	Are there new behavioral forms that can be used for existing functions? Describe new forms and functions.
5. Modify symbolic forms to be more conventional. Real objects Miniature objects Replicas Photographs Pictures Line drawings Manual signs Written words Speech Other	Describe existing symbolic forms.	Are more conventional or recognizable symbolic forms needed? Describe new symbolic forms.
6. Add new content (vocabulary).	List the existing content.	Is there new content that can be used with existing functions? List the new content.
7. Add new functions.[c] Behavior regulation Social interaction Joint activity	List the existing functions.	Can the same behavioral form be used for a new function? Describe the new functions that existing forms will serve.
8. Decrease the level of assistance. Instructional versus natural cues Response prompts	Describe the existing level of assistance.	Do instructional cues or response prompts need to be faded? Describe how assistance will be faded.

[a]Currently in use.
[b]Ways to expand system.
[c]See Wetherby and Prizant (1989).

Table 6.2. Ideas for expanding Mary's initial communication system for requesting food/leisure items by reaching for or touching

Expansion option	Existing[a]	New[b]
1. Add new contexts/ activities.	Request food at lunch and snack. Request leisure at arrival and centers.	*Can new contexts/activities be added using existing partners, functions, and forms?*[c] Request food: Nothing new Request leisure: Ten minutes of free time prior to 3 P.M. dismissal
2. Add partners.	Request food at lunch—teacher snack—teacher Request leisure at arrival—peer centers—education assistant	*Can new partners be added in existing instructional contexts/activities?* Request food at lunch—education assistant snack—peer Request leisure at arrival—two new peers centers—two new peers
3. Modify behavioral forms to be more conventional.	Reach for or touch symbols.	*Are more conventional/ recognizable behavioral forms needed?* Reach or touch, then look at communication partner.
4. Select new behavioral forms that serve existing functions.	Reaches or touches symbols to request; pushes objects away to protest; requests a walk by leaving her seat	*Are there new behavioral forms that can be used for existing functions?* At recess, she stands beside playground equipment as a form of request. This can be a new behavioral form to request (in this case, playing on the equipment).
5. Modify symbolic forms to be more conventional.	Real objects: food, tape recorder, audiotape, computer, computer disk Part of object package: front of graham cracker box, label/cellophane of cookie package, front of milk or juice carton	*Are more conventional or recognizable symbolic forms needed?* Real objects: Substitute part of package for audiotape (cover of holder) and computer disk (part of the box in which disks come). Part of the object package: Decrease size of partial package for all objects.
6. Add new content (vocabulary).	Same as above	*Is there new content that can be used with existing functions?* At recess, playground equipment that she requests to play on is new content.

(*continued*)

Table 6.2. *(continued)*

Expansion option	Existing[a]	New[b]
7. Add new functions.	Request (initiate) food and leisure activities.	*Can the same behavioral form be used for a new function?* Use "reach for/touch" to get attention of another
8. Decrease the level of assistance.	Items placed within reach; wait for her to initiate. No instructional cues or response prompts	*Do instructional cues or response prompts need to be faded?* Place symbols farther away (e.g., on an adjacent desk, at the other end of the lunch table) so that she must move closer to them to signal.

[a]Currently in use.

[b]Ways to expand system.

[c]See Mary's schedule in Chapter 3 (pp. 39–41).

could make requests. If she and a few peers would quickly get ready for dismissal, they would have almost the full 10 minutes to participate in several leisure activities of Mary's choosing.

Introduce New Communication Partners

Some individuals have a limited number of communication partners who can understand their communication attempts. This might occur because less familiar partners have difficulty understanding the signals, or there may be a limited number of partners available in the contexts in which the initial training occurred. The more communication partners there are, the stronger and more legitimate the communication system becomes. It may, therefore, be necessary to add partners in the initial training contexts, such as training more peers to be partners, or to increase the number of contexts in which communication training occurs. Adding new partners is also a way to overcome attitudinal barriers. By involving new partners in the communication process, they gain new respect for the individual and his or her abilities. Table 6.2 illustrates how Mary's system might be expanded by involvement of new partners in existing contexts and activities.

Modify the Behavioral Forms to Be More Conventional

A behavioral form that is more conventional is one that is recognized more easily by members of the individual's cultural community without providing the community members with specific training. Chapter 5 stressed the need to identify existing behaviors that can be given communication value and to observe these behaviors as having communicative intent. The initial behaviors selected, however, are often not conventional in appearance. The use of a more readily understood behavior to communicate often affords the individual more opportunities to interact with a larger group of communication partners. For example, if the existing behavioral form consists of looking at a desired item and touching it in order to request that item, an even clearer form in many cultures is touching while alternating gaze between the item and the person who can obtain the item. To achieve the new response, the partner might, after the individual points and looks at the item, bring it closer to the individual and wait, hoping that the individual will look at the partner in a puzzled manner. If the individual does, then the object is provided. If the individual does not, prompting might be needed initially (e.g., shaking the object next to the partner's face) to elicit the behavior of looking at the partner.

As another example, if requests are being made by looking at a desired object, a more conventional form is to reach for the object. This might be taught by bringing an object, at which the student is looking, within reach, but not providing it until the youngster moves his or her arm toward the object. If this does not occur initially, prompting (e.g., physical guidance) might be provided and then faded. Whatever new forms are selected, they must be ones that the individual can readily display or can be easily prompted. If a new form is too difficult, it may become a barrier to communication, rather than a means to expand the system. The team must make certain that the behavior is culturally appropriate. Also, if the individual has physical impairments, a therapist should be consulted to be sure that the form can be displayed without disruption of appropriate physical positioning.

Mary

Mary's existing behavioral form of reaching or touching was recognizable to familiar people, but not to unfamiliar people (see Table 6.2). Therefore, a new form for her would be to reach or touch while looking at her partner.

Select New Behavioral Forms that Serve Existing Functions

When new behavioral forms are added, they should serve existing functions. In other words, the new forms should represent another means to achieve a familiar communication goal (e.g., request, protest, greet). Javier, for example, vocalized to request the continued actions of rocking and swinging. It was noticed that he often lifted his arms slightly in anticipation of being lifted up. "Arms up" was chosen as a new form for requesting that the adult continue the motion of picking up Javier. The adult would come near Javier with hands in position for picking him up and pause with hands firmly under Javier's armpits, lifting slightly. When Javier lifted his arms, he was using a new signal to request continuation. If possible, the adult can take advantage of an existing movement, so progress will be more rapid. Again, the physical form must be culturally appropriate and not in conflict with any needs related to the individual's physical positioning and movement.

Mary

In Mary's example (see Table 6.2), a new behavioral form was selected in order to expand her system. In addition to her now established system of requesting by reaching for or touching objects or object containers, she would take a partner (a new behavioral form) to a playground apparatus on which she wanted to play.

Modify Symbolic Forms to Be More Conventional

The symbolic form is the representation used as a code for the meaning of the message. Symbolic forms may be quite abstract, such as spoken or written words, manual signs, or line drawings, or, they may closely resemble the item to which they refer, as with photographs or colored catalog pictures. The forms also may be quite obvious in meaning, such as actual objects or realistic replicas of the objects.

At least two scenarios are possible with individuals who have disabilities. First, an individual may have the potential to learn the representative value of the more abstract symbols mentioned (Sevcik, Romski, & Wilkinson, 1991). In this case, gradual changes from more obvious icons to more abstract forms are targeted in successive steps. For example, if the individual currently points to actual objects, changing the symbolic form to pictures might be the new form. This might be achieved by interjecting a picture whenever the individual points to an object and prompting him or her to touch the picture before giving the requested object. The picture might be provided concurrently with the object (e.g., beside it) or after the object has been touched. Jeremy's story (see Chapter 15) illustrates this process and also how difficult it can be to introduce a more abstract symbol system.

Mary

Mary (see Table 6.2) presently uses both real objects and parts of packages in which objects come. More conventional (and easier to use) symbolic forms would be pictures. At this time, however, Mary does not recognize the meaning of pictures. Furthermore, before moving on she needs to build her vocabulary at this current symbolic level so that she has a firm foundation. The next step, then, would be to capitalize on her ability to utilize parts of packages by adding the number of objects requested using the partial package symbol system. Then, to make more choices available at one time, another goal would be to decrease the size of existing packaging used as symbols. This could be done by cutting the package so that it includes only the most essential part (e.g., product title or logo).

Numerous articles have been written about hierarchies of symbol types. The term "transparent" is used for symbols that are icons and easily recognized by everyone (Fuller et al., 1992). "Opaque" refers to symbols that are abstract; the link between the symbol and its referent must be learned. There is general agreement that real objects are transparent, whereas written words, Blissymbols, and the majority of manual signs are opaque. Somewhere between these two points fall the rest of the symbol types—parts of objects, colored pictures, photographs, black-and-white line drawings, and miniature objects (Fuller et al., 1992; Mirenda & Locke, 1989; Sevcik et al., 1991). Also, there is general agreement that life-size representations are more transparent than smaller sizes. The exact hierarchy of abstractness or opaqueness of these symbols, however, may vary from one individual to the next.

How is this information used to select the next symbol form? After considering the general guidelines, the selection should be individualized. As mentioned, not all individuals find photographs to be more like icons, or transparent, than line drawings. Photographs can be confusing to someone with figure–ground perception difficulties. One might find that an individual who does not recognize any two-dimensional drawings has learned two or three sight words through the repeated use of a stimulus-response-reinforcement instructional approach (Sevcik et al.,

1991). Team members should remain open to using multiple symbol types with an individual. It should never be assumed that he or she is unable to use a particular symbol type.

The second scenario involves individuals who may be slow to develop representational awareness or who have immediate needs for communication in order to participate in settings with partners who may be unable to recognize their current symbol system. For example, a picture or list of words might be used to order food in a restaurant. These symbols are meaningful to the restaurant worker, while the act of using the symbols has meaning for the individual with a disability because it is a tool to reach a desired goal. Although the individual has learned when and where to use the symbols, he or she may not have understood the usual meaning attached to each picture or word.

Sometimes, changes in the symbolic form occur without specific planning. The individual may accidently discover a form that others understand. For example, Jenny, who has visual and hearing impairments, was crawling around her house one day and found a metal tube on the floor. She held it up, vocalized, and headed toward the bathroom. When she arrived, she reached for the metal bar surrounding the toilet, dropping the metal tube. Her mother, who observed this, added a small metal tube to Jenny's object board. Jenny immediately began to use it to request "bathroom."

Add New Content

Increasing the number of objects, actions, and people to which one refers in communication is comparable to expanding the vocabulary. When new content is added, it should serve existing functions. The schedules that were completed during the assessment stage may be a good resource in identifying new content. By examining familiar routines, it may be evident that the individual has been exposed to other vocabulary and he or she might want to express some of these. For example, Maria consistently reaches toward a milk carton to request "milk." Now she has begun to reach toward the soft drink vending machine that she walks by on the way to the bus (i.e., she has expanded her vocabulary to include soft drinks).

Mary

While observed on the playground, Mary seemed to request playing on the playground equipment. (Because she needed assistance to play on the equipment, this also could be regarded as a request for help.) Playground equipment could become new content to be used as part of the existing communicative function of requesting (see Table 6.2). Mary's example also illustrates how new content often accompanies other forms of system expansion. In this case, as described previously, the new content was associated with a decision to expand the behavioral forms (e.g., standing next to the equipment) used to serve existing functions (e.g., requesting).

Add New Functions to Existing Behavioral Forms

Communication is powerful and efficient. Efficiency is reflected by the fact that a single form can often do several jobs. For example, "more" can function as a request in many different situations, and it can function as a comment that there *is* more. "Mom" can be used to gain attention, request, protest, label, or comment.

Using Wetherby and Prizant's (1989) listing of functions, an individual's existing forms can be examined for the variety of functions served. For example, if vocalization combined with looking at an adult is used to request a social routine, an examination of daily routines might indicate that this same behavioral form also might be used to request food at lunch or to comment on an object or activity by drawing one's attention to it. The more functions a behavioral or symbolic form can serve, the more efficient the communication system.

In Mary's case, it was decided that the reach for or touch behavioral form could serve a new function of getting someone's attention (see Table 6.2).

Because the system will change and new partners, as well as ongoing ones, will need training in how to interact with the individual, it may be helpful to standardize a training system. One approach is always to videotape someone demonstrating the changes. It is useful to have a designated person who ensures that necessary partners are trained. Because of the staff turnover rate in some programs, this assignment should be given to a person whose role in the individual's life is stable, such as a parent or teacher.

Decrease the Level of Assistance

The system can be expanded by changing or fading the instructional assistance to less intensive levels. By examining the details of routines, the team can become aware of the balance between instructionally cued responses and naturally cued initiations. An *instructional cue* is a stimulus that occurs before a particular behavior is performed. A *response prompt* is extra assistance to help the student correctly respond to the natural or instructional cue. Often it is assumed that "teaching" should involve numerous instructional cues. Researchers (e.g., Falvey et al., 1980; Halle, 1985; McDonald, 1985) have challenged this assumption. Many of the cues used for communication arise from natural conditions such as hunger or needing help. When a high percentage of instructional cues is used, in essence, individuals are taught to ignore the natural cues and wait for a cue from the instructor.

To illustrate, a common training method is to hold up a desired item and ask, "Sammy, what do you want?" When the adult provides such verbal (i.e., asking for a label) and gestural (i.e., holding up the item) cues, he or she needs to be aware that Sammy's chance to initiate has been eliminated. The passivity often described in case studies of individuals with mental disabilities may, in some cases, be a result of overuse of instructional cues. A better approach is to see what Sammy does when, for example, the juice is present but out of reach. If Sammy wants the juice because he has just had a salty snack and the adult holds it back looking expectantly, Sammy is likely to reach for the juice. This allows him to initiate communication without a cue.

If instructional cues are used, there are methods for systematically fading their use that are similar to the way instructional prompts are faded. One approach is to gradually increase the time between the occurrence of the natural and instructional cue (i.e., time delay procedure) (Wolery, Ault, Gast, Doyle, & Griffen, 1990). For example, if the instructional cue consists of holding a desirable object out of reach and asking the student what he or she wants, the cue could be faded by placing the object on a shelf out of reach, directing the student's attention to it, and then waiting expectantly for a response. Initially, one could wait 1 second, and then provide the instructional cue if the student does not respond in that time or if he or she begins to respond incorrectly. Gradually, if the student consistently waits for the instructional cue or occasionally responds correctly, the length of the "wait" interval could be increased to 2 seconds, then 3 seconds, then 4 seconds. Four seconds is usually the longest interval needed, because most students begin to respond spontaneously by 4 seconds. Of course, more time may be needed if the individual has any physical impairments.

There are many other approaches to fading the cue, just as there are with fading response prompts (e.g., verbal, modeling, and physical prompts). For example, less of the instructional prompt could be given over time (e.g., "What do you want?", "What?", and finally, no cue and wait for an independent response). Because of the time needed to fade instructional cues and response prompts, it is preferable to omit them in the first place, if possible, and have the youngster communicate in the presence of the natural cue only.

Mary

In Mary's example (see Table 6.2), neither instructional cues nor response prompts were utilized. However, a certain amount of arranging of the instructional setting was required, making certain that objects she wanted were nearby. A more natural scenario would be to leave the objects where they are typically located, such as on the classroom shelves and in closets. Mary would then have to go to the objects before making a request. One must be careful in making adjustments such as this one. If the new system takes too much effort (i.e., it is no longer as efficient for Mary), she may refuse to use the system or will utilize some other form to communicate, such as displaying problem behavior.

PRACTICAL CONSIDERATIONS

Successful augmentative communication systems take into consideration the practical factors surrounding everyday use of the system. Some of these factors are portability, audience, time required to make noncommercial systems, maintenance, and expansion. A number of questions are listed below to assist in the process of choosing an appropriate system. Addressing these questions prior to the final design and selection of the system will help ensure the design of a successful system with minimal oversights.

Portability

Portability refers to the ease with which the system can be moved or carried. Because voice and hands are usually "built in"—a part of the individual—they are the most portable. Systems other than the voice or hands present an added burden in terms of portability. A goal, then, is to minimize this burden if such "external" systems are being considered. The following questions can assist with this goal:

1. Is there a way (other than holding it) to transport the system? Possibilities include the following:
   a. Attaching it to a wheelchair
   b. Carrying it in a backpack, purse, wallet, pocket, notebook, or waist pack
   c. Attaching it to a belt
   d. Having someone else carry it
   e. Having copies of the system in numerous places

2. Can the size and weight of the system be limited? Possibilities include the following:
   a. Designing the system for a 3-inch × 5-inch or 5-inch × 7-inch holder
   b. Removing and adding items so that all vocabulary does not have to be carried to all places (e.g., when going to recess, remove the classroom items and add the items that relate to communication on the playground)

Audience

Audience refers to the people with whom the user will send and receive messages. Consider the following points to ensure that the system(s) uses means that are readily understood:

1. Will adults, including those who are familiar and unfamiliar with the system, readily understand the specific meaning of the message? Would written words attached to the symbol help with comprehension?
2. Will same-age peers, including those who are familiar and unfamiliar with the system, understand the messages that are sent? For nonreading peers, will there be someone nearby to interpret the message to them?
3. Will one system meet the needs of the audience, or are different systems needed for different audiences?
4. Is the system usable by others who wish to send messages paired with words to the person with a disability? Would this enhance comprehension by the person with a disability? What is needed to enable use of the system by partners and to ensure comprehension by the person with a disability?

Time Required to Make Noncommercial Systems

Communication systems that require a substantial investment of time or resources for construction or modification may be a disincentive to modifying or expanding the system to keep pace with the individual's communication needs. Some issues to consider in designing the system are the following:

1. Are materials (e.g., symbols, holders) readily available?
2. Can the same materials be utilized when expanding the system without the need to reconstruct the entire system?
3. Can computer-generated symbols (e.g., line drawings) be utilized so that they can be easily modified (e.g., changes in size, modification of the symbol such as highlighting or deleting certain features)?
4. Can others construct or modify the system in case the original developer leaves?

Maintenance

After a communication system has been constructed, procedures and personnel should be identified for ensuring that it remains in good condition. Systems used during meals and breaks typically require cleaning after each use. Likewise, their use during recess, community outings, and transporting can be particular hard on systems and result in the need for more frequent repair. To help ensure that systems remain in good condition, consider the following issues:

1. Can the cleaning of the system be incorporated into any of the individual's existing cleaning routines so that the system is regularly maintained?
2. Who will take primary responsibility for cleaning and repairing the system? How will the user be involved in these activities?

3. Is the system durable enough to withstand the use it will receive? Will moisture or rough handling cause it to deteriorate? What can be done to minimize the damage from such use (e.g., selection of durable materials, use of protective overlays)?
4. Are there additional symbols (e.g., line drawings) and symbol holders readily available so that the system can be repaired quickly without long periods of time in which the individual is without a system?
5. If the system cannot be quickly repaired, is a back-up system available? This could be a duplicate of the original system or a alternative system that still permits the individual's communication needs to be met. An extremely important rule is always to have a back-up system available.

Expansion

Expansion refers to the design and use of a more complex communication system. As described in the next chapter, there are many ways in which a system can be expanded. However, there are some basic questions that, if addressed in the initial design of the system, can make the system expansion go more smoothly:

1. Can the layout and organization of the system facilitate larger utterances (e.g., use of two-word combinations such as "want drink")?
2. Are the symbols that are selected for use readily available (e.g., line drawings)? If not, could a combination of symbol types be used, such as photographs and line drawings, so that the system can be used in the absence of available symbols?
3. Will expansion substantially increase the bulk of the system and hinder its portability? If so, could vocabulary for specific settings be kept in that setting and added whenever it is appropriate?
4. What procedures are in place to ensure continued input from the family, user, and others into the expansion of the system?
5. What evaluation system will be used to determine the current success and problems with the communication system? Can the evaluation system be used when the system is expanded?
6. Who has primary responsibility for expanding the system?

POSSIBLE PROBLEMS WITH THE SYSTEM

It is necessary to remain flexible when expanding the communication system in order to solve problems that arise. It is possible to overlook a critical problem that blocks the further development of the system. Some of these problems have been discussed already, such as adult-initiated interactions that preempt communication and lead to the individual being a respondent rather than an initiator of communication.

Individual Does Not Seem "Motivated"

A common problem is that the individual does not seem "motivated" to use the communication system. In this case, several factors should be examined. First, the individual's awareness of his or her ability to manipulate others through communication should be examined. If the individual does not know he or she has an effect on others, he or she may appear unmotivated. This awareness can be achieved only if the partners consistently respond to communicative attempts.

Second, the functions served by the communicative signal and the contexts in which the signals are used should be reviewed. The signals and functions must address the *individual's* needs, not the needs of the partners; that is, the system must afford the individual power over his or her partners. Power means being able to make requests, protest, and otherwise join in conversations without being prompted with questions. It means that the individual initiates the interaction, relying on natural cues as much as possible (Falvey et al., 1980; Halle, 1985; McDonald, 1985). It means that the individual communicates about things he or she believes are important, not about things the partners believe to be important. When we attempt to teach communication out of context, such as sitting at a desk teaching a youngster to point to pictures as we say, "Show me the ___," we relegate the individual to the role of a responder (not an initiator) and we teach the individual that communication is a test unrelated to daily needs and interests.

Third, the vocabulary (content) of the communication system should be examined. The individual may have lost interest in the choices represented by the vocabulary. The vocabulary may be too simple or too complex. Perhaps the vocabulary has been used so much that the individual is bored with it, or, the vocabulary may not allow the individual adequate control over his or her environment.

Physical and Sensory Needs of the Individual

Some problems are a result of the physical and sensory needs of the individual. If a youngster's sitting position is unstable, this can interfere with pointing accurately to objects. Placement of symbols, relative to physical or visual abilities, and lighting and noise characteristics of the environment are other factors that may affect use of the system (see Chapter 4). These issues point out the need to have all relevant team members involved in examining problems associated with the use of a communication system.

Dreams of the Future Linked to Present Needs and Abilities

More schools and other agencies are using a future-oriented, quality of life approach to planning for individuals, such as Person-Centered Planning (Mount & Zwernik, 1988) and Planning Alternative Tomorrows with Hope (PATH; Pearpoint, O'Brien, & Forest, 1994). These approaches focus on the quality of an individual's life by pursuing goals he or she chooses or would choose if he or she were able to do so. Often these are dreams of the future, unfettered by present constraints and traditional ways of thinking about what one needs to learn or develop within particular discipline areas, such as personal communication. Team members may include those who know the individual (e.g., friends) or people who are willing to invest in helping him or her reach personal goals (e.g., neighbors, extended family, professionals).

Professionals on the team may participate in a discipline-free manner (Giangreco, Cloninger, & Iverson, 1993) whereby they help plan ways to achieve the goals, regardless of whether there is a communication, motor, or other component related to their specific discipline. A plan might involve, for example, working with an agency to acquire funding for a wheelchair lift in order to provide more freedom for the individual or helping the individual develop a friendship network for evenings and weekends. Professionals might also function in a more discipline-specific manner when necessary. Communication development, in particular, is crucial because of its role in promoting independence and control over one's life. The communication goals must, however, fit within any larger goals related to the future.

The long-term goals established through this process may not be realized for many years, but they provide a destination. The challenge is to chart a course to that destination from the individual's present location. In terms of communication, the present location for some individuals consists of limited comprehension and few means to express one's self. In many cases, the concept of communication is not even established, so awareness of being able to control one's environment is absent.

The first task, then, is to establish a system, such as the one described in Chapter 5. Once the system is in use, however, we need to chart a course to the destination established through the person-centered planning process. This course helps establish how the system is expanded, as discussed previously in this chapter.

The following is one approach to using the future planning information for expanding the communication system:

1. After the top priorities have been identified by the team, identify potential settings in which the individual might participate and the communication needs of those settings—functions, minimal level of behavioral and symbolic forms, and potential partners.
2. Determine whether the communication goals in these settings can be attained best by instructing the individual, adapting the physical environment, or working with people in those settings.
3. When planning how to expand the individual's communication system, use the communication needs for the future to help identify partners, contexts, functions, and forms. These needs, however, must be balanced with the need to firmly establish a communication system. Otherwise, if expansion is too unrelated to *present* needs, the individual may cease to use the system.

Future goals are not static. As the student matures, as parents and others get to know the individual better, and as the individual develops in terms of communication and other areas, future goals may change. Future goals should be reviewed annually and the course from the present to the future must be redesigned to reflect these changes.

SUMMARY

A communication system can become more useful when the system is expanded. The following eight options for expanding a communication system, which were discussed in this chapter, include adding new contexts or activities, adding partners, modifying behavioral forms to be more conventional, selecting new behavioral forms that serve existing functions, modifying symbolic forms to be more conventional, adding new content, adding new functions, and decreasing the level of assistance that is needed to use a system. In addition to expanding the communication system, practical considerations that surround the everyday use of a communication system help enable both the individual and partner to understand what the individual is trying to convey. These considerations are portability of the system, audience, the time required to make a noncommercial system, maintenance, and expansion of the system.

CHAPTER 7

Communication in the Classroom

Students once placed in separate classrooms because of their disabilities are now being taught in general education classrooms along with their same-age peers. When students with disabilities become part of the general education classroom, the classroom teacher faces new challenges as a teacher and as a role model for the students without disabilities. What and how to teach a student with a disability, how to adapt curricula, how to work with a team, how to accommodate physical and/or sensory disabilities, and how to include this student in all aspects of the classroom activity are some challenges the general education teacher faces. A teacher's skills and ability to problem-solve will help him or her to meet those challenges successfully.

But, what if the student has severe or multiple disabilities; wanders around the room and does not respond to verbal directions; or does not appear to understand any gestures, pictures, or activities that are presented? Then the teacher's first challenge will be determining how to communicate with that student, using both formal and informal systems, to help the student move forward to reach his or her full potential as a member of the class and a member of his or her community.

How a teacher communicates with this student will not only affect the student educationally, but it will also set the stage for the inclusion of that student in the overall classroom activity. Communication with the student must demonstrate respect, understanding, and an acceptance of how the student communicates if he or she is to be a valued member of the class.

Often, it is a peer without a disability who will lead the way in communicating with a student who uses an unconventional communication system. Although adults use a limited number of communication styles and a limited number of interaction styles with people of different ages, children typically use a wide array of behaviors to communicate. Hitting, biting, kicking, yelling, spitting, screaming, and crying, as well as less demonstrative behaviors (e.g., staring, pointing, not talking, glaring, touching, gesturing) are still comfortably within the repertoire of children, especially when dealing with peers and siblings. Whereas adults may find certain methods of communication inappropriate and bizarre, children are willing to listen to those behaviors and give credence to their communicative intent. The following illustration of a student, Charles, provides an example of a student with limited communication who is taught to play catch by a peer without a disability.

Charles

When Charles entered the classroom he ran over to play with a large ball. The teacher instructed one of the children to "play with Charles." The child looked at Charles and asked the teacher what they should play. The teacher answered, "Why don't you play catch with him."

The child went over and took the ball from Charles, who was hitting the ball repeatedly with his hand. She then rolled the ball to Charles, telling him to roll it back to her. Charles took the ball back and started hitting the ball again. After several attempts to get Charles to follow her verbal and gestured instructions, the student moved over so that she was next to Charles. She then began imitating Charles's behavior and she, too, hit the ball. The teacher looked dismayed, but chose not to interfere. As the teacher watched, she noticed that each time the helping student hit the ball she pulled it away from Charles a little more. Charles would then reach for the ball to get it back, hit the ball a few times, and then stop, waiting for his friend to take the ball and hit it. After a while his friend stopped hitting the ball, held it for a moment, and then rolled it back to Charles. Charles would hit the ball a few times, stop, and then push the ball toward his friend. Within 15 minutes, the two children were playing catch.

The peer communicated successfully with Charles because she started with behaviors that Charles already had and communicated using behaviors that he understood. The student in the illustration was able to teach Charles because she did not have any set "rules" about teaching the game of catch. She was more than willing to adapt the game to what Charles could do and change the game slowly to a more traditional game of catch. Because children without disabilities are not bound by a set of appropriate behaviors, children with disabilities have less trouble communicating with them than they do with some adults. Because of this, it would be wise for the general education teacher to watch children and determine how they communicate across systems.

Communication between students is an important part of successfully including a student in the classroom. It is just as important that the teacher is able to communicate successfully with the student with a disability. When the student attempts to communicate with the teacher, that communication must be heard, must be seen, and must lead to an appropriate response. If the student tries to communicate and that communication fails (e.g., perhaps the instructional assistant is told to take care of the student), the possibility of the student benefiting from the general classroom placement is jeopardized. If the teacher is unable to understand the student, to respond meaningfully to the student, and/or to discontinue efforts to communicate, then the teacher inadvertently has devalued that student in the eyes of his or her peer group.

Such devaluing does not have to occur. While using creative problem-solving skills and working with team members, new ways to communicate with the students can be discovered. Below are a series of processes that other classroom teachers have found to be successful.

STARTING NOW: IMMEDIATE CONCERNS

How the General Education Teacher Fits into the Team

There are some concerns that need to be addressed immediately when a student with limited communication skills becomes part of the classroom. It is important that the teacher identify and express those concerns to the team of people who work with the student. Teachers must realize, however, that the methods offered here are very different from the methods they would use to resolve a similar concern for a student who does not have a disability. The student's behavior, the classroom environment, the educator's actions and reactions, and the student's needs all need to be examined. The educator will be expected to work with a team, including parents, who will expect to give input into the plan of action. The teacher's needs, in terms of classroom management, may appear to have a low priority. Educators need to have an open mind and remember that everyone is an equal member of the team. The solutions that are offered may be inappropriate given the context of the general education classroom.

Teachers who have not taught students with limited communication skills may be overwhelmed by the prospect of having a student who not only has limited communication skills, but who also uses aggressive, inappropriate, and/or disruptive behavior to communicate.

All Behavior Communicates

Before a teacher decides that he or she can successfully include a student with disabilities in the classroom, the communicative cause of the behavior must be observed. The teacher must accept that the student is using his or her behavior to communicate with the world around him or her, regardless of how different that behavior may appear; this acceptance does not mean the behaviors will continue indefinitely or increase, but rather that the intent of the behavior needs to be acknowledged.

The first step in accepting that all behaviors may be communication is for the general educator to set aside some of his or her own behaviors and reactions that are based on students with higher cognitive abilities and more sophisticated communication systems. When a student tells a teacher that he or she is frustrated, whether by using speech or a typical behavior that indicates frustration (e.g., crying, sitting passively and refusing to complete a task, sharpening a pencil until it is a fourth of an inch long), the teacher's response can be 1) adapting the task so that the student can complete it without being frustrated, 2) reteaching the task because the frustration is caused by a lack of understanding, 3) motivating the student to attempt a task that is difficult by offering a reward of a more preferred activity or item when the task is completed, or 4) using authority to insist that the student do the task even though it will be difficult because the student needs to learn to work through his or her frustration.

When a student uses other, more aggressive, less manageable behaviors to communicate frustration, teachers may find that they do not use the same responses. Often, educators get so caught up in the behavior that they forget to respond to the behavior in terms of what the student just told them. For example, if a student sits quietly at his or her desk, and then stops working and a tear slides out from the corner of his eye, the teacher probably would go to the student and ask him if he is having trouble with the assignment. But, if a student picks up his desk and tips it over, the teacher may find herself unable to go quietly to the student, place the desk upright, and ask, "Are you having trouble with the assignment?"

Theoretically, the second student's behavior has given the same message. The teacher's response may not be based on the message, but on her own interpretation of the behavior as aggressive or disruptive. Because tipping a desk over is not allowed, the student is taken from the room and dealt with in a traditional manner.

Consequences of Ignoring the Message

Two things happen when educators allow themselves to disregard the message: 1) they respond with a behavior that probably is not understood by the student (e.g., the student is asked to leave, is taken from the room, or is placed in time out without ever understanding that the behavior had been dangerous to him- or herself and other students), and 2) the student learns that the consequence of his or her behavior relieves the frustration and somehow gets the desired response (e.g., the student does not have to do the assignment).

The student learns that certain behaviors get certain results. In the second example, the child knows, "If I tip over my desk, I get to leave." The teacher says, "If he does it again, he'll be out of here until he learns that he can't get away with it." Will the student tip over the desk again? Only if he wants to leave the room.

Dealing with the Message

Educators should consider reframing the child's behavior in terms of communication. Teachers should ask themselves if the student is communicating a need or is simply being disruptive. The team is available to help teachers determine which behaviors are communicative and which behaviors are inappropriate and what needs to be done about each behavior. Chapters 2, 3, and 4 discussed assessing behavior as communication. Educators should review these chapters if they are working with a child with disruptive behavior. The team can discuss the implications of the child's behavior in terms of communication.

Once the team has determined how each behavior will be interpreted, it needs to be communicated to the other students, parents, and caregivers who come in contact with this student. The easiest and most effective way to do this is to talk through the communication when the student uses an inappropriate behavior. For example, some very common disruptive behaviors that may signal frustration are making loud noises, nonverbal yelling, or screaming. When these behaviors occur, the communication partner can say, "You are frustrated," "You are angry," or "You would like me to stop and pay attention." This provides a verbal label for the behavior so that others can understand the intent, and it provides feedback to the student that someone is attending to his or her message. The following scenario illustrates how Jesse tries to communicate using what is perceived to be inappropriate behavior.

Jesse

Jesse has cerebral palsy and very limited voluntary movement. He had been placed in a self-contained classroom at the public school. Because of his screaming, the school staff and the group home staff decided to have Jesse taught where he lived. Jesse continued screaming at the group home, and the staff and the teachers decided to respond to his screaming by placing him in time out.

Time out did not decrease Jesse's screaming. The teachers decided to look at the behavior as communication. They decided that Jesse could look steadily at a picture for 10 seconds and associate that picture with an object, activity, or person. Using a Polaroid camera, a series of pictures was taken of all the activities and people to which Jesse could have access. When he started to appear agitated (the staff tried to get to him before he started screaming), he was shown the pictures one at a time. If he followed one picture as it moved across his gaze from midline to the right, it was determined that he wanted that activity or person. Only the choices that were available were shown to him. If he continued to be upset, the staff would let him know that they realized that his needs were not being met and if he would relax they would work with him to figure out what he wanted.

This approach led to a decrease in Jesse's screaming for two reasons. First, Jesse knew that someone understood that he wanted something and he would have the opportunity to make some choices and have some control over his life. Second, if the staff were to be responsive to Jesse, they had to have him near a staff person who was available to respond. Because some of his screaming was to get attention because he was bored, Jesse spent less time by himself and more time with other people.

As illustrated in this example, if the team determines that the student is screaming to signal distress, frustration, or the need to change activities, the teacher will have to show the other students how to interpret this behavior as communication. In Jesse's case, the teacher would notice that Jesse was getting upset. She would walk over to Jesse and say, "I can see that you are trying to tell me something, Jesse. Is anything wrong? Let's get your pictures out and see if you can tell me what you need."

As the teacher talked, the other students began to watch for the behavior that the teacher was interpreting as frustration. They also watched as the teacher showed Jesse the pictures one at a time. The teacher also verbalized the response for which she was looking. "I'll know what you want, Jesse, when you look at one of the pictures and keep looking at it while I move it in front of you." The other students started to pick up on the first signs of frustration (e.g., a slight tensing of Jesse's face, a quiet sound). Jesse then had less need to scream. Jesse learned that a quiet sound, rather than screaming, evoked the response he needed. The other students were able to show the pictures to Jesse and determine what he needed. They modeled their behavior after the teacher.

Old Systems in a New Setting

In the next scenario, Mary's communicative behavior is observed.

Mary

The first part of the day in the first-grade classroom usually was spent sitting in a circle on the floor. The teacher would discuss the day of the week and the weather. Following calendar time, the children would spend a few minutes telling their classmates about items that they had brought to school. Mary often brought an item and, because she could not speak, the educational assistant would help her share. When sharing time was over, the children would go back to their desks and the teacher would present a lesson to the class. At the end of the lesson she would give directions for a desk assignment that related to the lesson. On this particular day, several children were walking around the classroom getting books and other items that they would need to complete the assignment. Mary got up and went behind the teacher's desk while glancing at the educational assistant. The assistant asked Mary to sit down, but Mary appeared not to hear her. As the educational assistant got up and started walking to the left of the teacher's desk, Mary started moving to the right. When the educational assistant changed direction, Mary moved away in the opposite direction. This continued until the educational assistant was chasing Mary around the desk. The children stopped working and watched Mary and the educational assistant. The classroom teacher waited until the educational assistant firmly had Mary's hand and had taken her out of the classroom.

What behaviors did Mary use to communicate when she ran behind the teacher's desk? What was Mary communicating when she ran around to the other side of the desk, engaging the educational assistant in a chasing game? Perhaps Mary was trying to establish an interaction that made sense to her; what was happening in the classroom did not make sense to Mary. Sharing time was highly structured and Mary could see what was expected. The directions at the end of the lesson, however, and even the lesson itself were confusing to Mary. She was using her behavior to tell the educational assistant that something was not right. She used a behavior (e.g., running) that would be sure to get the attention of the teacher and the educational assistant.

When the teachers listened to what Mary was saying and responded to her behavior as communication, they changed their behavior. They gave Mary more cues to help her understand what was happening in the classroom. The activity was adapted to fit Mary's educational needs. When Mary got up from her chair, the educational assistant responded to Mary by quickly taking her hand, acknowledging that the activity was new or different. She directed her to look at the teacher or the behaviors of the other students, reintroduced the materials Mary needed for the activity, and helped Mary understand what was being done and what she needed to do to participate.

Mary's ensuing behavior changed, reflecting a better understanding of what was happening in the classroom. When she did not understand what was happening, rather than get up and run, she began to remain in her seat and look around for the educational assistant so that she could get help.

Although Mary's "chase" behavior was a problem for the teacher and the other students in the class, her behavior was really a form of communication. The system Mary used was one that had worked for her for many years, but it did not fit in the general classroom. The solution was to replace the system Mary used with a system that was compatible with the general classroom setting.

Inappropriate Behavior

What happens when a student uses a form of communication that appears inappropriate in the general classroom setting? Should that student be asked to stop using a form of communication that has been effective for him or her in other settings? Should a student be allowed, or even encouraged by responding positively, to use a communication system that is perceived as disruptive in the classroom?

In Chapter 2, (see p. 13), the communicative intent of behavior is discussed. Teachers, are the experts on what behaviors are inappropriate for the classroom setting. With the assistance of the team, they can attempt to discern the message behind an inappropriate behavior and find a substitute behavior that can communicate the same message more appropriately. The steps for doing so are as follows:

1. *Identify the communicative behavior.* Observe the student and describe the behavior that is inappropriate. Note how often the behavior occurs, what happens right before the behavior takes place, and how other adults and students react to the behavior. Observe the students without disabilities. Do they ever display this behavior? The following is an example of Mary's behavior being observed in the classroom:

Mary

After Mary had been in the general education classroom for several months, she no longer ran from the room or tried to involve the educational assistant in chasing her around the room. However, Mary still got out of her seat frequently and wandered to other areas of the room. The teacher found this very distracting. She took this concern to the team and asked if someone could come in and collect some data on the amount of time Mary was wandering and out of her seat.

When Mary was observed, it was noted that Mary was out of her seat at least twice every 15 minutes. She would wander to the front of the room and watch what the teacher was doing. The teacher would ignore Mary and continue with the lesson. On most occasions, Mary returned to her seat when asked by the educational assistant. It also was noted that more than half the other students got out of their seats at approximately the same rate. They would sharpen a pencil, get a book, get a piece of paper, and examine a classmate's work. The difference was the duration that they were out of their seats and the reasons they were out of their seats. The movement by the students without disabilities appeared to have purpose, but Mary's movement did not. Because the teacher did not know why Mary was up and walking around, Mary's behavior was more distracting.

---

2. *Note what the student is communicating.* Try to discern what the student could be communicating with the behavior.

Mary

When the team looked at Mary's behavior they decided to interpret Mary's behavior as curiosity and a request to be more involved in what was going on in the classroom. The next time Mary wandered toward the front of the room, the teacher moved over to Mary, acknowledged her presence, invited her to sit close to the teacher, and had Mary participate in teaching the lesson.

3. *Make sure responses to the behavior are appropriate and made in a reasonable time frame.* Often a student communicates a need using a behavior that is very appropriate, and, if no one responds he or she will proceed with a more disruptive inappropriate behavior. Because the teacher responded as if Mary were curious instead of disruptive, Mary did not have to escalate her behavior to get the desired results.
4. *Teach the student to use another behavior to communicate the same need.* In the first case, in which Mary ran around the desk, Mary's behavior was her means of communication but also was inappropriate and disruptive. It was necessary to teach Mary a new way to communicate her lack of understanding of the classroom activities. It was necessary to find another behavior or to modify the behavior she was using if she was going to be successful in the general education classroom.

   In the second case, in which Mary walked up to the teacher who was in the middle of teaching a lesson, Mary's behavior was interpreted as distracting. On further examination, it was determined that the behavior was appropriate in the classroom and Mary was communicating a very important message in a very appropriate way. When the teacher responded to the behavior as appropriate communication, Mary's wandering ceased to be a problem.

A TEACHER'S KNOWLEDGE BASE

Examining a General Educator's Ability to Teach a Student with Disabilities

Many general education teachers feel that because they have not received specific training to teach students with special needs they need to rely on the decisions of other colleagues in determining how and what a student with special needs should learn, how these concepts should be taught, and who should do the teaching. In contrast to this feeling, when the team comes together to make these decisions, teachers are expected to be fully participating members. They are asked to contribute suggestions and their opinions regarding who should teach the student, what the student needs to learn, and how that student can learn best in their classrooms.

In order to feel confident in doing this, general educators must take some time to examine their own teaching skills and beliefs. They should ask themselves what their strengths are and in what areas they need additional training or information. For example, they may look at the students in the classroom who have the most success. There may be patterns to help teachers gain insight into their teaching skills.

Once a teacher has identified his or her own strengths and skills, those skills can be reframed in terms of teaching a student with special needs. These questions also can help:

- What do you need to know about the student or the student's disability to help you teach that student?
- What additional teaching skills do you feel you need?
- What personal philosophies do you have that may need to be adjusted or modified to include this student?

What does this have to do with communication? Communication is one subject that an educator will have to teach when this student enters his or her classroom. Communication is very personal and very individualized, especially with students who have more involved impairment. So, what do teachers know and what do they need to learn? The following are some questions that may provide answers:

1. *How does the student communicate?* Everyone communicates through different forms: gestures, body language, sounds, and gaze. A student with disabilities will have an array of communication forms even though he or she may not use verbal communication. Similarities between how this student communicates and how all students communicate need to be discovered. What does the student like or dislike? Who does the student like or dislike? Communication is making choices. Knowing a student's likes and dislikes is important in order to understand his or her communication. Being able to say, "I know what he or she wants," is part of being an effective communicator and an effective teacher.
2. *How does the student's disability affect communication?* People communicate using a variety of methods including facial expression, gestures, body language, and posture as well as formal communication systems. Many informal communication methods help others to interpret what is meant. For example, when a person communicates that he or she is angry, the person may raise his or her voice, talk faster, slam down an item on the desk, get up and walk out of the room, or simply glare at the speaker. But what if the person has cerebral palsy and his or her motor skills are very limited. How can that person show that he or she is angry? The person may not be able to raise his or her voice because when he or she is really angry the person may not be able talk at all; cannot talk faster because he or she is very difficult to understand, even when speaking slowly; does not have the fine motor skills to pick up an item and release it fast enough to slam it anywhere; cannot walk out of a room because he or she is dependent on someone else to push him or her; and cannot glare because he or she cannot hold a fixed position.

   When looking at how someone's disability affects communication, teachers need to be open-minded. How do people with disabilities communicate anger, surprise, happiness, or frustration? How will their communication appear different because of their motor, speech, visual, or language limitations?
3. *What will help teachers communicate more effectively?* Teachers want to communicate with every student in their classrooms, but they have a limited amount of time so they want each communication to be meaningful. If a teacher tries to communicate with a student and does not have enough information about the student's disability, the teacher may be unsuccessful. There is a good chance that the teacher will stop trying to communicate and allow others who

seem "to know more about it" communicate with the student. If this happens, the teacher needs to stop and ask him- or herself why someone else is able to communicate with the student.

Once the system of communication a student uses is learned, a teacher will need to determine what new skills he or she must learn to use that system. If the student uses an augmentative device that needs to be programmed for a variety of settings, it will be helpful to the student if the teacher can program that device. If the student uses sign language, then the teacher will need to learn sign language. The need to learn so many new skills may seem overwhelming, especially if using the student's communication system is very time-consuming or involves technology that is new. Teachers must remember that the student's system is the only means for him or her to communicate what he or she is learning in the classroom.

4. *What information should a teacher learn about working with students with disabilities, working with their families, and where the students will fit into the community?* Some disabilities have specific characteristics that are common in most students with the disability. For instance, having information about teaching students with Rett syndrome will help in teaching students with that syndrome, particularly in terms of the approach. Likewise, individuals with fragile X syndrome are known to have a *sensory integration dysfunction*. A common approach for students with fragile X syndrome in working on academics, speech, language, and other skills is for an occupational therapist to design a program in which the student is provided gentle sensory stimulation concurrently with the lesson.

   Information about families that have children with disabilities and knowledge about what the families' dreams are for their children provide insight into the parents' needs and help teachers develop meaningful programs for the students. Information from students without disabilities, articles, stories, and accounts from parents show how other students communicate with students who have a particular disability and can help teachers build meaningful interaction among all of their students.

   Perhaps some of the most important questions that need to be answered in order to provide meaningful education for a student with a disability are "Where does he or she fit into the community?", "With whom will he or she need to communicate?", and "Where will he or she be communicating as an adult?" The skills a teacher gives his or her students, including the youngest students, are meant to prepare them for the future. Although the future is unknown, the teacher has an idea and the student has a dream. Students with disabilities, even those with the most severe disabilities and even the most extreme limitations, have dreams and futures. (See Chapter 6 for a discussion on personal futures planning.)

5. *What personal philosophies do general educators have that may not be compatible with what a particular student needs to be an effective communicator?* When general educators teach students with disabilities, they often confront their personal philosophies on what is appropriate communicative behavior, teaching, and inclusion. The behaviors that teachers consider important in communication are determined by their cultures. A teacher's culture is influenced by where he or she lives, family background, and shared values with a com-

munity of people. Within each teacher's community are individuals who hold the same general values but who demonstrate those values in ways that do not fit the teacher's cultural perspective. For example, in some cultures, it is appropriate to make eye contact during a conversation to indicate attention and respect for the speaker. In some communities, however, there are families whose culture teaches that averting gaze is the way to indicate attention and respect, particularly for elders. Therefore, it would be inappropriate to teach a child with disabilities from one of these families to make eye contact to request an item. Thus, it is important for teachers to think about and discuss cultural values, teaching philosophies, and views on inclusion with colleagues and students' parents.

Asking the Right Questions

The answers needed to help a teacher communicate with a student are not always easy to obtain. Sometimes people repeat information they have given you already, using different words and/or different examples. When this happens it is a good idea to provide a scenario (see the following example involving Mary).

Mary

Mary's first-grade teacher came to the team meeting distraught. "Mary is running all over the classroom. She is distracting the children, and I can't teach. I need someone to help me, or she needs to be in the self-contained classroom where she has more freedom."

Mary's mother said, "Mary's just confused. Tell her what you want her to do."

The special education teacher said, "Mary is used to getting up and going to what she wants to do. This is just another example of that."

The consultant said, "Just don't let her run around."

The first-grade teacher remained distraught.

Another approach to getting answers is to say, "I'm not getting the information I need from your answer. Will you come into the classroom and observe the problem that I am trying to describe because I cannot see how the solution you offered me is going to work?" Often a shared observation with another person will help the teacher communicate his or her concerns more effectively.

Relating the Information to the Classroom

In the previous example involving Mary, the information given by her mother, special education teacher, and consultant was correct, but it was not useful to the first-grade teacher because it was incomplete and did not discuss implementation. Some of the frustration teachers feel regarding inclusion is because the information they are given does not help them resolve problems. Ironically, Mary was having a problem in the classroom for the same reason. She, too, was being given information that was correct, but it was not helping her understand what was happening in the classroom.

After Mary's mother, special education teacher, and consultant observed Mary in the classroom, they were able to answer the teacher's question completely with both the information she needed and solutions for implementation.

Mary

When Mary's first-grade teacher came to the next team meeting, she was still very distraught. She carefully explained Mary's behavior: "Mary sits very well during sharing but then darts behind my desk and waits for someone to chase her. It is very distracting to the other children and to me when I am trying to do whole-group instruction. Can you give me any advice?"

Mary's mother responded, "Mary often acts like that when she does not understand what is happening in the classroom. We need to develop a plan so that we can explain the activities or give her a choice that makes more sense to her."

The special education teacher, who observed Mary in the first grade, said, "We have to allow Mary to get up and find a way to allow her to use this form of communication in the general classroom."

The consultant, who also observed in the first-grade classroom, said, "I think that the educational assistant needs to be close enough to Mary so that she can reinforce her when she is sitting and can prevent her from running if she does get up. When Mary stands, try to get her to sit back down and explain the activity to her. If she will not sit down, hold her hand and walk quietly around the room with her. Give her the opportunity to choose a different activity."

The first-grade teacher said, "I think that this will work. Knowing that Mary is telling me something when she stands up makes it easier for me to respond correctly. It really helps knowing that we will all respond the same way. I'm sure it will help the other children in the class also."

What about the other students? How should they be taught to interact appropriately? Much has been written about benefits of inclusion for the student without disabilities. There are several friendship programs (e.g., Circle of Friends, Good Friends and Advocates) that have been used to structure interaction between students with disabilities and their same-age peers. It is unnecessary to use a structured program to encourage students to interact. Having a child with special needs in the classroom is a time for both the teacher and the students to learn together. Most teachers today have never invited a friend with multiple disabilities to their birthday parties, have not taken a friend with autism to the mall, and have not invited a friend with cerebral palsy to a sleepover. Teachers should be prepared to learn with the students in their classrooms. By being creative and accepting, teachers and their students without disabilities will learn how to open their circle to include a more diverse population; meanwhile, their students with disabilities will learn to take the risks that come with being included in a new group of friends and participating in new activities.

What if the student has no way to communicate with the teacher? There will be students with disabilities in the classroom who have such limited communication that teachers might feel that there is no way for those student to communicate with them. If teachers act on that belief, then they will never give those students the opportunity to have any control over any part of their lives. Teachers need to imagine having everything done for them and never having the opportunity to stop an activity or let someone know they like a particular activity, and they can imagine how empowering it is for someone to "listen" to their most subtle communication signals and interpret them as legitimate messages. One role teachers and other team members need to learn is that of more skilled listeners. For example, one student with spastic cerebral palsy had minimal voluntary movement and did not appear to be able to communicate what she wanted. The teacher called the team members together to discuss how they could give this student the opportunity to express herself and make choices. The team members examined their own behavior and saw that they automatically made choices for this student without regard for her preferences. They fed her, changed her, took her in and out of her chair, washed her face, and put music on and off for her without ever considering what she wanted.

To determine if the student would communicate, the team members decided that they would do all activities by placing their hands over hers and guiding her through each activity. If she resisted in any way, they would interpret her reaction as "no." If she showed any sign of wanting an activity to continue, they would honor that request.

The first "yes" and "no" responses they got were during lunch. Rather than simply feeding the student, the second-grade teacher placed his hand over hers and had her bring the spoon to her mouth for each bite. When she wanted more food, she would open her mouth in anticipation and the teacher would ask, "Do you want some more?" When she had enough, the student stopped opening her mouth and the teacher said, "You must have had enough. We are finished."

The most surprising communication came when the student was offered a choice of music from her tape recorder or a toy. She knew that the cassette tape represented music and was able to look directly at a cassette tape to let a partner know she wanted music. The team members were excited that they could interpret these existing behaviors as meaningful. The teacher was surprised by how easy it was to use this system, and he became an advocate for implementing these strategies with other students.

Determining What to Do Next

Once a thorough understanding of the student and his or her communication needs has been established, it becomes time to use communication to teach new skills. A team composed of the teacher and other professionals should work together to determine what to teach and how to expand the communication system for the student.

Working with a team—any team—takes time and energy. Teaming skills can be reviewed by using the Teaming Checklist in Appendix C at the back of this book. The team will include a variety of professionals, some of whom have experience working in general education classrooms and many of whom do not. The team also will include the student's parents and/or caregivers. Parents of children with disabilities are often very knowledgeable resources, and they play a very important part in developing their children's programs. Teachers should be present at all staffings, multidisciplinary team meetings, individualized education program (IEP) meetings, and conferences. The team should be aware that it is important for the teacher to be present if the student's IEP is to be implemented successfully. The teacher knows what the student needs to be successful in the general education classroom. Many of the skills identified will also be needed for the student to be successful in the community. Communication is the most important skill that students will learn.

To determine how the student's communication system will be expanded, the student's present communication skills must be assessed first. Then it should be decided what skills the student should learn in the next year, in 2 years, or even further in the future. Chapters 5 and 6 focus on implementing those skills. Once a goal has been established, steps the student will have to accomplish to reach that goal should be analyzed before moving ahead. Each step must be functional for the student. If, for some reason, the student does not reach the final goal, he or she should always have learned skills that helped him or her communicate more effectively. The student should never be taught nonfunctional skills that may (or may not) generalize into useful skills. For example, teaching a student to reach and touch any object when it is placed on the tray of his or her wheelchair is nonfunctional. Teaching a student to reach and touch his or her spoon when he or she wants more, however, is a very functional communication skill.

Learning the Student's Communication System

A student may come into the classroom and have a communication system in place. It will be the teacher's role to use that communication system to teach new skills and to determine how to expand that communication system. The teacher needs to learn all he or she can about the student's communication system. For example, if it is an electronic device, the teacher should learn to use it and to program it. If the student uses a communication board, a communication book, or an object board, the teacher should learn what items and activities are in the student's system and design some of the classroom activities to fit the limitations of the system. The student should have messages on his or her system for talking about and requesting activities that are specific to the classroom. The student should be given opportunities to use his or her communication system by allowing him or her to initiate requests without prompts and to communicate about things other than the immediate topic. All the students in the classroom should be taught what the communication system is and how to use the system if the individual wishes them to do so.

Evaluating the Current System

It is possible that the student will have a communication system that is not functional for the general education classroom. A picture communication system that is not portable will not work in the general education classroom because the students typically spend much of their day out of the classroom in music, physical education, and art. A communication system that is difficult for same-age peers to use because it is very technical or involves waiting a long time for responses should be modified. If it is not used by the peer group, the student's opportunities to practice and learn the system will be limited.

If a student is going to learn to use a communication system effectively, he or she must practice. Teachers will have to provide opportunities for practice to take place. Teachers can start by writing a list of activities that take place across the school day and then considering those activities in terms of communication. For example, a teacher may start the day by asking the students, "Who wants hot lunch." The teacher should consider whether the student with disabilities has any way to communicate whether or not he or she wants hot lunch. This activity remains an opportunity for the student to communicate even if that student will never get hot lunch. All activities that happen in the classroom can be considered as opportunities to teach communication. Chapter 3 provides checklists and suggestions to examine classroom activities more closely.

Finding New Opportunities to Communicate Using the Current System

In order to communicate using the current system, teachers will need to contrive some opportunities. For example, if a teacher wants the student to learn to communicate with his or her peers during an academic activity, the teacher will have to work with the students to determine what part of a cooperative learning project this student can do and how they can use this activity to encourage the student to communicate more with his or her classmates. If the teacher wants the student to ask for items, the teacher may have to make the items (e.g., spoon, jacket, book) be missing. Once the student has learned the new skill, it will be maintained within the context of the classroom activities.

SUMMARY

Students with disabilities are now attending general education classrooms along with their same-age peers. Educators face many new challenges to make this successful. This chapter discussed some of those challenges and suggested specific strategies for determining what and how to teach communication skills in the general classroom.

How well students with and without disabilities interact and the opportunities they have for interaction play an important role in the success of any program that includes students with disabilities. When a student with limited communication skills becomes part of the general education classroom, teachers may have some concerns that need to be addressed immediately. Teachers can identify and express their concerns to the team of people who work with the student.

These questions are important to keep in mind:

- Is the student communicating a need, or is the student simply being disruptive?
- Why is the student using a particular behavior to communicate a need?

When the teachers listen to students and respond to behavior as communication, both the student and the teachers change their behavior.

The general education teacher is part of the educational team that comes together to make decisions for the child with a disability. The teacher is expected to be a participating member of the team.

As teachers plan programs for their students, one of the most important questions they need to answer to provide meaningful education for a particular student is "Where does he or she fit into the community?" Education for this student must be directed to improve the quality of life for this student and give the student every opportunity to become a fully participating member of the community.

As teachers face these new challenges they often confront their personal philosophies on what is appropriate communicative behavior, teaching, and inclusion. Having a child with special needs in the classroom is an opportunity for both the teacher and the students to learn together.

SECTION IV

MENTORING AND COLLABORATION

Section IV discusses and illustrates mentoring and collaboration when assessing communication skills in different cases. The vignettes in Section V should make it apparent that the authors of this book have acted as mentors and collaborators on many school teams. The explanations and definitions of mentoring and collaboration provided in Chapter 8 are based on the experiences of the authors during these activities. An example of one collaborative effort is then shown in Chapter 9. The example is meant to capture some of the characteristic trends in mentoring and collaboration and to illustrate the complexities that always exist when educators and families implement innovations in schools. The process of mentoring and collaboration is critical to designing communication systems and, as discussed in this section, is a process that has evolved to enhance communication system design and implementation.

CHAPTER 8

A History of Mentoring and Collaboration

A glimpse back into the late 1970s would allow educators and professionals to view many school districts beginning to serve students with severe disabilities for the first time. Some of these districts were searching for experts to provide information, advice, and, if at all possible, *the* answers for what and how to teach these newest members of their learning communities. Also seen would be experts providing just those things: what and how to do it right. In that era of educational history, it was common to view mentoring and collaboration as a hierarchical system. Experts saw themselves as people who had the answers on how best to conduct services. Contractors of these expert services were viewed as needing information about the "nuts and bolts" of curriculum and instruction. After 10 years of these efforts, it became apparent that the consultants, educators, and other "reformers" were energetic in their efforts and in inventing new ways to achieve recommended practices. But, it also was evident that changing practices in systems was difficult. Even when changes occurred, they were difficult to maintain or replicate.

Sheila Tobias (1992) captured the past reform efforts and outcomes of experts in her statement: "They shake, but nothing moves." Educators, reformers, and other experts were at a point at which they realized the complex nature of implementing change in systems. Previous reformers assumed there was a best curriculum or pedagogy waiting to be discovered, and once discovered, it would universally become practice regardless of the teacher, resources, climate of the educational setting, and attitudes of the participants. In essence, the history of educational changes, including changes in implementing communication strategies, was one of reforming again, and again, and again. Looking at the barriers to lasting change was critical to discovering how to do it better.

Educators and reformers now realize that change and innovation require bargaining, negotiating, and collaborating to get needed support. In the business world, this is referred to as "buying into" local input and control. Educational researchers addressing change documented that innovation is not a replication of others' efforts or models, but rather combines thoughtful processes of extrapolation. The extrapolation involves at least three processes. The first is understanding why changes are needed as well as the theories and assumptions underlying new practices. The second is instituting a process of "buying in" to areas in which local participants see or feel a need to change. The third is personalizing the mission and changes to match the understandings and needs of the people within the system. Studies demonstrate that changes do happen when educators review model programs and theories, distill what they like and value from the models, and then systematically determine how best to implement changes within their own system. The result is a series of locally controlled and structured efforts that move within the political structures of schools and classrooms. The results are outcomes that may look very different from district to district and classroom to classroom but that are implemented and sustained. The result is not perfect innovation as viewed from an objective standpoint, but rather innovation with a realization that "the way it is supposed to be" really does not exist.

MODELS OF CHANGE

Two models of change, the expert and the collaborative models, are discussed and illustrated in Figures 8.1 and 8.2. The first model, a linear process, represents past efforts to implement change using a hierarchical expert approach. The second model represents the current collaborative approach that features both commitment and problem solving.

A Linear Process of Change

In Figure 8.1, the process of change toward recommended practices is illustrated as a linear process. The goal is assumed to be 100% understanding and 100% performance of those practices. Typically, goals and objectives are written to describe the actions that need to be taken to reach the end or the predetermined goal. In Figure 8.1, the starting point for changing varies, but all directions of change and the efforts of the expert are toward a predetermined ending point—the goal of understanding and using the recommended practices. The existing conditions of the system (e.g., resources, attitudes and willingness of people, climates and norms of the systems) are not addressed by the expert or those in the system and are not integrated into a starting point, determining how best to proceed or how to set up local goals. There is also a judgment value embedded within this change model: Districts, schools, or classrooms in which the goal is met are good, while those not attaining the goal are not as good. Thus, regardless of the process, commitment to change, or resource allocation, the outcome is valued significantly more than the process. In this model, the way it is "supposed to be" and how that must look is defined and is assumed to be a universal goal.

An Interactive Collaborative System of Change

Figure 8.2 illustrates the concept of a system of change that is more interactive and collaborative than the linear one. Unlike the linear graph, Figure 8.2 has an elongated "whiffle ball" shape. The changes that are desired, valued, and envisioned

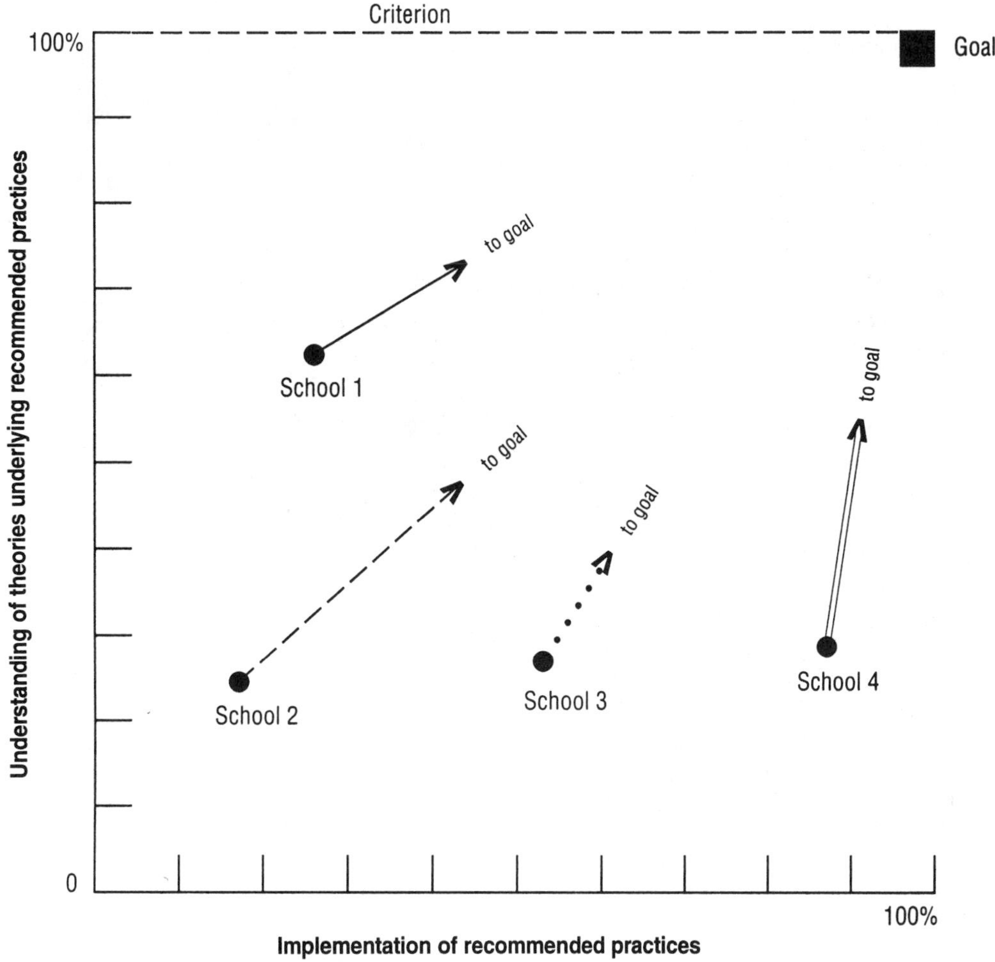

Figure 8.1. The Expert Model.

are on the inside of the shape. Educators and consultants start somewhere on the outside of the shape, while the goals or outcomes are somewhere inside the shape. In this model, each person or team must specify what his or her goals are in relation to theories and professionally recognized practices, and then he or she must specify actions to take in relation to these goals. Theories are reviewed, and an understanding of the person's goal and the direction of change is developed. The openings on the surface of the illustration represent various starting points for the change process. The illustration in Figure 8.2 represents the multitude of origins that are possible within this interactive model. Implicit within this model is the assumption that leaving the surface and moving "inside the ball" not only constitutes change but also offers a new perspective on desired goals and outcomes and thus may alter future directions of change and even previously specified goals. In essence, this illustration considers that the actual process of changing interacts with an understanding that may influence goals, desired outcomes, and directions for change.

The path of change in Figure 8.2 is undefined also. There are routes that may or may not be linear. Likewise, the outcome itself (somewhere in the center) is not

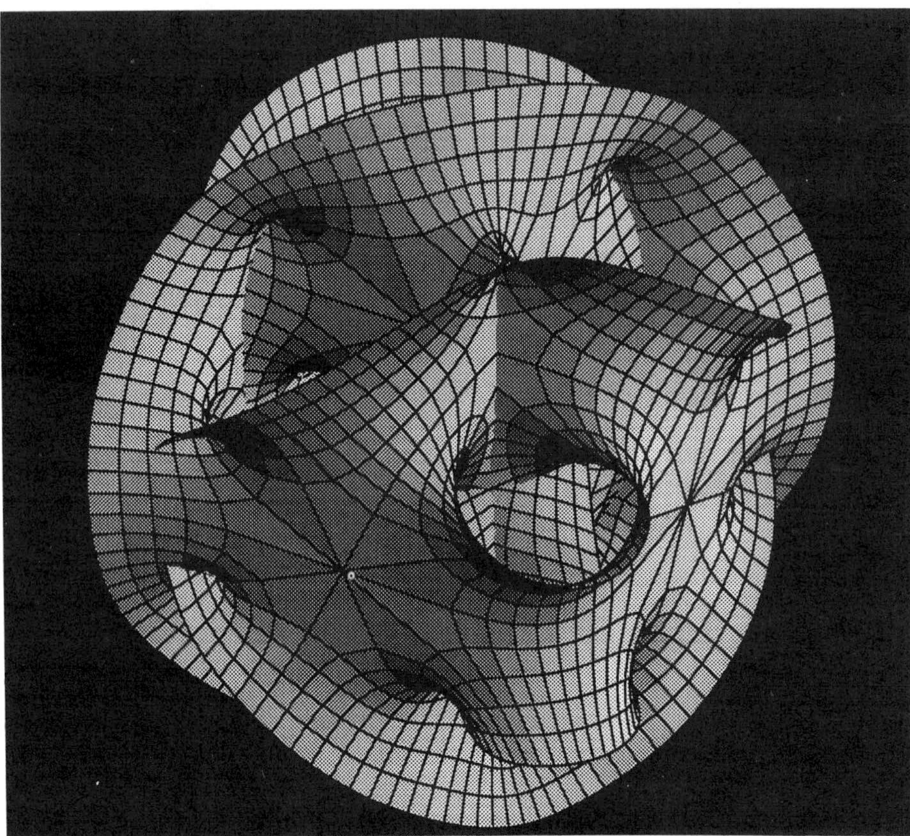

Figure 8.2. The Collaborative Model. (From Hanson, A.J., & Dickson, S. [1994]. A construction for computer visualization of certain complex curves. *Computers and Mathematics*, *41*(9), 1156–1163; reprinted by permission.)

exact and may be different, depending on the starting conditions, resources, changing understandings of those involved, and tolerance for change that exists within the system and participants. Within this model of change, it is expected that the outcomes and processes attained will be different. These differences are not judged as better or worse than a predetermined standard. The notion of a recommended practice or "the way it is supposed to be" is replaced by the notion that knowledge is a road always under construction. Movement and change are driven by ideas and missions. Their results can and are typically very idiosyncratic.

NEW ROLES FOR MENTORS AND COLLABORATORS

Within the changing concept of how innovation and change can and do happen, there emerged new roles and definitions of mentors and collaborators. The notion of the hierarchical expert who tells others how and what to change in the linear model was replaced (Reeve & Hallahan, 1994). Experts became *collaborators* or *mentors*, and the terms *collaborative consultation* and *transformative mentoring* were used to describe the change process in the interactive collaborative system of change. Unlike the linear model's *consultant* and *consultee* (or *mentor* and *protégé*) relationship, the interactive, collaborative model assumes that both the consultant and consultee are actively problem solving together and share responsibility for all stages of the process (problem identification, implementation strategy, outcomes, and evaluation). This model has many proponents and is referred to as *mentoring* in the following discussion.

During mentoring, the mentor assumes a support role to colleagues. Rather than exchanging expert information, the relationship assumes shared responsibility for identifying goals, barriers, processes, and outcomes. The relationship consists of discourse between partners that is characterized by reflection, conversation, and actions. The mentor assumes colleagues are working to change and that support is needed to enable an individual or team to change. The following roles in mentoring are support and inquiry (Fosnot, 1989):

1. The mentor learns the perspective of the person or team through skillful listening, conversation, and observation.
2. The mentor challenges the thinking of the person or team and facilitates feelings of imbalance between understandings and practices.
3. The mentor relies on the body of professional knowledge to enable him- or herself and the team to develop personalized and an ever-expanding basis of understandings related to professional practices.
4. The mentor acknowledges the intellectual abilities and freedom of the protégé or team to adopt and adapt theories and practices to meet the needs of his or her students within his or her system.

The roles and responsibilities in mentoring are underscored by caring and commitment to working and learning. An analogy used by Gehrke (1988) is that mentoring is like gift giving in the term's best sense. Dialogue and commitment are parts of the gift, and the understanding is the actual gift. Like most exchanges between close friends, the gift comes without an obligation and its value is in the giving rather than in the tangible object. It is frequently the case that the mentoring results in a bonding similar to a friendship and yet different because of the professional focus. The complex process of this inquiry-based learning requires balancing personal qualities of humility, honesty, creativity, and courage with professional knowledge and a vision of professional excellence.

Where Can One Get a Mentor?

One assumption about mentors and the mentoring model is that the mentor must come from outside of one's current system. It certainly can be energizing to have mentoring occur with professionals from other places. The roles of collaborator and mentor are often assumed by professionals who are external to the system; state department consultants, higher education faculty, and consulting teachers are typical examples. However, these roles also can be assumed by team members at the same school or within the same district. What is important is valuing the process of understanding and resisting the urge to view progress as time limited, as someone else's responsibility, or as limited by someone's poor skills or deficits in an area. People are different, and these differences are what we bring to the change process and are what drives locally determined, idiosyncratic outcomes. Time is too often spent discussing how good things could be if certain conditions did not exist. Mentoring, when it works, requires suspension of judgment and concentration on inquiry and creative problem solving. Sometimes this process is easier when either the expert is from outside the system or a facilitator is initially used to get teams up and running in a collaborative process. Regardless of how mentoring is initiated, time and energy are invested in valuing and understanding where people are in the process and in pinpointing areas of agreement in which resources and sustained efforts to implement planned changes can enhance the life outcomes for students.

CHAPTER 9

A Snapshot of a Collaborative Project

This chapter describes a 2-year collaborative venture between Kathy, a special education teacher, and Diane, a professor of special education. The project was a collaborative endeavor to review curricula and schedules for two students with disabilities and alter the students' programs to enhance their learning. The North Idaho Special Education Consultant arranged for Diane and Kathy to meet in the spring. Kathy's struggle as she began the process of implementing theory and related new practices and the professional reconstruction of both Kathy and Diane as they engaged in collaboration are documented here. The need for effective strategies to support the implementation of new practices in schools is definitively shown.

The chapter is presented in parts, which were written either separately or jointly by Kathy and Diane. Many of the complex issues that arise as changes are implemented in schools and classrooms are demonstrated. The shared perspective of the authors affirms the need for multiple perspectives in forging changes and the need to capture essential professional and personal strengths within this process.

HISTORY AND TIME LINE OF THE PROJECT

Presented first are the changing phases that occurred as Kathy and Diane shifted from a traditional student–professor relationship to a collaborative relationship and began to implement theory into ongoing practice. The phases represent the initial impetus for the project, environmental circumstances that affected the interactions, and the strategies and rationale for changes that occurred throughout the project. Kathy organized the project into four different phases. Each phase is briefly described below and then is followed by narratives about findings and outcomes that occurred within each of these phases.

Phase I: The Including Exceptions Systems (IES) Project

The Including Exceptions Systems (IES) Project (Ferguson, 1991–1994) is a program that is designed to assist teachers in planning curricula that are functional, age appropriate, and activity based; it was a focal point for the initial collaboration between Kathy and Diane. The IES program contains assumptions regarding the learning characteristics of students with severe disabilities. The program assumes that even though all students with severe impairments are individuals with their own strengths and skills, they have several important similarities: 1) these students often have too few behaviors and too few consistent behaviors on which to build effective participatory behaviors, 2) these students are alert for learning only at certain times, and 3) these students often do not respond consistently to instructional stimuli.

Phase I consisted of formal data collection on two students, Brent and Holly, as part of a review of their instruction. The IES process included 4 months of data collection in Kathy's elementary school. The IES forms and strategies used to review students' behaviors and a summary of the data are contained within the stories of Brent and Holly in the next section.

Phase II: A Beginning of Collaboration

Phase II involved a change from IES data collection on Brent and Holly to journal writing and oral and written reflections on the journal entries. This stage was initiated 6 months after Phase I, and Diane suggested a change in format and focus.

Phase III: A Turning Point: Making Sense of It All

Phase III consisted of reviewing the journal entries and reflections and listing themes that were evident in the written journal entries and reflections. The themes and code words that emerged from the journal and reflections are embedded in the dialogue below between Kathy and Diane.

Phase IV: The Fruits of Collaboration

Phase IV was the final phase. The first three phases offered information that was helpful in planning for students and effecting changes in how to teach. The journal reflections and interactions over these entries comprise the authors' findings, along with changes in the teaching styles of both Kathy and Diane. The findings are reviewed in the dialogue and in Kathy's and Diane's reflections at the end of this chapter.

KATHY'S PERSPECTIVE

I was teaching in a self-contained classroom for students with moderate and severe disabilities during the spring of 1989. I had very little specific training in teaching students with severe disabilities. I heard that there was consultative help available through the University of Idaho. I reluctantly requested that someone assist me in developing a program for a student who had very disruptive behavior. I say "reluctantly" because I felt very intimidated by having an expert come into my classroom. I knew that some of my teaching practices were satisfactory, but I believed there was a "right" way to teach students with disabilities and I didn't know what it was exactly. The thought of having a college professor in my class to observe me made me nervous.

When I met Diane, I was pleasantly surprised. She was very easy to work with and she gave me a lot of encouragement. Instead of giving me advice to change things, she showed me how to evaluate the existing schedule and set up small areas of change. Her ability to relate to all the students, especially our students with such difficult behaviors, amazed me. She really knew how to teach these students. Our consultation was a big success. The small changes really worked, and I felt like I learned a lot.

I began taking graduate courses at the University of Idaho, Coeur d'Alene Center, in the fall of 1989 with Diane as my instructor. I continued teaching and took classes at night and during the summer break. The coursework was very demanding, but always proved to be very applicable to the students I was teaching. I gained knowledge and skills that I actually could use in my class.

The IES Project

In the fall of 1992, Diane and I started on a joint data collection project. Diane approached me about being involved in a project that assisted teachers of students with disabilities to evaluate curricula and school schedules. She indicated that there would be federally funded assistance from the University of Oregon to teachers of students with multiple disabilities. She asked me if I might be interested in becoming involved in such a program. I needed help designing functional programs for several of the students in my classroom. I agreed to meet with Diane and a representative for the IES project from the University of Oregon.

Brent and Holly, who are described as having severe disabilities as well as other complex health care needs, are both students in my class. Both students are nonambulatory. Brent has cerebral palsy, receives physical therapy, and requires adaptations to minimize his rigidity and facilitate some control of his movements. He moves his eyes voluntarily and indicates choices and interest through gaze. His gaze responses are inconsistent, and he seems to look away from activities to which he responded favorably in the past. I referred Brent to IES because of his inconsistent response pattern, his need for a communication system, his crying, and the frustration staff felt in ensuring they were meeting his needs.

Holly also has cerebral palsy and requires full physical assistance in order to reach, grasp, or hold onto items. She uses a gastrostomy tube system for meals and liquids and has a visual impairment. She does orient her head toward sounds and people. She is a very social girl and likes a lot of attention. Holly was referred to IES because the staff believed her curriculum and schedule needed to be enhanced, she needed a communication system, and she often cried loudly in school. It seemed she cried for no apparent reason and staff wanted to explore her crying behavior. I had some ideas about why Brent and Holly were crying, but I welcomed the assistance to review their behavior and curricula. They were challenging students for me. The project was discussed with Holly's and Brent's families and care providers, and after they agreed to the involvement, a visit was arranged.

In October of 1992, I met with Mike Young, IES Field Consultant from the University of Oregon, and Diane. I was introduced to the data recording sheet and the data sheets Diane would be using as well. Both Diane and Mike observed the students for over 2 hours and then we all met to review the project and my role. I identified behaviors that were of concern to me and those I wished to observe more closely. Mike assisted in generating a data sheet that listed typical environmental conditions that might be influencing these behaviors. My task with the team was to list the daily schedule at the top of each data sheet and collect anecdotal data.

At first I was concerned that this data recording sheet was too complicated. I explained it to the staff in the classroom and asked that they give it a try. They were very receptive, and once they had used the data recording system, had many positive comments. We began recording behaviors of Brent and Holly in November. The data collection in itself became a tool that the team used to collaborate on the students' individual programs. The process of keeping data encouraged the team to pay attention and focus on the target behaviors.

At the end of the 6 weeks of data collection, I reviewed all the information and began to organize and make some sense of it. Patterns of behavior that I had anticipated were confirmed by this data recording system. Diane and I had tentatively listed some patterns emerging after 2 weeks of data collection and then confirmed these and others over the remaining weeks of the semester. Diane had summarized the data and listed emerging patterns because she had not been as integrally involved in its collection. I reviewed these patterns and summarized them according to the time of day that they occurred and the possible intent of the behaviors in regard to written comments by staff members. Diane and I shared our data summary over the telephone in January, 1993, and discussed implications for student schedules and programs. We took notes of our telephone conversations and exchanged these along with the data.

Results of Data Collection

In early January, I had the following information on Brent and Holly from the IES system: Holly cried often in our class. I had hypothesized that she wanted attention or was communicating a specific need. Diane and I discussed the implications of the data collection and I shared this with our school team. It appeared that both Brent and Holly wanted to be with people more and were using their behaviors of crying and turning away from work to signal rejection of assigned tasks when they were alone with a teacher for instruction. Diane suggested that both Brent and Holly probably would benefit from more time with their peers and that I might look at moving their mealtimes to the cafeteria and at least some of their instruction time into the classrooms of their peers without disabilities.

We ended the conversation with the idea that I would follow through with finding a buddy for Brent to give him the opportunity for, as Diane called it, "noncontingent social interaction." I would alter his schedule somewhat to accommodate this and look into classroom and cafeteria times with his fifth-grade peers. We decided to set up a telephone session for February. I would call Diane and schedule staff to cover the class while we talked.

It was not until the end of February that I got in touch with Diane to set up an appointment to consult with her over the telephone. I had a number of excuses as to why I had not been in contact sooner, but the truth was that I was feeling very stuck in my routine. I had not made many schedule changes or contacts for peer buddies for Brent or Holly and had lost my drive to try new things. I was avoiding talking with Diane because I knew I had little to say to her. Brent and Holly were still crying and fussing in the room. I had lost my drive.

A Beginning in Collaboration

During the telephone conversation with Diane, I had no encouraging success stories to relay. Brent's chair was not renovated, and he and Holly were still crying and fussing. The staff had the flu, the elementary grade teachers were not receptive to having Brent and Holly in their classrooms, and I did not have time to go to these classrooms. I was spending a lot of time complaining about problems. Diane picked up on my attitude and suggested we make a change.

Diane suggested that I keep a journal about my classroom and stop the IES data collection. I could write about Brent's and Holly's progress, relationships with other teachers, issues concerning including these students anywhere outside my classroom, and, basically, my thoughts about my school and classroom. I had never kept a journal before and did not enjoy writing. The idea of writing down my thoughts and then having Diane read them scared me, but I decided to give it a try. I knew I needed to get out of the rut I was in, and journal writing was something I had never done before. I was not convinced it would help.

I began my journal on February 23, 1993. I quickly noticed how much I had to say. As I wrote, my concerns just materialized on the page, and I began brainstorming ideas and solutions. Usually by the end of the journal entry I had a plan for solving a problem or at least I was beginning to work out one. The following is an example of something I wrote when I first began the journal:

> I always have such a hard time getting myself to sit down with the pen and write down my thoughts. I usually can find many excuses as to why I don't have time (even the laundry is calling?). But usually when I do sit down and get busy, it surprises me as to how much was on my mind. Why, even just while I have been writing this paragraph, a couple of ideas popped into my mind as areas I want to explore. Explore those thoughts!!! And when I am all written out (or out of writing time), I usually feel inspired or at least directed in a particular area. I guess my actual feelings vary depending on the topic, but it always feels good!

Journal writing for me became a creative outlet. As I wrote about daily concerns, other ideas would surface and inspire me. An assignment that I thought would be a chore became an activity I enjoyed and supported me to grow professionally.

DIANE'S PERSPECTIVE

I met Kathy during a consultation with her in her classroom and later contacted her and other educators about master's-degree coursework and tuition waivers available on a federal grant. Through the grant, I began teaching weekend courses at North Idaho in the fall of 1989, and Kathy, along with seven others, was funded on this project and began coursework in the area of severe disabilities at the Coeur d'Alene Center, approximately 100 miles from the University of Idaho. Over the first three semesters of her master's program, Kathy and I developed an ongoing teacher–student relationship. The relationship was congenial but defined by the parameters of a hierarchical professor–student relationship. My role as professor seemed to give me influence and authority in Kathy's eyes. I met this role by essentially directing, with democratic input, the content and assignments of courses. In my classes, I focused on understanding why changes had been occurring in special education curriculum and on the importance of involving families in how and what to teach. Kathy was a conscientious student and worried about doing well in her courses (only an "A" was acceptable) and implementing changes in her classroom.

I visited Kathy's classroom many times throughout her courses and noted she was a traditional teacher, well versed in applied behavior analysis, constructing instructional programs, and evaluating students. Kathy was very skilled within her classroom, and her concern for her students and their education was always apparent. Rearranging instruction to include settings outside her classroom was hard for Kathy, as was looking to families for input into curricula. Kathy had been prepared to be an expert on her students, and she struggled with gathering input from some of her families. I saw changes in Kathy over the years and thought of her as a very good teacher.

The IES Project

The IES project was initiated with Kathy in the third year of our professional relationship. I had received a sabbatical leave for the 1992–1993 year. I intended to focus on learning qualitative research methods with colleagues at the University of Oregon. I also wanted to revisit and rethink college teaching. I was dissatisfied with the teaching format, process, and outcomes. I was in a rut about college teaching and felt there must be a better way. Part of the sabbatical leave also was allocated to a federal grant (IES) awarded to the University of Oregon. I was a field consultant on the grant and in this role investigated a curricular approach for students with severe disabilities and other health impairments. I contacted Kathy and two other Idaho teachers to assess their interest in the project and data collection.

I had not spent much time with Brent and Holly, the two students in Kathy's classroom, and the collaboration regarding the two students began quite formally. Kathy was insightful in her hypotheses regarding Brent and Holly, and we exchanged the data as agreed. As Kathy put forward ideas, I could feel the tension even over the telephone. It was hard for her to express her ideas, ideas with which I might not agree. I resisted the urge to share my thoughts first, as I worried she might not take the chance to lead the conversation and the data collection. I felt the need in our first conversation to withdraw from offering suggestions and merely make comments affirming her ideas. We had agreed at the meeting with Mike, the Oregon consultant, that I would work *with* her and not act as an expert who already knew the answers. I had mentioned my need to follow her direction because she was the actual teacher in the situation, and thus my ideas would be only ideas that may or may not work in the situation. We both talked about valuing one another's insights and resisting domination of the outcomes or process by one of us. I had started reading about mentoring and collaboration and the work of Fosnot (1989) in this area. I knew this collaborative venture would require a considerable shift in our professor–student relationship. I was excited about the opportunity to make the shift, but, in retrospect, I realize Kathy had not had the same opportunity to explore collaboration or mentoring, and, inadvertently, I was leading us in this collaborative venture.

After the first few telephone calls, Kathy gradually began to suggest hypotheses about the meanings of Brent's and Holly's behaviors, and I gradually put forward my interpretation of the data as well. We agreed that Holly was indicating she wanted more social interactions and Brent preferred to be learning within peer group settings rather than individually with teachers. Discussions about how to arrange more social time for these students were somewhat strained between us. I mentioned situations that could be used with Brent and Holly (e.g., eating lunch in the cafeteria rather than the classroom, going to the library, participating in recess and a grade-level classroom for social interactions with peers). Kathy was unusually silent after suggestions about peers from outside of her classroom, and I did not force any resolution. I saw her as a good teacher, somewhat cautious about leaving the special education setting. She had peers coming into the room, but reported this solution was not working well. I left the selection of schedules and the time line to Kathy. I knew she really cared about her students in all ways and felt that, in time, she would propose solutions to enhance programs for these students and other details would be worked out.

I was surprised when we talked in February that neither Brent nor Holly was going to the cafeteria. Schedule changes are very hard to accomplish after the academic year is rolling so I was expecting Kathy to explain difficulties with changes in staffing assignments. Instead, Kathy seemed to avoid the issues. I was perplexed and wondered what the real issues behind her past stressful weeks at school had been. A change in our communication seemed important. I thought the IES data system had taken us as far as it was going to in rethinking programs and schedules for students. I was frustrated by the formal data system. The system had been helpful, but a new focus was needed—more on Kathy's concerns than on the students' behavior. An informal yet supportive means of communication seemed necessary. I suggested journals partly because I thought it would free Kathy from focusing just on the students and refocus her on system issues and barriers and on herself and how she made decisions. I also believed that Kathy, as the teacher in the system, was the best problem solver for the students in this system. I loved the idea of giving her support without any semester time line for when we would start or stop our discussions. I felt my role was to support her in recognizing the solutions within her school context. I was not surprised that the journals and reflections were helpful to us both, but I was surprised at the direction in which our reflections took us. I also was reminded of the incredible efforts and the time, reflections, and support needed to implement new ideas in actual schools and classrooms.

A TURNING POINT

The following excerpts are from Kathy's journal and Diane's responses about how this mentoring process affected their teaching. The format of a reconstructed conversation, centered around key journal entries and parts of taped conversations, is used to illustrate the change process that occurred during 1993. At this point, the writing had been on hold for a year while Kathy and Diane met and reviewed past entries and reviewed themes extracted from the journals. The journal process was continued for another year to record teaching style changes on the behaviors of Brent, Holly, and Kathy's other students. The conversation begins with a discussion of a pivotal meeting that occurred on April 27, 1993.

Diane: Let's start with our late April meeting in 1992. It was a critical turning point in our teaching styles for both of us.

Kathy: Yes, you had asked me to review my journal and our reflections on our telephone conversations from early February. My journal entry after that meeting sums up my reactions very well.

> May 6, 1993
> I had three themes from my journal for the meeting: 1) Brent's needs for more vocabulary and his fussings may mean that he doesn't understand; 2) Holly's crying is her communication mode and is very frustrating for me; and 3) it is all a process, there is no quick fix or miracle. I have been feeling that things weren't moving fast enough. I saw lots of things I wasn't doing. I saw short-

comings that I hadn't fixed yet. So, Diane really surprised me. I was expecting to discuss more things that I should do for each student. I was expecting to examine all other possibilities that might work for Brent and Holly and come up with more work. Instead, she [Diane] basically talked about going with the flow. She said I tended to write like it was my fault that Brent had a bad day when, in fact, it might be that he was sick, had high muscle tone, or was fussing to tell me something.... She talked about going with the flow and teaching the kids, not the IEP goals and objectives.

Diane: I was *really* nervous about that meeting. I wasn't quite sure how to broach the themes I had noted in your journal. I wrote my themes down before the meeting and wrote later in my journal as well:

April 26, 1993
Themes:

1. Kathy tends to blame herself for the behaviors (crying and fussing) of Holly and Brent. She brings these frustrations to the teaching task and sees their task "failures" as her failures. She is getting depressed with this line of thinking.
2. Kathy has a fear of conflict or rejection by her elementary education colleagues. She knows that she has this fear now. She avoids more inclusion because inclusion involves talking with her colleagues. She feels bad about this.
3. Kathy longs for a place (a school) where it is how it is *supposed* to be...principals and administrators set the direction and tell teachers to do it...
4. The area of school restructuring is vague. Kathy may see inclusion as only a disability issue and not part of a larger school restructuring effort.

May 3, 1993
I was nervous about that meeting! These themes seemed so personal and I wasn't sure how I was going to talk about them.... I didn't want to talk about personal issues! I was committed to bringing them up and still wonder if Kathy was okay with the talk....

Kathy: This was an emotional meeting for me. I don't like talking about myself. But, (at the April 27th meeting) I didn't feel threatened or criticized. I felt relieved! We weren't going to talk about what I was doing wrong or what I was not doing for Brent or Holly. In a sense, it was a weight off my shoulders. What really did strike me during our conversation was my teaching style. I began to see how my philosophy and beliefs about teaching were very different from my teaching practices. I wrote a lot about this after that meeting.

May 5, 1993
My teacher training taught me to specify goals and objectives, break those goals into steps, and teach those steps. Remember mass trials? That was great stuff...you could get percentages...that showed improvement. Teachers like me still feel responsible for the data! I feel a pressure to run those programs and the child's needs seem to get in the way. Diane is reminding me to keep looking at the needs of the child, the perspectives of the child. That is what a good teacher does. A good teacher teaches to the child, not to the curriculum. This was just a part of our meeting, but this part about teaching style was the deepest and personally most challenging.

Diane: Are you saying you don't feel that goals, objectives, or data are all that important?

Kathy: No, quite the opposite really. Goals and objectives are essential to good planning. They are the backbone to meeting the needs of my students. But, a teacher must not let the wording of a particular objective dictate how a child is allowed to respond. A teacher should always be willing to adapt and change methods in order to assist students to meet their goals.

In my case, I was disregarding my student's behaviors because these behaviors did not fit into the programs I had written for them. I have since learned to look at those behaviors as communication. I use the information students communicate to me to make changes in the programs in order for my students to achieve their goals.

Diane: How did our talks and the journal assist you? What was going on for you this semester?

Kathy: Conversing with you and reflecting on my journal entries helped me to examine my beliefs about teaching and how they related to my practices. My struggle to see Brent's and Holly's behaviors as communication became very evident as I reviewed my journal. As a teacher, I wanted to control the programs, and I expected students to respond in the ways I dictated. I remember writing in March about Brent and his lunch program. I had his communication system of making food choices by looking at the foods all set up. Then he got all upset and started fussing and would not sit in his chair and follow my programs! We had to bag lunch and feed him his soup using the gastrostomy tube so he could get out of his chair. I wrote about being so frustrated and being mad at him! Now, it doesn't seem like I was that teacher.

Diane: Really, you *had* accomplished so many things. In the fall, you had hypothesized about the meaning of their behaviors and actually you were right. The data confirmed what, in a sense, you already knew. You had the coursework and "on paper" knew what to do. You were just hitting things that for you, in your school, were hard to do! What papers had you read that told you how hard it was to implement theory into practice? Where in the articles about model programs does it tell us how isolated one can feel being a changer? But, you are a good teacher; you were thinking about changes and to your credit you tried something new. When I came back and observed after our April meeting it was like seeing new kids.

Brent was going to recess and the cafeteria with his buddies. He ate in the room and went to the cafeteria to hang out. You had a "no teachers allowed" rule so these times were not controlled by teachers. He had a great picture schedule board that you and the speech-language pathologist had designed. He watched everything you pointed to and when he fussed you pointed to a "no" picture; stated, "Oh, you're tired of that"; and went onto something else until he ate or just stopped and went on to the next activity. It was great to see the aide using it conversationally but not requiring Brent to point to no in addition to fussing to say "no." He could use behaviors he already showed and be understood.

Holly was waiting at the door for peers who walk with her to collect the attendance sheets. She fussed and cried while waiting. An aide went over and explained the girls were a little late. She stopped crying! I went over and waited and chatted with her. When her coworkers appeared down the hall, she beamed at them and gave them all her attention. I saw them later, when I came in from recess, making the rounds. They were on the side of her wheelchair so she could see them just chatting away. She was still smiling! I was genuinely pleased at all I saw.

Kathy: Things had changed, yes. But I was still expecting you to give me more to do. The discussion of my teaching styles and of school reform really hit me. I was such an advocate of child-directed learning for my own children. Your description of some schools as a large conveyor belt was a really good analogy. Bad apples are pulled off and put on a slower belt to be fixed. If they are fixed (ha ha) they are returned to the conveyor belt. If not, they are separated to a smaller, slower belt. Many of these apples never get back onto the belt! I related this to my own son. He is in a Chapter 1 reading program for reading and writing. His skills always have been just a little below grade-level stuff....Every year he had received services to "catch him up." Each year he has made significant progress but is still eligible for services the next year! I was requesting that he not be pulled out and that his teachers look more at his motivation and skills rather than what to teach in their curriculum. I began to actually see similar structures in my own teaching. You told me I tended to write about Brent and Holly crying like it was my fault. Instead, I should be thinking "what could they be trying to tell me?" (Kathy laughs out loud here.) I have always been a strong supporter of nongraded primary schools and child-directed learning. How many times have I said, "We must meet the needs of our students and not the first- or second-grade curricula. All kids develop at different rates." I wanted that for my son. Yet, I was determined to write programs and run them in special education. I saw my son and my students as the bad apples off the conveyor belt and locked in a separate place because the main belt needed to be fixed, not them. I began to see that including Brent and Holly was not just my responsibility to get them in and make them fit.

Diane: I was so pleased and really amazed with the changes in your journal and how you approached teaching in later May and June. The whole following year was different.

Kathy: I guess things just came together more at the meeting in April. I gained insight into my own style of teaching over the spring. Instead of getting more to do, the meeting and reflection helped me see the expert in me. I was expecting a list of expert advice and instead I got an awakening that I had all the answers. I needed to stay focused on teaching kids. I knew that, but somehow I had gotten caught up in looking for the way it is supposed to be.

Diane: The way it is supposed to be?

Kathy: Believing the answers are out there in some model and an expert already knows them is what I believed. Now I see how experience, philosophy, and reflection are part of what an expert draws on and not a list of answers.

Diane: The collaboration and mentoring really helped me understand how idiosyncratic change really is. In every school and for every teacher it will look a little different. Our professional and personal abilities interact with the system we are in, and change happens in different ways. We set the goal to have a student communicate. The steps and strategies are basically the same, but the process of doing it is different every time.

Kathy: I am reminded by all this that becoming a good teacher is in the process. In May I had such fun giving up control. During one session Brent had made a choice to play with a switch-operated doodle art drawer. I got it all set up on his tray and turned it on. Brent went into extension, which, at first, I though meant he didn't like it. Then I wondered if the noise and movement was scaring him. I turned it on and put it on a separate table where he could still see it. He was calmer, but still tense. I turned it off and placed it on his tray. He tensed up and his arms moved and sometimes caught on the plastic toy parts. I pulled it away and held it up at eye level for him to look at. He relaxed considerably. He looked and examined it intently as I turned it upside down for him. I told him I was going to turn it on and showed him where the button was. I turned it on and held it for him to see. He was calm, happy, and attentive. The lesson changed from "doing doodle art" to "how does the battery-operated machine get that pen to go around?" I was beginning to implement my child-directed behavior as communication philosophy. I can now see that the way it is supposed to be doesn't exist. As a good teacher I just keep searching for all the right ways to meet my students' needs.

THE FRUITS OF COLLABORATION

Kathy's Viewpoint

When I started this collaborative project with Diane, I held the belief that a good teacher was one who used teaching techniques that were considered to be recommended practice. I wanted to be a good teacher, but knew under this criterion, I did not measure up. I was constantly searching for the way it is supposed to be.

My approach to teaching came from my former preparation as a teacher, which was a very traditional teacher-directed college program. In contrast, the classes and studying that I did during my master's program at the University of Idaho helped me to change my educational beliefs toward a child-directed approach. This was good in theory, but I had a hard time putting my beliefs into practice in my classroom.

During this project I was able to explore my own teaching practices. Through journal writing I was able to reflect on my own personal teaching beliefs and examine how I was implementing what I believe in my own classroom. Diane offered support and feedback along the way. She guided me to a deeper understanding of what a good teacher really is. I now can see that a good teacher is someone who is committed to meeting the student's needs. A good teacher might not have all the answers but is willing to search, learn, and grow.

This project in itself is a good example of student-directed learning. I was able to focus on my skills as a teacher. I was encouraged to draw upon my own experiences to improve my teaching style. Diane did not compare me with the "expert" teacher. She did not have a list of competencies for me to complete. She allowed my learning to be very personal and meaningful for me. I gained a deeper understanding of the concept of child-directed learning, and I was able to implement this knowledge in my own teaching situation. My theory and practice began to be one.

As I finished the rest of the school year, I continued to write in my journal. Many of the entries focused on listening to the needs of my students and responding to their nonverbal communication—their behaviors as communications. The students' pleasure at being heard and responded to was mixed with the excitement I was feeling in becoming a child-directed teacher.

As I continue this search, I am reminded that becoming a better teacher is a process. It is not something that will happen overnight. It is not a set of new skills, books, or devices to use with students. I continue to relearn and revisit concepts when I see them being implemented through my teaching. It becomes a peeling off of old habits and a building of new methods. The method of questioning and searching for the "right" answer is a continuous process as teachers and students face new situations and experience growth and success. I now can see the way it is supposed to be does not exist. To be a good teacher I will not settle only for how it is done somewhere else, but will continue to search for all the right ways to meet my students' constantly changing needs. As Diane and I met for what was "almost" the last time to review this written project, I reflected on my old and new teaching style. It is a good example of how I have changed and I would like to end with this:

> During the spring of 1994, I was taken off guard when a student with a history of severe behavior outbursts started taking off his shoes and socks on a bus while on a field trip. My first reaction was to keep him "on the program" and get those shoes back on! After all, I'm sure wearing shoes is a school bus rule. Instead, I watched and listened. He began to tell me about a friend who had been cut on the foot that weekend. As he relayed his story using his limited verbal vocabulary and pointing to his foot, I understood him and expressed my concern. After this short, but meaningful conversation, he immediately put on his socks and shoes without any directions from me. Yes, I was amazed. I was close to labeling this behavior as inappropriate and then would have missed his message and isolated him by not listening. This is child-directed learning and teaching. The way it is supposed to be on the bus and other places does not exist.

Diane's Viewpoint

Kathy's writings really helped me to work through how I wanted to change as a college teacher. This was my sabbatical year and I had decided to look at my college teaching. I was really tired of the way it was being done, but the "good college teaching suggestion lists" left me cold. Be more organized? Come to classes 10–15 minutes early and talk with students? Give students more choice in assignments? These things were just doing more of what I already was doing. I went back to my philosophy and looked at good teaching, at child-directed teaching, and behavior as communication. I read. I saw Kathy, an excellent teacher with good coursework, struggling to implement theory into practice and having a hard time. I realized I was having the same hard time, but my kids were college students! I read a description of mentoring that was different from what I had previously read and liked it. In this mentor system, correct practice is viewed as an illusion. So, the way it is supposed to be never really is. What happens in the mentor process is that the mentor constructs a line of inquiry and supports the other's intellectual freedom and capability to understand, adopt, or modify. I was going to try it and stay with it all the way.

The next fall I had the students in my class organize the syllabus. I had them interview teachers, parents, and young adults with disabilities and use that as a starting point to determine what they wanted to learn. At the time I thought that was enough of a change, but as I listened to them more and more, I realized that fundamentally my understanding was based on my already-attained experience base. I began to see that what you need to know can be very situation driven. I began to realize that course sequences and content may not need to be so filled with meeting predetermined competences. More time was needed for trying things in schools with students and reflecting upon it. Next semester I will be coteaching a classroom with a district teacher. We will both work with university students. Some of the content for the semester will be predetermined (e.g., legal issues, determining and writing IEPs), but the remainder will be situation driven as students enounter interesting and frustrating challenges in teaching. It should be interesting. I am sure I will have as many questions as the students as we explore our notions of the way it is *supposed* to be and how it really is.

Section V

VIGNETTES

In this section, vignettes, or case studies, are presented as examples of how assessment data were used to set up communication systems. A cross section of environments, partners, and individual abilities is presented. The individuals featured in these vignettes spent their time in a variety of settings, including natural homes, group homes, elementary schools, junior high and high schools, special recreational programs, and supervised work settings. Each of these environments led to unique communication needs, while at the same time many communication needs were similar across settings.

As might be guessed, the partners varied considerably among settings not only in their roles but also in their level of training and, particularly, in their attitudes toward the individual. In some cases, barriers to the growth of the communication system were identified and targeted for change.

The individuals described in the vignettes were chosen because their needs for communication support ranged from extensive to pervasive. In addition to this range of needs, the individuals varied in degree of mental and physical ability. These thorough descriptions provide examples with which the reader can identify. Although the characteristics presented here may not exactly match those of an individual about whom the reader is concerned, enough detail is provided so that ideas from several vignettes can be synthesized.

The assessment methods varied according to the consultant's individual preferences, the distinctive characteristics of the team, prior assessment data, and, of course, the individual's characteristics. Nonetheless, data fitting the assessment model presented in Section II of this book can be identified readily. Resulting communication systems varied from nonsymbolic, gestural systems to more complex computerized devices. This section provides numerous examples of how the assessment, implementation, and ongoing adjustments were made in natural contexts (Calculator & Jorgensen, 1992).

The final chapter in this section addresses the lessons learned from working with individuals whose vignettes were presented in *Augmentative and Alternative Communication Systems for Persons with Moderate to Severe Disabilities* (Baumgart, Johnson, & Helmstetter, 1990). The authors revisited as many of the individuals as possible in order to address long-term outcomes. Without giving away too much, it can be said that not all outcomes were as positive as expected. There remains a significant need for ongoing advocacy as individuals make transitions among settings and partners.

Chapter 10

Kevin

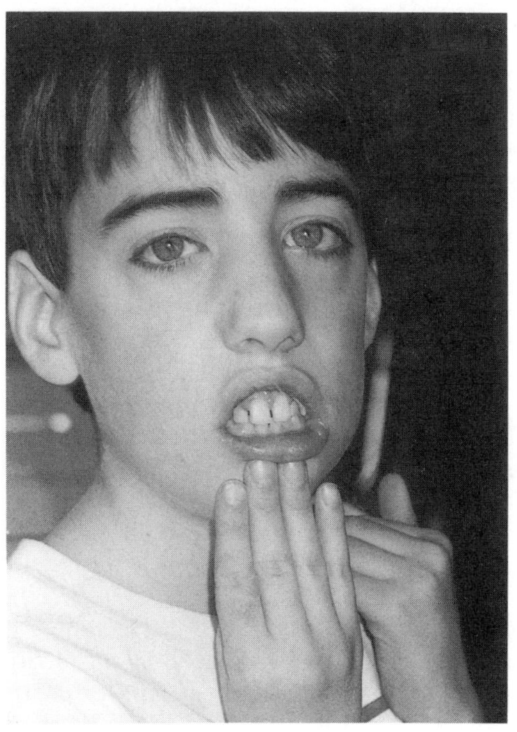

Name: Kevin
Age: 9 years
Teacher: Sandy
Consultant: Jeanne Johnson
System: A multimodal system that includes a communication book with sight words, a wall-mounted system of picture symbols representing daily events, vocalizations, pointing, physical manipulation of partners, and some signs

When the consultant first met Kevin, he had just made a transition from a private program for children, from birth to 3 years of age, to the public school setting. Many things have changed for Kevin since that time. He is 9 years old now. As he has grown and moved into different school settings, his abilities and needs have changed. This chapter chronicles the path his communication system has taken.

OVERVIEW

Kevin has myotonic dystrophy, a rare, slowly progressive, hereditary disease characterized by atrophy of the head and neck muscles. As a result, Kevin's subtle facial expressions are difficult to read, particularly for those who do not know him well. For example, as a young child, when he was happy or excited, he showed a slight raising of his lower eyelids. Now, he has more facial movement with his smile; although it is still difficult for partners unfamiliar with him to identify this signal. To his benefit, he continues to express enjoyment in other ways, such as becoming more active and vocalizing.

Kevin has been receiving special services since birth. He has delays in the areas of motor skills, cognition, and communication. At 3 years of age, he scored at about the 12- to 24-month level for adaptive, cognitive, social, and communication skills on a criterion-referenced developmental checklist. Now at age 9, according to standardized and nonstandardized assessments, he scores at about the 36- to 48-month level in all areas except communication. His current speech-language pathologist, Sherry, estimates that his receptive communication skills are at the 20- to 30-month level according to results from the Sequenced Inventory of Communication Development–Revised (Hendrick, Prather, & Tobin, 1984) and the Peabody Picture Vocabulary Test–Revised (Dunn & Dunn, 1981). Sherry feels that standardized tests are inappropriate for measuring Kevin's expressive communication skills because they rely so heavily on verbal responses. Instead, she has documented his skills in a detailed, descriptive manner. This information is described in detail later in this chapter.

Kevin has been walking since the age of 2. He generally has adequate motor skills for walking, running, and jumping as well as for manipulating small objects, pointing, and performing other conventional gestures. According to his most recent IEP, he is working on improving balance and range of motion in his ankles. His vision and hearing are normal. He has received direct services from speech-language pathologists, occupational therapists, and physical therapists throughout his educational career.

ORIGINAL REFERRAL AT AGE 3½ YEARS

Kevin's preschool teacher, Kathy, contacted the consultant because she and Kevin's parents were concerned about broadening his communication skills. Kathy had conducted a detailed nonstandardized assessment of Kevin's skills as part of a class on augmentative communication that the consultant taught and Kathy attended. As a result, Kathy was considering changing Kevin's system of communication from sign language to something else.

Kevin had been taught to sign at an early age, but little progress had been made. His signing vocabulary was limited to three signs used spontaneously and five signs used with prompts. He rarely initiated communication with sign. At home, he used only one sign—MILK—to request milk. He also would bring a desired object or food to his parents or pull them to the refrigerator and touch what he wanted as he vocalized.

At age 3, his speech consisted of vowel-like sounds, and he did not imitate novel sounds. When he was frustrated, he would run away, vocalizing "eeee" as he waved his hands in front of his chest. Kevin had been receiving direct communication therapy aimed at increasing the variety of his vocalizations, but little progress had been made.

Kevin's parents recognized many different types of idiosyncratic communicative signals Kevin already used, and they tried to respond to the signals in a meaningful manner. However, all of the communication partners, including Kevin, expressed frustration over the inadequacy of this system. His parents wondered, at that time, if a communication book would be appropriate because Kevin was interested in pictures.

ORIGINAL ASSESSMENT AT AGE 3½ YEARS

Standardized assessments had been attempted with Kevin; however, he had difficulty performing the required tasks. The school assessment team decided to use, instead, Kathy's detailed nonstandardized assessment of sensorimotor and communication skills to determine eligibility for programs and to establish appropriate goals. In addition, a communication consultant assisted in the assessment by observing, interviewing, and eliciting certain behaviors from Kevin.

Kevin's Environments and Partners at Age 3½ Years

As mentioned, Kevin started in a birth-to-3 program and made a transition to a half-day public school preschool program at the age of 3. In the preschool program, his primary communication partners were his teacher Kathy and two educational aides (EAs). Parents of the children in this class volunteered their time to help Kathy, so Kevin's mother was often present in class. Kathy had established a regular sequence of routines for her students that included morning greetings, circle time, small group activities, snack, recess, free play time, small group activities, and preparation for going home.

Kevin's home schedules were also comfortably predictable such that he could anticipate upcoming daily events. Within this framework, his family allowed him to make choices and honored his requests if they were appropriate.

Kevin's Abilities at Age 3½ Years

Content: Sensorimotor Abilities and Receptive Vocabulary Kevin played with objects in a manner typical of a child who is about 24 months old. He explored the novel aspects of toys, he used common objects (e.g., comb, telephone, keys) conventionally during play, and he showed indirect means–ends skills in problem solving. His receptive vocabulary abilities seemed tied to the routine; that is, within familiar routines, Kevin would respond correctly to an adult's one-word verbal instructions. During transitions in activities and in unfamiliar routines, Kevin did not show that he comprehended the same words. As for his comprehension of nonverbal symbols, Kevin's mother noted that he seemed to enjoy looking at pictures, but she was not sure that he understood the meaning of the pictures. Kathy agreed with his mother's observation.

Form and Use: Expressive Communication A Form and Use Assessment Sheet was used to document Kevin's expressive communication signals (see Figure 10.1). As noted, he used the vocalization "eeee" with fluctuating pitch and loudness to distinguish between enjoyment and protest. His partners interpreted these signals as requests to continue or terminate an activity. Some communication partners were better than others at successfully interpreting his vocalizations and gestures. If the partner misinterpreted, Kevin would either ignore the adult's interpretation or express frustration and protest again.

Kevin was observed to verbalize "dada" clearly as he held up his arms prior to being lifted. This was interpreted as a request for action. In addition, he was observed to say "nana" when his mother moved around in the room. This was interpreted as a comment on her presence or activity.

Kevin also touched or reached for desired objects and often alternated his gaze between the object and the adult who was assisting. All partners interpreted these gestures as requests for the object or requests for them to name the object for Kevin. Kevin's facial expression sometimes influenced his partner's interpretation of his level of interest in an activity. If they misjudged his actions, Kevin would vocalize his protest as he ran away.

Social Interactions: Intentionality and Communication Roles There was absolutely no doubt that Kevin was intentionally trying to interact with peers and adults by using vocalizations and gestures. He not only initiated interaction, but he also sought to maintain joint activity routines by taking the next turn in the interaction. For example, Kathy had a tickle routine with Kevin that he seemed to savor. He would stand near her, arms slightly away from his body. Kathy would tickle his sides saying, "tickle, tickle," and then she would pause. Kevin would then lift up his shirt to request more. If Kathy did not respond quickly, he would lean toward her hands. This interactiveness was also seen with vocalizations. If an adult imitated one of his vocalizations, he would look at that adult and vocalize again.

Kevin's ability to manipulate others so positively and appropriately in interactions was supported by the structure of Kathy's classroom routines. In morning circle, for example, he filled in the hand motions for a favorite song when the teacher paused midsong and looked expectantly at Kevin. His interactiveness also encouraged new partners to engage in conversation with him. Whenever someone new came into the room, he would run to them saying "eeeee!"—a greeting not easily ignored.

ORIGINAL COMMUNICATION SYSTEM RECOMMENDATIONS AT AGE 3½ YEARS

A *right-now* system of using actual objects was first recommended because it was not clear that Kevin understood the symbolic representation of pictures. He was shown two or three objects representing choices within various activities and he would touch the one he wanted. He was then given the actual object while the representation remained in front of him. As anticipated, Kevin was able to do this immediately. All partners were involved in the decisions as to when to make choices available and what types of choices he should have so that he could use this system in all settings throughout the day. Kevin's signs and gestures also were encouraged. He added many prompted signs to his list and added EAT, WANT, COOKIE, and CRACKER to his spontaneous repertoire.

Individual's Name: Kevin (Age: 3-6) Date: 11/94
Observer: J. Johnson Location: Preschool

Context	Partner	Individual's signal	Partner's response	Discourse function	Pragmatic function
Play time: Cue: OK, go get the monkeys, Kevin."	Kathy	Looks at Kathy	Looks at Kevin, eyebrows raised, points, and asks, "Monkeys, Kevin?"	Maintain	Request for clarification or repair
		Goes to toy shelf and takes out monkeys	"Uh-huh."	Maintain	Acknowledgment
Small group: Sitting at small table with two peers and two adults playing with Play-Doh	Educational aide	Says, "Eee," looks at aide, and holds up Play-Doh	"Oooh, a pancake."	Initiation	Comment or show off
Aide makes a snake with Play-Doh, holds it up for Kevin, and asks, "See?"	Educational aide	Says, "Eee," with lower eyelids raised	"A snake."	Maintain	Acknowledgment
		"Says "Eee" and gives educational aide his Play-Doh	"What?...You want a snake?" (Makes snake)	Initiation	Requests action
	Peer	Reaches for cookie cutter	Says, "It's mine!" and pulls cookie cutter away	Initiation	Requests object
		Says, "Eee!" and runs away waving hands on chest	Says, "You can't have it!"	Termination	Protest

Figure 10.1. Kevin's Preschool Form and Use Assessment Sheet.

At the same time, Kathy spent about 2 weeks preparing pictures for Kevin. She found pictures in school supply catalogs for most of the toys with which he liked to play and magazine pictures of food and drink items. She added photographs of home and family members also. All pictures were laminated on 3-inch × 5-inch notecards and arranged according to his daily schedule of events. Kathy also collected objects to match some of the pictures and was prepared to do a Match-to-Sample assessment with Kevin.

Kevin readily embraced the picture system, using it without any special training on the first day it was attempted. One of his first responses when he saw a picture of some plastic monkeys was to take the picture to the toy it matched and bring both the picture and toy to Kathy. Kathy interpreted this series of signals as a request to play with the monkeys and Kevin seemed satisfied with Kathy's response. The challenge then was to keep up with his many and varied preferences. The number of pictures grew astronomically. Kathy abandoned her plan to do a Match-to-Sample assessment because Kevin was already demonstrating his symbolic capability to comprehend these representations.

Because Kevin was ambulatory, a communication board or notebook was deemed too unwieldy. His family and his teacher devised a shoebox file system in which all his choices were organized chronologically according to the daily schedule of events. Kevin went right to the section in the shoebox with the picture he wanted, pulled it out, and gave it to Kathy. He also enjoyed taking out a whole section of cards just to look at each one before replacing them, much like other children examine their baseball card collections. Kevin had a shoebox at home and one at school with numerous catalog pictures, photographs, and colored line drawings representing choices within his daily routines.

Kevin had an ideal situation in the preschool because both his teacher and his mother were present to teach and model this system to the EAs and other parent volunteers. Each day there were multiple opportunities for new partners to observe more skilled partners using the system. Thus, teaching partners was not an issue of concern. Moreover, by modeling their attitude of acceptance of these signals, Kathy and Kevin's mother influenced the other partners' view of Kevin as a legitimate communicator.

Kevin's story was characterized as a *Pollyanna* case—supportive environment, eager child, eager parents, and eager teacher. His story was an excellent example of how the weight of success depended on those who communicated with him. Before Kevin's consultants first met him, some of his partners felt he was not motivated enough to communicate. His partners at the preschool never considered his lack of facial expression or clear verbalization to be an indicator of low motivation, but rather they sought to match a system to his *right-now* level of skill. When they did so, Kevin appeared extremely motivated to communicate.

WHAT HAPPENED TO KEVIN AND HIS SYSTEM?

Kevin is now 5½ years older and has remained in the same school district. In the last year of preschool, he had a new teacher who had more difficulty implementing his communication system on a consistent basis. Kevin's communication did not change much during this time, and he began to have behavior problems involving protesting the actions of others. He then made a transition from preschool to a nearby elementary school. The information about his communication system was not shared with the elementary school staff, and, as a result, his communication system was not used at all. For several years, the focus for communication was on increasing Kevin's verbalizations and sign proficiency. Kevin's communication skills, again, did not show much improvement.

A New School—A New Start
During his ninth year, Kevin transferred to another school within the district; he spends his school day either in a special education classroom or with his peers in a third-grade classroom. His new teacher, Sandy, has a positive attitude toward Kevin's communication system. She researched his past communication systems and has reestablished them. She feels that "he has a lot more to say than he can express" and wants to continue expanding his system.

Communication Abilities at 9 Years

Expressive Communication: Speech, Signs, and Gestures Kevin's expressive communication has expanded since he was 3. His speech has not changed dramatically since his consultants last saw him. "Eee" is still his favorite thing to say, particularly when he is excited. He has a few other variations on vowel-like sounds and some consonant plus vowel utterances. None of these vocalizations have specific symbolic meanings attached. It was noted that every now and then he says a single word clearly.

He also has continued to work on learning signs. The team believed that if he concentrated on signs, he might learn them better; but so far, he has added only a few more signs to his spontaneous repertoire. He spontaneously signs WANT, EAT, CRACKER, COOKIE, CANDY, BOOK, and SCHOOL to request or comment. The signs for CANDY, BOOK, and SCHOOL are new on the list from when he was 3 years old.

The vocabulary was chosen based on his daily schedule and choices within the schedule. He still needs prompts, in the form of cue cards showing the written word, for MILK, BATHROOM, CHEESE, COMPUTER, GRAPES, DRINK, MUSIC, PHYSICAL EDUCATION, and OFFICE. Sherry, the speech-language pathologist, reports that hypotonia affects his ability to articulate these signs clearly, but that they are identifiably separate from his other signs.

The team has decided that signs are worth the effort: They are portable, most people in his environment can interpret his signs, and he has shown progress since this has become a focus and consistency of partner response has improved. The team members plan to make a videotape of Kevin's current sign vocabulary so that new partners can learn his system.

Another reason the team wants to pursue improving Kevin's sign repertoire is that he is very gestural in his natural communication. He points and vocalizes to establish joint attention to an object, person, or event.

Now Kevin has a communication notebook at school, which has replaced the shoebox (see Figures 10.2 and 10.3). He still uses his shoebox at home. He does not use these systems all the time—only when his partner does not understand his gestures. During these times, he finds his book or, when at home, his shoebox, and takes it to the person with whom he is trying to communicate. Most of the time, he prefers to point, pull, or show partners what he wants or means. He may take the partner's hand and manipulate it to point to a picture. For example, when he is being emphatic about requesting, he takes the partner's index finger and points to what he wants and where the event will occur. For example, the consultant was sitting with Kevin during free time. Kevin wanted to change the cassette tape to

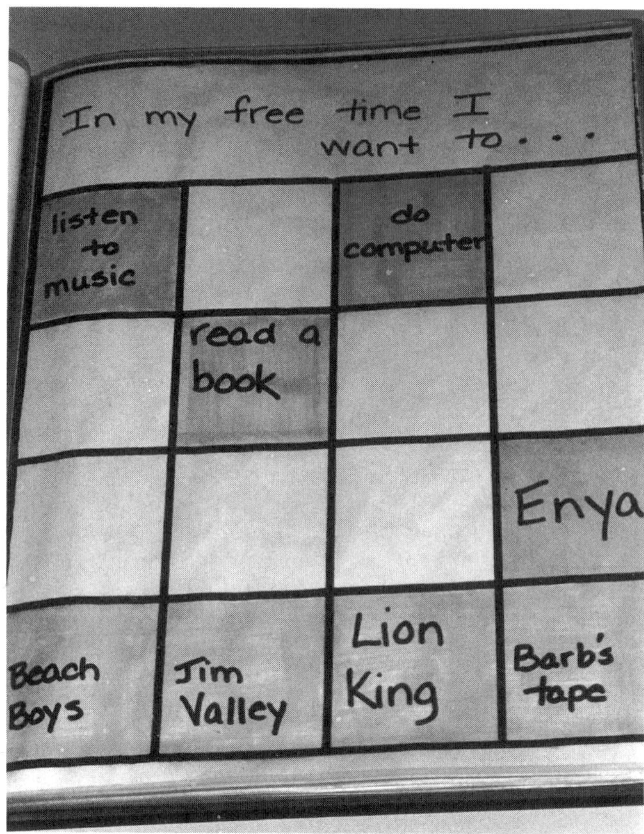

Figure 10.2. A page from Kevin's communication notebook, which features free-time activities.

which he was listening, so he pointed to "Beach Boys" in his communication notebook and selected the matching tape (see Figures 10.4 and 10.5). When the consultant played the wrong tape, he took the consultant's hand, moved it to the "Listen to Music" message, the "Beach Boys" message, and then to the tape recorder. When the consultant again put in the wrong tape, Kevin persisted by taking her hand, putting it on "Beach Boys,"and pushing her hand toward the tape recorder.

Expressive Communication: Pictures and Written Words Kevin's vocabulary represented by pictures is much more extensive that when he uses signs. Kevin's picture communication system has undergone several transitions from the shoeboxes previously mentioned. His mother says, "After a couple of years of fumbling around, we finally have a system that seems OK." Kevin's shoebox picture system stayed with him for several years; however, not all his partners used it consistently with him. As a result, the pictures available at school did not represent his changing preferences and needs. While he was still in preschool, he tried using a Wolf board for activity choices, but it seemed to be too limited given his considerable vocabulary.

A communication and schedule board (Figure 10.6) is posted on the wall of Kevin's classroom; this board shows picture choices for aspects of the schedule. These symbols are used by many of the children in the class. Kevin uses this to request activities and to respond to adult queries regarding the next scheduled event

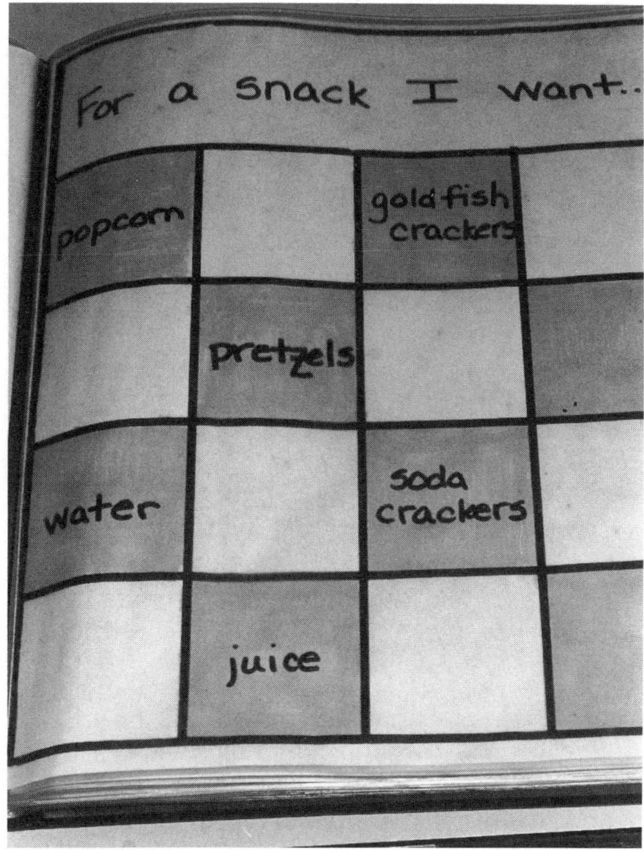

Figure 10.3. A page from Kevin's communication notebook, which features snack-time options.

in his day. As an example, Sherry reports that when she enters the room, Kevin often comes over to the wall and points to the picture for speech therapy as a request to work with her. Sometimes his request is honored, and sometimes Sherry tells him that it is not his turn. Kevin seems very disappointed when this happens. The consultant suggested adding a clock face to the wall symbols, showing the time he gets to go with Sherry, so Kevin can work on matching the clock representation to the real clock in the room. This fits with his academic objective of matching clock hand positions. When he is done with therapy or when therapy is not an option, the symbol is covered. It was suggested that a routine be implemented at the beginning of the day to decide whether it was a therapy day. Kevin could then cover the symbol himself as further reinforcement of the idea that speech therapy was not an option on that day.

The biggest change since the consultant's last visit with Kevin is that he is using written words. He has about five pages of 152 sight words and phrases in his notebook that he is reported to use spontaneously to repair misunderstandings in conversation. These words and phrases have been rearranged recently so they are grouped by topic or by the event in which they are likely to occur. For example, on his page for leisure choices, he has the following messages: "Listen to Music," "Do Computer," "Read a Book," "Beach Boys," "Enya," and "Barb's tape" (of his

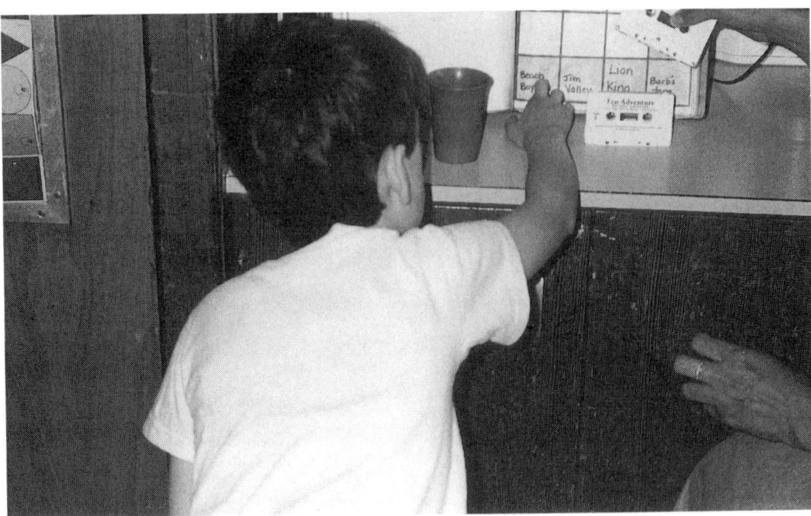

Figure 10.4. Kevin pointing to the "Beach Boys" message in his notebook.

favorite tapes), "Jim Valley," and "Lion King." Pages from his rearranged communication book are shown in Figures 10.4 and 10.5, and a recent Form and Use Assessment Sheet is shown in Figure 10.7.

The leap from pictures to written words is not a minor one and could not have been predicted by looking at test scores indicating levels of development. Kevin has somehow learned these words through repeated exposure to printed media. He cannot spell, but he can reliably recognize these sight words and has assigned specific meanings to these words. This ability can be explained by the ecological model in which Kevin learned to assign meaning based on his need to use a particular symbol at a particular time.

Kevin's mother described the process by which they discovered Kevin could recognize sight words. While at home, the family gradually realized that Kevin was

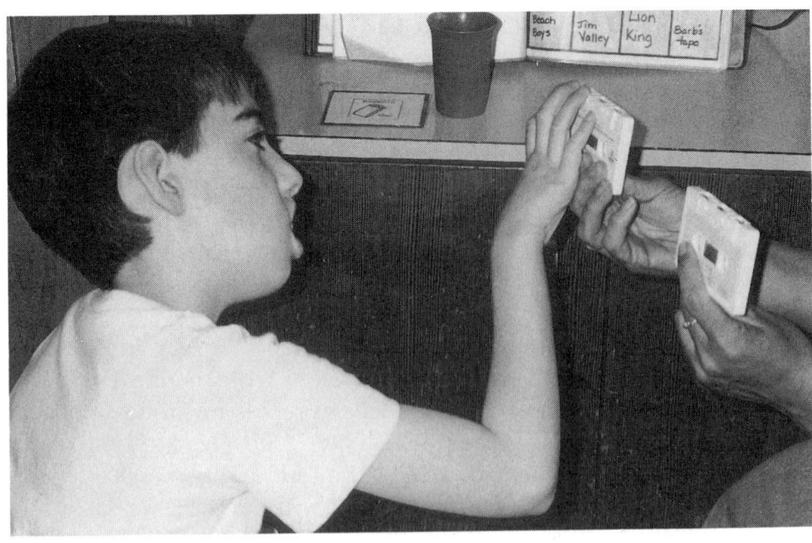

Figure 10.5. Kevin selecting the matching Beach Boys tape.

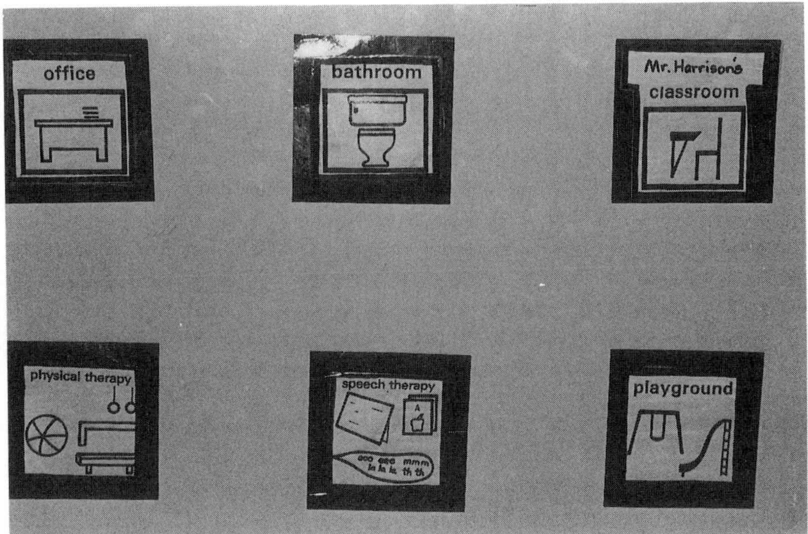

Figure 10.6. The communication and schedule board posted in Kevin's classroom.

using written words, not just pictures, to communicate when he would pick out a word from printed matter and match it to an object, particularly when he wanted that object. A private reading specialist then suggested trying a more comprehensive sight-word approach with Kevin. The family had a moderate degree of success with this method and were anxious to share it with the school staff. Kevin's mother described her frustration in trying to convince previous school staff members that Kevin really did comprehend some sight words; she felt that no one at school believed he could do it. After a convincing demonstration during a visit to school, the previous staff began to believe her. They conveyed this information to Sandy, his current teacher, who was able to remain open to the idea that Kevin could perform at this level of abstraction.

Sandy emphatically agreed with Kevin's mother. She is working with Kevin to expand his sight-word list to include developmentally and ecologically appropriate vocabulary. Specifically, she plans to add names of familiar communication partners, body parts, prepositions, and some action words. These will allow Kevin to be more specific about emergency needs, locations, and interesting events. About 95% of the sight words are nouns. Sandy is enthusiastic about Kevin's sight-reading skills and the avenues that are open to him as a result of this skill. The fact that he can use sight words indicates Kevin has the propensity for assigning meaning to arbitrary symbols.

After the consultant visited Sandy's classroom to discuss Kevin's progress, further suggestions were made for expanding his communication system. First, it was suggested that Sandy try voice output for some of Kevin's choices to see if he responded positively. A low-tech suggestion was to have two tape recorders connected to a switch on which a picture of Kevin's choice could be attached. When he touched his choice, one of the tape recorders would be activated to say "I want ____." Sandy planned to find a boy in Kevin's third-grade classroom to record the messages so they would sound age- and gender-appropriate.

If Kevin responded positively to the recorded messages, it was suggested that Sandy contact the local special technology resource center in order to borrow an

Individual's Name: Kevin (Age: 9) Date:
Observer: J. Johnson Location: Special education classroom

Context	Partner	Individual's signal	Partner's response	Discourse function	Pragmatic function
Transition to leisure time: Sitting at table, looking at communication book, asks, "What do you want to do today?"	Sandy	Points to "Listen to music"	Says, "OK, you want to listen to music."	Request	Maintain by answering question
		Takes Sandy's hand and points to "Beach Boys"	Says, "OK, you want your Beach Boys tape. Let's go."	Request	Maintain; initiation of subtopic
Kevin walks over to tape recorder with Sandy, carrying his communication notebook.		Picks up basket containing all the tapes and gives it to Sandy	Asks, "You want me to find the right tape?...OK."	Request	Maintain; initiation of subtopic
Sandy puts in a tape that is mislabeled.		Opens notebook and points to "Beach Boys" while saying, "Eee!"	Takes out tape and looks at it closely	Request	Repair attempt (unsuccessful)
		Takes Sandy's index finger and puts it on "Beach Boys" and pushes her hand toward the basket of tapes	"You're right. That wasn't the Beach Boys. Here it is."	Request	Repair attempt (successful)
Beach Boys music begins to play.					

Figure 10.7 Kevin's Classroom Form and Use Assessment Sheet.

array of devices. To get started, an Alphatalker (by Prentke-Romich) or a Digivox (by Sentient Systems) was suggested because these two devices are similar in their capacities and are a bit more flexible than a Wolf board in programming. It also was suggested that Kevin try a Dynavox (by Sentient Systems) or a similar device because it has a greater capacity for vocabulary that could grow with his abilities.

As a final note, it is a pleasure to report that the relationship between Kevin's family and his teacher, Sandy, is very solid. Although there have been problems during the transitions, they seem to have been resolved by the move to this new school and the presence of a teacher with positive regard for Kevin's abilities. Sandy feels that Kevin's parents provide "excellent follow-through" on her suggestions. Kevin's mother feels Sandy listens to her opinions and incorporates them in her planning.

LESSONS LEARNED

Because Kevin was followed for several years, it is appropriate to reflect on what did or did not work and why. The following is a list of what was learned through this process:

1. Using a *right-now* system, such as the object system, did not prevent progress with a higher-level system, such as the pictures. Similarly, the use of pictures, gestures, and signs did not prevent progress to sight words. Adults' attitudes, not Kevin's skills, were the barrier.
2. Educators must listen more openly to parents. The previous school staff may have assumed that Kevin's parents were overestimating his abilities. This caused friction and dissatisfaction with the program. When this information was considered legitimate, Kevin's system leapt forward, as did the relationship between the family and school staff.
3. Development is not always linear. Educators must remain open to the possibility that an individual can learn a skill even though he or she appears not to have the foundation skills in place.
4. Multiple modality systems are appropriate. Gestures, in particular, are too often overlooked as a powerful means of communicating naturally. They serve an excellent role in communication because they are fast, portable, and understood by many. Paired with other, more structured means of communication, they provide richness and emotion that are often lacking in stark picture systems. In more than one instance, individuals have temporarily abandoned their fancy systems of communication in favor of direct gestures. It is a common means of communicating even when people *can* verbalize proficiently.
5. Transitions are a way of life. When plans for transition do not include a systematic, multimodal means of training new partners to use a communication system, the individual's ability to communicate will be impaired. The individual's right to communicate is significantly hindered.

Chapter 11

Angela

NAME: Angela
AGE: 5 years, 9 months
TEACHERS: Teri and Brenda
CONSULTANTS: Chris Curry, Ed Helmstetter, and Jeanne Johnson
SYSTEM: The initial communication system consists of tactile representations of objects that are used to make choices and objects that represent upcoming events. The objects are attached to the communication board with Velcro. A subsequent system consists of gestures and vocalizations associated with familiar routines.

Angela was first seen by the consultants in February of 1993. She was referred for an AAC consultation by her family, the school staff, and a special education consultant who wanted to facilitate the development of her communication skills. Many of Angela's communication partners felt that she comprehended more than she could express and they wanted her to be able to express her needs.

Angela had orthopedic impairments, severe developmental delays, and cortical blindness. She spent most of her time in her wheelchair, moving occasionally to an adapted stationary chair or prone stander. Her learning objectives included eating lunch and going on field trips with peers, making choices of food or drink items at mealtimes, greeting others by raising her hand, feeding herself with a spoon, and tapping her lunch tray to signal when she wanted more food.

ANGELA'S ENVIRONMENT

Angela lived at home with her family, where she was cared for by both parents. Angela attended a kindergarten classroom, which was appropriate for her chronological age. Her kindergarten schedule, however, differed from those of the other students. For example, she ate lunch alone in a separate room and had time set aside for physical therapy.

Angela was assigned to one educational aide for most of the day. A second aide worked with her during mealtimes so that the first aide could have breaks. She also interacted with the kindergarten teacher, classmates, and, of course, family members. When asked what meaning particular signals had, the partners responded inconsistently. For example, some partners were interpreting head shakes as meaning "no," whereas others were not assigning this signal a meaning. Some partners were letting Angela touch choices before giving something to her and others were just giving her items.

Angela had developed some signs and gestures that were interpreted in the same way by all partners, but the partners often chose to ignore her attempts to communicate. For example, when Angela tapped on her tray for more food or for an activity to continue, her partners, although they knew what she wanted, would give her more or not give her more based on what they felt was appropriate, not on her request. Both adult partners and peers led the interactions, responding inconsistently to Angela's communication.

ANGELA'S SKILLS

Comprehension

Angela's comprehension of spoken language was unclear. Some of her partners believed she understood most of what they said, whereas others felt she did not understand any words at all. During the observational process, it became clear that Angela "understood" spoken words if they were used during familiar routines. Her comprehension seemed to depend not only on the sequence of the activities within the routine but also on the contextual support of objects and gestural cues; that is, as partners were telling her what to do, they were also helping her move her hands to touch familiar objects. She would then use the rule of "do what you usually do" with these objects once she had them in her hands, regardless of the verbal instructions given.

The best characterization of her comprehension abilities was seen during transitions. For example, her communication partner would say, "Time for lunch" or "Let's wash up" and then take her to the lunchroom or washroom. In each case, when Angela felt her chair begin to move she started yelling, crying, and biting her hand. She stopped these behaviors when she arrived at her destination and was given an object (e.g., spoon, soap) related to the new location. It seemed clear that she did not comprehend the spoken words only.

Forms and Functions

Angela demonstrated many different types of intentional communication signals in specific contexts. She had a variety of vocalizations that she used to call others and to express pleasure, frustration, and discontent. If no one answered or if her partner responded with a nondesired item, she would persist in signaling or protesting. The vocalizations for frustration and protest were followed closely by head shakes and hand biting. Angela also had some imitative verbal approximations that were being interpreted as meaningful. They included "guhgu" for "good girl," "mamam" for "mom," and "duh" for "done." Angela used gestures such as clapping her hands when she had done well, tapping on her tray for more food, touching objects and people to establish joint attention, and leaning toward her communication partner in anticipation of being hugged.

Physical Abilities

Angela had good control of her trunk and head; thus, she also had good control of her hands and arms. She seemed to have some interest in brightly colored objects and black–white contrasts placed on a light box. Her hearing had not been checked for several years, so a hearing evaluation was scheduled with an audiologist who could assess her with electrophysiological measures.

SYSTEM RECOMENDATIONS

Because of Angela's cortical blindness, it was decided that the system needed to afford her tactile feedback. The representations of choices would be the actual objects she was to receive. At the beginning of the routine, the partner was to help her feel her two choices and then wait for her to reach out and touch what she wanted.

The aides believed that Angela did not always make clear choices. It was suggested that the positions of the objects should be changed and the partner should provide specific assisted physical cues regarding location (e.g., "Angela, drink is *here* and potatoes are *here*").

Choice-making times included two snacks, lunch at school, and meals at home. After this system was working, the staff added choices of music versus listening to a story. These choices were represented by headphones, which Angela always held prior to listening to music, and a book, which she also held during the activity. For the first system, it was decided that Angela would get the item she touched. Later, it was decided to make her system a bit more symbolic by having her touch an item just like the one she would receive. The item used for choice making would be attached with Velcro to a communication board.

To ease transitions, it was decided to mark the salient portions of events for Angela by having her feel items related to that event. For example, before going to wash her hands, she was given a washcloth to hold as she was wheeled to the washroom; before going to lunch, she was given a cup; before she was taken out of her chair and placed on the mat, she was given a piece of her green, orange, and black soft mat; and before changing and toileting, she was given her underwear. To mark the end of one activity before moving on to another activity, it was suggested that her partners help her sign ALL DONE by crossing her forearms and opening them widely.

TEN MONTHS LATER

Impressions

After working with the system for 10 months, these impressions were noted by Angela's teachers, assistants, and parents:

1. Angela appeared much more responsive to those around her and voluntarily involved herself more in classroom activities. Her responses seemed more contingent on the actions of others than they did during the first visit. She spent less time fussing and more time vocalizing and/or using gestures for communication than she had previously. She commented and requested more and protested or rejected less.
2. Angela's educational aide and her second-grade teacher established some consistent routines for Angela that blended into her daily schedule. The routines allowed her to anticipate and even control her environment. Examples included the following:

   a. Routine of transferring from wheelchair to chair: The aide had Angela touch the back of the chair to which she was to move. Angela then put her hands out for assistance in getting out of the wheelchair. This was the aide's idea. She took it back to the team so that it could be established as a part of her program.
   b. Routine of transferring from a chair back to her wheelchair: The aide had Angela touch the curved metal bar of the seat support on the wheelchair before she was moved. Angela again put her hands out in anticipation of receiving assistance in moving.
   c. Routine of "shake your head for 'no'": Both the teacher and aide prompted Angela when it appeared that she was protesting or rejecting. They used the verbal prompt, "shake your head for 'no'" and touch prompts to the head to get her to shake her head. They then either allowed Angela to move on to another activity or ceased the activity.
   d. Routine of "say 'done'": When Angela was reading a book with a peer and began to vocalize loudly in protest, the aide gently closed Angela's mouth and said, "If you're done, say 'done.'" Angela immediately replied, "du." This same sequence was used several times and seemed to meet her needs for being understood. The sign for ALL DONE did not seem necessary.

New Recommendations

1. Angela is ready for a multicomponent communication system that facilitates, as her second-grade teacher so aptly stated, "what Angela is already trying to tell us." The system should include aspects already present in her communication and some new components, as follows:

   a. Angela's vocalizations and verbalizations should be encouraged, responded to, and even imitated. Her approximations of "mom," "good girl," and "done" are fairly intelligible to those who work with her. Her vocalization for protest is a sure sign of her feelings. Pairing head shakes and "done" with these protests is a good strategy. These forms may show up spontaneously in the future.

b. Angela is ready for speech output paired with a communicative gesture or vocalization. To achieve this, a simple system could be set up using two switches. Each switch would be attached to a different tape recorder. The tape recorders could have tapes with short, simple messages recorded by another girl in Angela's classroom to make the voice age- and gender-appropriate. The spoken messages might include, "no," "stop," "up, please," "book, please," "lightboard, please," "sleep," "sing," "go," "want out," or "want ball." The messages should be set up so that within an activity Angela has a choice of two messages. An important connection for her is the symbol used to represent the spoken message. Her comprehension of spoken language is questionable. It would help her to understand speech if she had two tangible icons attached to her switches. The icons are objects that represent Angela's experience with the choice activity or item. For example, the book could be placed on one switch and the plastic wheel from the lightboard could be placed on the other. She is familiar with the way these feel and seems to associate them with the respective activity. As she touches the object, the switch would be activated and the spoken message matching that object would be played. Angela would receive immediate feedback regarding her actions.

c. The school staff also should try a Unicorn board. The Unicorn board can be programmed with more choices than a tape recorder system because it is attached to a computer. The state technology center might loan these items. The drawbacks to the Unicorn board are that the speech is computerized so it is less natural, and the device is not portable.

d. If Angela seems to enjoy the flexibility of the Unicorn board in terms of vocabulary or if she seems to be motivated by the speech output of the two tape recorders, then the next step would be to consider purchasing a portable communication device. The device should have the capability of providing speech output that is prerecorded and have the capability of expanding to meet current and immediate future needs. Angela can use direct selection because she already has learned to press a switch. (Direct selection implies that she presses on the square that has the message she desires.) Icons or parts of icons that have been learned should be used as the symbols on each square. These can be attached with Velcro.

   Several options were available: 1) the Cheap Talk 4 and/or 8 (from Toys for Special Children), 2) the AlphaTalker (from Prentke-Romich), and 3) the Macaw (from Zygo). It was suggested that Angela, her family, and those who work with her try each of these, if possible, to make an informed decision.

2. The school staff and family should continue using routines with Angela. The group may wish to collaborate on their schedules, looking for moments at which new routines could be established or when Angela could participate more actively. To encourage more active participation, prompts can be faded or the adult can pause midroutine and wait for Angela to become active.

CHAPTER 12

Lutero

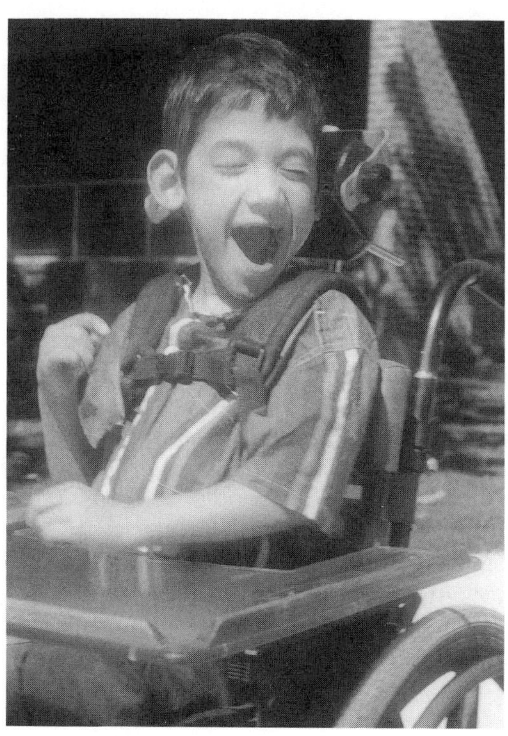

NAME: Lutero
AGE: 6 years, 2 months
TEACHER: Tim
CONSULTANTS: Chris Curry, Ed Helmstetter, and Jeanne Johnson

SYSTEM: The communication system is composed of tactile symbols attached to a communication board with Velcro. The symbols are used to make choices.

When Lutero was first seen by the AAC consultants, he already had been the focus of much team effort. The team included his teacher, an instructional aide, the speech-language pathologist and her assistant, a special education consultant, a vision specialist, an interpreter, and the family. The family's first language is Spanish. The team was concerned about moving Lutero toward a more conventional system of communication so that he could be a more independent communicator.

Lutero has a chronic seizure disorder, spastic quadriplegia, hydrocephaly, severe developmental delay, and blindness. When the consultants first met Lutero, he spent most of his day in a wheelchair or lying in a prone or sidelying position. His hands were constantly clenched, and he could not spontaneously relax them for grasping. He mouthed objects that were placed in his left hand. He enjoyed being assisted to do things with his hands, such as shaking a noisemaker or pushing a pressure switch. When he was in the prone position, sounds, especially novel or funny ones (e.g., talking to him in a teasing manner), often caused him to lift his head, turn it to the left, and vocalize. When seated, he would sometimes flex his arms and vocalize with a happy voice whenever someone talked to him or he heard a novel sound.

His education program included such goals as using happy sounds (e.g., "Yaa") as requests in response to questions (e.g., "More music?"), greeting peers with smiles and/or vocalizations, relaxing during dressing, using a pressure switch to activate toys, and increasing the range of motion of his arms.

LUTERO'S ENVIRONMENT

Lutero's environment was bilingual. Some of his classmates were Hispanic, so he heard both Spanish and English in the classroom. He spent half of his day in a general kindergarten and the remainder in a special education classroom. His peers used Spanish when they talked among themselves and English when they spoke to the teacher or aide. When the AAC consultant first visited, there were no adults who were fluent in Spanish in the room. It was reported and observed that Lutero followed simple instructions in English. For example, when told to "relax," Lutero relaxed his arms. It was difficult to ascertain, however, whether the relaxation was voluntary or the result of therapy being conducted concurrently to help him relax. It also was observed that classmates sometimes repeated the teacher's instructions in Spanish to Lutero, although most of their interactions with him were in English. At home, the family spoke Spanish.

Lutero's partners were inconsistent in how long they waited for him to signal, what signal they interpreted as being meaningful, and which language they used to talk to him. This happened, as it often does, because of good intentions: His partners were trying very hard to interact with him. As a result, individual partners tried one technique after another until they had a successful communicative interaction. These successes were sometimes, and sometimes not, shared with the other team members, depending on the partner's status. For example, Lutero's peers rarely shared what worked with Lutero with any of the adult partners. The communication aide and the classroom aide did not feel they had the education or authority to suggest to others how to interact with Lutero.

LUTERO'S SKILLS

Comprehension

Lutero's comprehension of spoken English and spoken Spanish was difficult to discern. The vision specialist had some success having him follow directions during her evaluation. For example, she said, "Make a long sound if you like this color," to which he responded by making a long sound. Other instructions to which he responded were "relax," "stretch your arm," "turn your cheek," "reach," "use your voice," "use your hand," and "find me." During the AAC consultant's visit, Lutero was observed to respond to directions given in Spanish to push on a switch and find (reach for) a ball. He did not consistently respond by vocalizing or turning his head when peers and adults attempted to interact with him. He seemed to respond consistently, however, to one of his teachers, turning and vocalizing whenever the teacher spoke in novel ways. He also would vocalize when the teacher rubbed his back, stopped, and asked if he wanted more.

Forms and Functions

Lutero was observed to vocalize "mmm," "aaa," and "mmuumm"; however, these sounds did not have specific meanings. He appeared to use these vocalizations to express pleasure, to get attention, and to request "more." Gestural signals included smiling to indicate pleasure or in response to the attention of others and reaching out toward people and objects. Because of his spasticity, reaching was slow; if he became excited in the process, he would contract both arms and have to begin all over again. The school staff identified that he turned his head away from people or objects to reject activities or objects. When this was observed, it was difficult to determine whether this either caused or was the result of an asymmetric tonic neck reflex (ATNR). The consultation of a physical therapist was requested. The vision specialist suggested that a lack of response be taken as a rejection.

The school staff had been working on a schedule board with tactile icons for "kindergarten," "diaper," "home," "mat," and "wheelchair." In addition, they were using tactile symbols as *name signs* for the common partners in his life.

Physical Abilities

Lutero already had been using a box with two switch inputs signified by different tactile representations for music box versus audiotape. He used his left hand in an overreaching, distal, slapping motion to activate the switches. Sometimes this movement caused an ATNR, but when his arm moved straight forward and his head was stabilized, he could move his arm voluntarily.

According to all reports, Lutero's vision was limited. An ophthalmologist assessed Lutero and believed he had cortical blindness. His right eye rested inward and his left eye outward. Some nystagmus was present. The vision specialist who visited the school found that Lutero responded to particular colors when acetate filters were placed on a light box. When a spinner with black and clear sections was placed on the light box, Lutero reached toward it to spin it with a gross swiping motion. He similarly explored other surfaces with different tactile characteristics.

One other physical characteristic that affected Lutero's communication system was that he sometimes startled easily. When no verbal warning was given, he was observed to startle when people touched him and when he heard loud noises.

SYSTEM RECOMMENDATIONS

Lutero clearly was trying to communicate via primitive means. The first step was to set up a tactile symbol board with choices attached using Velcro. The choices were represented by putting a part of the object on his board. In choosing the symbols, the team tried to keep in mind his perspective toward the object or activity such that the icon was something with which he had firsthand experience. When Lutero was given a choice, the partner would help him touch both symbols and then wait for him to touch the one he wanted again. It also was suggested that the team think of more choices to give him. It seemed that he became tired of the same choices after a few experiences.

Members of the school staff wanted to have Lutero learn a signal for "yes" and a signal for "no." This, however, was in conflict with their desire to make him a more independent communicator because the use of these signals required that the partner initiate the interaction with a question. Furthermore, Lutero already had a signal for rejecting and accepting choices, but these signals did not always result in a consistent response from partners. It was decided that giving him choices, rather than asking him "yes/no" questions, was more empowering. It was decided that all partners needed to learn his current signal system.

Next, it was suggested that Lutero be given experience with voice output when he made a selection. To do so, a small Unicorn board was set up with the same symbols as those used on the tactile board. The voice output was in Spanish. Spanish was chosen because it was his dominant language. It was hoped that he would continue to learn English, but without a strong foundation in one language, he likely would continue to have difficulty in both.

It was suggested that, if Lutero seemed to enjoy the voice output using the Unicorn board, he try a portable communication device that could be with him at all times, such as the Digivox (by Sentient Systems) or the Macaw (by Zygo). These types of devices allowed for Spanish to be recorded in age- and gender-appropriate voices and for tactile icons to be placed on the device in varying arrangements. It was suggested that the family try these devices before purchasing one and that family members and the school staff receive training in programming the device selected. It also was suggested that Lutero's choices be reassessed continually, just as for the back-up nonelectronic board, to circumvent boredom.

In relation to his environment, it was recommended that his partners speak to him using simplified, correct Spanish. This would help him isolate important word-to-referent relationships to increase comprehension. In addition, his partners, as mentioned, were asked to identify other types of choices based on his daily routines and schedules.

To decrease Lutero's startle responses, his partners were asked to make a routine of approaching him by talking to him as they approached and telling him, in Spanish, that they were going to touch him. When moving Lutero from one position to another, the partners were asked to use, in Spanish, a "1-2-3-lift" verbal routine each time.

ONE YEAR LATER

One year later, Lutero began to attend a first-grade classroom on a full-time basis. Many of the recommendations made by the consultant the previous year were implemented. All partners, both children and teachers, were very consistent about speaking to him as they approached and telling him they were going to touch him. This was usually done in Spanish. Lutero not only decreased his startle response but also began to anticipate activities and would vocalize if the anticipated activity did not occur. For example, each morning during the opening activity, the children would greet Lutero in unison. If the children did not greet Lutero, he would become very vocal until the greeting took place.

An attempt was made to introduce the use of a tactile communication board to allow Lutero to make choices. Several factors affected the limited success of this system. The change in the classroom environment from a self-contained program to a fully inclusive program had a major impact on his communication. First, the number of partners who interacted with him increased. These partners, mostly children, continued to use Lutero's "yes/no" response to interpret what he wanted. Because they preferred this method of communication and Lutero preferred communicating with the children, the "yes/no" response was highly reinforced. Communication that involved making a choice required more effort and was less rewarding to him. Consequently, his response was inconsistent.

Because this was the first year that Lutero was attending a general classroom on a full-time basis, he was assigned a full-time assistant. The assistant often interpreted his choice without asking him to use his system to make a choice. Also, an effort was made to include him in all the activities that the other children were doing. His choices were limited to choices within the activity rather than choosing preferred activities.

By the end of the year, both the school staff and Lutero had adjusted to a fully inclusive program. An effort was made to use the system more consistently. Lutero's responses were still very inconsistent when he was asked to make a choice using his system. He was primarily interested in people and the activity around him. He also enjoyed new activities and did not show a consistent preference to any one activity. His range of motion and his ability to reach also were issues. On some days it appeared very difficult for him to reach and touch an object, whereas on other days he was able to reach easily.

Because the year featured so many changes for both the teachers and Lutero, the team decided to continue working with the system with two choices until he was more consistent in his response before introducing a portable communication device.

CHAPTER 13

Alex

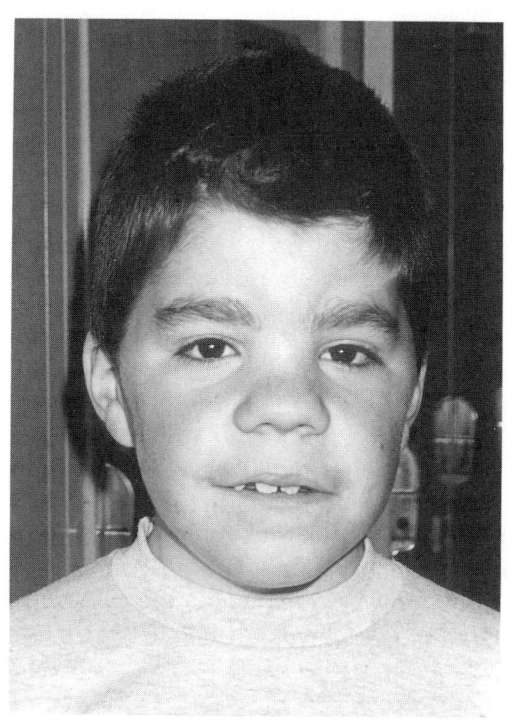

NAME: Alex
AGE: 8 years
CONSULTANTS: Jeanne Johnson and Diane Baumgart
TEACHERS: Mrs. K and Ms. McNally
SYSTEM: Signs, a few verbalizations, a picture notebook, and separate picture cards are used to communicate. Alex is trying out different augmentative devices so that he will have voice output for his messages.

Alex's communication partners were at a crossroad. They did not know what to do next for him to facilitate better communication. Alex was expressing frustration, as were his partners. The first consultant, Dr. Johnson, was contacted in November to assist the team in planning the next phase of his communication program. The second consultant, Dr. Baumgart, was contacted in January, following a change in special education teachers, to assist in generating ideas for Alex's academic instruction while in the second grade and to facilitate his membership in the second-grade classroom. Dr. Johnson's assessments and Dr. Baumgart's additions are presented in this chapter.

BACKGROUND

Alex has been receiving special education and communication services since he was very young. He was identified at birth as having oral-motor difficulties resulting in feeding problems, although the etiology was unknown. He was referred by his pediatrician for oral-motor therapy with a private speech-language pathologist (SLP), Kathy. As Kathy worked with Alex in his first year, she became concerned that he was not developing speech as expected. Through continued longitudinal evaluations, Kathy found that he had severe dyspraxia. This meant that he had a serious oral-motor planning impairment with a neurological origin, which interfered with his ability to say anything other than highly routine and often repeated phrases. Kathy began to use augmented communication in the form of objects and pictures with Alex when he was about 1 year old.

Since that time, it has become apparent that Alex has cognitive delays as well, although the exact level of his abilities has been difficult to pinpoint. The school psychologist has been unable to obtain a valid measure of baseline performance on standardized tests of cognition.

Alex has been using sign language and pictures as an augmented form of communication for the past few years. These systems are described in detail later in this chapter. A Liberator (by Prentke-Romich) was tried last year. Although Alex liked the clear voice output, the means for generating messages was too complicated for him and, it is important to note, his family. This device uses a special means of combining icons to represent messages that requires in-depth training—a resource that was not available at the time.

ASSESSMENT: FIRST CONSULTANT

Dr. Johnson was asked to help the team determine the best communication system for Alex. The team wanted a system that would be flexible enough to encompass communication demands in different environments and be understood by peers and adults.

Alex's Environments and Partners

Alex lives with his mother, father, and two brothers and is very close to his grandmother. Alex's two favorite activities are going for drives with his grandmother and staying overnight with her.

When Dr. Johnson visited Alex, he was spending most of his day in Mrs. K's special education classroom with a 30- to 40-minute period in the second-grade classroom. He attended second grade during the morning group discussion, which included calendar time, weather, and preparation of the lunch report for the main office. His participation involved being called on to choose the date or weather symbol. This was done with verbal and physical prompts by the second-grade teacher. Peers were involved in a similar manner, only without prompts. In the special education classroom, Alex worked individually with his teacher or with one or two other students on academics. He also had pull-out therapy with the physical therapist and the speech-language pathologist.

When the data were combined from peer participation patterns and his own daily schedule, the opportunities for communication and barriers to communication were clarified. Alex's barriers to participation included lack of opportunity to interact with same-age peers without adult supervision and limited ability to express more than simple requests within daily routines. Most choices were predetermined.

Alex's Skills and Needs

Dr. Johnson compiled data about Alex's communication skills and needs from interviews, school records, and direct observation. The data were divided into the topics of comprehension, forms and functions, and sensory abilities.

Comprehension Alex's comprehension of spoken language was shown by his school speech-language pathologist, Betsy. She shared information pertaining to cognitive-related language skills. At the beginning of the school year, Alex showed symbolic play and comprehension of spoken utterances at the 24- to 36-month level according to nonstandardized developmental scales. Betsy also administered the Peabody Picture Vocabulary Test–Revised (Dunn & Dunn, 1981) to determine Alex's single-word comprehension. He scored at about the 4-year level, and Betsy believed Alex's test performance was a valid reflection of his abilities even though this score was higher than those obtained from other measures.

Other partners believed Alex understood everything. During Dr. Johnson's visit to the school, it appeared that Alex did understand much of what was said by his partners based on his appropriate responses to their directions or to the topic of the discussion. It was noted, however, that his adult partners were using short sentences, which was appropriate for his comprehension ability. Also, many of his partners were signing one or two key words as they spoke or pointed to pictures representing concepts key to the topic. This seemed to facilitate Alex's comprehension. He definitely had more difficulty, however, when spoken language input exceeded five to six words per utterance. In these instances, he nodded "yes," did not respond, or engaged in disruptive behavior. Alex's comprehension of connected speech, then, was not as strong as his understanding of single words. Furthermore, the verbal directions given to him usually were in the context of a familiar routine. In order to follow these directions successfully, Alex was taking his cues from the one or two words he did understand, in addition to the rich contextual support of the routine.

Forms and Functions Alex had many forms of communication that he used successfully with partners who were familiar with his system. Some of the consultant's observations are summarized on the Form and Use Assessment Sheet shown in Figure 13.1. Gestures included nodding his head for "yes" and shaking his head for "no," pointing, taking his partner's hand, showing, giving, and holding his palm up to receive an item. He had an estimated 40-sign vocabulary with prompts and a somewhat smaller spontaneous sign vocabulary. Alex also used pictures to represent broad concepts and categories of items, activities, animals, or people. Spoken utterances included "mama" and "no." Alex did vocalize when he laughed or be-

Individual's Name: Alex | Date: 11/94
Observer: J. Johnson | Location: Elementary school

Context	Partner	Individual's signal	Partner's response	Discourse function	Pragmatic function
Second-grade morning discussion	Sign interpreter	Points to clock, looks at partner	Signs: NOT TIME NOT YET	Initiation	Requests permission
"Hot or cold lunch, Alex?"	Mrs. K., second-grade teacher	Signs: EAT	"Eat? Eat what? Hot or cold?"	Maintain	Answers
		Points to picture of hot lunch on desk	"Hot lunch, OK."	Maintain	Gives information
Walking down hall toward custodian	Rita, custodian	Waves and says, "Momma"	"Hi, Alex."	Initiation	Greeting
Discussing his schedule for the day	Renee, special education consultant	Opens book, points to book, looks at Renee	"No, we don't have library today."	Initiation	Requests event
		Points to grooming picture and points down the hall toward the restroom	"Yes, you need to go wash up and get ready."	Maintain	Requests permission or gives information about preferences
		Goes to locker, takes out grooming basket, and points to "wash hands" card	"You're going to wash your hands. OK?"	Maintain	Gives information

Figure 13.1. Form and Use Assessment Sheet summarizing some of the consultant's observations regarding Alex's communicative abilities. (Form adapted from Duchan, Hewitt, & Sonnemeier, 1994; Wetherby, Cain, Yonclas, & Walker, 1988.)

came excited, but few voluntary vocalizations were evident, which was in keeping with the condition of dyspraxia. Most of Alex's multimodal productions were one or two units in length. For example, he said "Mama" and then signed DRIVE to indicate that his grandmother had taken him for a drive the day earlier.

Alex was observed to use all aspects of his communication system when trying to express an idea. He combined a verbal word with a sign or a sign with a picture. In addition, he had some overlaps of symbol types; for example, he used pictures and signs for the same concepts and indicated "no" by saying "no" or shaking his head. His former special education teacher, Mrs. K, noted that Alex's signs began to develop more quickly when the pictures were introduced and that the use of pictures was facilitated by the use of sign. The children in Alex's second-grade classroom also had learned a few of his signs.

Alex's signing showed some articulation errors; that is, when he signed, his hand shape, the movement of his hands, the orientation of his palm, and/or the location of the sign were not always exact. These four distinctive features of signs are similar to manner, place, and voicing—the distinctive features of phonemes or speech sounds—and can be used to record baseline performance and progress. Several informants reported that his signing had improved in clarity over the previous 2 years. This improvement might have been related to the emphasis in physical therapy on improving fine motor dexterity and strength.

During the consultant's visit, Alex spontaneously used signs for ALL DONE, DRINK, DRIVE, EAT, DAD/BOY, PLAY, COOKIE, GRANDMA, WASH, WORK, DOG, and ME. He most often executed the sign in the correct location (e.g., forehead, mouth, in front of his chest); the other three distinctive features were approximated, but not produced clearly (see Figures 13.2 and 13.3). With only one or two clues from a familiar partner, a person fluent in sign language might be able to understand these signs after seeing them only once. For those who knew only a few basic signs, however, identifying the correct meaning was more difficult. Alex had been observed to use about 50 signs spontaneously, usually in one- and two-sign combinations. Some of the signs were politeness words; most were nouns.

Figure 13.2. Alex spontaneously signs EAT to his teacher.

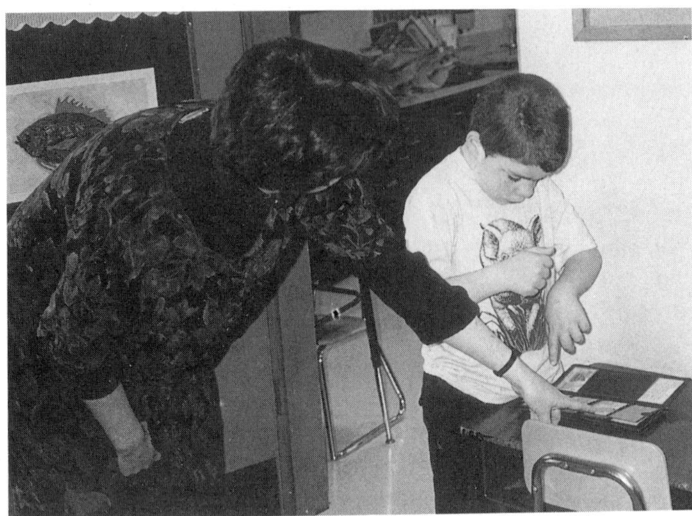

Figure 13.3. Alex signs WORK to his teacher.

Alex used the previous forms of communication for a variety of purposes: 1) to request objects, action, and "more"; 2) to protest or reject activities; 3) to comment or label things of interest in his environment; 4) to talk about future or past events; 5) to establish joint attention; 6) to maintain interactions (see Figure 13.4); 7) to repair misunderstandings by repeating his signal; and 8) to terminate conversations.

Alex took both an active and passive role in communication as dictated by the circumstances. For instance, in Figure 13.5, Alex initiated a request to go wash his hands. Given the limitations in the types of forms he had available, Alex was quite versatile in his communicative interactions.

Alex's September IEP goals for communication focused on increasing vocabulary through signs and pictures, increasing the number of signs or pictures com-

Figure 13.4. Alex uses previous forms of communication to maintain interactions.

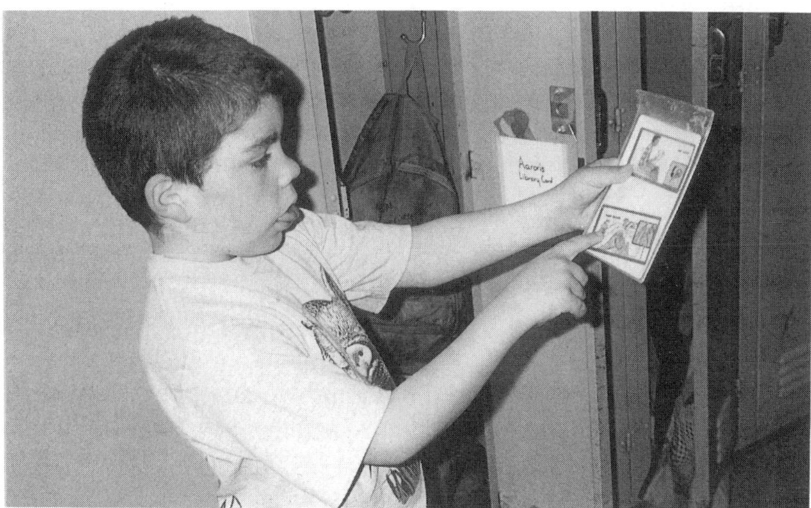

Figure 13.5. Alex spontaneously finds a picture of "wash hands."

bined from two to four in order to convey messages more clearly, continuing work on oral-motor patterns, and investigating the possibility of an AAC device with voice output. From September to November, Alex was able to increase the number of units in his communication messages to an average of three. For example, he would point to himself, sign EAT, and point to the picture for "lunch."

Sensory Abilities Alex's speech-language pathologist reported that Alex had passed a hearing screening test at the beginning of the school year as he had every year. His vision was noted as normal by the school nurse.

SUMMARY OF ASSESSMENT

Alex had a multimodal augmentative system in place that served most but not all of his purposes in a general sense. The one area that needed to be augmented was his ability to express very specific messages with voice output. Given his severe dyspraxia, the prognosis for significant improvement in speech in the near future was guarded. Alex relied on touching to get someone's attention. If he had voice output, he could get attention in a more age-appropriate manner. In addition, clear age- and gender-appropriate voice output would allow those unfamiliar with Alex's signs to understand his messages and afford him even greater social acceptability with his peers and unfamiliar partners.

Recommendations

1. It was recommended that Alex continue using signs, gestures, and pictures for communication.

   a. *Signs* Because it is difficult for newcomers to understand Alex's signs, the consultant suggested that a videotape be made of him using his signs in their normal context. Those who are new to the school and who would be working with Alex could watch the tape and learn his version of the signs while they learn the correct production themselves. The videotape also could be used to track improvements in the formation of his signs and serve as a baseline and end-of-year follow-up for the number of signs.

Alex was mostly using one-sign utterances, although he was combining signs, speech, and pictures in a single utterance. Within-modality expansion was targeted on his IEP. Betsy worked on having him use two-, three-, and four-sign utterances. Given that he has an adequate vocabulary base, this approach to expansion seemed appropriate. By the end of the school year, Alex was observed to spontaneously use four-sign utterances occasionally.

b. *Pictures* Alex's pictures seemed to serve him well in his interactions. He had both a notebook with his pictures arranged by routine or topic and individual cards to help him remember the steps for particular tasks (e.g., grooming routine). As seen in Figures 13.2, 13.3, 13.4, and 13.5, Alex pointed to these pictures in order to perform all the functions listed previously for signs, but usually he just points to one picture.

Dr. Johnson suggested continuing to combine pictures to make longer utterances, just as the signing system is being expanded. (Dr. Baumgart later concurred.) Some pictures were affixed to cards placed in individual plastic pockets that were lined up on the table surface. Alex was expected to organize the pictures to make longer messages; however, moving the pictures into various strings was slow. To make this process faster, small adhesive magnets were attached to the back of the plastic pocket containing the picture. A lightweight metal board was made available in each of his rooms with the vocabulary appropriate for that room or location so that he would not have to carry a board with him. Alex could then combine the pictures in novel ways, a process assisted by the fact that they were all available on the board and easy to slide into the correct order.

2. Alex needed a better means for communicating with unfamiliar partners and for communicating in depth to his familiar partners. A device with voice output would afford him this ability and greater respect as a communicator. Because the Liberator was not successful, a less complicated device was recommended. The device needed to have the following features:

   a. Age- and gender-appropriate voice output that is clear to naive listeners even when the maximum number of messages is stored (Some devices provide more message recording time at the expense of message clarity.)
   b. Capability of displaying different overlays related to the activity in which Alex is participating
   c. A range of 15–40 selection squares with which to begin
   d. Activation by touch (membrane switch)
   e. Capability of accepting one word or a whole message in each square of the overlay
   f. Portability, light weight, and durability (Alex is ambulatory and needs to carry the device with him as much as possible.)
   g. Capability of using pictures as icons for messages

   Also, if the voice is digitized, it should be possible to record one new message without having to re-record all the messages.

   It was suggested that Alex have access to an array of devices so he could demonstrate his ability and preferences. The following devices were suggested to be used on a trial basis before being purchased: MessageMate 40 (by Words+),

Alphatalker (by Prentke-Romich), Macaw or Parrot (by Zygo), Digivox or the Dynavox (by Sentinent Systems), and Attainment 15 Talker (by the Attainment Company) (see Appendix D for a list of manufacturers). These devices have the features, in greater or lesser detail, mentioned in the list of needs.

Shortly after Dr. Johnson's visit, Alex was able to try out an Alphatalker. According to Betsy and Mrs. K, Alex became very excited and quickly learned how to use it. He not only tried out each message, but immediately began using the message for meaningful and appropriate communicative exchanges. He was able to try the Alphatalker at home as well with similar results. The next device he tried was the Dynavox, which has a computer screen on which "overlays" appear. His family expressed a preference for this device because they felt it would best fit Alex's needs and preferences currently and as they grow over time. Alex expressed his preference for this device by becoming even more excited about this device than the Alphatalker. Although the Dynavox was not on the original list of recommended devices, Alex demonstrated that he was ready for a more complex system than was first thought. It was a pleasant surprise that Alex was able to do more than the consultants anticipated, particularly because there were no solid data on his cognitive abilities.

The family and school staff were referred to the state Adaptive Technology Service Center to explore available assistance for funding the device. The family would like Alex to have the device available at home and at school. It was hoped that the funding source would permit this. (Sometimes, when a device is purchased by a school district, the individual is not allowed to take the device home.)

Once the device is received, Alex and his partners will need to be trained in *device competence* (e.g., turning it on, charging, programming) and *interactive competence* (e.g., how to carry on a conversation). Betsy will spearhead this effort until Alex's parents are trained. At that point, they will take over as the primary trainers. Again, videotapes would be a useful way to show others how to interact with Alex when he is using his device.

3. The use of scripts was suggested to initiate use of the device. By using scripts, Alex could learn how to engage in conversation with his device while still using signs and pictures. At first, the script could be used with a familiar partner who is having a moderate amount of difficulty understanding his usual signals. In other words, he has a new form to express existing meanings and existing functions with a familiar partner. As an example, the following messages could be programmed for a small group morning activity in the classroom:

   a. "Hi guys!"
   b. "Can I have a turn?"
   c. "Is that right?"
   d. "Let's do it again."
   e. "I'm all done."
   f. "Time to clean up."
   g. "What's next?"

   At first, a helper could show Alex when to use the messages with his peers during the normal sequence of the academic activities. This is preferable to having the listener show Alex how to talk to him or her because it maintains the sender and receiver roles more clearly. Other messages can be added as needed and the helper can encourage Alex to augment his device's messages with signs and pictures, thereby increasing the quality of his communication.

The next step would be to identify scripts that naturally occur in his day and that involve unfamiliar partners. For example, Alex's class goes to the library once a week to check out books. A script could be anticipated in which Alex greets the librarian, asks for help in finding a book, and then thanks her for her assistance. In this case, Alex is using the forms (the pictures and voice output of the device) with which he is becoming more and more familiar to express existing meanings for existing functions with a new partner. This follows the sequence proposed in Chapter 6 on expanding the communication system (see p. 101).

REASSESSMENT: SECOND CONSULTANT

In February, Alex had a change in special education teachers. Mrs. K left the school, and Ms. McNally replaced her. Ms. McNally and the family collaborated to extend Alex's time in the second-grade classroom. With the change in teachers came a request to the second consultant, Dr. Baumgart, for temporary staffing support. Dr. Baumgart, together with a university student, met with teachers and observed Alex between 11 A.M. and 12 P.M. when assistance was requested. This was a time when Alex had not previously been included in second grade so the routines and content were new to him and Ms. McNally. His previous communication system did not encompass these changes.

Peer Participation Patterns

Because Alex's daily schedule had changed so much, it was important to examine what his peers did in the course of a day. The classroom activities of second-grade peers consisted of verbal book reports by children, silent reading, reading seat work, and math. These were taught via teacher demonstrations, lecture, and math worksheets.

Assessment of Alex's Participation in Daily Routines

Alex was intrigued with his second-grade classmates and with the second-grade teacher. He enjoyed second grade. He did have difficulty attending to lectures and doing paper-and-pencil tasks during this time interval. He often signed EAT, a request to leave and go to the cafeteria, and then pushed his chair backward until he was against the wall. He then would make verbal and tapping/clapping sounds to get the attention of his classmates, and put his head down or walk around to avoid class work.

After the observation, the teachers, Dr. Baumgart, and the university student met to discuss options. The second-grade teacher requested that during this time, Alex perform similar tasks in the same academic subject as his second-grade peers. Ms. McNally discussed how she would adapt materials and the level of work for Alex and requested academic work suggestions from the university student as the remaining 3½ months of the semester progressed.

Additional Information on Forms and Functions

Dr. Baumgart hypothesized that because Alex was not able to tell time and, thus, the passage of time, his disruptive behavior could be related to not knowing how long he needed to attend to particular tasks. The academic tasks were unfamiliar work and his behaviors could be his way of expressing boredom. Eating was a favorite activity for Alex. His behaviors could have been communicating, "Will it *soon* be time to eat?" or "Have you forgotten about eating?"

Dr. Baumgart suggested that a schedule system be developed that would 1) assist him with initial time-telling using the 11 P.M.–12 P.M. interval; 2) take advantage of Alex's existing communication forms; and 3) continue to encourage him to combine signs, pictures, and gestures into longer utterances. The team discussed what his disruptive behaviors might be communicating, and a system for marking time and communicating expectations for both him and his classmates was developed.

The previous success with pictures suggested the device incorporate line drawings of classroom activities and clock faces depicting the changing time intervals (see Figure 13.6). The objectives for the 11 P.M.–12 P.M. interval included the following:

- **Objective 1:** Given a watch, picture board, two to four line drawings, a line drawing of the current time, and the question, "What are the teacher and class doing now?", Alex will select the drawing that matches the teacher's and his classmates' instructional activities. He will select the correct pictures and put them in correct sequence without teacher prompts on 4 consecutive days.
- **Objective 2:** Given a watch, picture board, two to four line drawings, adapted materials, a line drawing of the current time, and the question, "What do you need to do now?", Alex will select the line drawings of his activities and put them in correct sequence without teacher prompts on 4 consecutive days.

Figure 13.6. Alex's schedule system for 11 A.M.–12 P.M. in second grade.

Collection of Data

Data was collected twice a week during April and May. The first accomplishment was that Alex quickly learned to use the clock on the classroom wall instead of the watch. He initially did not select the correct pictures, but his inattentive behaviors decreased and he attended to instruction on the pictures and some of his adapted academic work. By the end of May, he was scoring 94% accuracy for selecting pictures of the ongoing activities and maintained this for 3 data collection days when the school year ended. He also learned to count to 3 by rote and to match the numbers 1–3 to the correct number of real and pictured objects. By the end of the school year, Alex selected pictures of his classmates' activities (e.g., reading in a small group) and used the signs WANT, ME, and THERE to indicate he wanted to join an activity.

The Alphatalker (by Prentke-Romich) was again requested from the Easter Seals organization to be used for verbal book reports to the class. The Dynavox had been requested from the school district, but a decision had not been finalized by the end of the school year.

SUMMARY

Alex taught his partners many things. First, he made it clear that multiple systems are effective means of communicating. Second, his excitement over his new systems showed how motivated he was to communicate. His partners also were reminded that family feelings about all aspects of the system must be considered. In doing so, the potential for successful implementation of a system was increased significantly.

A third lesson Alex taught is that it is easy to over- or underestimate an individual's skills in relation to device needs. The consultant underestimated Alex's ability and began with a device that was too basic. Being able to use devices on a trial basis clarifies exact skill levels that cannot be assessed through other means.

A fourth lesson had to do with how a change in one team member can lead to significant changes in environments, daily schedules, and communication needs. Alex's new special education teacher advocated for inclusion, which occurred much to Alex's benefit. She modeled for other team members how to adapt materials for the curricula and make Alex more a part of his second-grade classroom. She also showed how to integrate a schedule board, such as that developed for the 11 P.M.–12 P.M. period, with communication systems for maximal effectiveness. Her efforts led to decreases in what had been viewed as disruptive behavior. Alex's behavior was acknowledged as legitimate communication signals, and partners became more adept at interpreting them. A side benefit has been a positive change by the second-grade teacher in attitude toward children with special needs.

Finally, Alex had been a delightful teacher in patience for all of his partners in that he continued to make extraordinary effort to communicate even when he was extremely frustrated. All of these ingredients have led to a more successful communication experience for Alex and all his partners.

Chapter 14

Brent and Holly

Names: Brent and Holly
Ages: 10 years
Teachers: Kathy and Laurie
Consultant: Diane Baumgart
Systems: Gaze, body orientation, and line drawings

When the consultation began, Brent and Holly were 10 years old. The consultation ended 2 years later, when both children were 12 years old. The two students are presented together because they share the same teachers and because their programs were considered and implemented using similar methods by the same team.

This vignette focuses on Brent's and Holly's behavior and communication, as well as the data collection system used to design and select their communication systems. Issues and barriers encountered in the system implementation are discussed and linked to initial oversights in the assessment processes.

OVERVIEW

Brent and Holly attend the same elementary school in an urban area (population 7,000) in Idaho. The school is not their neighborhood school, but rather one in which the district has clustered services for students with severe and multiple disabilities who require a pervasive system of supports. The classroom of 11 students is taught by two special education teachers, Kathy and Laurie.

Brent resides with his parents and younger sister. He was diagnosed with cerebral palsy at birth and was hospitalized and treated for medical complications throughout most of his first 5 years. He attended a developmental center for early childhood services and has attended his present elementary school for the past 6 years. When Brent is 13 years old, he will begin attending his neighborhood junior high school. Brent receives special education and speech-language services, as well as physical therapy. He attends music, library, physical education, science, lunch, recess, free time, and drug awareness classes with his sixth-grade peers.

Holly is a foster child living with a family that includes 10 brothers and sisters who also have disabilities. One of Holly's sisters attends the same elementary school as Holly, and her other siblings attend the neighborhood junior high school and senior high school in the same district. Holly has been diagnosed with cerebral palsy, seizure disorders, and mental retardation. She uses a wheelchair, which is pushed by others, and a continuous feeding pump for her meals and most liquids. Holly receives special education and speech-language services as well as physical therapy. She attends music, band, science, and reading classes with her sixth-grade peers. Holly has a skin condition that makes her very sensitive to sunlight and, at the request of her parents, spends recess indoors. She has a friend from the sixth-grade class who spends most of her recesses indoors with Holly.

Additional information on Brent and Holly is in Figures 14.1 and 14.2.

Brent's Initial Communication Systems

Brent uses two systems for communication. The first system involves gaze and head and body orientation to indicate his preferences for visible objects and events in his environment. These gestures typically are understood by his peers, family, and the school staff for routine events and requests. His second system is used during structured classroom routines (e.g., lunch, break, free time). It consists of 2-inch × 2-inch line drawings that are mounted on a 16-inch × 16-inch piece of plexiglass and his gaze, which he uses to select from at least three options (see Figure 14.3). Line drawings are also mounted on a schedule board and used by the school staff and his peers to inform him of events and activities (i.e., to enhance his receptive vocabulary and model use of his system) (see Figure 14.4). The plexiglass is used because it enables his communication partners to watch and locate the direction and location of his gaze.

Holly's Initial Communication Systems

Holly also uses two systems. She uses vocalization and facial gestures for spontaneous communication, and she uses 8-inch × 11-inch, high-contrast, black-and-

Cognition: Brent's social and cognitive functioning is estimated at about 18 months of age. He appears to understand simple cause-and-effect relationships, as determined by his difficulty/lack of interest in activating lights and switches. It is hypothesized that his difficulty with causal relationships is more the result of his physical condition and/or lack of motivation than of his cognitive ability.

Motor: Brent has cerebral palsy with spastic and athetoid components. With support to maintain his body and head position, he can move his head from side to side. He has restraining straps to assist with grasping and pointing motions and to prevent skin damage and cuts from a bite reflex.

Vision: Brent uses gaze to indicate his preferences and can scan three to five objects horizontally and across the midline. He is not able to scan vertically, most likely because of lack of head control. With support to maintain head control, he can visually track and follow teachers/peers moving around the room. He has the ability to fixate at distances ranging from 1 to 20 feet.

Medical: A gastrointestinal tube is used for nutritional supplements. He eats soft foods of a variety of textures, and liquids should be offered periodically during the day.

Language: Brent uses gaze to indicate interest and his preferences. He has a range of vowel sounds and crying sounds that he uses to gain attention and/or indicate dislike.

Figure 14.1. A selection from Brent's school records.

white line drawings during routine activities (e.g., opening, free choice, lunch) to make selections (see Figure 14.5). Her vocalizations indicate she wants something, and her smile and gaze indicate she likes someone or something.

Behaviors

Consultative services for Brent and Holly were requested by Kathy, in part, because of disruptive behaviors. Teachers and staff reported Brent often cried at school for

Cognition: Holly is an outgoing student who functions at a level between 6 and 18 months of age. This level is approximated because of Holly's limited motor and vision abilities.

Motor: Holly uses a Mulholland-type chair and has some volitional hand motion that she uses to activate switches. She has the ability to reach out and move either hand to the mid-line. She is learning to relax, which enables her to have better motor control, including range of motion and directional reaching and grasping. She uses an orthotic device that assists her in holding pencils and markers.

Vision: Visually, Holly functions at about the 6-month level. She has nystagmus (i.e., involuntary eye movement) and a hypoplastic optic nerve (i.e., congenital underdevelopment of the optic nerve). Her central vision is estimated to be between 20/200 and 20/1000. She responds to visual stimuli; fixates for extended time intervals; and tracks items, people, and pictures for limited durations of time. Her optimal vision is at central forward gaze, rather than at downward gaze. A raised platform and light box are used to enhance perception and decrease the frequency with which her head drops forward.

Medical: Holly has seizures that are partially controlled by medication. She uses a continuous feed pump for nutrition.

Language: Holly uses vowel sounds to verbalize and obtain the attention of others. She indicates choices by reaching out and touching preferred items. Her responses are inconsistent.

Figure 14.2. A selection from Holly's school records.

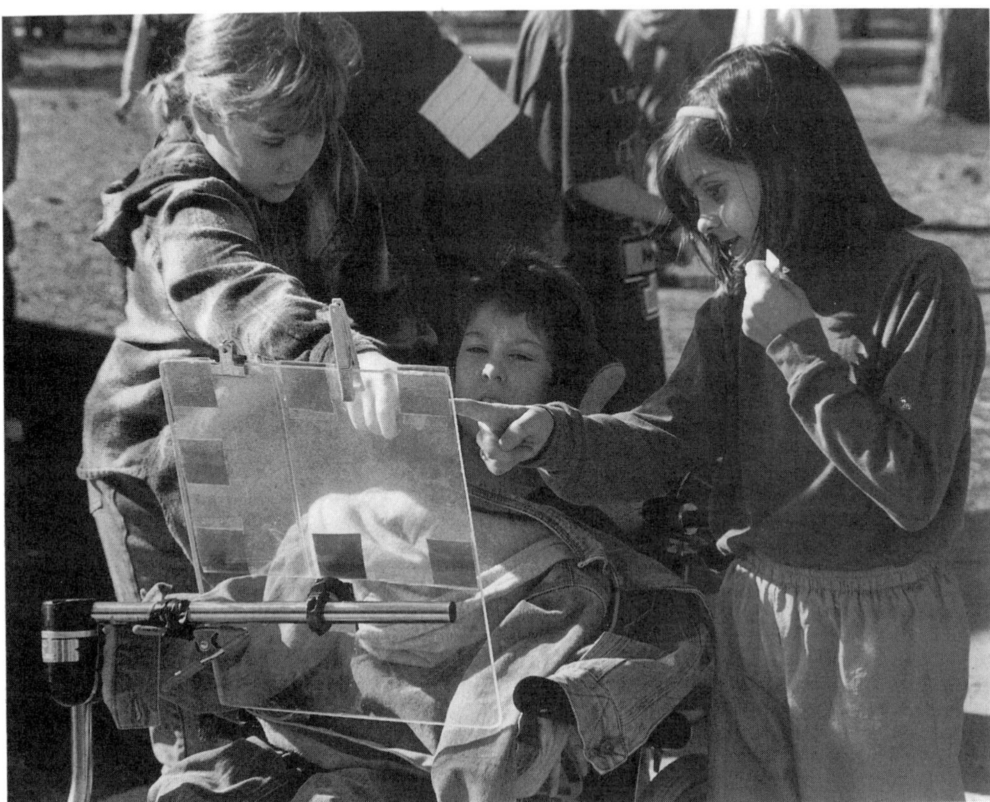

Figure 14.3. Brent uses his second communication system, which requires that he gaze at various line drawings to make selections.

unknown reasons. His mother said he had tantrums at home when something that he wanted was taken away. Returning the item or reengaging in the activity with him (e.g., returning to him and looking at a magazine together) seemed to stop his crying; however, he sometimes cried for reasons that were not apparent. These behaviors had continued through the last school year and everyone was concerned. Brent was being fitted for a new wheelchair, and staff worried that the fit of his present chair was causing discomfort. In addition, Brent seemed to turn away from some activities (e.g., lessons with the teacher, lunch), but he was not consistent in this behavior. More information was needed to determine if his crying and turning away behaviors were intentional or were related to being physically uncomfortable or in pain, and to plan appropriate responses.

Holly also engaged in crying behavior, and the staff wanted to review her curriculum. She seemed to cry when asked to engage in tasks independently. Sometimes the crying ceased when staff came over, while at other times she seemed to cry because she had bitten her lip and was in pain. Keeping Holly in a one-to-one ratio with staff seemed to decrease crying, but this was not a consistent or realistic possibility. More information was needed to determine if other conditions were related to her crying and if her crying and lip biting were intentional and/or preceded by other behaviors.

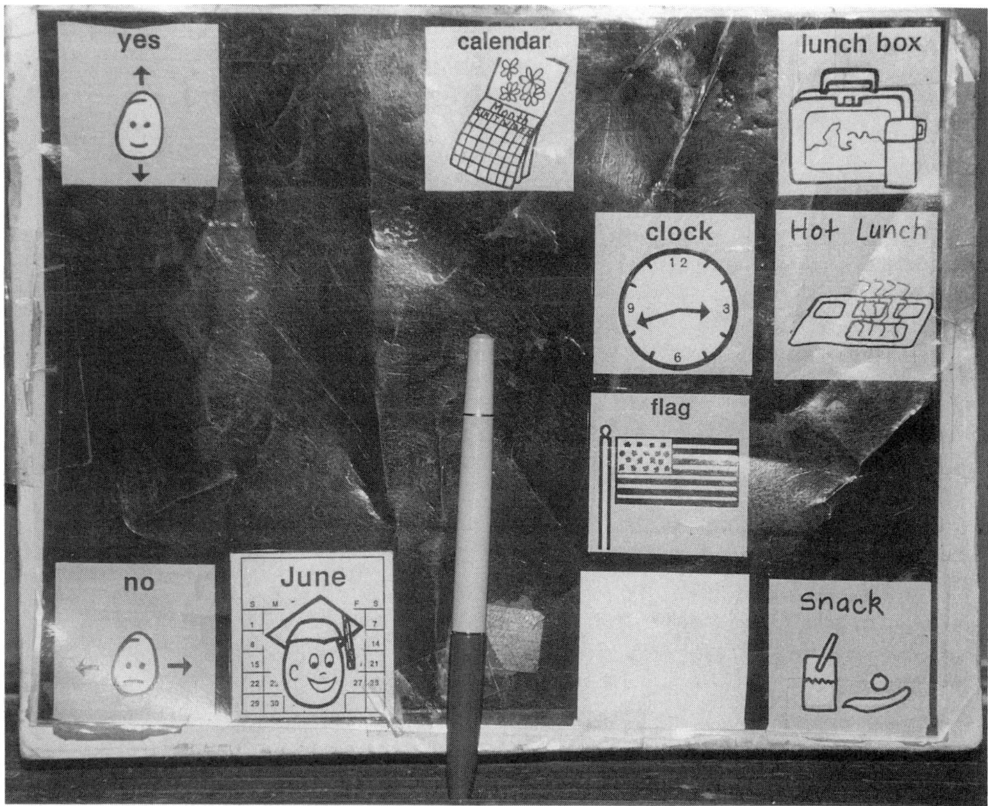

Figure 14.4. Brent's communication system set up for school arrival.

ASSESSMENT FOR COMMUNICATION PLANNING

Prior to the design and implementation of a communication system for both Brent and Holly, a number of additional assessments were required to address concerns and personalize communication systems. The team formulated the following specific concerns and questions regarding the behaviors of Brent and Holly:

1. Are there consistent times or activities during the day or week when Holly's crying or Brent's crying, turning away, and extension patterns are most frequent? Are there consistent times or activities when Holly is most content/smiling or Brent is more alert and less distracted?
2. What environmental conditions or circumstances, besides the activities, are present when Holly is crying or engaged in activities or when Brent is crying and/or distracted or alert and attending? Are loud noises and people talking things that distract or overstimulate Brent?
3. Are there behavioral indicators that occur before Brent escalates to crying or turning away or that seem to precede Holly's escalation to crying or lip biting? If so, what are they and how do staff respond?
4. Do the staff underestimate Brent's understanding of his environment? Are staff putting him into a role of a passive observer? Is Holly's program stimulating enough for her? Is she too alone or bored?

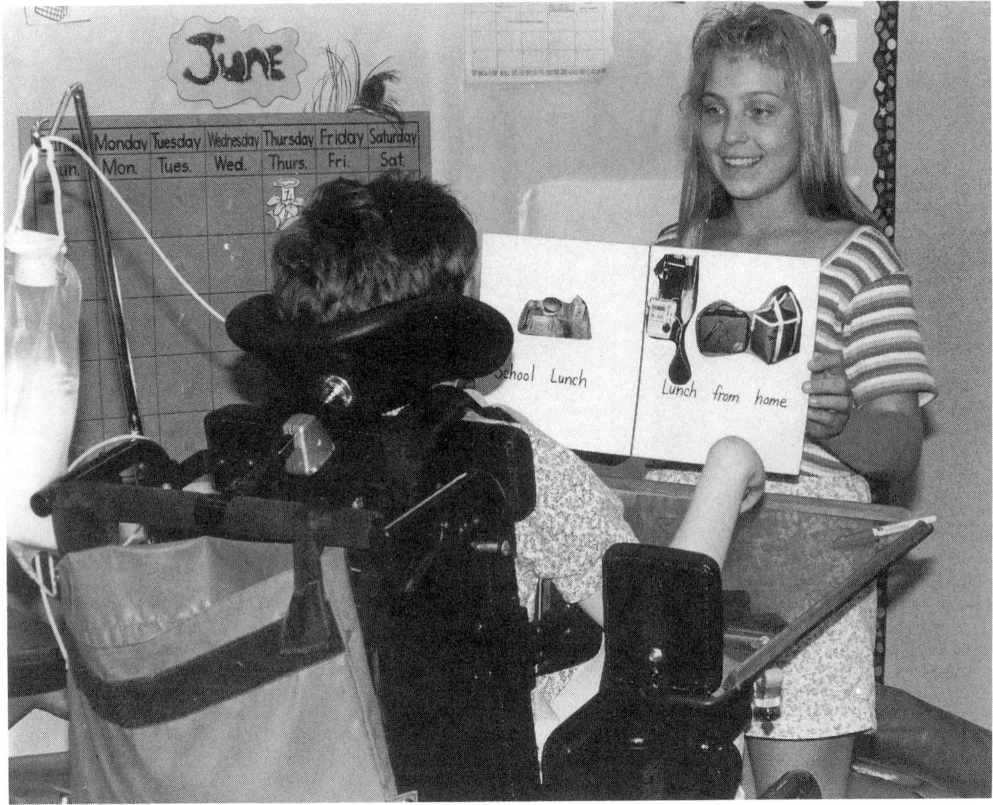

Figure 14.5. Holly uses her communication system to indicate preferences.

The team decided to gather information to respond to the first three questions prior to attaining additional cognitive assessments to answer the fourth question and before revising any curricula or schedules. Ideas about the students' cognitive abilities and intentions would be recorded during data collection in daily routines. The assessment procedures, data summaries, and conclusions are described below.

Retrospective Recollection

Before beginning assessments during daily routines, the team met to reconstruct information from past observations. The discussions resulted in the following examples.

Brent

School attendance was taken each morning by using 5-inch × 7-inch cards containing each student's picture and printed name. Brent often was crying or vocalizing and going into extension during this time, so he was not often asked to take attendance. One morning, because he was attentive, Laurie held up a card and, without stating the classmate's name, asked Brent if this classmate was at school. Brent looked at Chelsie, then back at Laurie, smiled, and then looked back at Chelsie. His response was a real surprise. He was asked about another student and, again, by using gaze, he indicated the student was present. In this manner, he proceeded to take attendance and appeared to be able to read the cards and match the information with each student present. He had observed this many times, although often crying, and Laurie and Kathy wondered if he had learned this just by observing. Later that same day at a table in the classroom with some classmates present, Brent was shown the card and asked to look at the student if he or she were present. Brent looked away, went into extension, and cried.

A second incident involved Brent's reaction at lunch. Brent was eating lunch he had brought from home (not using his gastrointestinal tube) and was eating very well. He had pudding toward the end of the meal and enjoyed it. He was shown each spoonful and asked if he wanted more. He smiled, the spoon was brought to his mouth, and then he swallowed. When he returned his gaze to the teacher and the pudding, the process was repeated. The next day, pudding was offered early in his meal. He was asked to gaze at the spoon if he wanted pudding—he turned away. The request was repeated and he cried. He was given some pudding to make sure he knew what was on the spoon and the request was repeated. He cried, went into extension, and refused the remaining lunch.

These two examples illustrated the changes staff saw in Brent from day to day, even with the same materials and teacher. Kathy hypothesized that Brent understood all that was asked of him. She hypothesized that his behaviors of refusal (e.g., turning away from tasks, crying, extension) were his way of trying to gain control over his life. She also shared her concern about his not eating, as Brent had become dehydrated in the past. Mealtimes needed to be constructed so he would eat and take in enough fluids, yet both Kathy and Laurie believed mealtimes offered excellent opportunities to extend Brent's communication. The recollections ended with the teachers concluding that mealtimes would be reexamined after more data collection. It appeared from recollections that all staff members had experienced Brent's changing behaviors.

Holly

Holly's behavior consisted of crying, vocalizing loudly, and sometimes biting her lip. Sometimes she bit her lip hard enough to cause bleeding. On occasion, the bleeding required the attention of the school nurse. One such incident was during the initial morning group instruction. Kathy and Laurie were assisting other students in reviewing the daily schedule. Holly was vocalizing and started to cry. Her crying escalated and was so loud she was removed from the class until she quieted.

A second incident was during free time. Holly had selected an activity by looking at an object and had been given the object for the remainder of the class interval. Kathy went to other students to offer choices and soon Holly was crying and had bitten her lip. Kathy was not able to assist her to calm down, and Holly was removed from the class and care was given to her bleeding lip. Holly missed the entire 30-minute class interval and the aide was left with the other students. Holly was congested on that day.

The two instances described here illustrate the behaviors about which staff were concerned and the dilemma staff faced when requiring Holly to work independently. Staff shared their conflict about either being with Holly (and limiting the teaching they could provide to other students) or not requiring Holly to learn to perform some tasks independently. Likewise they were concerned about her lip biting and worried that she cried because she was congested and not feeling well. Concern also was expressed that her crying and/or being upset might precipitate a seizure and lip biting. The staff concluded that they would reexamine the schedule and determine if crying and lip biting occurred when Holly was asked to be independent and if the behaviors were associated with additional specific tasks or situations, including being congested.

Assessment of Daily Routines

The Including Exceptions Systems (IES) data collection sheet was used for this process. The data sheet is designed to collect anecdotal information of concern and interest across the day. The information is collected by whomever is with the student, is rated on a scale of "little" to "a lot," and is reviewed to look for patterns of responses related to partners, activities, and/or environmental conditions. Figures 14.6 and 14.7 show data collected over the course of 1 day for Brent and Holly. Brent's behaviors of interest are attending (e.g., gazing, looking), inattention, turning his head away (e.g., refusing to work), distractibility (e.g., intentional turning away from instruction or tasks and/or gazing at other students/activities instead of doing his own work), crying, vocalizing, reaching out, smiling, and/or extension. The behaviors of interest for Holly were her smiling, vocalizing, crying, reaching out with arms/hands, gaze, body orientation, and excitability. Data were also collected on whether she was congested.

Environmental conditions included the daily schedule and other environmental conditions that the team hypothesized might be influencing behavior. These included the noise level in the room, peer interactions, adult interactions, and, for Brent, instructional arrangements (e.g., alone with teacher versus in a small group) and whether he was being asked to perform a specific task by a teacher. Tasks included making a choice with photographs, activating a switch, and grasping objects. The daily schedule and staff initials were written across the top of the data sheet; and environmental conditions, student's behaviors, and other things of interest were listed along the left side.

Data were collected for 2 weeks and were then reviewed by Kathy and Diane and shared with the team. Data review steps are listed in Figure 14.8. Some of the findings for Brent and Holly include the following:

First Data Review for Brent Brent cried and looked away (i.e., was distracted) when he was alone for instruction with an adult and peers were nearby or when he was in a group of classmates with disabilities and was not actively engaged. In most one-to-one situations with a teacher, Brent was distracted (i.e., looked toward what others were doing), cried, and/or turned his head away from the task (possibly refusing to do what was requested of him).

	Date 11/2 Period/Staff	9:45 ms	10:00 ms	10:15ms	10:30 kh	11:00 ls	1:20 ls	2:00 _	2:15 _	
	Description of activity	Choices Bowling →	Opening →	Drink →	Flex →	Lunch room	Matth	Recess PT	Flex	
	Position	Chair	Varies	Varies	Varies	Chair	on teacher's lap			
What he or she does	Turns head away					• •	•	•	•	lots none
	Reaches out arm					• •	•	•	•	
	Activates switch					• •	•	•	•	
	Attempts grasp					• •	•	•	•	
	Makes choice with photographs					• •	•	•	•	
	Vocalizes					• •	•	•	•	
	Cries					• •	•	•	•	
	Extension					• •	•	•	•	
	Laughs/smiles					• •	•	•	•	
			→	→						
What mood he or she is in	Attends to person/activity					• •	•	•	•	
	Distracted					• •	•	•	•	
	Inattentive					• •	•	•	•	
How he or she does things	Alone with teacher								•	
	With peers							•		
	Small group		→	→			•			
Other things going on	People noise					• •	•	•	•	
	Other noise					• •	•	•	•	
	COMMENTS	Got too hot—vocalization				Needed to get out of chair once—too hot	Upset—out of chair Schedule mix up			

Figure 14.6. Brent's IES data sample. (The placement of the dots within each cell in the shaded grid is significant: Placement at the top of the cell indicates that the behavior occurs with high frequency; placement in the middle of the cell indicates less frequency; and placement at the bottom of the cell indicates that the behavior does not occur.) (Form adapted from IES Project, D. Ferguson, Project Director, University of Oregon, College of Education.)

	Date 11/11 Period/Staff	9:45 ls	10:00 ls	10:15 ot	10:30 +c	11:00 k	12:30 pt	1:20 ls	2:00 k
	Description of activity	Music	Opening	OT	Watch movie	Group time	PT		
	Position	Chair	Chair	Chair	Chair	Chair			
What he or she does	Reaches out	•	N.A.		•	•	•		
	Orients to people/object	•	•		•	•	•	No data	No data
	Vocalizes	•	•		•	•	•	No data	No data
	Smiles	•	?		•	•	•		
				No data					
				No data					
What mood he or she is in	Cries	•	•		•	•	•		
	Fussy	•	•		•	•	•		
	Happy	•	•		•	•	•		
	Congested	•	?		•	?	•		
	Excitable	•	•		•	•	•		
How he or she does things									
Other things going on	Adult interaction	•	•		•	•	•		
	Peer interaction	•	None		•	•	N.A.		
	People noise	•	•		•	•	•		
	Other noise	•	•		•	•	•		
	COMMENTS		I was not paying close enough attention to notice smiles or interaction.			Was very quiet through movie, gave movie box to her—was content with that.	Bit lip—bleeding; wouldn't stop crying; mad cry.		

lots

none

Figure 14.7. Holly's IES data sample. (The placement of the dots within each cell in the shaded grid is significant: Placement at the top of the cell indicates that the behavior occurs with high frequency; placement in the middle of the cell indicates less frequency; and placement at the bottom of the cell indicates that the behavior does not occur.) (Form adapted from IES Project, D. Ferguson, Project Director, University of Oregon, College of Education.)

Data Review

Step 1	Review the data, read the comments section (which contains teachers' notes), study the activity descriptions (student's schedule), and the list of behaviors.	**Step 6**	Compare and analyze the results of Steps 3, 4, and 5. Form a basic hypothesis based on the results of comparing the target behavior with other variables. Then determine from a review of data if a. A pattern is found in the data to support the hypothesis *or* b. No pattern is found in the data to support the hypothesis. If no pattern is found, return to Steps 3, 4, and 5 using a new variable. If a pattern is found, go to Step 7.
Step 2	Identify the target behavior—the behavior that needs to be modified because it has been identified as a learning roadblock.	**Step 7**	Summarize conclusion/hypothesis.
Step 3	Identify correlations between the high-level target behavior (i.e., where "lots" is indicated) with the presence of other variables (e.g., a group or individual activity, time of day, noise level). Such variables are noted in the behavior list, in the descriptions of activities, and in the teachers' comments sections. These variables may affect the level of the target behavior. The data about the correlation between the target behavior and the variables will be used to determine changes that should be made in the student's schedules and programs. Graph the results.	**Step 8**	Ask collaborator to complete Steps 1–6 for the same target behavior.
		Step 9	Have a conference with collaborator and compare conclusions and hypotheses.
		Step 10	Plan with collaborator. Discuss the following questions: 1. Are there new data to be collected? Why? 2. What data collection should be continued? 3. What schedules and/or programs need to be refined? What do you expect from these changes? 4. What teaching directions (e.g., your own expectations of the student, your teaching style) should be changed?
Step 4	Repeat Step 3 using the low-level target behavior (i.e., where "none" is indicated) or where desired behaviors occurred.		
Step 5 (Optional)	Repeat Steps 3 and 4 using a contrasting behavior (e.g., contrast "crying" with "happy").		

Figure 14.8. Steps in data review.

Brent smiled and was attentive when he was with his peers or when he was actively assisted by a teacher to participate within a group of students. The behaviors were not consistently associated with any particular teacher, task, or noise level.

The team agreed that the findings were tentative because Brent had been absent for 3 days and data had not been collected during community instruction intervals. Two more weeks of data collection would confirm or refute these first findings and also provide more information on Brent's behaviors throughout the day and over the course of the week. The behaviors of reaching out, activating a switch, attempting to grasp, and making a choice with photographs were initially of interest but were not viewed as offering additional information to this process. These behaviors were, therefore, deleted from the second 2 weeks of data collection.

First Data Review for Holly Holly did cry often during the day and throughout the week. Time of day, day of the week, and noise were not factors related to her crying. It appeared she cried when alone and/or when she was not receiving attention while in a group (e.g., while watching a movie with her classmates with disabilities). She also had been absent, as had been teaching staff; and more data were needed to determine if her lip biting was intentional and if other behavioral signals occurred prior to crying or lip biting.

Two more weeks of data were collected for both Brent and Holly.

Second Data Review for Brent Review of the second data set indicated that Brent was often inattentive to teacher instruction when alone for instruction with a teacher *and* a group of peers or classmates was nearby doing other things. The percentage of his distractibility was figured by dividing the number of times he was recorded as being distracted by the sum of the number of times he was recorded as being distracted plus the number of times he was noted as being attentive, then multiplying that number by 100. This data review indicated that during one-to-one or group instruction he was looking away or "refusing" to perform his work during 81% of the activity intervals during this second data review. In the one-to-one or group situations in which he was attentive, he was alone in the room with the teacher or was actively participating in the group with teacher assistance. Notes from the teachers and staff on the data sheets indicated that Brent seemed to look toward the other activities going on in the room and seemed to refuse to look back at his own work. Work also included his meals and choices at mealtime. The team concluded that noise was not problematic for Brent, because when he was with peers without disabilities or was actively engaged in group activities, he attended regardless of the noise level. Three data entries indicated Brent combined inattention, crying, and extension (when in one-to-one instruction and alone in the classroom) to indicate he needed to be changed or was uncomfortable in his chair. The data from the first and second data reviews for Brent are summarized in Figure 14.9. This summary indicates that Brent was inattentive or distracted 48% of the time.

Second Data Review for Holly The data review for Holly indicated that she did cry at various intensities during most of the day. She vocalized before crying and seemed to cry softly before she escalated to loud crying and tears. The team had hypothesized that crying was her way of seeking attention or requesting a change. The data summary indicated that Holly cried when alone with her tasks or when she was not actively engaged in a group activity (e.g., was expected to observe others). She also vocalized when alone (e.g., expected to work independently), and these vocalizations were ignored by staff until she cried. Her lip was bleeding nu-

Behaviors	Instances in two data collection intervals																													
Distracted/in-attentive Looks away from work	x[a]	x	x	x	x	x	x	x	x	x	x	x	x[b]	x	x																
Attends																x	x	x	x	x	x	x	x	x	x	x	x	x	x	x	x
Vocalizes				x																x											
Cries	x												x																		
Extension		x									x		x	x		x				x											
Laughs		x	x											x			x						x								
Other considerations																															
People noise	x	x	x	x	x	x	x	x	x	x	x	x	x	x	x	x	x				x		x	x		x		x			x
Other noise		x	x	x							x	x		x	x	x	x				x			x							x
Peer interactions							x	x				x						x		x			x	x		x		x			
Group activity classmates with disabilities											x	x				x	x	x	x	x	x		x	x		x	x	x			x
Work one-to-one		x	x	x	x	x	x	x	x	x				x	x							x			x				x	x	

[a]Brent needs to get out of his "new" wheelchair.
[b]Brent needs to be changed.

Figure 14.9. Summary data for Brent.

merous times when staff went to her. It was not clear from the data if the lip biting was intentional and her means of getting attention or a result of a seizure or rigidity caused by being upset. Data on lip biting would continue to be collected and written in the comments section on the data sheet. The data from the first and second collections for Holly are summarized in Figure 14.10. The data summary indicates that Holly was crying or fussing 30% of the time.

INTERVENTION AND IMPLEMENTATION OF A PLAN

The data reviews were helpful. Teachers were not surprised by the findings, and in fact had guessed that Brent was refusing to perform as teachers requested and Holly was crying to seek attention. The team agreed Holly was seeking attention and preferred not being alone and that Brent's inattentive behavior might be Brent's way of asking to be with other students or more involved in activities, as well as a way of seeking to have some control over his environment. The following section describes suggested changes for both students.

Suggested Changes for Brent The team concluded that Brent's crying and nonattending behaviors were his means of stating, "I don't want to do this. I want to be with others over there." Staff would respond as listeners by honoring his requests. In addition, at mealtime they would use his system to communicate with him and honor his gaze response to the food items rather than requesting that he communicate choices using photographs or line drawings. Staff hypothesized this might take the pressure off Brent at lunch time. The changes they would try to implement included the following:

1. The staff would decrease their requests for Brent to respond to teacher programs when he refused his work and looked at peers nearby. Instead, if he looked at peers nearby and refused his work, staff would assume he was saying, "I want to go there" or maybe, "That's more interesting. How about pushing me over there?" Staff would respond affirmatively to this request and view his gaze and behaviors as a choice, not as distractive or inattentive behaviors.
2. Staff instruction requiring Brent to respond in specified ways at lunch to make choices would be terminated (e.g., when cued, "look at the pudding," Brent will scan the three containers and look at the pudding container). Brent's line drawings at lunch would remain, but they would be used by teachers in talking to Brent. Brent would not have to use gaze to get an item or to proceed to the next activity. Essentially, the line drawings would be used receptively to communicate with Brent.
3. A talkative buddy would be found for Brent and would give Brent a lot of attention and verbal input about activities in his environment. In this way, he would receive social attention from others besides teachers. Inclusion with his fourth-grade peers was suggested as a means to accomplish this as well as eating in the cafeteria during mealtimes. This last suggestion would require schedule changes for Brent and redesigning staff schedules.

Suggested Changes for Holly The team agreed to respond to Holly's vocalizations and crying as behaviors that meant, "I do not want to be alone. I want to be with others." The suggested changes noted here were designed to respond to her behaviors and put her into a more social instructional arrangement:

1. The staff should tune into Holly's vocalizations before they escalate into crying or to her soft crying and respond as if she were saying, "I want to be with

	Behaviors noted during two data collection intervals																										
Situation	Crying					Fussing			Smiling																		
With adult, but passive																					x						
With adult, but active											x	x		x	x	x			x			x	x	x	x		
Alone in group		x	x		x	x	x	x		x																	
In group with someone																	x			x						x	x
One-to-one	x			x					x				x					x									
Bites lip	x					x		x																			

Figure 14.10. A data summary for Holly.

someone, not alone." The staff examined the schedule and found times when she could be more included in group activities. When she could not be physically taught or assisted, she would be positioned near other students and within arms' length of teachers. At these times, teachers would verbally attend to her as they instructed other students and involve her in their instruction.
2. Kathy would review the schedule and consult with elementary teachers and find times when Holly could be with her same-age peers in their activities and classes.

Follow-Up

Decisions regarding follow-up for both students are described below.

Brent Schedule changes had been implemented for Brent. Brent's crying had decreased during mealtime, but his refusing and crying behaviors remained during instructional times. His teachers reported he was still crying during much of the day.

Holly In February, almost 3 months after the last team meeting, few schedule changes had been attempted. Kathy had observed the staff interactions with Holly and confirmed the hypothesis that she was crying for attention. Staff were listening for her vocalizations, responding to her verbally, and bringing her closer to them and the students they were teaching. This was effective: Holly's smiling increased and her crying decreased during these times of the day. However, there were still times during the day (e.g., mealtimes, recess, transitions to and from the room, instructional intervals) when staff could not attend to her; thus, she continued to cry, which disrupted the class. Holly was required by her foster family to remain indoors at recess and this time was especially difficult.

Summary In retrospect, the staff realized there were a number of assumptions embedded within the initial suggestions. As a result, the initial plans were not implemented and a procedural change was necessary. As noted in Chapter 9, which describes the change process associated with this story, Kathy did not make any schedule changes and lost her drive to try new things. She avoided initiating follow-up contact with Diane and was still frustrated with the students' behaviors and the teaming process. Luckily, the lack of progress was not viewed as anyone's fault but was seen as resulting from assumptions and system constraints that had not been addressed. A list of these issues and restraints were gathered from the journals of team members.

One assumption was that an assessment of the communication partners was not needed. Because staff had so readily interpreted Brent's and Holly's behaviors as communication, it was assumed they would be able and willing to act differently during instructional intervals with Brent. Teaching based on a belief that behavior is communication demands an understanding of interactive, child-directed teaching. This is in direct contrast to teacher-directed instruction (prescribing all aspects of instruction without allowing for student input and/or variations in responses), which was the mode of instruction used by Kathy and her teaching staff. Over time, Kathy revealed that she believed Brent's behaviors were communication but she 1) did not like that he was refusing to perform her programs as she had written them; 2) did not understand how to interact with Brent as his communication partner *and* as his teacher; and 3) knew that his behavior communicated what he did not like, but she did not understand that honoring his dislikes really meant changing his schedule and teaching approaches.

Kathy felt that Brent was not learning unless he was giving a response that she had specified. She felt the mealtime program changes were good. One day of using the new techniques resulted in Brent eating, smiling, attending, and not crying or refusing to look. However, she felt that Brent was being allowed to be even more of a passive observer and this bothered her. Because she did not feel she was teaching and because she did not have any data to record on Brent's responses to teacher requests, she discontinued the changes.

The consultant assumed that a barrier to changing students' schedules would be a time and staffing issue only. What was not considered initially was the climate and history of the school with regard to collaboration and previous conflicts between special education and elementary teachers. In her journal, Kathy mentioned she was avoiding discussion with her elementary education colleagues about including Brent in general education classrooms. She was afraid they would reject the idea and, in effect, reject her. Also, she was unsure she could control Brent's behavior in her colleagues' classrooms and was unsure of her role in "their" classrooms. *Collaboration* was a word and a concept, not a practice, for Kathy, the team, and other colleagues at this school. Collaboration requires a very big change in educational practice, and "overlooking" system barriers and support necessary to collaborate was a large error. Assuming that *knowing what to do* and *knowing how to do it in a specific situation* were the same almost stopped further interventions for Brent and Holly. It was at this point that the mentoring process discussed in Chapter 9 was reviewed and implemented.

Changes with Collaboration

Chapter 9 discussed the results of 6 months of journal writing and periodic reviews and discussions of Kathy's perspectives on Brent and Holly, her teaching and teaming situation, and assumptions regarding these situations. This 6-month interval was a time in which the focus on students and their behaviors was replaced by a focus on teaching and beliefs about how and why staff taught as they did. Gradually, as ideas of staff collaboration were explored, and as Kathy and the team were willing, a plan was redeveloped. The process was slow, considering what already had been successful with Brent and Holly; however, the process of how to do it with other team members, including elementary education teachers, required a change in pace to understand collaboration, to respond to behavior as communication, and to work within the existing school climate to plan more.

In mid March, the consultants reviewed the journals and concluded that the school team assumed Brent could understand everything that was said. The assumption was checked by scheduling a test of syntax comprehension to be conducted by the speech-language pathologist, Mindy. Reviewing the results of the test indicated that Brent did understand some of what was spoken, but not nearly as much as was assumed. Mindy and Kathy enjoyed their first collaboration and implemented a program together. Although the program was similar to the first one outlined previously on page 206, the process of collaboration and jointly owning the program contributed to its implementation over the remaining school year.

In April, after attending a workshop together, Kathy and Mindy began using line drawings during Brent's mealtimes as a means of conversing with him that did not require him to respond in specified ways. Although this had been suggested earlier, it had not been implemented. Now, Brent watched as staff members pointed to drawings as they talked with him. According to Kathy, Brent was a different person. The crying, refusing food, and extension had essentially ceased. Other times during the day remained problematic and frustrating, however. Likewise when staff could readily involve Holly in activities, her crying ceased. Other times remained problematic and a higher staff-to-student ratio was viewed as the solution.

The journal continued to be reviewed throughout the spring, and, by May, Kathy was changing from a practice described as teacher directed to one that was interactive and more child directed. The journal and conversations continued for another year and 6 months with changes in student's schedules, programs, and partners occurring throughout the interval.

A summary of Brent's and Holly's schedule, systems, and behavioral changes is described next. These changes were made as this vignette was written, but ongoing assessment and changes in students and teachers have continued.

Results

Information on Brent, Holly, and Kathy was collected over 2½ years. The changes included altering the teaching style of teachers and other communication partners,

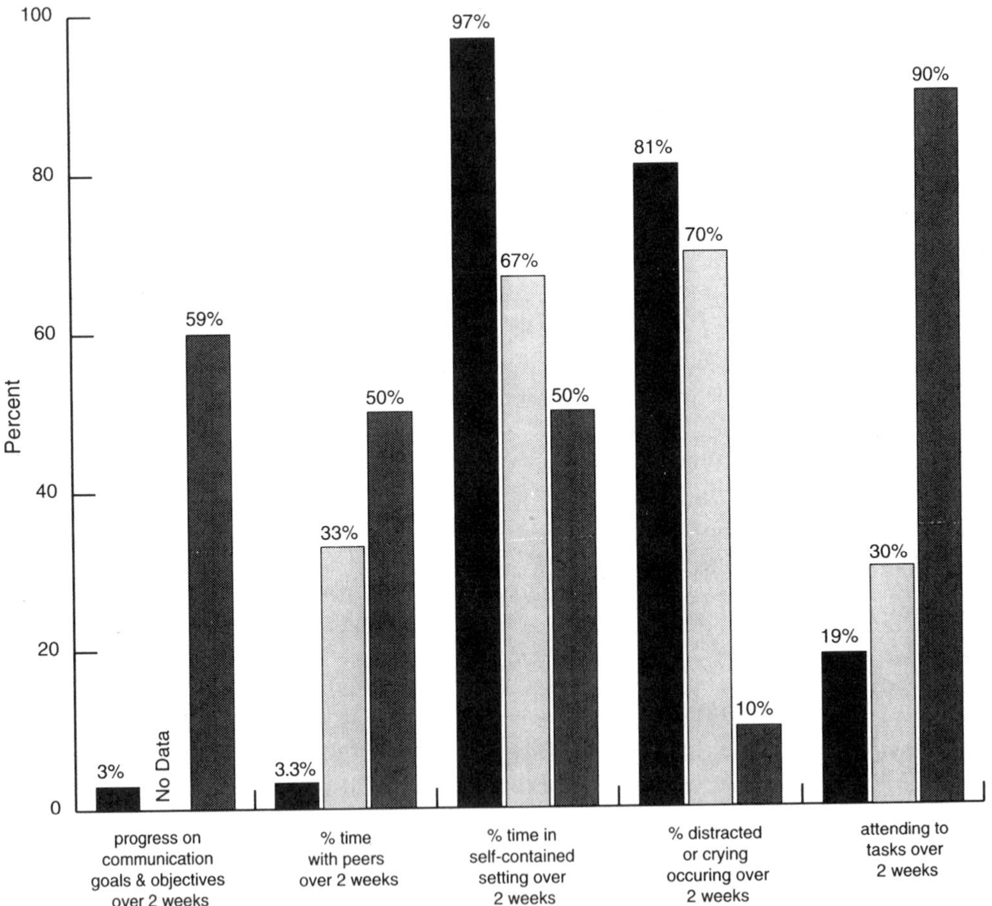

Figure 14. 11. Outcomes for Brent. (■ = Phase I, during the IES data collection with no intervention or schedule changes; □ = Phase II, 6 months after initiating IES data collection and during some changes; ■ = Phase III, 17 months after initiating IES data collection and with changes in teaching style and placement.)

changing the schedule, and changing the goals and objectives for each student. Some documentation of the changes and outcomes are summarized in Figures 14.11 and 14.12. The outcome data were collected by Diane as she visited and observed the students and by Kathy, who periodically collected student performance data. Both students realized an increase of time in classes with their peers without disabilities as well as increases in appropriate behaviors. The increased time in classes, for these students, is directly related to both the recognition of behaviors of these students as legitimate communication and the level of commitment by the school staff required to enhance the school experience of Brent and Holly.

SUMMARY

The vignettes in this chapter illustrate some of the barriers that are encountered as teachers proceed through the complex task of assessment and change. The recognition of each student's behaviors as communication and the willingness of Kathy and the school team to reflect and change were critical to the students' success and

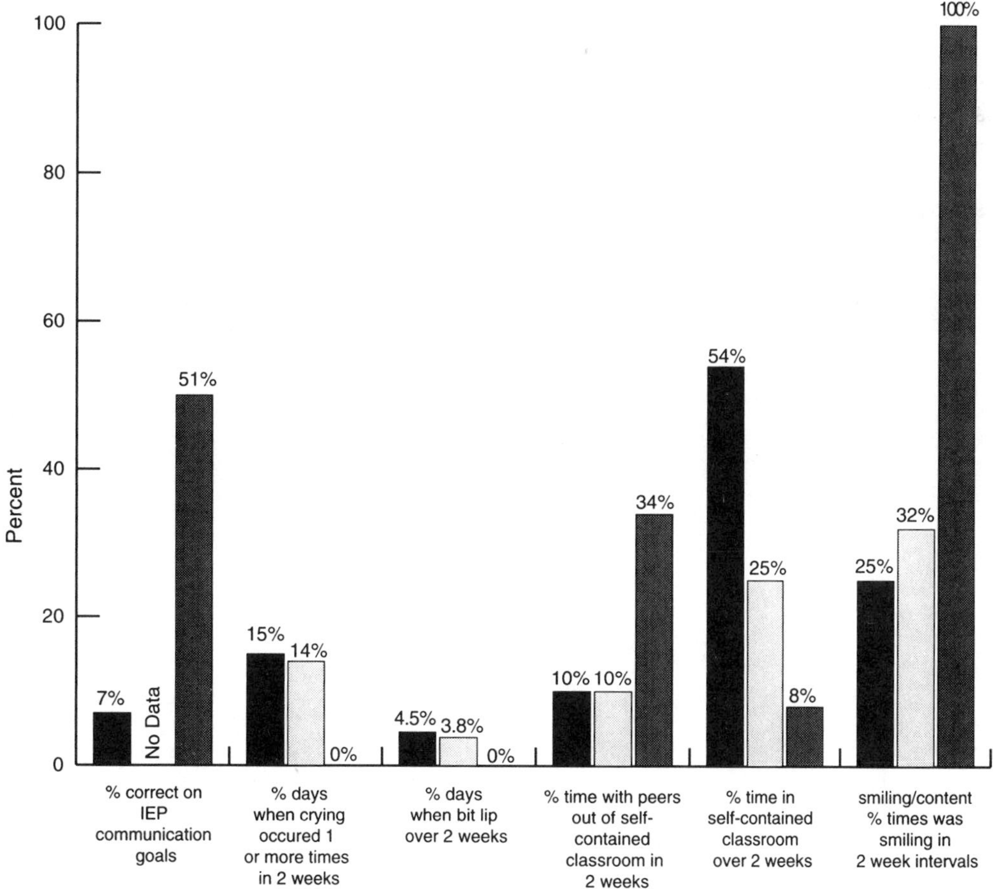

Figure 14.12. Outcomes for Holly. (■ = Phase I, during the IES data collection with no intervention or schedule changes; □ = Phase II, 6 months after initiating IES data collection and during some changes; ■ = Phase III, 17 months after initiating IES data collection and with changes in teaching style and placement.)

the maintenance of their communication systems over a 2-year period. As both Brent and Holly make transitions to the middle school next fall, the maintenance of their systems of communication will face a critical test. The continued use and expansion of these communication systems will require knowledge of their systems, how they are used, and why they were selected, along with an understanding of how interactions of various communication partners can affect the students' use of their systems.

As the last quarter at elementary school began, Kathy and each student's family initiated meetings regarding the upcoming transitions. They have met individually and collectively with the current junior high school teacher. Their conversations included scheduling visits to the junior high for both Brent and Holly as well as opportunities for the teams at both schools to exchange information and make observations. Transitions are typically difficult times for students and families and often result in communication systems being either literally or figuratively left behind. The planning and involvement of the team members are critical components for the maintenance of the systems throughout these upcoming transitions. In addition, both Brent and Holly attended this elementary school because services were assigned there by the district and thus did not attend their neighborhood elementary school. Although their time in school has been positive, both academically and socially, these students will make transitions to their neighborhood junior high school in the fall, which is a different school from the one their current sixth-grade peers will attend. The friendships developed over the last 2 years will be disrupted and the transitions will be a time of making and seeking friendships among strangers.

CHAPTER 15

Jeremy

Tom Weddle

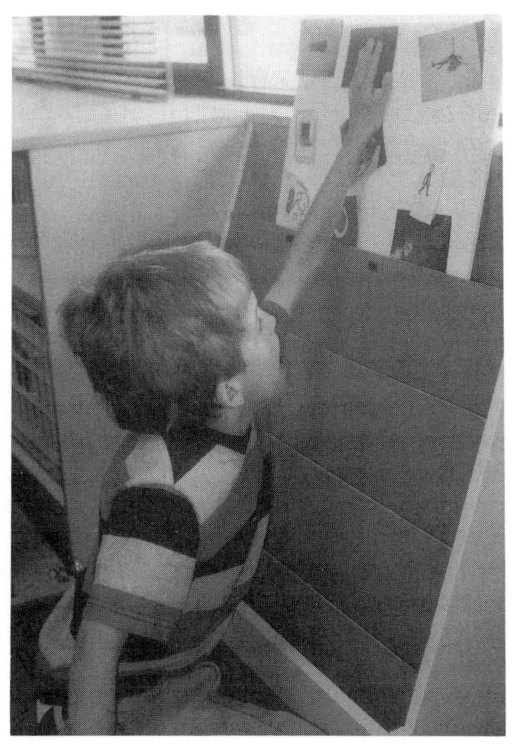

NAME: Jeremy
AGE: 9 years
TEACHER: Tom Weddle
CONSULTANT: Jeanne Johnson
SYSTEM: Thirty-five millimeter color photographs of daily activities, preferred foods, and play items were collected. Choice photographs were attached to foam boards with Velcro, and the boards were placed in accessible areas of Jeremy's school en-

vironments. Transition photographs were placed in sequence in a plastic communication book. The book was carried by the staff, and the photographs were shown to Jeremy whenever he moved from one activity or setting to another.

Jeremy spent 3 years attending a special education preschool before joining a classroom for children with multiple disabilities at an elementary school in September of 1990. Tom became the teacher in Jeremy's class in September of 1992. When Tom first met Jeremy, Jeremy was able to push himself into the classroom, and with help getting out of his wheelchair, proceed to scoot along the floor to an isolated corner. He refused to join group activities, was resistant to leaving his corner, and wanted only to play with his plastic toy cow.

Jeremy was born with hydrocephaly. He loves playing with toy cars and balls and has adequate use of his arms and hands for most daily living activities. He is nonverbal; incontinent; reluctant to use utensils for eating; does not dress or undress himself; prefers isolated, self-stimulatory play; and walks with difficulty. His adaptive skill level, as measured through the Vineland Adaptive Behavior Scales (Sparrow, Balla, & Cicchetti, 1984), is in the 12- to 18-month range.

He does not have a diagnosis of autism or fragile X syndrome, but he does exhibit numerous autistic-like behaviors, including difficulty with transitions, severely delayed verbal and nonverbal communication, limited social and play skills, insistence on sameness within his physical environment, a narrow range of interests, and visual and auditory stereotypies. In addition, Jeremy has cortical visual impairment. Jeremy's visual cortex was damaged at birth and he has some difficulty attending to and processing visual information. This impairment does not affect visual acuity, but it often makes it difficult for Jeremy to process novel or unfamiliar visual information.

According to Jeremy's father, Jeremy's primary need was communication. He saw Jeremy's inappropriate behavior as being a result of his inability to communicate his needs. Jeremy's individualized education program (IEP) included the goal areas of communication, mobility, academics, and functional daily living skills. During Jeremy's past school years he had made little progress in any goal area other than walking.

ASSESSMENT FOR COMMUNICATION PLANNING

The previous year, Jeremy had been taught to touch a 4-inch × 6-inch card with the word "yes" printed on it in response to the question "Do you want ____?" The "yes" was always placed on his right side and the word "no" on his left. The consultant assessed this communication at the beginning of the school year to see how much of this skill Jeremy had maintained over the summer. Jeremy did not look at the cards placed in front of him. He merely hit or slapped the table with his right hand, touching the "yes" card each time he was asked if he wanted a particular item.

The procedure for teaching appropriate discrimination between "yes" and "no" consisted of giving Jeremy the item presented when he touched "yes," even if it was an undesirable item. Jeremy became very angry when he was assessed using this same procedure. He had been taught to touch the word "yes" in response to specific stimuli (i.e., the card placement and the instructor verbalization). He responded appropriately as long as the "yes" card was placed on his right side and as long as his behavior resulted in a favorable outcome. Unfortunately, he had acquired a rote and rigid communicative response. Through daily observation of Jeremy's responses to verbal directions, it was determined that Jeremy probably did not attend to or comprehend novel, noncontextual spoken language. Attempts to teach "yes/no" discrimination had failed as a result of his inconsistent comprehension of spoken language and his inability to gain meaning from the printed words "yes" and "no." This information suggested that spontaneous, mutual communication would have to be taught at a lower level of abstraction—less spoken language and more visual, concrete cues for comprehension.

Through interviews with Jeremy's former teacher, parents, and aides from the previous year, the team discovered that Jeremy had only one highly motivating interest that could be used to encourage communication—a plastic cow. From reports, all other toys or items, including food, were of minimal interest to Jeremy. Jeremy regularly refused lunch or snacks, would not seek out a toy or activity other than his cow, and became quite angry when anyone touched or attempted to remove the cow from his grasp.

These reports were verified through observation of Jeremy during structured choice making. During the course of ongoing, daily activities such as snacktime and play, Jeremy was presented with choices that were of possible interest to him, such as the cow, Cheerios, fruit, juice, and crackers. Jeremy was encouraged to indicate his choice through pointing, reaching, or vocalizing an interest in the items presented. Jeremy would reach for or grab these items if and when he desired them. Any attempt to delay his acquisition of a desired item or to encourage him to point to or touch the item led to escalating agitation, which usually led to crying, scratching, and escaping to another part of the room. During these choice-making activities, his ability to use photographs to ask for desired items was assessed. A photograph of an item of interest was placed near or in front of Jeremy and the actual item was placed within his sight but out of reach. Jeremy did not attend to the photographs. He became frustrated when he was unable to reach the desired item and would attempt to scratch anyone near him or cry.

During the prior school year, Jeremy had been encouraged to look at line drawings of activities prior to transitions and to make choices among food items graphically displayed on a computer, but he was inconsistent in visually attending to the transition drawings or touching the computer graphics for choice making. Most of the time Jeremy communicated his needs and desires physically and vocally by crying, screaming, scratching, grabbing, and biting. The Motivation Assessment Scale (MAS) (Durand, 1990; Durand & Crimmins, 1988) was used to determine the functional basis of these disruptive behaviors. This behavioral tool measures the likelihood of specific behaviors given specific circumstances through a series of questions that are answered by individuals who are familiar with the child. The user can determine the general function of a target behavior—whether it serves to gain a tangible item, to provide escape from an activity or setting, to provide sensory stimulation, or to gain attention. When Jeremy was unable to escape a situation or to gain a desired item or activity, he would scratch, grab, or bite. The screaming and crying were used most often to gain attention. Jeremy also enjoyed vocalizing loudly in hallways just for fun. Much of his disruptive or inappropriate behavior seemed to have a communicative basis. There were times when Jeremy cried for undetermined reasons, but his teacher later discovered that he was subject to severe headaches and that he periodically suffered from allergies. As he became a more capable communicator, the staff members were able to decide whether he was sick or whether he had a specific, addressable need, such as attention.

How could Jeremy be taught to use a formal system when he chose not to attend to or participate in a training session? In spite of his diagnosis of cortical visual impairment, his cognitive ability to utilize photographs did not seem to be the issue. According to reports from both his physical therapist and his occupational therapist, who had worked with Jeremy for the preceding 5 years, Jeremy had some experience and success using line drawings to communicate choices in preschool. Attempts by staff to control his communication by denying him access to choices when it was not appropriate or convenient resulted in Jeremy's refusal to use the drawings. Past training sessions with the "yes" and "no" cards also had served to lessen Jeremy's interest in and tolerance for attending to anything that interfered with his immediate gratification. The team felt that control and motivation were major issues for Jeremy. Consequently, teaching sessions were set up with Jeremy to maximize his interest and his control.

Formal communication training began with Jeremy seated at a table. Jeremy's teacher, Tom, would place items in front of Jeremy and wait for him to make a choice. Jeremy was willing to choose between the cow and any other items placed in front of him by reaching and picking them up. He would then play with the cow by holding it at arm's length just above his head and shaking it. He became frustrated if Tom took the cow from him too often, but as the sessions progressed, Jeremy began to realize that he could get the cow back from Tom quickly and easily by reaching for it. This format allowed Jeremy control and invited participation. The team hoped that establishing sessions as nonthreatening and rewarding would allow the shaping of more appropriate and potentially useful behaviors, such as pointing or touching. The long-term goal was to introduce photographs as a communicative medium. Line drawings had met with limited success and were perhaps too abstract for Jeremy to use them readily as a communicative form. The team hoped that the photographs would provide Jeremy with clearer, more concrete information and allow him relatively easy access to an appropriate communicative mode.

How could Jeremy be taught to use a formal system when he had such a limited range of interests? The initial sessions lasted for no more than 5 minutes because of Jeremy's disinterest in any item other than the cow and his lack of tolerance for teaching trials that necessitated the continual removal of the cow from his grasp. In order to lengthen the sessions and to increase his range of interests, the team altered the presentation format to encourage Jeremy's contact with and use of other toys that might interest him. The toys selected were chosen based on age appropriateness and Jeremy's interest in toys that provided him with auditory or visual stimulation.

Rather than place the cow on the table as a first option, his teacher would show Jeremy other toys, demonstrate how to make them work, and encourage him to try. Within a few weeks, as his comfort level with the sessions increased, Jeremy began exploring these toys. Through this approach Jeremy became interested in about 10 different visually and auditorily stimulating items and toys. A few of these toys, a talking basketball hoop and a switch-controlled truck and soldier, later became Jeremy's favorites. In addition, the amount of time spent in direct instruction per session increased to 15 minutes.

How could Jeremy be taught to use a formal system when he had so few useful and appropriate communicative skills, such as pointing, touching, attending to photographs, or gaining listener attention? Having established some interest in a range of toys, Jeremy's teacher moved the items presented out of Jeremy's reach so that he could not obtain them without assistance. Jeremy still did not look at Tom to gain his attention in order to communicate his interest in an item, but he was tolerating having to wait a few seconds for Tom to hand him the item for which he was reaching. At this point, Tom began to pair the item reached for and its photograph by placing the photograph just in front of the item. No attempt was made to have Jeremy touch the photograph, but as the item was handed to him, the photograph was shown to him and labeled verbally.

After a few moments, Tom would then take the item from Jeremy. When he attempted to get the item back by reaching for it, Tom held a photograph of the item next to the item just in front of Jeremy so that he could see both. Jeremy was asked to touch the photograph to get the item back. If he did not, Tom would show the photograph to him and touch the photo to his hand. Tom would then immediately hand him the item. After several weeks, he began to touch the photograph as soon as he wanted the item back. He still was not attending to the photograph with any genuine interest or attempting to gain Tom's attention, but he had learned to touch the photograph as a necessary step to get what he desired.

Having established this behavior, his teacher continued to place the items within view and just out of reach. Two items and two photographs representing those items were placed in front of Jeremy. Jeremy was asked to touch a photograph of an item in order to obtain it. Jeremy did not look at the photograph and reverted to slapping whichever one was on his right.

Tom felt they had reached an impasse. Jeremy still communicated his choices through the most direct route (i.e., reaching for an item, rather than looking at it and communicating to another person by means of a photograph). The staff attempted to remedy this problem by placing all the toys out of sight in a basket. Jeremy was allowed to see the toys going into the basket, but the basket was placed behind the instructor. A photograph was placed on the table in front of Jeremy and he was encouraged to touch it. As soon as he did, the pictured toy was handed to him and he was allowed to play with it. He immediately caught on to this approach, so they introduced another photograph. The plastic cow remained Jeremy's favorite toy for many months. In order to teach Jeremy to discriminate between two photographs, the staff used the cow photograph as a means to judge whether Jeremy was actually making an informed choice. Again, Jeremy tended to touch the photograph on his right side, but now he was actually looking at the photograph on occasion to see which one was the cow. When he touched the cow photograph, he immediately was handed the cow, but when he chose the alternate photograph, his teacher held the photo up in front of him with the item he had chosen to let him know that he had not picked the cow. If he reached for the item anyway, he was given it, but more often than not, he refused the item by pushing it away, and then he was redirected to touch the cow photograph and was quickly handed the cow.

Through trial and error, Jeremy began to check more often before touching the photographs. After approximately 2 months, he was attending to groups of three to four photographs and picking out the cow photograph without a problem. Soon after, he began to select other photographs in order to play with other toys. The teaching sessions were moved to the play area of the classroom and the photographs were scattered loosely in front of Jeremy. All the toys were placed behind the instructor and Jeremy was asked to hand a photograph of the toy he desired to the instructor. Jeremy caught on to this additional demand quickly. The instructor then began using the photograph to ask Jeremy for a chance to play with the toy. Jeremy was given the photograph and the toy was taken. Jeremy was shown that if he handed the photograph back, he would receive the toy back. Once this behavior had been established with one instructor, other staff members were brought into the sessions so that Jeremy could generalize these skills with them. The mutual use of photographs between Jeremy and the staff was introduced so that Jeremy would learn that the procedure worked both ways. The staff wanted him to communicate with photographs and let him know that they worked for them as well.

How should communication instruction be incorporated into the natural flow of the school day? For communication to generalize and to become motivating, it is necessary to continually develop activities and settings that promote and necessitate communication between the student and possible listeners. Jeremy was now making choices when working directly with staff. The team wanted to encourage him to use his communicative skills in a variety of settings and for a wider range of purposes than just selecting toys. The team also wanted to provide Jeremy with information about his day using the same photograph format. Transitions between activities and choices within activities served as natural opportunities for teaching communication throughout the day.

The photographs were placed on a foam board using Velcro once Jeremy began using the photographs in the play area to obtain toys. A board displaying his preferred toys was placed in the play area. The same toys were placed in a clear plastic bin out of reach. When Jeremy was allowed free time, he was asked to choose a toy, by picking a photograph from his play board, and hand it to his instructor. He was allowed to choose other toys during these sessions, but he had to use his board to indicate his new choice. The staff watched Jeremy carefully during these free times so that if he approached his board, someone was there to communicate with him. His teacher was adamant that Jeremy not be expected to wait for staff to find the time to attend to him. The connection between the use of photographs and their communicative purpose would be quickly lost if the staff did not reinforce their use consistently and immediately. Another board was placed near the door of the classroom and Jeremy was encouraged to use this board to ask for desired activities outside of the classroom, such as buying a soda from the soda machine and taking walks around the school. As his interests developed over the course of 2 years, staff were able to add more age-appropriate photographs to his choice boards, such as snack and lunch items, water, a computer, picturebooks, and magazines. The photographs were placed on his board in accordance with his daily schedule: Lunch items were placed on the board just prior to lunch, and his walk photographs were placed on the board just prior to his scheduled walk.

Concurrent with the development and teaching of Jeremy's expressive communicative system, a receptive communication counterpart was developed. Some 4-inch × 6-inch photographs of Jeremy's daily activities were placed into a Mayer-Johnson communication book. The photographs were placed in sequence to follow the course of the day's activities and were updated each day to reflect his changing daily schedule. These photographs always showed Jeremy involved in the activity. The visual information in some of them was dense (i.e., sometimes they depicted classroom activities with numerous people). A conscious attempt was made to simplify the content of the photographs when possible, but the contextual information provided by these shots of Jeremy involved in actual activities seemed to enhance his comprehension rather than to detract from it. They were shown to Jeremy by the staff to augment their verbal instruction when it was time for him to move to another activity or setting.

Previously, Jeremy had been given verbal instruction and immediately prompted physically to begin making a transition to the next activity. The physical prompting had been necessary because Jeremy rarely responded to verbal cuing alone, but he generally responded to physical prompts by scratching, screaming, or hitting. The photographs had been used not only to provide Jeremy with additional information when he was being asked to make a transition, but also to create a routine that allowed Jeremy to process the request with a temporally stable cue (e.g., photograph); the photographs also had encouraged the staff to wait for Jeremy to initiate the transition on his own. The inappropriate behaviors seemed to have been prompted by Jeremy's uncertainty about the content of the verbal request and his discomfort with immediate and unsolicited physical interaction with staff. Over time, the use of the transition book reduced Jeremy's confusion and frustration dramatically. By the end of the first year of using the book, Jeremy was consistently self-initiating appropriate behavior to a request within seconds after the transition photograph was shown to him.

How are appropriate communication skills maintained with a child who has not acquired any long-term appropriate communicative strategies in the course of numerous years of direct intervention? Often, the spontaneous or child-initiated use of communication is overlooked when the use of augmentative modes or devices is taught. In order to facilitate this outcome, the staff must encourage the child to initiate the use of the communicative mode by providing motivating activities and a reasonable amount of freedom for requesting and choosing. If the staff use an approach that is too rigid (i.e., complete control of communicative opportunity and content), the child may remain a passive, adult-directed communicator or may refuse to use the system and revert to less appropriate communicative behaviors.

After 5 months of teaching, Jeremy was making choices when presented with photographs of options during free time or snack, but he made choices only when staff structured the communicative opportunity by presenting his communication board to him. Choices were allowed only at specific times and for specific items; the staff were controlling the communication. This approach had worked very well in teaching Jeremy about getting his needs met when there was a narrow range of options, but his teacher wanted Jeremy to seek out and use the communication boards spontaneously to move from simple structured choice making to self-initiated requesting, so that he would no longer be dependent on staff to facilitate his choice making by physically guiding him to or providing him with the communication board. The first spontaneous, independent request occurred in conjunction with another of Jeremy's primary interests and needs—learning to walk independently.

At the beginning of the school year Jeremy was unable to walk without someone supporting him as he moved forward. Progress in this area had been slow and painful for a number of years. Jeremy loved to walk, but it was often difficult to interest him in walking to specific places or at specific times. His aide always had walked him indiscriminately through the halls, and frequently Jeremy would protest not only because he tired easily but also because he wanted to go somewhere other than the direction in which his aide was moving him or because he wanted to do something else. The use of the board for out-of-the-classroom activities gave Jeremy control of the walk. He was able to choose an alternate activity, such as using the computer, in lieu of walking, and he was shown photographs of possible destinations from which to choose if he did choose walking.

Initially, the walk photograph was almost always on display, but Jeremy most often was guided to the board and allowed to choose it. He had not taken a spontaneous interest in seeking out his communication board to select any photograph, much less the walk photograph. But at the end of the fifth month of instruction, Jeremy scooted along the carpeted floor toward Tom, grasped his pant leg, stood up, and led him to the outside board. He requested walk and looked back to hand Tom the photograph. From that day on, Jeremy began using photographs as his means to communicate. Photographs on walls, halls, bulletin boards, magazines, postcards, or in photo albums became an obsession. He would stop and look carefully at any photograph that was within reach. He seemed to feel that there was a chance for something personally meaningful within each and every photograph.

Before the end of Jeremy's second year in Tom's class, Jeremy began to walk independently. He began to explore the classroom. He walked or scooted about constantly. As Jeremy became more mobile, he began to seek out photographs from the bins in which they were stored. The photographs were to provide choices, but the staff had selected choices and requests that fit their scheduling needs. He learned that the foam boards were useful when they reflected his interests, but that if they did not, he could seek out the necessary photograph elsewhere. The photographs were used as an incentive for him to move about the room. He had progressed by this time to being rather easily redirected, so staff members were able to give him alternate choices or send him to another area of the room without triggering tantrums when they were unable to fulfill his request.

Jeremy's progress seemed limited only by the staff's ability to provide meaningful activities and choices. He seemed content with a world that was sensitive to his needs and that was structured to keep him involved through choice-making opportunities. Jeremy was capable of more, and staff members attempted to move him from photographs to line drawings. An icon of walking was used to teach him to begin using line drawings. At first it seemed to work for him, but only if the walk drawing was the only choice. Jeremy did not seem to progress to choosing between two line drawings or between the walk drawing and a photograph of another activity. Because Jeremy reacted so poorly to frustration and because the photographs mediated that frustration so effectively, the staff did not push Jeremy to use line drawings.

Not all of Jeremy's frustration was eliminated through the use of photographs. There were still times when he became frustrated for reasons the staff could not ascertain. At such times he was not expected to communicate spontaneously to them. The foam board would be given to him so he could choose an activity. If he was unable to choose as a result of stress or if he showed no interest in anything that was offered, an instructor would pick a photograph of an activity that he might enjoy, such as free time in the play area, and use that photograph to direct him to the activity. Frequently, he would calm down very quickly. If he did not, it usually meant the staff had failed to guess his need and that he was not pleased at the choice. At such times he was encouraged to show what he needed by going to the item he desired. More often than not he was able and willing to do so. If he could not be given what he wanted, such as lunch at 10 A.M., substitutes (e.g., a snack) were offered or the photographs were shown in the necessary sequence of events before he could get or participate in his desired activity. His ability to temporally sequence events through photographs and delay his own gratification progressed nicely during the 2 years the consultant worked with him. His reaction to frustration had moved from immediate and often aggressive tantrums to looking for a means (e.g., photograph) to express his need more clearly and emphatically. He would persist for several minutes and vocalize loudly if he had a photograph, but he rarely was aggressive.

After Jeremy began using the photographs spontaneously, the staff began experimenting with the Wolf board to see if Jeremy would enjoy having a "voice" with which to augment his communication. The Wolf board is an augmentative, electronic device that measures approximately 1 inch × 12 inch × 12 inch. The device is programmed to allow the user to press specific points or cells on the front surface of the board, which results in the activation of a digitalized voice. This robotic voice then verbally labels the photograph placed at that particular cell and allows the user to communicate verbally as well as graphically. Several weeks of experimentation resulted in failure. Jeremy did not seem to attend to the photographs when they were presented as a part of the augmentative device. Instead, he wanted to touch and examine the device itself. He played with the speaker and with the plastic backing, but would not attend to the photographs. Jeremy has a very strong interest in any device that makes noise or that contains a light source (e.g., a light bulb). He will attempt to stare into the light source or cause the noise to be repeated for extended periods of time. He does not attend to the device's functional purpose. The Wolf board was just another noise-making device for Jeremy, and he was distracted by its robotic voice.

How can a photograph communication system be used in settings other than a special education classroom (e.g., the home, a general education setting)? Jeremy's parents were thrilled with Jeremy's communicative progress, but they were somewhat reluctant to implement the use of photographs at home. Jeremy's consultant and teacher met with them in their home to explain Jeremy's communicative system and how they might use the photographs to help generalize his skills in the home setting. Their reluctance seemed to result from a belief that their home life was not predictable enough for using photographs to make transitions, choices, and requests. Also, they were not comfortable with Jeremy having unlimited free choice of activities or items. The consultant explained that they could modify the transition photographs by using just a few for the major transitions that might occur during any given day. Jeremy's choices were limited only by displaying photographs of activities and items that would be provided at any given time. It was suggested that the family put up a few photographs in a consistent location for available snacks when they could provide them conveniently. They did implement the use of photographs to a limited extent, but not as often as the school. Jeremy used the photographs at home when they were available.

Jeremy attended a second-grade classroom for about 45 minutes per day as part of his curriculum. In the past, attempts at integrating Jeremy into general education settings had led to frustration and temper outbursts. The staff found that by allowing Jeremy to participate in center activities of his choice, chosen through photographs, his frustration dropped dramatically. Jeremy participated in his second-grade setting with no incidents of aggression or outbursts of temper for the entire year that he used his communication board.

FUTURE DIRECTIONS WITH THE SYSTEM

After the team's attempts at teaching Jeremy to use line drawings and the Wolf board failed, they concentrated on teaching Jeremy to be more spontaneous and to expand his communicative range. Jeremy had demonstrated competence with the system as it existed and was able to request a number of items and activities. Attempts at making the system more formal (e.g., using an electronic device) or more abstract (e.g., using icons or words) had only served to distract or frustrate Jeremy. Because easing his frustration was the primary reason for communication intervention, the staff concentrated on expanding the number of settings in which he communicated and the range of activities that he could enjoy and request. This horizontal expansion of skills and abilities became a goal during Jeremy's second year in Tom's classroom.

The addition of a computer site at Jeremy's school led to a new avenue of hope for further abstraction and portability. It was possible to use a video camcorder to download pictures (e.g., photographs) into a computer. These digitalized photographs then could be altered through a paint program. It became possible to videotape anything, download it, highlight salient information through the use of extraction and contrasting backgrounds, shrink or expand the images, and print them in color. The resulting output was nearly photographic. The printouts looked more like line drawings than photographs but were just similar enough to the videotaped items to be recognizable. The child care staff and his current teacher are working to implement the use of these digitalized images in the hope that they can be mounted on a higher quality augmentative device, perhaps a Macaw (by Zygo), Alphatalker (by Prentke-Romich), or Digivox (by Sentient Systems) (see Appendix D for addresses of manufacturers), and achieve a more satisfying and impressive communicative mode for Jeremy. These devices function similarly to the Wolf board but use recorded human voice as speech output rather than the robotic, difficult-to-comprehend digitized speech of the Wolf board. By using these computer images and reducing them in size, many more options can fit onto an augmentative template than would be possible using the unaltered 3-inch × 5-inch photographs.

Jeremy cannot move away from the current low-tech approach unless he can become comfortable with and demonstrate the cognitive capability to use an augmentative, high-tech device. There will need to be further technological advances before Jeremy really can benefit from a high-tech approach, but he can be ready for the possibility of using a portable, sturdy, and flexible voice output device.

In review, the steps involved in teaching this system are as follows:

1. Create an instructional setting that allows for motivation and control by the child.
2. Increase range of student's interest by actively teaching the use of different, but potentially appealing, toys and items.
3. Teach the use of photographs as a communicative mode by making highly desirable items available contingent on attending to them and touching photographs of those items.
4. Increase training opportunities for the use of the system by providing natural opportunities for both expressive and receptive use of photographs by and with the child.
5. Teach spontaneous use of the system by providing the student with motivating opportunities and a wide range of freedom for initiating and choosing activities.
6. Generalize the use of the system by transferring photograph communication to the general education classroom and the home setting.
7. Begin to explore more sophisticated augmentative devices after basic communicative skills have been taught and generalized.

SUMMARY

Jeremy presented a challenge for several reasons: He frequently communicated frustration and anger in a very aggressive manner, he chose not to participate in training sessions, and he had an extremely narrow range of interests. The approach used to teach him to communicate took all three of these limitations into account. The staff members were forced to modify every aspect of teaching to accommodate these obstacles. Within a classroom it is sometimes difficult to see the need for such a degree of accommodation, but many years had been wasted attempting to fit Jeremy into a communicative mode and a teaching regimen that he could not and would not accept. Even with the willingness of the staff to be accommodating, it took many months for Jeremy to acquire and initiate communication in an appropriate manner. The time spent and the effort expended were obviously worthwhile, but there were many who questioned whether Jeremy would attain the goals envisioned. Jeremy is now a spontaneous communicator and those working with him on communication are rewarded daily by his subtle but constant growth, which is both social and communicative.

Chapter 16

Jacob

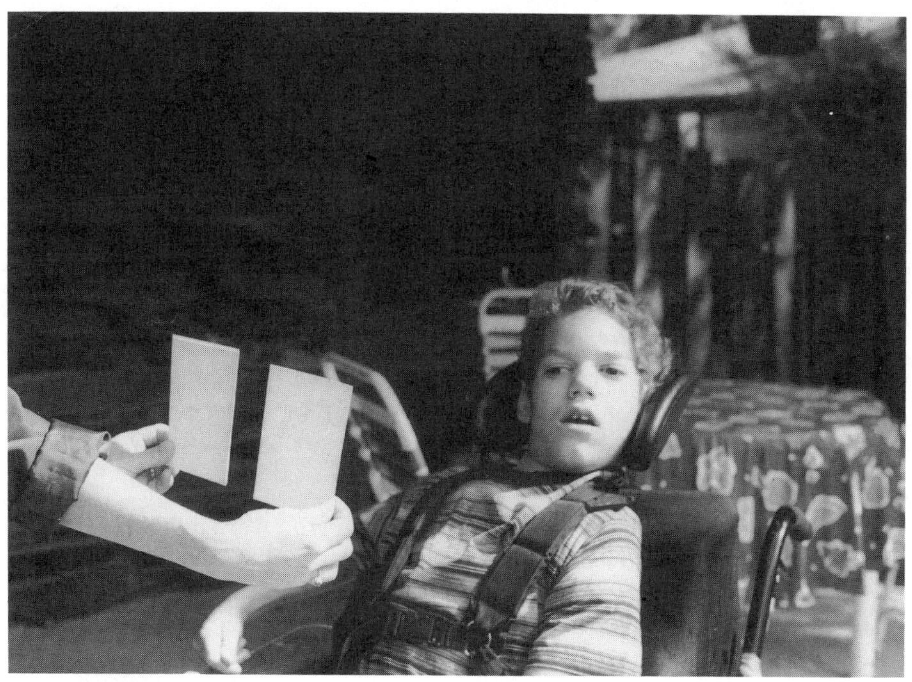

Name: Jacob
Age: 11
Teacher: Tim
Consultant: Chris Curry and Jeanne Johnson
System: Jacob's first communication system involved a partner holding up several objects or objects that represented activities. He communicated by

looking at one of the objects or by staring at his partner without making a choice. Eventually, the objects were replaced with picture representations.

Jacob was 11 years old when he was first seen by an AAC consultant. He had spastic quadriplegia and significant cognitive delays. He was living in a home for children with complex health care needs and multiple disabilities, although his family was very involved in his schooling and care.

ASSESSMENT OF COMMUNICATION SKILLS

The team working with Jacob to assess his communication system included his mother, special education teacher, instructional assistant, occupational therapist, physical therapist, and speech-language pathologist. They had formulated the following list of questions to discuss with the AAC consultant:

1. Is Jacob intentionally communicating?
2. If so, what level of symbolic representation is appropriate for choice making?
3. What format should his communication system follow?
4. What are some existing choices and preferences?
5. What behavioral signal should be used with the symbols?
6. Who will coordinate the efforts to establish the system?

These questions addressed only Jacob's skills and did not focus on the environments in which the skills were expressed nor the partners with whom he showed these skills.

Environment

Jacob's environment included several other children who were nonverbal, the teaching staff during the day, and caregivers after school and in the evening. He had little contact with peers without disabilities. He spent his mornings in a classroom that was part of the residential setting, and in the afternoon he went upstairs to his living quarters.

Communication Skills

Through interviews, observations, and elicited responses, a clearer picture of Jacob's skills emerged. In answer to the team's first question, it was clear that Jacob was intentionally trying to affect others with his limited repertoire of signals. For example, he gained attention by yelling, protested or rejected activities by crying and screaming, and requested things by gazing alternately at an object and at his partner. If the partner did not respond as he wished, Jacob persisted and continued alternating his gaze between the object and his partner, but not all partners recognized this signal. When he was satisfied with the partner's response, he stopped signaling. Although this showed intentionality, some of his partners still found it difficult to interpret his signals.

In answer to the second question, Jacob's symbolic skills were related to the here and now. He did not attend to pictures but enjoyed looking at objects and seemed to anticipate upcoming events based on the presentation of an object related to that event. For this reason, it was suggested that Jacob use objects to expand his communication.

The format of the communication system (question #3) needed to be informal at first. Jacob's partner would hold up two choices and wait for Jacob to look at his choice. This format was selected because Jacob could not reach out toward the choices. During the consultant's visit, Jacob made clear choices between milk and pudding using this system, so it was clearly a right-now system.

The system included interpretations of existing behaviors as well. If Jacob stared at the partner without looking at the objects, it would mean that he was "all done." Jacob had been using a tongue extension to request "more," but the occupational therapist and physical therapist suggested that another signal be selected to avoid reinforcing an abnormal reflex. It was decided that a vocalization that was already in his repertoire would be used to request "more." This was easily elicited during snack time. When he gazed at the pudding, he was given just a taste. The partner then waited for another signal from Jacob, holding the pudding-laden spoon where he could see it. He looked at the pudding, then looked at the aide, then looked back at the pudding, and then vocalized. The aide immediately gave him the pudding.

Jacob's preferences were easy to identify because he liked eating. The "drink" versus "cracker/cookie/pudding" choice gave him the opportunity to choose between two liked items. His family, caregivers at his residence, and team members at school decided to start with presenting choices during mealtimes.

Jacob's mother wanted to add choices for preferred activities. She and the school staff agreed that Jacob showed preferences for listening to music, watching television, and listening to stories in the library. They tried to come up with ideas about what visual representation meant "music," "television," and "read aloud" from Jacob's perspective. They decided to try two types of icons. First, a tape cassette, a television remote control, and a book were paired with the presentation of the respective choices. Many of his partners wanted him to be able to respond to pictures, so they decided to try an associative conditioning paradigm in which pictures of a cassette recorder, television, and book were placed right on these objects. Again, each picture was paired with the presentation of the activity.

Question #5 from the team concerned behavioral signals that would be interpreted. In addition to those described previously, the team decided to formalize the interpretation of his existing signals by agreeing on the following:

- Cooing vocalization = pleasure, enjoyment
- Yelling = displeasure
- Body tensing = anticipation of upcoming activity
- Calming/quieting = acceptance or anticipation

The team's last question to answer dealt with coordinating training and system adjustments. System adjustments included finding new communication environments, encouraging partners to provide new choices, and making sure symbols for choices were appropriate. Jacob's teacher felt she had the time and resources to do this; although, when Jacob made a transition out of her class, she would need to invest effort to smooth the way.

COMMUNICATION SKILLS 2 YEARS LATER

During the next 2 years Jacob continued to use the same communication system. Opportunities to communicate and activities remained the same for Jacob. For a short time, he attended a public school classroom, but he began to scream for extended periods of time at school and the team decided to return him to the classroom at the residential setting.

The caregivers at the residential setting were frustrated because Jacob screamed for much of the time that he was with them. The teaching staff at the residential setting also were concerned with the screaming that Jacob seemed to do for no reason. Once he began screaming, he was unable to relax and his body would arch into an abnormal reflex that was very painful.

After talking to the staff, it became apparent that Jacob screamed to communicate when other methods had been ignored, but because of Jacob's abnormal muscle tone, he was unable to relax once he became upset. The staff responded inconsistently to the screaming; some of them attempted to determine what Jacob wanted, and others would ignore him until he stopped screaming.

Jacob still used cooing, body tensing, yelling, and calming to communicate. He still indicated choices by gazing at the object that he wanted, and he still had the same likes (e.g., television, music, books). There were some differences, however, that gave some indication as to why the screaming was becoming a problem. Jacob's range of motion had decreased and it was more difficult for him to remain physically relaxed. He wanted to change position frequently and did not want to be in his wheelchair, and he seemed to become bored with activities that used to entertain him. Because of increased abnormal muscle tone, eating was more difficult for him than it had been previously. Eating, which had always been so reinforcing, was now a less-preferred activity.

Jacob was reassessed by the consultant and the other team members. He had learned to identify pictures and would gaze at a picture of a person or an activity that he wanted. Activities that he preferred now included outings to stores and taking walks around the neighborhood.

Reexamination of Communication Skills

A staff training was held that centered around Jacob. The focus of the training was to reexamine his communication skills, look at the possibility of using a picture communication system, identify events that preceded his screaming, and develop a consistent response to his screaming that would involve replacing the screaming with another form of communication. Because Jacob's behavior had become a problem for the entire staff, everyone who worked with Jacob attended the training.

The staff examined their feelings toward Jacob. They discussed the fact that Jacob was no longer responding to them affectionately and that he was moody and difficult. They resented the fact that he was demanding. The staff training included a discussion of how personnel interacted with Jacob. Some of them thought of Jacob as a very young child because they had been with him for several years. The new staff treated him as a 13-year-old, expecting behavior that was more mature. They realized that Jacob had changed both physically and emotionally during the preceding 2 years and that he had developed some new skills. They also discussed the fact that at school Jacob was given a wide range of choices that was not always available in the living unit.

Implementation of Communication System

The staff implemented several changes that were instrumental in decreasing the screaming. First, everyone responded to Jacob consistently when he began to yell by saying, "I know that you want something. I will try to help you, but you must relax so that I can understand what you are saying to me." A series of photographs was shown to Jacob one at a time, slowly crossing the midline from right to left. When he saw the photograph of the object or activity he wanted, he would continue looking at that photograph as it moved in front of him. Only photographs of items or activities that were available to him were shown. If he continued to get upset, the partner would repeat, "I am trying to help. Let's get you relaxed so I can understand you."

The staff began talking to Jacob more often, offering explanations prior to a change in activity. Jacob spent more time with the staff when he was on the living unit and he began spending minimal time in his room alone. The staff began to treat him as an older child, making reasonable demands, including that he wait to have his requests met, and respecting Jacob's right to refuse activities or items. These changes in the partners' communication style and the introduction of photographs into Jacob's system had a dramatic effect on his behavior. The screaming decreased and was no longer identified as a problem behavior. Jacob's ability to communicate successfully increased as his partners used the photographs consistently.

CHAPTER 17

Ronnie

Tom Weddle

NAME: Ronnie
AGE: 14 Years
TEACHER: Tom
CONSULTANTS: Tom Weddle and Jacqueline Weddle
SYSTEM: A communication book containing photographs of Ronnie's daily sequence of activities and choices he could make during each activity

Ronnie is a 14-year-old boy of medium height and build who has a diagnosis of pervasive developmental disorder–NOS (not otherwise specified). Ronnie displays many characteristics associated with this diagnosis, such as insistence on rigid routines, perseverative types of play, and limited language and communicative skills. In addition, Ronnie loves to wrestle and interact physically through hugs and play with others.

This chapter is adapted from an article by Weddle, T., & Weddle, J. (1991). Communication: A tool for choice and change. *TASH Newsletter*, *17*(1), 1, 3; adapted by permission of The Association for Persons with Severe Handicaps.

ASSESSMENT FOR COMMUNICATION PLANNING

Assessment with Ronnie was done primarily through observation and interview with his parents and the school staff who worked with him daily. As reported, Ronnie was independent in many domestic skills, such as dressing, snack preparation, and hygiene, but was relatively unskilled socially, communicatively, and vocationally. He had few leisure skills and interests and rarely occupied his own time independently. Most often he insisted that someone be with him and attend to him at all times.

Communicatively, Ronnie used a few signs and words, vocalized in conjunction with pointing and gesturing, and led others to items of interest, but he was generally unable to express his choices and needs efficiently and flexibly. He performed most verbal one- to two-step requests given within a familiar context or routine, but when he was excited or angry, his ability to respond appropriately to verbal direction decreased dramatically. At such times, Ronnie would have tantrums for periods up to 30 minutes. He would scream, hit himself or others, or throw chairs or other items until he was restrained, placed in secluded time-out, and medicated.

Ronnie attended a private school for children with developmental disabilities. The school provided excellent community and recreational programming for the children it served (e.g., daily community outings to stores and fast-food outlets, swimming, horseback riding). But the classrooms were small (10 feet × 12 feet) and there were six children in Ronnie's classroom, all of whom were diagnosed as autistic. This overcrowding was an issue for the staff as well as the students. Ronnie's behavior had escalated to two tantrums a day and their severity had changed such that staff were unable to control his outbursts without emergency help from trained ancillary staff who were on call for emergency interventions throughout the school. The staff reported that they were no longer able to provide effective educational programming because of the overall intensity of Ronnie's disruptive behaviors.

The consultants' initial step was to gain some insight into the communicative function of these behaviors. Ronnie's behaviors were charted for a period of 2 weeks using a modified version of a scatter-plot analysis (Touchette et al., 1985) in order to determine the pertinent antecedent events and circumstances of his disruptive behaviors. The consultants were specifically looking for trends and patterns in both his responses and the circumstances in which they occurred.

An analysis of the data indicated that the behaviors were being used across all environments, people, and activities, but the intensity and frequency of the behaviors varied depending on the degree of Ronnie's frustration and his physical state. The behaviors were being used generally to protest change in routine, to reject activities or items offered, and to request social attention or desired items from others. If he was content (had just had a lot of one-to-one attention) or his needs could be guessed and satisfied quickly, the frequency of the behaviors was low and the intensity did not escalate. He might toss one item to the floor or tip his chair over and then allow himself to be redirected to an activity or item of choice. If he was not content or his needs could not be met quickly, the frequency of his behaviors was high and the intensity would escalate quickly. He would not be able to be redirected to an activity and suddenly would strike out or attack a person or item, such as a television, in the room. Those working with Ronnie were unable to communicate efficiently and effectively with him at all times, but communication was especially difficult and hazardous during these disruptive episodes. As his problem behavior escalated, he no longer attended to requests or possible options for meeting his needs. As a result, it was often necessary to use physical restraint and time-out to protect Ronnie and the other people in his environment. Physical restraint and time-out angered Ronnie and escalated the intensity of his physically aggressive and self-abusive behaviors.

Illustrative of this sequence was his typical behavior while waiting in line to order fast food. Ronnie was very impatient when waiting in a line to be served. There was no clear way to communicate to Ronnie that he needed to wait just a few minutes to order his food and wait for it to be prepared. He wanted his food immediately and would reach over the fast-food counter to grab it or throw a tray. These behaviors often resulted in Ronnie being physically removed from the restaurant. He would then begin to hit others, grab and throw any objects that he could reach, kick, fall to the floor, wet his pants, hit himself, and rip his clothing.

Through structured activities such as choice making during snack and leisure, it was determined that Ronnie was able to use photographs or line drawings functionally to represent items, people, and activities symbolically. He did not tolerate delay or uncertainty when he wanted something. In addition, his comprehension dropped precipitously when he was stressed. No mode of communication provided him with the support he needed to communicate at such times. It was imperative that any system the staff attempted to implement feature speed and clarity of communication among its qualities. Color photographs of the actual people, items, and activities that comprised Ronnie's days were used, so that it would be easier for Ronnie and everyone involved in his day to understand quickly and easily the messages the photographs represented.

The primary goal of the intervention was to provide Ronnie with a means for lessening his anxiety about change and expectations and for expressing his needs appropriately. Operationally, this goal meant that he and the primary people in his world would be trained in the use of a shared and mutually acceptable and comprehensible system for communication. The secondary goal would be to decrease Ronnie's dependence on, but not his interest in, one-to-one attention from favorite people.

THE COMMUNICATION SYSTEM

A communication book was made containing the necessary photographs and was updated daily to reflect each day's particular sequence of activities and the items and people who would be available. The variety and number of photographs grew as Ronnie showed the team more of his interests and abilities. Photographs needed in specific settings for choice making, such as leisure time, were placed in a clear plastic sheet near him.

Ronnie's classroom was providing an age-appropriate, community-referenced, functional curriculum with an emphasis placed on structured choice making. The content of the classroom program was not an issue, but Ronnie's awareness of activity sequence and choice making within activities was an issue. Ronnie's behaviors would be more appropriate if he were provided with continuous and clear information about daily routines and if he were given easy and immediate access to an appropriate means for communicating his needs.

How can appropriate educational programming be provided by enhancing a child's awareness of daily activities, sequence, and opportunities for choice? The first task was to make Ronnie aware of the daily routine and the choices available to him during his day. This was done by going over the photographs of his daily activities with him as soon as he entered the classroom in the morning and sat at his desk. Then, as a classroom group lesson, the day's activities were rehearsed using photographs. Each task or activity was displayed in sequence on a portable, wipe-off board. Ronnie indicated his awareness and understanding of the photographs by pointing, categorizing, signing, and occasionally verbalizing. His tolerance for such group activities was increased by his enjoyment of the signing and socializing done to help pace the content of the lesson.

Each community outing was rehearsed with a group lesson about the sequence of the coming events, such as driving or walking to a fast-food outlet, ordering and eating, and walking or driving back. Choices were given based on student preferences. Money and augmentative communication aids were distributed. The emphasis of the group activity was always on the sequence of events and the choices that were available. This group training augmented the use of a portable communication book containing the day's photographs. This book always accompanied Ronnie and was a mutually shared, easily obtained, and readily comprehensible communicative mode for Ronnie and those communicating with him.

The book was used instructionally to provide Ronnie with information about transitions and choices during the course of the day. Whenever a transition occurred, Ronnie was given verbal direction to look at and point to a photograph of himself participating in that activity. Then he was given verbal and gestural input, such as, "Look, Ronnie, we're going to McDonald's." The book was carried by staff working with Ronnie (at Ronnie's insistence), but it was shared with Ronnie whenever he chose to use it. He used the photographs to make structured choices based on preferences at certain times of the day (community training), but was not required to use the photographs to satisfy primary needs, such as water or bathroom.

How can the use of augmentative modes of communication be encouraged with an individual whose tendency is to react physically and disruptively when his or her needs are not met? Ronnie and his teachers used the photographs as visible referents whenever possible while communicating. Ronnie's communicative use of the photographs was honored whenever possible. This mutual sharing and honoring of the communicative content of the photographs encouraged and fostered the development of two-way communication. Ronnie was more apt to use the photographs when his teachers consistently modeled the appropriate use of the photographs and when use of the photographs led to reinforcing consequences. The advantage of mutually utilizing the same mode was illustrated most clearly when Ronnie refused to make a transition to an activity or to wait for a desired item. At such times, Ronnie would take or be given the book. If he could not find a photograph that expressed his need, he was asked to show what he wanted. Negotiations with Ronnie often proceeded in the following manner:

1. A photograph of the activity being requested would be shown to Ronnie.
2. Ronnie would use the photographs or gesturally show what he wanted to do or get.
3. If his needs could be honored, this was done.
4. If he wished an activity or item that was not scheduled for that time, the photograph of the activity being requested would be shown to him again and an instructor would say, "Look, Ronnie, first you do this."

5. Then the instructor would point to the photograph of the activity or item Ronnie wished and would say, "Then you do or get this!"
6. This sequence would be rehearsed with Ronnie to ensure that he comprehended the message by having him point to the photographs in sequence while the instructor verbally labeled and/or pointed with him.

If the instructor did not force the issue (i.e., use physical prompts), Ronnie did not become aggressive. He occasionally fell to the floor but generally followed along after a few seconds. If he consistently refused to make a transition to a particular activity, the activity or demand would be analyzed and modified to fit Ronnie's tolerance or interests.

How can augmentative modes of communication be used to encourage and maintain independent activity for a child who demands and invariably gets adult attention through his or her disruptive behaviors? The secondary goal of lessening Ronnie's dependence on others was addressed during leisure time and capitalized on Ronnie's growing communicative ability. During leisure time Ronnie sat at a table in an area of the room containing low, open storage shelves on which were kept the items and activities (e.g., magazines, catalogs, a variety of manipulatives with which he would build block structures) that Ronnie enjoyed. Photographs of Ronnie's teachers, favorite activities, and personal needs were placed on this table for him to use as he wished. Initially, a teacher would sit with Ronnie and immediately respond to his use of the photographs by getting the item he desired or making it possible for him to obtain it himself. Delay of response and independence were gradually worked on by having Ronnie's teacher get up and attend to other students or activities around the area of Ronnie's table. If Ronnie gesturally or vocally indicated a need for attention or activity, he was encouraged to use his photographs or signs to make his request more specific. For example, when staff members were standing nearby, if Ronnie pointed to a photograph of a particular staff member, that person would go over to Ronnie's table and say, "Hi, Ronnie. What do you want?" Ronnie usually would point to a chair and sign SIT or he would point to a photograph of a particular item that he wanted. Eventually, it was possible for staff to attend to other tasks and children while Ronnie attended to his interests for 15–30 minutes. As his independence with and interest in leisure activities, such as magazines and electronic games, increased, it became possible to build in longer delays by telling and showing Ronnie that the teachers were busy. For example, when Ronnie was involved in a leisure activity, his teacher would begin attending to other children or doing chores around the room. Then, when Ronnie indicated a need for attention or help, the teacher would respond by saying, "Hi, Ronnie, I'm busy. You need to wait." She would then finish whatever she was doing before attending to Ronnie's need. If he engaged in disruptive behavior, such as lifting the table, throwing an item, or falling to the floor, he was attended to by having him put things back in order and having him tell what he wanted in a more appropriate communicative manner, such as gesturing or using his photographs. His instructors were cautious not to trigger explosive behaviors by slowly lengthening the amount of time that Ronnie would tolerate sitting and being engaged in independent activity. This behavior was carefully shaped by requiring more of Ronnie in terms of appropriate communication and patience and by exposing him to more and more activities in the classroom and the community to increase his leisure options and to minimize his boredom.

FUTURE DIRECTIONS WITH THE SYSTEM

Ronnie's range of communicative behaviors (e.g., gesturing, vocalizing, signing, using photographs) provided him with a potentially adequate system for communicating basic needs, but his discomfort with change in routine or environment often overwhelmed his ability to use appropriate forms of communication.

For example, a trip to Disneyland was a near disaster when Ronnie's excitement about the rides overwhelmed his patience for waiting in lines with or without a photograph. He was able to wait for a few minutes in the line for Space Mountain, but soon began to push his partner from behind and hit him intermittently on the head when they did not move through the crowd to get nearer to the front of the line. Ronnie and his partner were able to get to the front of the line quickly when people moved out of their way to avoid contact with a rather physically insistent Ronnie.

A wonderful example of his need for routine and his successful use of communication with photographs, once it was established, occurred at home. Ronnie loved putting the laundry in the dryer and was used to doing this chore every night after dinner. One evening, his parents were involved with friends and did not help Ronnie do his nighttime chore. Ronnie became agitated and ran to his room. His parents followed, fearing the worst, only to find Ronnie searching frantically through his belongings. He pulled out his communication book, opened it to the picture of laundry, and handed it to his mother. She was quite relieved and quickly followed through on Ronnie's request.

Naturally, a goal for the next school year was to promote more spontaneity and independence in Ronnie's use of the photographs across a greater variety of settings.

SUMMARY

The consultants worked with Ronnie and the classroom staff from January through June of the school year. Training with the photographs began immediately, but it took approximately 1 month before all the photographs needed to sequence his day were developed. During those 6 months, the frequency of his tantrums decreased from two times daily to approximately one time per week. During the last 3 months of the consultant's involvement, Ronnie's disruptive behaviors averaged 1–2 minutes and only rarely involved hitting himself or others. By June, Ronnie was sitting without one-to-one attention in the leisure setting for 5–30 minutes depending on his physical state, the amount of one-to-one attention he had experienced already, and his motivation for the activity.

Ronnie still fell back on his physical "language" when he was in an unfamiliar environment without established routines, when his needs could not be met, or when there was a sudden change in routine. Nevertheless, the intensity and frequency of the maladaptive behaviors were much reduced when he had readily comprehensible and accessible communicative options and a receptive listening audience.

Fortunately, Ronnie's faith in photographs increased to the point that he was able to wait in a fast-food line if he was allowed to hold a photograph of the food item that he was going to order. The photograph served to reassure Ronnie that having to wait did not mean that he was being denied his food.

The strategies utilized for Ronnie (i.e., teaching an awareness of routine and providing comprehensible, accessible, and preferred communicative options) are particularly pertinent to and effective for children who have language disabilities and who react unpredictably and volatilely to change in routine or environment.

Chapter 18

Lessons Learned

In *Augmentative and Alternative Communication Systems for Persons with Moderate and Severe Disabilities* (Baumgart, Johnson, & Helmstetter, 1990), the augmentative communication needs and systems of many individuals whose stories are not presented in this book were discussed. In this chapter, information is reviewed and updated on a few of the individuals who were introduced in the previous book. Such information includes communication systems originally recommended, how those recommendations were implemented, and how the systems changed in expected or unexpected ways. In looking at this updated information, it is hypothesized that pertinent lessons can be extracted to guide partners in future decisions.

JESSE

Overview

Jesse was 21 years old and in the last year of his school program when his consultant, Dr. Helmstetter, first met him. Jesse's school records indicated that he had autistic-like tendencies and he was categorized as having mental retardation requiring him to need extensive to pervasive support. Although his comprehension of language was good, Jesse had no recognizable means to communicate expressively. Jesse's teacher requested help from Dr. Helmstetter because of Jesse's problem behaviors, which included prolonged bouts of screaming, aggression toward others, destruction of materials, running from the classroom, and self-abuse.

The Initially Recommended System

Initially, some of Jesse's existing gestures were interpreted as communicative requests for highly preferred objects (e.g., touching his cheek as a request for skin lotion, placing his hand to his mouth to request water) or actions (e.g., touching his groin to request going to the bathroom). After the gestures were established, Jesse was required to vocalize using a sound that was already in his repertoire (e.g., "wah" as an approximation for "water") in addition to using a gesture. Also, his teachers began to shape his gestures to resemble American Sign Language forms.

After 24 weeks of instruction, Jesse was appropriately initiating 43 vocalization/sign/gesture combinations to request objects, people, and actions in school and community settings. His problem behaviors had diminished significantly and occurred mostly in situations in which his partner was unable to respond appropriately to his attempts to communicate.

Changes Resulting from the System

Success with this first system did not last long. After graduation from high school, Jesse continued to reside in a small group home and began to attend a sheltered workshop. The people in both his work and living settings attempted to reduce his problem behavior by manipulating contingencies—a system that had proved ineffective in the past at school and at the group home. When this book was written, Jesse had high rates of problem behavior and he no longer used gestures, signs, or vocalizations to communicate.

Lessons to Be Learned

The staff working with Jesse have learned the following lessons:

1. It is important that the people and agencies in Jesse's life work together. This is particularly crucial during the transition from high school to adult residential and work programs. In Jesse's case, the school staff had worked for years prior to graduation with residential staff members to find an effective intervention for the problem behavior. The residential program staff, however, had not encountered sufficient information or training on alternative approaches to behavior problems and had not begun to reexamine or change their values and practices toward Jesse and his behavior. The staff were convinced that all that was needed was more consistency in the implementation of the contingency program for behavior reduction at school and the group home.
2. Another issue was the failure to establish a productive interagency collaborative relationship. While school and residential staff met and discussed issues, there was competition as to who was in charge of Jesse and who was right. Healthy interagency relationships are characterized by a lack of such territorial issues and a trusting relationship among participants. In Jesse's situation, the entities involved had not taken the time to build a more positive relationship that ultimately would have benefited Jesse.

KYLE

Overview

Kyle was 7 years old and attending his neighborhood elementary school in a rural town (population 290) as his communication system was developed. When this book was written, he was residing with his family in the same town and attending the neighborhood junior high school.

The Initially Recommended System

A 3-inch × 5-inch communication binder with miniature representations of choices for activities throughout Kyle's day was developed. Line drawings also were included to represent "no" and "drink." In addition to using already existing vocalizations and gestures, Kyle needed prompts to use his binder to communicate his needs. A schedule board also was developed using the same type of symbols.

Changes Resulting from the System

Kyle's communication system had changed in complex ways. The most obvious is that the symbol form became different: Photographs have been substituted for the miniatures and line drawings. This resulted from a change in attitude about how to use the communication board. Kyle had been using the miniatures and line drawings to request, a powerful communicative function. A new speech-language pathologist was assigned to Kyle's school, but she had not encountered the training needed to continue Kyle's communication system. She believed Kyle was not ready to communicate until he could match identical miniatures or point to a miniature upon request. By having him use his system in this manner, she changed the communicative purpose of the system. She also changed the communication environment by having Kyle use the system in a pull-out therapy session rather than in the integrated setting in which he had been using it successfully. Kyle then began to resist using the system.

The family and Kyle's teaching aide, who both were familiar with the success of the original system, decided to try using photographs as a new symbol set. They thought that perhaps new symbols would motivate Kyle to use the system again. Unfortunately, the photographs were used only as a means for Kyle to respond to the questions of others; that is, during lunch his partners worked to teach him to point to food items that they verbally labeled (e.g., "Show me macaroni"). This strategy was unsuccessful, and Kyle began to throw the photographs and resist the task. The communication system was not reintroduced.

Another change that affected Kyle's ability to communicate was that he had a new teacher. The teacher assigned Kyle a teaching aide for instruction. His instructional programs were written by a resource room teacher in the building and were carried out by the teaching aide. This resource teacher designed his learning tasks following a developmental, rather than functional, model. The focus was on foundation skills, at the expense of learning relevant skills for the social environment. Kyle's ability to communicate age-appropriate needs was severely hindered.

Kyle's parents have stayed very involved with Kyle and his communication, but they have not been able to influence the program as much as they would like. They have been successful in having Kyle included in some general education activities, such as lunch and physical education, but they feel frustrated with their level of input to the team.

Lessons to Be Learned

The team members working with Kyle have learned the following lessons:

1. A change in partners is a potential weak point for systems, a time when breakdown is most likely. New partners come with new attitudes about communication, even if those partners come from the same facility. Attitudes are carefully constructed based on experience. Experience must include training and collaboration with former partners. Without transition collaboration between partners, communication systems are destined to fail.
2. Without being taught to provide functional opportunities, many partners resort to using communication only for labeling. Labeling is not as powerful as requesting. It puts the individual in the role of a responder as opposed to that of

an initiator. In other words, communication initiation is given over to the adult, who directs the interaction by asking questions. The individual must demonstrate knowledge to that partner—knowledge that already is shared, not new. This is a much weaker function for communication than requesting, and it affords the individual little control over the actions of others.

ERNIE

Overview

Ernie, at the age of 37, lived in an intermediate care facility for people with mental disabilities who were making transitions out of state institutions. The team's main concern was that he did not initiate appropriate interactions with others; he usually used yelling and hitting to express protests.

The Initially Recommended System

The system developed for Ernie was a 3-inch × 5-inch communication binder with one photograph. The system fit in the back pocket of his pants and was used to purchase a beverage at a fast-food restaurant. Later, a photograph representing a restroom was added so Ernie could inform people he was going to the restroom. The booklet was expanded further with line drawings representing other needs and preferences that he could request.

Changes Resulting from the System

After Ernie had used his system for about 1 year, a statewide policy change resulted in his moving from a community-based day program to a segregated day center for adults. As noted in the original case description, the communication booklet was not seen as necessary in Ernie's new day program. In addition, during the ensuing 5 years, the facility had many staff transitions and three different executive directors.

In the transition to the segregated program with new staff, Ernie's yelling and hitting behaviors recurred and were viewed as problematic and inappropriate. At this same time, the agency was expanding and building new homes. As sometimes happens, energy and time were directed toward reorganization and expansion rather than Ernie and his communication needs.

More recently, the expansion and turnover in staff has slowed and a new director has been in place for 2 years. In the last year, the staff have gained a new perspective on Ernie as a communicator. The new director, who has a background in special education as well as experience in community living, shared the following perspectives on Ernie's behaviors:

> It has taken us awhile to realize that Ernie is not just like us in what he wants to do and how he will say things to us. Ernie likes to spend time alone and in quiet situations and we have had to realize that a Friday night out on the town may be a staff request more than a request on Ernie's part. We have done more to look at what Ernie likes and not just expect him to like what is fun for most people.
>
> Another thing we have planned for is to listen to Ernie when he says he doesn't like something. This is hard because he is not able to tell us in advance what he likes, for example, whether he wants to go to the football game. We have learned to plan staffing so if he says at the entrance (by acting upset and pushing away from the entrance) that he doesn't want to go in, we are ready to honor this and take him back home. In the past we weren't ready to have him say no and so his behavior was a problem. Now, we just need to be ready for last-minute changes and we now plan for these.

This discussion with the executive director and other staff who work with Ernie was a positive change in how his behaviors were viewed. His behaviors are now seen as communication and staff interpret for others what his behaviors mean. In Ernie's current situation, his behaviors constitute his communication system, which seems to be a satisfactory outcome.

Lessons to Be Learned

The team members working with Ernie have learned the following lessons:

1. Transitions were the weakest point in the structure of social events surrounding carefully constructed communication systems. Careful collaborative training during the transition to the new living environment might have influenced the attitudes and beliefs of the new partners.
2. A system that works, even though it is not ideal, is far better than no system at all.

SUMMARY OF LESSONS LEARNED

The communication issues for Jesse, Kyle, and Ernie are summarized in Table 18.1. Using the Sociocommunicative Filter Model, many of these problems, or barriers, were predictable. By definition, a change in the individual's living, educational, or vocational placement leads to changes in communication partners. With a change in partners comes new attitudes toward the individual's abilities and toward augmenting communication. The only answer is to advocate for making better transitions and training. This is certainly not a new idea. It is, certainly, a significant, continuing barrier to effective communication.

What happened with these individuals also reflects barriers resulting from the collaborative process. In some cases, such a process was never established. In others, the efforts to maintain the process were not continued as team members changed positions and as new people joined the team. Ongoing efforts to collaborate on transitions not only between settings but also within the same setting with new partners need to be prioritized in order to make communication successful.

Many researchers and authors have provided detailed descriptions of successful transitions. Transitions work when staff members are given the time by administration to collaborate, when at least one staff member from each setting is determined enough to make sure information is passed along, when team members

Table 18.1. Summary of lessons learned

Communication issues	Jesse	Kyle	Ernie
Living environment changed	X		X
Daytime environment changed	X	X	X
Staff changed	X	X	X
Staff attitudes changed	X	X	X
Administrative barriers (transitions)	X	X	X
Staff not trained to use or be aware of communication system	X	X	X
Team collaboration not established	X	X	X
Partners not consistent in responding to communication	X	X	X
Vocabulary in system not changed	X	X	X

feel ownership and respect for their opinions as legitimate contributions, and when time is given for attitudes to be influenced by education and training.

Chapter 5 on implementation discussed ways in which new staff can be trained to use an augmented system with an individual. The stories presented in this chapter reinforce the idea of using videotapes. If staff from two facilities only have time to talk on the telephone, the videotape can provide an excellent substitute for live modeling of the system.

Other predictable problems emanate from the changes in the individual's skills over time. It is clear that flexibility is key to having a generative communication system that satisfies the constantly changing needs of the individual. Flexibility is possible when staff have the time to prepare new symbols, program new messages, and talk with all communication partners to ascertain any new vocabulary needs. In other words, if they are given time and encouragement, communication partners can be responsive to the individual's changing needs.

Change is the essence of communication. For example, people do not use the same phrases to describe something they really like now as they did when they were 5 years younger. People do not have the same things to say about familiar topics (e.g., foods, television shows, favorite activities) as they did yesterday, last month, or last year. People have new friends and go to new places and events. A communication system should be a constantly evolving system that reflects current needs and interests. Only then can it remain a seminal tool for communicative interactions. It is the AAC consultant's job to ensure that the individual's right to communicate and right to be seen as a legitimate communicator are not compromised by external barriers.

Section VI

APPENDICES

APPENDIX A

Interview Approach to a Functional Analysis of Problem Behavior

Structured interviews can be used with someone knowledgeable about an individual's behavior in order to learn about the behavior and the conditions in which it occurs. The interview questions in this appendix cover a range of factors that are critical to a functional analysis of problem behavior.

INFORMATION ABOUT THE BEHAVIOR OF CONCERN

1. Describe what the behavior looks like.
2. Describe how much the behavior occurs (e.g., number of times per day, length of each occurrence, intensity of behavior)
3. Describe any other problem behaviors that might occur just before, just after, or at the same time as the behavior of concern.
4. If behavior escalates over time, describe the escalation so that one could predict that the problem behavior would occur.
5. Determine at what point in the individual's life the behavior began.
6. Determine whether the behavior changed over time since it began and describe how it changed.

HEALTH FACTORS

1. Note the following about medications:

   - Name of medication, time given, amount of each dose, and possible side effects
   - Drug interactions that might occur, including the drug combinations and the possible side effects of the particular drug combination

2. Make note of any other conditions that might affect behavior:

   - **Medication:** Side effects of seizure medications and decongestants include hyperactivity; irritability; lethargy; and, rarely, hallucinations (Gourash, 1986). Antiasthmatic drugs containing theophylline can cause sleep disturbance, restlessness, irritability, and depressed mood (Gourash, 1986). Corticosteriods (used to treat asthma and arthritis) can cause psychotic symptoms (Gourash, 1986). Other side effects of various medications include drowsiness, lethargy, poor coordination, dizziness, thirst, frequent urination, blurred vision, eye pressure, nystagmus, itchy or tingling skin, and tics (e.g., winks, grimaces, repeatedly touching things, sniffs).
   - **Syndromes and diseases:** Some conditions are associated with higher-than-usual rates of problem behavior. *Lesch-Nyhan disease*: Individuals chew their own lips and fingers until there is tissue damage or amputation. *Cornelia de Lange syndrome*: Individuals appear predisposed to self-mutilation. *Rett syndrome*: Individuals exhibit, among other things, repetitive hand washing, hand wringing, hand clapping, and hand mouthing. *Tourette syndrome*: Individuals show involuntary twitching and other motor movements and uncontrollable vocalization. *Prader-Willi syndrome*: Individuals may experience insatiable appetites that can lead to foraging for food. *Fragile X syndrome*: Individuals may be temperamentally difficult, displaying tantrums, irritability, hyperactivity, repetitive speech and behavior, and aggression.
   - **Ear infection** can cause odor, ear rubbing, and head hitting.
   - **Glaucoma or other severe visual problems** can cause eye poking or pressing.
   - **Hearing or vision loss** can lead to problem behaviors used to avoid auditory or visual tasks that have become difficult to perform.
   - **Skin disease** can cause severe scratching or picking.
   - **Allergies** can cause restlessness, rubbing and scratching, irritability, lethargy, crying, whining, and tantrums.
   - **Weakness or poor stamina** may result in problem behaviors to avoid physical tasks.
   - **Inappropriate diet** may affect activity level and/or allergies.
   - **Sickness** can lead to pain, nausea, headaches, crying, whining, and/or tantrums.
   - **Thyroid gland** problems can cause such behavioral changes as lethargy, anxiety, and/or psychotic behavior (e.g., hallucinations) (Gourash, 1986).
   - **Seizures** can be in the form of motor activity or behavioral outbursts (e.g., repetitive mouth movements, jumping out of one's seat, aggression, yelling) or lapses in attention.

- **Headaches** can lead to self-injury (e.g., head hitting), crying, whining, having tantrums, and/or inattention.
- **Toothaches and decay** can cause unusual oral behavior (e.g., sucking on objects), irritability, crying, whining, and displaying tantrums.
- **Gastroesophageal reflux** is the abnormal regurgitation of gastric contents into the esophagus, often due to anatomical abnormalities (Gourash, 1986). This complication may exist in people who frequently vomit or ruminate.
- **Urinary tract infection** can lead to constant urinary dribbling and/or frequent urination.
- **Diabetes mellitis** is the inability to maintain normal blood sugar levels. In insulin-dependent diabetes, symptoms of hypoglycemia (which could be caused, for example, by not having meals or snacks on schedule) are excessive sweating, faintness, confusion, paleness, nervousness, irritability, headache, nausea, and fatigue. Treatment consists of 10 grams of a quick-acting carbohydrate. Symptoms of hyperglycemia are thirst, increased urination, increased appetite, weakness, itching, dry skin, and blurred vision. Treatment consists of insulin provided by a physician.

QUALITY OF LIFE

Determine to what degree the individual is

1. Provided learning opportunities based on abilities and interests.
2. Treated with dignity and respect.
3. Involved in friendships and long-lasting relationships.
4. Involved in choices, self-determination, and control over his or her life.
5. Participating in settings with peers without disabilities.
6. Feeling safe and healthy.

COMMUNICATION

Answer the following questions:

1. How does the individual usually communicate?
2. What can she or he communicate to you?
3. How do you communicate to her or him?
4. What can she or he understand (comprehension)?
5. What is a typical day like? Describe the events of such a day, indicating time and activity (e.g., 8:30: arrives in homeroom). Include each daily activity, writing down the following information about the problem behavior:

   - Time
   - Context (partner, location, activity, what is said and done)
   - Child's signal
   - Partner's response
   - Function

   When describing each daily activity, also indicate whether the problem behavior does *not* occur during part or all of the activity and the context in which the behavior is not occurring.

SETTING EVENT CHECKLIST

Check any of the following events that occurred last evening (P.M.) or this morning (A.M.):

	•A.M.	P.M.
Was individual informed of something unusually disappointing?	____	____
Was individual refused some requested object or activity?	____	____
Did individual fight, argue, or have negative interaction(s)?	____	____
Was the individual disciplined or reprimanded? Was behavior or disciplinary action atypical?	____	____
Was the individual hurried or rushed more than usual?	____	____
Was the individual's sleep pattern (including duration) unusual?	____	____
Was the individual under the care of someone new? Was a favorite caregiver absent?	____	____
Did the individual experience other major changes in the living environment?	____	____
Did individual learn about visit or vacation with family or friends (will or will not occur)?	____	____
Did visitors arrive or fail to arrive?	____	____
Were medications changed or missed?	____	____
Does the individual have her menstrual period?	____	____
Did individual appear excessively tired or lethargic?	____	____
Did individual appear excessively agitated?	____	____
Did individual appear to be in a bad mood?	____	____
Did individual appear or complain of being ill?	____	____

Figure A.1. Setting Event Checklist. (Adapted from Gardner, W.I., Cole, C.L., Davidson, D.P., & Karan, O.C. [1986]. Reducing aggression in individuals with developmental disabilities: An expanded stimulus control, assessment, and intervention model. *Education and Training of the Mentally Retarded*, *21*[1], 7; adapted by permission.)

6. What communication symbols can/could she or he use—verbal words, written words, manual signs, line drawings, photographs, or part or all of actual objects?

SENSORY INPUT

Determine whether the behavior is an attempt to obtain desired sensory stimulation, and, if so, in which modality (e.g., auditory, visual, tactile, kinesthetic, olfactory, gustatory)?

DISTANT EVENTS

Determine whether events elsewhere could influence behavior (e.g., something at home influences behavior at school). Figure A.1 may be helpful in making this determination.

Immediate Events

Answer the following questions:

1. Are there particular places where the behavior is more likely to occur?
2. Are there certain *physical aspects* (e.g., noise, temperature, lighting, novelty) of these places that might cause the behavior?
3. Are there certain *social aspects* (e.g., presence of teacher, other adult, or peer who is disliked; size of group; crowdedness of the setting; types and amounts of interactions that occur) of these places that might cause the behavior?
4. Are there particular *curricular or instructional aspects* (e.g., dislikes the task, material, or activity [indicate why]; does not acquire sufficient reinforcement [indicate why]; cues, prompts, or correction procedures are aversive or confusing [indicate why]; task is too difficult or boring [indicate why]; task taxes visual or auditory limits; pacing or duration of activity is disliked; dislikes format [e.g., sitting, standing, active, passive, repetitive, changing]; tasks seem meaningless) that occur that might cause the behavior?
5. Are there any particular places where the behavior is *un*likely to occur in terms of physical settings, activities, and people present?
6. Does the behavior occur during transition times?
7. What typically occurs immediately after the behavior?

OTHER INFORMATION

Answer the following questions:

1. What interventions have been tried, and what was the outcome of each?
2. If you could structure the day so that the problem behavior would not occur, how would that day unfold?
3. What does the individual like the most?
4. What does she or he like the least?

APPENDIX B

Checklists for Assessing Partners and Environments

This appendix contains the following checklists for assessing the interactions of communication partners and the environments in which communication interactions are likely to be facilitated:

1. Overall Checklist for Assessing Partners and Environments
2. Assessing Peer Participation Patterns
3. Assessing the Individual's Daily Routines
4. Determining Opportunities and Barriers
5. Choosing Roles in the Assessment Process
6. Assessing Interactional Styles of Partners
7. Self-Rating Partner Interaction Styles (Self-Rating Scale for Young Children [Johnson, 1989])

Readers are granted permission to photocopy and/or adapt these checklists for educational or clinical purposes.

OVERALL CHECKLIST FOR ASSESSING PARTNERS AND ENVIRONMENTS

Target individual: ______________________________

Assessment period dates: ______________________________

Completed date: ________________

_____ Assess peer participation patterns

_____ Assess the individual's daily routines

  _____ Partners: Parents

  _____ Partner: Teacher

  _____ Partner: Aide

  _____ Partners: Specialists

  _____ Other partners

_____ Determine opportunities and barriers

_____ Choose roles in the assessment

_____ Assess interactional styles of partners

_____ Perform self-rating of partner interaction styles

ASSESSING PEER PARTICIPATION PATTERNS

Target individual: ______________________________

Settings/times of day: ______________________________

____

____

1. In what ways do peers participate in daily events:
   - Do they initiate activities? If so, describe:
   - Do they have responsibilities for certain aspects of an activity? If so, describe:
   - Do they work individually or cooperatively? Describe:
2. What types of communication are used during the activity?
   - Do they give instructions? If so, describe:
   - Do they ask for information, assistance, or particular items? If so, describe:
   - Do they have choices? If so, describe:
   - Do they refuse to participate? Is this appropriate? Describe:
   - Do they express their pleasure or displeasure with the activity? If so, describe:

(continued)

Assessing the Individual's Daily Routines. *(continued)*

ASSESSING THE INDIVIDUAL'S DAILY ROUTINES

Target individual: ______________________________

Partner(s): ______________________________

Instructions: Please fill out the schedule below for the time you spend with the individual named above. Specify the general activity and the usual sequence of events within that activity (e.g., snack: set table, make food/drink choices, eat, clean up).
Return this form to ______________________.

Time	Event/activity

(continued)

Assessing the Individual's Daily Routines. *(continued)*

ASSESSING THE INDIVIDUAL'S DAILY ROUTINES

Target individual: ____

Instructions: Compile all the schedules and combine the data on the chart below.
Return this form to ____________________________________.

Time	Setting/who	Setting/who	Setting/who

(continued)

Assessing the Individual's Daily Routines. *(continued)*

ASSESSING THE INDIVIDUAL'S DAILY ROUTINES

1. Which activities seem to go well? In which activities does the individual get involved and show enjoyment?

2. Does the individual express a choice in these activities? What are the choices?

3. In which activities could the individual express a choice and what would be the choices?

4. In which activities is the individual independent?

5. In which other activities could the individual be independent?

6. Is there a rationale for the sequence of behaviors within a specific activity?

7. Are there certain activities or settings in which the individual communicates more or less?

8. Are there certain partners with whom the individual communicates more or less?

DETERMINING OPPORTUNITIES AND BARRIERS

Target individual: ______________________________

Person completing form: ______________________________

Instructions: Answer the following questions from your personal perspective and provide details for each response.

Return this form to ______________________________.

1. Even if the individual signals clearly, do partners have a preconceived notion of the individual's competence?

2. Do partners feel this individual needs to be taken care of, or do they feel that the person should be able to control what happens to him or her?

3. Would the partners be willing to honor a choice that, although allowable, is not what they see as the "best" choice?

4. Do partners see their role as one in which they must follow exact schedules and routines, regardless of the individual's desires?

5. Can partners be comfortable with the unpredictability and loss of control that accompany allowing the individual to make choices?

CHOOSING ROLES IN THE ASSESSMENT PROCESS

Team member: ______________________________

Instructions: Along with your other team members, please decide which role you will play in the assessment of ______________ [individual whose communication is to be assessed]. Please check all roles you wish to take.

Return this form to ______________________________ .

_____ *Receiver of information:* I would like to receive information from the team about the assessment results.

_____ *Observer of behavior:* I am willing to be trained to quietly record behaviors as they occur.

_____ *Informant:* I have information about this individual that I would like to share.

_____ *Describer of daily life:* I would like to share my descriptions with the team.

_____ *Interpreter of behaviors:* I have some ideas about why the individual behaves in certain ways.

_____ *Validator of opinions:* I would like to hear others' opinions about this individual and offer my experiences as evidence so we can decide as a group if the opinion is appropriate.

_____ *Active participant in the assessment:* I am willing to perform any aspect of the assessment for which I am already trained or for which I will be trained.

_____ *Evaluator:* I want to be involved in the evaluation of data from the assessment process.

ASSESSING INTERACTIONAL STYLES OF PARTNERS

Target individual: ______________________________

Partner: ______________________________

Instructions: This form should be completed by each partner who indicated on the Choosing Roles in the Assessment Process form that he or she wishes to be involved in assessment in any capacity other than, or in addition to, Receiver of Information. Respond to each of the questions below, providing details as needed.

Return this form to ______________________________.

1. On what days and at what times do you interact with this individual?

2. Are you willing to spend time observing others as they work with the individual?

3. Are you willing to make anecdotal descriptive notes about the successes you observed?

4. Are you willing to learn to count directive and nondirective adult behaviors by watching a training videotape?

5. Are you willing to count directive and nondirective behaviors in one time period of the day when someone else is interacting with the individual?

6. Are you willing to have someone else observe you as you interact with the individual? Are you willing to have someone else make anecdotal records about your successes with the individual?

7. Are you willing to have someone else count your directive and nondirective behaviors as you interact with the individual, or would you prefer to watch a videotape of your interactions and count your behaviors yourself?

SELF-RATING SCALE FOR YOUNG CHILDREN

Overall, how good are you at talking and playing with this child?

Not very						Very
1	2	3	4	5	6	7

How interested were you in what the child was doing?

Not very						Very
1	2	3	4	5	6	7

How interested was the child in what you were doing?

Not very						Very
1	2	3	4	5	6	7

How often did you communicate with the child?

Not very						Very
1	2	3	4	5	6	7

How often did the child communicate to you?

Not very						Very
1	2	3	4	5	6	7

How often did you talk about the toys or materials?

Not very						Very
1	2	3	4	5	6	7

How often did the child talk about the toys or materials?

Not very						Very
1	2	3	4	5	6	7

How often did you talk about what you or the child was doing?

Not very						Very
1	2	3	4	5	6	7

How often did the child talk about what either of you was doing?

Not very						Very
1	2	3	4	5	6	7

How much did you enjoy playing with the child?

Not very						Very
1	2	3	4	5	6	7

How much did the child enjoy playing with you?

Not very						Very
1	2	3	4	5	6	7

How often did you tell the child what to do?

Not very						Very
1	2	3	4	5	6	7

How often did the child tell you what to do?

Not very						Very
1	2	3	4	5	6	7

From Johnson, J. (1989). *A nonintrusive intervention technique for mother–child interactions.* Paper presented at the annual convention of the American Speech-Language-Hearing Association, St. Louis, MO; reprinted by permission.

APPENDIX C

Checklists and Forms

Included in this appendix are the following forms and blank data sheets useful for assessing interactions with communication partners and environments:

1. Written plan
2. Teaming Checklist
3. Pupil Educational Team Communication (ETC) Form
4. IES Data Sheet

Readers are granted permission to photocopy and/or adapt these checklists and forms for educational or clinical purposes.

WRITTEN PLAN

Pragmatic and discourse functions	Symbol system	Procedure

Pragmatic and discourse functions	Symbol system	Procedure

TEAMING CHECKLIST

Teaming is playing an increasingly significant role in educational settings, ranging from the involvement of teams focused on restructuring to teams focused on dealing with student learning and behavior. Although teams are important, educators and professionals seldom take the time to step back and evaluate how well teams work and, if necessary, to change how the teams function.

The following checklist provides a means to examine a team's effectiveness. The checklist is based on what some professionals say are healthy attributes of teams.

DIRECTIONS FOR USING THE TEAMING CHECKLIST

The Teaming Checklist can be completed in different ways; for example, each team member may assess the team and then a group discussion may follow, or the team members may complete the checklist together. For each entry (row) on the checklist, one corresponding evaluation box ("adequate," "needs work," or "does not apply") should be checked.

1. Begin by assessing Overall Team Effectiveness (the first four entries [rows] on the checklist). If the ratings for all four of these entries are "adequate," there is no need to proceed with the remainder of the checklist.
2. If one or more items in the first section is scored "needs work," proceed with the remainder of the checklist in order to identify aspects of teaming that limit effectiveness.
3. Upon completion of the ratings, analyze the results. Select areas that need work and develop strategies for improving team effectiveness.

TEAMING CHECKLIST			
	Team rating		
Team assessment	Adequate	Needs work	Does not apply
Overall team effectiveness			
1. Team completes tasks set out to do.			
2. Team completes tasks in timely fashion.			
3. Completed tasks are of high quality.			
4. Team has built a climate of trust and interdependence.			
Goals			
5. Team has clearly stated goals.			
6. Members agree on goals.			
7. Members feel ownership and commitment to goals.			
Roles			
8. Members are assigned roles (e.g., facilitator/leader, timer, recorder) that support the team process.			
9. Roles vary from meeting to meeting.			
10. Responsibility for tasks is shared, rather than concentrated among a few members.			
11. All the necessary people are represented on the team (e.g., those with needed information or skills, those affected by decisions).			
12. Best possible use is made of each member's strengths in completing tasks.			
Meeting procedures			
13. Meeting times and locations are determined by team members.			
14. Members feel that they have time to meet; they do not feel stressed by the need to meet.			
15. The team has established, agreed-upon rules for participation (e.g., arrive on time, stay for entire meeting, come prepared, no interruptions).			
16. Meetings start and end on time.			
17. There is an agenda for each meeting.			

TEAMING CHECKLIST			
	Team rating		
Team assessment	Adequate	Needs work	Does not apply
18. Agendas are sent to members prior to each meeting.			
19. Time limits are set for each agenda item.			
20. There is an established meeting format (e.g., approve agenda, approve minutes, old business).			
21. There are established procedures for addressing issues or for problem solving (e.g., brainstorming).			
22. Closure is achieved on agenda items before the team moves on to next item.			
23. Decisions are reached by consensus, not a vote.			
24. Ideas and decisions are recorded.			
25. Tasks to be completed are recorded and include person(s) responsible and time line for completion.			
26. Minutes are disseminated promptly following meeting.			
27. Team effectiveness is regularly assessed and discussed, and necessary changes are made.			
Communication and relations			
28. There is a sense of team identity and pride.			
29. Members see themselves as interdependent.			
30. A climate of trust exists; members feel free to express ideas, disagreements, and feelings.			
31. Members support each other by making positive statements, clarifying others' comments, and building on others' ideas.			
32. Members remind others when discussions are off task.			
33. Time is taken to recognize and work through negative feelings and disagreements.			
34. Members can challenge each other in ways that are not seen as personal confrontations.			
35. Humor is used during meetings.			

TEAMING CHECKLIST			
	Team rating		
Team assessment	Adequate	Needs work	Does not apply
36. Members readily volunteer in order to help accomplish tasks.			
37. Team celebrates individual and team accomplishments.			
38. Team regularly communicates with constituents about team activities and constituents' concerns.			
39. Team has positive relationship with constituents and other groups in the organization.			
40. Communication and relations are regularly assessed and discussed, and necessary changes are made.			

PUPIL EDUCATIONAL TEAM COMMUNICATION (ETC) FORM

Pupil: ______________________

Classroom: ______________________

Date	Concern	Procedure/action	By when	Major responsibility	Disposition/comments	Date

From Lynch, V. (1992). *Educational Team Communication (ETC) Form.* Seattle: Experimental Education Unit, Program Development Services, University of Washington; reprinted by permission.

Pupil: ____________________
Classroom: ____________________

Date	Concern	Procedure/action	By when	Major responsibility	Disposition/comments	Date

Lynch, V. (1992). *Educational Team Communication (ETC) Form.* Seattle: Experimental Education Unit, Program Development Services, University of Washington; reprinted by permission.

IES DATA SHEET

Date ____ Period/Staff								
Description of activity								
Position								
What he or she does								
What mood he or she is in								
How he or she does things								
Other things happening								
COMMENTS								

lots
none

IES data sample form. (The placement of the dots within each cell in the shaded grid is significant: Placement at the top of the cell indicates that the behavior occurs with high frequency; placement in the middle of the cell indicates less frequency; and placement at the bottom of the cell indicates that the behavior does not occur.) (Form adapted from IES Project, D. Ferguson, Project Director, University of Oregon, College of Education.)

APPENDIX D

Augmentative Equipment Resources

The following is a list of augmentative devices and materials manufacturers:

Ablenet, Inc.
1081 Tenth Ave. SE
Minneapolis, Minnesota 55414
1-800-322-0956

Adaptive Communication Systems
1400 Lee Drive
Coraopolis, Pennsylvania 15108
412-264-2288
1-800-247-3433

Attainment Company
Post Office Box 930160
Verona, Wisconsin 53593-0160
1-800-327-4269

Blissymbolics Communication International
Products distributed by EBSCO Curriculum Materials
Division of EBSCO Industries, Inc.
Box 1943
Birmingham, Alabama 35202
1-800-633-8623

Canon USA, Inc.
One Canon Plaza
Lake Success, New York 11042
516-488-6700

Crestwood Company
6625 North Sidney Place
Milwaukee, Wisconsin 53209-3259
414-352-5678

Daedalus Technologies, Inc.
7-12171 Bridgeport Road
Richmond, British Columbia V6V 1J4
CANADA
FAX: 604-244-8443

Don Johnston Developmental Equipment, Inc.
Post Office Box 639
1000 North Rand Road, Building 115
Wauconda, Illinois 60084-0639
312-526-2682
1-800-999-4660

Franklin Learning Resources
One Franklin Plaza
Burlington, New Jersey 08016
1-800-525-9673

Imaginart Communication Products
307 Arizona Street
Bizbee, Arizona 85603
1-800-828-1376

Independent Living Aids
27 East Mall
Plainview, New York 11803
1-800-537-2118

Innocomp
(Innovative Computer Applications)
26210 Emery Road, Suite 302
Warrensville Heights, Ohio 44128
216-464-3636
1-800-382-8622

Interactive Therapeutics
Post Office Box 1805
Stow, Ohio 44224-0805
216-688-1371
1-800-253-5111

Luminaud, Inc.
8688 Tyler Boulevard
Mentor, Ohio 44060
216-255-9082

Mayer-Johnson Company
Post Office Box 1579
Solana Beach, California 92075-1579
619-481-2489

Phonic Ear, Inc.
3880 Cypress Drive
Petaluma, California 94954-7600
707-769-1110
1-800-227-0735
or
10-7475 Kimbel Street
Mississauga, Ontario L5S 1E7
CANADA
416-677-3231

Pointer Systems, Inc.
1 Mill Street
Burlington, Vermont 05401
1-800-537-1562

Prentke Romich Company
1022 Heyl Road
Wooster, Ohio 44691
216-262-1984
1-800-262-1984

Sentient Systems Technology, Inc.
2100 Whorton Street, Suite 630
Pittsburgh, Pennsylvania 15203
412-682-0144
1-800-344-1778

TASH, Inc.
91 Station Street, Unit 1
Ajax, Ontario L1S 3H2
CANADA
905-686-4129
1-800-463-5685

TFH (USA) Ltd.
4537 Gibsonia Road
Gibsonia, Pennsylvania 15044
412-444-6400
1-800-467-6222

Tolfa Corporation
2660 Marine Way
Mountain View, California 94043
415-390-9566
1-800-332-4913

Toys for Special Children
385 Warburton Avenue
Hastings-On-Hudson, New York 10706
914-478-0960
1-800-832-8697

Words Plus, Inc.
40015 Sierra Highway, Building 13-145
Palmdale, California 93550
805-266-8500

Zygo Industries, Inc.
Post Office Box 1008
Portland, Oregon 97207-1008
503-684-6006
1-800-234-6006

Zygo Rehatele, Inc.
1829 Capilano Road
North Vancouver, British Columbia
V7P 3B5
CANADA
604-988-5899
1-800-663-1633

References

Armstrong, S., & Firth, G. (1984). *Practical self-monitoring for classroom use.* Springfield, IL: Charles C Thomas.

Bailey, D.B., & Wolery, M. (1989). *Assessing infants and preschoolers with handicaps.* Columbus, OH: Charles E. Merrill.

Bandura, A. (1971). Vicarious and self-reinforcement practices. In R. Claser (Ed.), *The nature of reinforcement* (pp. 228–278). New York: Academic Press.

Bates, E. (1976). *Language and context: The acquisition of pragmatics.* New York: Academic Press.

Bates, E., Camaioni, L., & Volterra, V. (1975). The acquisition of performatives prior to speech. *Merrill-Palmer Quarterly, 21,* 206–216.

Baumgart, D., & Giangreco, M.F. (1996). Key lessons learned about inclusion. In D.H. Lehr & F. Brown (Eds.), *People with disabilities who challenge the system* (pp. 79–97). Baltimore: Paul H. Brookes Publishing Co.

Baumgart, D., Johnson, J.M., & Helmstetter, E. (1990). *Augmentative and alternative communication systems for persons with moderate and severe disabilities.* Baltimore: Paul H. Brookes Publishing Co.

Bayley, N. (1969). *Bayley Scales of Infant Development: Birth to two years.* New York: The Psychological Corporation.

Beukelman, D., McGinnis, J., & Morrow, D. (1992). Vocabulary selection in augmentative and alternative communication. *Augmentative and Alternative Communication, 7*(3), 171–185.

Beukelman, D., & Yorkston, K. (1982). Communication interaction of adult communication augmentation system use. *Topics in Language Disorders, 2*(2), 39–53.

Bloom, L. (1970). *Language development: Form and function of emerging grammars.* Cambridge, MA: MIT Press.

Bruner, J. (1975). The ontogenesis of speech acts. *Journal of Child Language, 2,* 1–19.

Calculator, S., & Jorgensen, C. (1992). Integrating AAC instruction into regular education settings: Expounding on best practices. *Augmentative and Alternative Communication, 7*(3), 204–214.

Carr, E.G., Levin, L., McConnachie, G., Carlson, J.I., Kemp, D.C., & Smith, C.E. (1994). *Communication-based intervention for problem behavior: A user's guide for producing positive change.* Baltimore: Paul H. Brookes Publishing Co.

Chapman, R. (1978). Comprehension strategies in children. In J.F. Kavanaugh & W. Strange (Eds.), *Language and speech in the laboratory, school, and clinic* (pp. 309–327). Cambridge, MA: MIT Press.

Crais, E.R. (1993). Families and professionals as collaborators in assessment. *Topics in Language Disorders, 14*(1), 29–40.

Donnellan, A.M., Mirenda, P., Mesarsos, R.A., & Fassbender, L.L. (1984). Analyzing the communicative functions of aberrant behavior. *Journal of The Association for Persons with Severe Handicaps, 9*, 201–212.

Duchan, J.F. (1983). Autistic children are noninteractive: Or so we say. *Seminars in Speech and Language, 4*(1), 53–62.

Duchan, J.F., Hewitt, L., & Sonnemeier, R. (1994). *Pragmatics: From theory to practice.* Englewood Cliffs, NJ: Prentice Hall.

Dunn, L.M., & Dunn, L.M. (1981). *Peabody Picture Vocabulary Test–Revised.* Circle Pines, MN: American Guidance Service.

Durand, V.M. (1990). *Severe behavior problems: A functional communication training approach.* New York: Guilford Press.

Durand, V.M., & Crimmins, D.B. (1988). Identifying the variables maintaining self-injurious behavior. *Journal of Autism and Developmental Disorders, 18*, 99–117.

Erhardt, R.P. (1986). *Erhardt Developmental Vision Assessment.* Fargo, ND: Author.

Evans, I.M., & Meyer, L.H. (1985). *An educative approach to behavior problems: A practical decision model for interventions with severely handicapped learners.* Baltimore: Paul H. Brookes Publishing Co.

Falvey, M., Brown, L., Lyon, S., Baumgart, D., & Schroeder, J. (1980). Strategies for using cues and correction procedures. In W. Sailor, B. Wilcox, & L. Brown (Eds.), *Methods of instruction for severely handicapped students* (pp. 109–133). Baltimore: Paul H. Brookes Publishing Co.

Ferguson, D. (1991–1994). *Including exceptions: A system for educating students with dual sensory impairments and other extreme disabilities in general education settings* (Grant No. H025F10001). Washington, DC: U.S. Department of Education.

Fey, M. (1986). *Language intervention with young children.* San Diego: College-Hill Press.

Fosnot, C.T. (1989). *Enquiring teachers, enquiring learners: A constructivist approach for teaching.* New York: Teachers College Press.

Fratelli, C. (1993). *National students in speech, language, & hearing association clinical series: Vol. 11. Professional collaboration: A team approach to health care.* Baltimore: American Speech-Language-Hearing Association.

Fried-Oken, M., & More, L. (1992). An initial vocabulary for nonspeaking preschool children based on developmental and environmental language sources. *Augmentative and Alternative Communication, 8*(1), 41–56.

Fuller, D., Lloyd, L., & Schlosser, R. (1992). Further development of an augmentative and alternative communication symbol taxonomy. *Augmentative and Alternative Communication, 8*(1), 67–73.

Gardner, W.I., Cole, C.L., Davidson, D.P., & Karan, O.C. (1986). Reducing aggression in individuals with developmental disabilities: An expanded stimulus control, assessment, and intervention model. *Education and Training of the Mentally Retarded, 21*(1), 3–12.

Gehrke, N. (1988). Toward definition on mentoring. *Theory into Practice, 27*(3), 190–194.

Giangreco, M.F., Cloninger, C.J., & Iverson, V.S. (1993). *Choosing options and accommodations for children (COACH): A guide to planning inclusive education.* Baltimore: Paul H. Brookes Publishing Co.

Giraud-Birney, J. (1991). *The effect of self-rating on the directiveness of adolescent mothers of toddlers.* Unpublished master's project, Eastern Washington State University.

Gourash, L.F. (1986). Assessing and managing medical factors. In R.P. Barrett (Ed.), *Severe behavior disorders in the mentally retarded: Nondrug approaches to treatment* (pp. 157–205). New York: Plenum.

Guess, D., Turnbull, H.R., Helmstetter, E., & Knowlton, S. (1987). Use of aversive procedures with persons who are disabled: A historical review and critical analysis. *Monograph of The Association for Persons with Severe Handicaps, 2*(1).

Halle, J. (1985). Arranging the natural environment to occasion language. *Seminars in Speech and Language, 5*(3), 185–198.

Hanson, A.J., & Dickson, S. (1994). A construction for computer visualization of certain complex curves. *Computers and Mathematics, 41*(9), 1156–1163.

Helmstetter, E., & Durand, V.M. (1991). Nonaversive interventions for severe behavior problems. In L.H. Meyer, C.A. Peck, & L. Brown (Eds.), *Critical issues in the lives of people with severe disabilities* (pp. 559–600). Baltimore: Paul H. Brookes Publishing Co.

Hendrick, D., Prather, E., & Tobin, A. (1984) *Sequenced Inventory of Communication Development.* Seattle: University of Washington Press.

Horner, R.H., & Day, H.M. (1991). The effects of response efficiency on functionally equivalent, competing behaviors. *Journal of Applied Behavior Analysis, 24,* 719–732.

Johnson, J. (1989, November). *A nonintrusive intervention technique for mother–child interactions.* Paper presented at the annual convention of the American Speech-Language-Hearing Association, St. Louis, MO.

Johnson, J.M. (1995). *The Sociocommunicative Filter Model.* Unpublished manuscript. Washington State University.

Johnson, J.M., & Harrison, K. (1991, November). *A nonintrusive remediation technique for directive maternal behaviors.* Paper presented at the annual convention of the American Speech-Language-Hearing Association, Seattle, WA. (ERIC Document Reproduction Service No. ED 335 833)

Kangas, K., & Lloyd, L. (1988). Early cognitive skills as prerequisites to augmentative and alternative communication use: What are we waiting for? *Augmentative and Alternative Communication, 4*(4), 211–221.

Light, J. (1989). Toward a definition of communicative competence for individuals using augmentative/alternative communication systems. *Augmentative and Alternative Communication, 5*(2), 137–144.

Lynch, V. (1992). *Educational Team Communication (ETC) Form.* Seattle: Experimental Education Unit, Program Development Services, University of Washington.

Mahoney, G., & Powell, A. (1988). Modifying parent–child interaction: Enhancing the development of handicapped children. *Journal of Special Education, 22*(1), 82–96.

Marshall, K. (1991). *The effect of self-rating on the directive behaviors of mothers with developmentally delayed toddlers.* Unpublished master's project, Eastern Washington State University.

McDonald, J. (1985). Language through conversation. In S. Warren & A. Rogers-Warren (Eds.), *Teaching functional language* (pp. 89–122). Baltimore: University Park Press.

McEwen, I., & Lloyd, L. (1990). Positioning students with cerebral palsy to use augmentative and alternative communication. *Language, Speech, and Hearing Services in Schools, 21,* 15–21.

McLam, M. (1991). *Decreasing clinician directiveness in therapy.* Unpublished master's project, Washington State University.

Minnow, M. (1990). *Making all the difference: Inclusion, exclusion and Americal law.* Ithaca, NY: Cornell University Press.

Mirenda, P., & Donnellan, A. (1986). Effects of adult interaction style on conversational behavior in students with severe communication problems. *Language, Speech, and Hearing Services in Schools, 17,* 126–141.

Mirenda, P., & Iacono, T. (1990). Communication options for persons with severe and profound disabilities: State of the art and future directions. *Journal of The Association for Persons with Severe Handicaps, 15*(1), 3–21.

Mirenda, P., & Locke, P. (1989). A comparison of symbol transparency in nonspeaking persons with intellectual disabilities. *Journal of Speech and Hearing Disorders, 54,* 131–140.

Moll, L. (1990). *Vygotsky and education: Instructional implications and applications of sociohistorical psychology.* New York: Cambridge University Press.

Mount, B., & Zwernik, K. (1988). *It's never too early, it's never too late: A booklet about personal futures planning.* St. Paul, MN: St. Paul Metropolitan Council.

Musselwhite, C.R., & St. Louis, K.W. (1982). *Communication programming for severely handicapped: Vocal and non-vocal strategies.* San Diego: College-Hill Press.

Nelson, N. (1992). Performance is the prize: Language competence and performance among AAC users. *Augmentative and Alternative Communication, 8*(1), 3–18.

Newman, F., & Holzman, L. (1993). *Lev Vygotsky: Revolutionary scientist.* New York: Routledge.

Norris, J., & Hoffman, P. (1990a). Comparison of adult-initiated vs. child-initiated interaction styles with handicapped prelanguage children. *Language, Speech, and Hearing Services in Schools, 21*, 28–36.

Norris, J., & Hoffman, P. (1990b). Language intervention within naturalistic environments. *Language, Speech, and Hearing Services in Schools, 21*, 72–84.

Owens, R.E. (1994). *Language development: An introduction.* New York: Charles E. Merrill.

Owens, R.E. (1995). *Language disorders: A functional approach to assessment and intervention.* Needham, MA: Allyn & Bacon.

Pearpoint, J., O'Brien, J., & Forest, M. (1994). *Path training video: Planning alternative tomorrows with hope* [Videotape]. Toronto, Ontario, Canada: Inclusion Press.

Piaget, J., & Inhelder, B. (1969). *The psychology of the child.* New York: Basic Books.

Prizant, B.M., & Rentschler, G. (1983). Language-impaired children's use of language across three conversational situations. *Australian Journal of Human Communication Disorders, 11*, 5–16.

Reeve, P., & Hallahan, D. (1994). Practical questions about collaboration between general and special educators. *Focus on Exceptional Children, 26*(7), 1–12.

Romski, M.A., & Sevcik, R.A. (1988). Augmentative and alternative communication systems: Considerations for individuals with severe disabilities. *Augmentative and Alternative Communication, 4*(2), 83–93.

Romski, M.A., Sevcik, R.A., & Pate, J.L. (1988). Establishment of symbolic communication in persons with severe retardation. *Journal of Speech and Hearing Disorders, 53*, 94–107.

Scheuerman, N., Baumgart, D., Sipsma, K. & Brown, L. (1976). Toward the development of a curriculum for teaching non-verbal communication skills to severely handicapped students: Teaching tracking, scanning and selection skills. In L. Brown, N. Scheuerman, & T. Crowner (Eds.), *Madison's alternative to zero exclusion: Toward an integrated therapy model for teaching motor, tracking and scanning skills to severely handicapped students* (pp. 71–248). Madison: Madison Public Schools and University of Wisconsin–Madison.

Scholtes, P.R. (1988). *The team handbook: How to use teams to improve quality.* Madison: University of Wisconsin Press.

Schuler, A.L., Peck, C.A., Willard, C., & Theimer, K. (1989). Assessment of communicative means and functions through interview: Assessing the communicative capabilities of individuals with limited language. *Seminars in Speech & Language, 10*, 51–62.

Sevcik, R., Romski, M., & Wilkinson, K. (1991). Roles of graphic symbols in the language acquisition process for persons with severe cognitive disabilities. *Augmentative and Alternative Communication, 7*, 161–170.

Sparrow, S.S., Bala, D.A., Cicchetti, D.V. (1984). *Vineland Adaptive Behavior Scales.* Circle Pines, MN: American Guidance Service.

Tobias, S. (1992). *Revitalization Undergraduate Science: Why some things work and most don't.* Tucson, AZ: Research Corporation.

Touchette, P.E., MacDonald, R.F., & Langer, S.N. (1985). A scatter plot for identifying stimulus control of problem behavior. *Journal of Applied Behavior Analysis, 18*, 343–351.

Vygotsky, L. (1962). *Thought and language.* Cambridge, MA: MIT Press. (Original work published 1934)

Wetherby, A.M., Cain, D., Yonclas, D., & Walker, V. (1988). Analysis of intentional communication of normal children from the prelinguistic to the multi-word stage. *Journal of Speech and Hearing Research, 31*, 240–252.

Wetherby, A.M., & Prizant, B.M. (1989). The expression of communicative intent: Assessment guidelines. *Seminars in Speech & Language, 10*, 77–90.

Wolery, M., Ault, M.J., Gast, D.L., Doyle, P.M., & Griffith, A.K. (1990). Comparison of constant time delay and the system of least prompts in teaching chained tasks. *Education and Training in Mental Retardation, 25*, 198–220.

Suggested Readings

PROBLEM BEHAVIORS

Baumgart, D., Johnson, J., & Helmstetter, E. (1990). *Augmentative and alternative communication systems for persons with moderate and severe disabilities.* Baltimore: Paul H. Brookes Publishing Co.

Beukelman, D.R., & Mirenda, P. (1992). *Augmentative and alternative communication: Management of severe communication disorders in children and adults.* Baltimore: Paul H. Brookes Publishing Co.

Carr, E.G., Levin, L., McConnachie, G., Carlson, J.I., Kemp, D.C., & Smith, C.E. (1994). *Communication-based intervention for problem behavior: A user's guide for producing positive change.* Baltimore: Paul H. Brookes Publishing Co.

Durand, V.M. (1990). *Severe behavior problems: A functional communication training approach.* New York: Guilford Press.

Gourash, L.F. (1986). Assessing and managing medical factors. In R.P. Barrett (Ed.), *Severe behavior disorders in the mentally retarded: Nondrug approaches to treatment* (pp. 157–205). New York: Plenum.

Meyer, L.H., & Evans, I.M. (1989). *Nonaversive intervention for behavior problems: A manual for home and community.* Baltimore: Paul H. Brookes Publishing Co.

Mount, B., & Zwernik, K. (1988). *It's never too early, it's never too late: A booklet about personal futures planning.* St. Paul, MN: St. Paul Metropolitan Council.

O'Neill, R.E., Horner, R.H., Albin, R.W., Storey, K., & Sprague, J.R. (1990). *Functional analysis of problem behavior: A practical assessment guide.* Sycamore, IL: Sycamore Press.

Pearpoint, J., O'Brien, J., & Forest, M. (1994). *Path training video: Planning alternative tomorrows with hope* [Videotape]. Toronto, Ontario, Canada: Inclusion Press.

Reichle, J., & Wacker, D.P. (Volume Eds.). (1993). In S.F. Warren & J. Reichle (Series Eds.), *Communication and language intervention series: Vol. 3. Communicative alternatives to challenging behavior: Integrating functional assessment and intervention strategies.* Baltimore: Paul H. Brookes Publishing Co.

Reichle, J., York, J., & Sigafoos, J. (1991). *Implementing augmentative and alternative communication: Strategies for learners with severe disabilities.* Baltimore: Paul H. Brookes Publishing Co.

ASSESSMENT

Bailey, D.B., & Wolery, M. (1989). *Assessing infants and preschoolers with handicaps.* Columbus, OH: Charles E. Merrill.

Beukelman, D.R., & Mirenda, P. (1992). *Augmentative and alternative communication: Management of severe communication disorders in children and adults.* Baltimore: Paul H. Brookes Publishing Co.

Blackstone, S. (Ed.). (1988). *Augmentative communication: An introduction.* Washington DC: American Speech-Language-Hearing Association.

Langley, M.B., & Lombardino, L.J. (1991). *Neurodevelopmental strategies for managing communication disorders in children with severe motor dysfunction.* Austin, TX: PRO-ED.

McDonald, J.D. (1989). *Becoming partners with children: From play to conversation.* San Antonio: Special Press

Musselwhite, C.R., & St. Louis, K.W. (1982). *Communication programming for the severely handicapped.* Boston: College-Hill.

Rosetti, L.M. (1990). *Infant-toddler assessment: An interdisciplinary approach.* Boston: College-Hill.

Siegel-Causey, E., & Guess, D. (1989). *Enhancing nonsymbolic communication interactions among learners with severe disabilities.* Baltimore: Paul H. Brookes Publishing Co.

IMPLEMENTATION

Alberto, P.A., & Troutman, A.C. (1995). *Applied behavior analysis for teachers* (4th ed.). Englewood Cliffs, NJ: Prentice Hall.

Cooper, J.O., Heron, T.E., & Heward, W.L. (1987). *Applied behavior analysis.* Columbus, OH: Charles E. Merrill.

Zirpoli, T.J., & Melloy, K.J. (1993). *Behavior analysis: Applications for teachers and parents.* New York: Macmillan.

MENTORING AND COLLABORATION

Auster, D. (1984). Mentors and proteges: Power dependent dyads. *Sociological Inquiries, 52*(2), 142–153.

Baumgart, D., Gee, R., & Askvig, B.A. (1990). *Videotape self-monitoring as a social skill intervention: A single subject investigation* (Social Skills Research Project, U.S. Department of Education, Office of Special Education Programs, PR# G008730222). Moscow: University of Idaho.

Benner, S.M., & Cagle, L.C. (1987). The mentoring team approach: A new concept in undergraduate teacher education. *Teacher Education and Special Education, 10*(1), 26–30.

Brookes, J. (1990). Teachers and students: Constructivists forging new connections. *Educational Leadership, 47*(5), 68–71.

Cockran-Smith, M., & Lytle, S. (1993). *Inside/outside teacher research and knowledge.* New York: Teachers College Press.

Darling-Hammond, L. (1990). Teacher supply, demand, and quality. In C.A. Niebrand (Ed.), (1993). *A naturalistic study of variables in the mentoring of first year secondary teachers in a southwest Idaho school district.* Unpublished doctoral dissertation, University of Idaho, Moscow.

Davis, C., & Ferguson, D. (1992). Trying something completely different. Report of a collaborative research venture. In P.M. Ferguson, D.L. Ferguson, & S.J. Taylor (Eds.), *Interpreting disability: A quantitative reader* (pp. 124–143). New York: Teachers College Press.

Debolt, G. (1991a). *Helpful elements in the mentoring of first year teachers. A report to the State Education Department on the New York State mentor teacher internship program for 1988–1989.* New York: Author.

Debolt, G. (1991b). *Mentoring: Studies of effective programs in education.* Paper presented at the Diversity in Mentoring Conference, Chicago.

Donnellan, A., Mirenda, P., Mesaros, R., & Fassbender, L. (1984). Analyzing the communicative functions of aberrant behavior. *Journal of The Association for Students with Severe Handicaps, 9*(3), 201–212.

Esquivel, G., & Yoshida, R. (1985). Special education for language minority students. *Focus on Exceptional Children, 18*, 1–8.

Ferguson D., & Baumgart, D. (1994). Partial participation revisited. *Journal of The Association for Persons with Severe Handicaps, 16*(4), 218–227.

Ferguson, D., Meyer, G., Jeanchild, L., Juniper, L., & Zingo, J. (1992). Figuring out what to do with the grownups: How teachers make inclusion work. *Journal of The Association for Persons with Severe Handicaps, 17*(4), 218–226.

Fosnot, C.T. (1989). *Enquiring teachers, enquiring learners: A constructivist approach for teaching.* New York: Teachers College Press.

Gehrke, N. (1988a). On preserving the essence of mentoring as one form of teacher leadership. *Journal of Teacher Education, 36*(1), 43–45.

Gehrke, N. (1988b). Toward definition on mentoring. *Theory into Practice*, 27(3), 190–194.

Goossens, C., Crain, S., & Elder, P. (1992). *Engineering the preschool environment for interactive, symbolic communication.* Birmingham, AL: Southeast Augmentative Communication Conference Publication: Clinician Series.

Gray, W., & Gray, M. (1985). Synthesis of research on mentoring beginning teachers. *Educational Leadership, 43*(3), 37–43.

Hearn, K.A.J. (1994). *The way it is supposed to be: A collaborative mentoring project.* Unpublished master's thesis, University of Idaho, Moscow.

Hollingsworth, S. (1992). Learning to teach through collaborative conservation: A feminist approach. *American Educational Research Journal, 29*, 373–404.

Holt, L., & Johnston, M. (1989). Graduate education and teacher's understanding: A collaborative case study of change. *Teaching and Teacher Education, 5*(2), 81–92.

Hunsaker, L., & Johnson, M. (1992). Teacher under construction: A collaborative case study of teacher change. *American Educational Research Journal, 29*, 350–372.

Jackson, P. (1986). *The practice of teaching.* New York: Teachers College Press.

Murray, F. (1986). Goals for the reform of teacher education: An executive summary of the Holmes Group Report. *Phi Delta Kappan, 68*(1), 28–32.

Newman, J.M. (1990). *Finding our own way: Teachers exploring their assumptions.* Portsmouth, MA: Heinemann Educational Books.

Paterson, B., & Hart-Wasekeesikaw, F. (1994). Mentoring women in higher education: Lessons from the elders. *College Teaching, 42*(2), 72–77.

Perry, N.E., & Kamann, M. (1994). An amalgamated approach to support service delivery: Using resources effectively and efficiently. In J. Rogers (Ed.), *Hot topics series. Inclusion: Moving beyond our fears.* Bloomington, IN: Phi Delta Kappa, Center for Evaluation, Development and Research.

Reeve, P., & Hallahan, D. (1994). Practical questions about collaboration between general and special educators. *Focus on Exceptional Children. 26*(7), 1–12.

Routman, R., (1991). *Invitations changing as teachers and learners K–12.* Portsmouth, MA: Heinemann Educational Books.

Smyth, J. (1989). Developing and sustaining critical reflection in teacher education, *Journal of Teacher Education, 40*(2), 2–10.

Stokes, S.L., Jr. (1990). Building effective project teams. *Journal of Information Systems Management, 1*(3), 38–45.

Thousand, J.S., Villa, R.A., & Nevin, A.I. (Eds.). (1994). *Creativity and collaborative learning: A practical guide to empowering students and teachers.* Baltimore: Paul H. Brookes Publishing Co.

TEAMING

Larson, C., & LaFasto, F. (1989). *Teamwork: What must go right/what can go wrong?* Beverly Hills: Sage Publications.

Lippitt, G. (1982). *Organizational renewal: A holistic approach to organizational development.* Englewood Cliffs, NJ: Prentice Hall.

Lynch, V. (1990). *Educational teaming training kit.* Unpublished manuscript, University of Washington, Program Development Services, Seattle.

Maddux, R. (1988). *Team building: An exercise in leadership.* Los Altos, CA: Crisp Publications.

Shonk, J. (1982). *Working in teams: A practical manual for improving work groups.* New York: Amacom.

Thomas, C.C., Correa, V.I., & Morsink, C.V. (1995). *Interactive teaming: Consultation and collaboration in special programs* (2nd ed.). Englewood Cliffs, NJ: Prentice Hall.

Thousand, J.S., & Villa, R.A. (1992). Collaborative teams: A powerful tool in school restructuring. In R.A. Villa, J.S. Thousand, W. Stainback, & S. Stainback (Eds.), *Restructuring for caring and effective education: An administrative guide to creating heterogeneous schools* (pp. 73–108). Baltimore: Paul H. Brookes Publishing Co.

Index

Page numbers followed by *t* and *f* indicate tables and figures, respectively.

Sustainable by 2020?

A strategic approach to urban regeneration for Britain's cities

Michael Carley and Karryn Kirk

First published in Great Britain in 1998 by

The Policy Press
University of Bristol
Rodney Lodge
Grange Road
Bristol BS8 4EA
UK

Tel no +44 (0)117 973 8797
Fax no +44 (0)117 973 7308
E-mail tpp@bristol.ac.uk
http://www.bristol.ac.uk/Publications/TPP/

In association with the Joseph Rowntree Foundation

ISBN 1 86134 104 0

Michael Carley is a professor and **Karryn Kirk** is a research associate in the School of Planning and Housing at Heriot Watt University, Edinburgh.

The **Joseph Rowntree Foundation** has supported this project as part of its programme of research and innovative development projects, which it hopes will be of value to policy makers and practitioners. The facts presented and the views expressed in this report, however, are those of the authors and not necessarily those of the Foundation.

Cover design by Qube Design Associates, Bristol.
Printed in Great Britain by Hobbs the Printers Ltd, Southampton.

Contents

Preface

Many people made this research possible. Most importantly, we would like to thank the 100-plus key informants who gave freely of their time for interviews; unfortunately, they are too numerous to mention. We are also grateful to the Joseph Rowntree Foundation for funding the research; and John Low, Rowntree's Area Regeneration Coordinator and Michelle Powell, administrator, for their valuable assistance.

We would also like to thank the members of the Research Advisory Group who provided a substantial amount of their time to attend meetings, to review the material and to make constructive suggestions. These are Ted Cantle, Chief Executive, Nottingham City Council; Jim Coleman, Partnership and Urban Regeneration Manager, Wimpey Homes; John Dawson, European Institute of Urban Affairs, Liverpool John Moores University; Cathy Garner, Research Enterprise, University of Glasgow; Carol Hayden, Chief Executive's Department, Coventry City Council; Eoghan Howard, Wester Hailes Representative Council, Edinburgh; Alan Howie, Director, North Edinburgh Area Regeneration Programme; Liz Kerry, Director, Regional Assembly for Yorkshire and Humberside; Joel O'Loughlin, Chair, The Urban Forum, National Council for Voluntary Organisations; David Prior, Manager, Birmingham City Pride; Tom Russell, Assistant Chief Executive, Manchester City Council; and John Wilson, Tenants' Resource Centre, Glasgow. They are, of course, not responsible for the views set out in this report.

Finally, we would like to thank the four case study cities of Birmingham, Manchester, Glasgow and Edinburgh, and their residents, for their inspiration and for confirming that an urban renaissance is indeed underway in Britain. This process, which needs to extend to all citizens, is one of the foundation stones of national sustainable development for the country as a whole.

Executive summary

Despite some excellent local achievements, a compelling need for urban regeneration in Britain's cities has not been reduced by 30 years of policy initiatives. If deprived households, polarised sink estates and derelict landscapes are not to be with us 30 years hence, a new, strategic approach is required. To overcome persistent *failures of integration* we need to:

- integrate short-term initiatives within a long-term vision on the future role of our cities, and an investment framework to support that vision;
- evolve strategies for sustainable regional development which support city and local regeneration initiatives, and link cities and their hinterlands in a beneficial way;
- link physical development to economic and social regeneration;
- link policy streams, regionally and in local government, such as for the location of economic activity, education and vocational training and transport, to derive maximum benefit from inward investment;
- promote both leadership at the city level and devise means for genuine participation of all citizens in sustainable urban development, thus linking 'top-down' and 'bottom-up' in a new way which contributes to governance in the next century.

Perhaps the biggest challenge is that while the nation has become better at property-led regeneration of city centres, houses or heritage industrial buildings, we have not solved the problem of helping disadvantaged households, and their children, out of the deprivation caused by poverty and long-term unemployment. The challenges of regeneration are examined in Chapter 2. A key task is to make physical regeneration opportunities work to achieve social and economic development, and, once physical regeneration is accomplished, to devise more effective non-physical policy interventions.

This report summarises the results of a major research programme on strategic, city-wide urban regeneration, with case studies in Birmingham, Manchester, Glasgow and Edinburgh, reported in Chapter 4. It proposes an agenda of organisational innovation – a first step to sustainable cities.

Organisation innovation – the hidden resource for regeneration

Although well-financed initiatives can achieve good outcomes, managerial and organisational resources are important where finances are limited – almost always the case when regeneration challenges are examined at the city level. What is required is to make better use of existing resources, human and financial. Over time this could contribute to sustainable regeneration. This research makes recommendations for organisational innovation in regional development, city-wide regeneration and for neighbourhood initiatives. The dimensions of organisational innovation are discussed in Chapter 3, and key recommendations put forward in Chapters 5 and 6.

Recommendation 1: National action towards sustainable regeneration

Without pulling initiative back to the centre, central government needs to provide strong national leadership on urban regeneration through:

- establishment of basic principles of sustainable development and urban regeneration, which could provide a common agenda for a national programme of renewal of our cities;
- deriving rolling national and regional targets for regeneration, ranging from employment creation for disadvantaged households to amounts of derelict land reclaimed;
- enabling organisational frameworks at regional and city levels, including for emerging non-traditional urban areas, such as the M4 Corridor in England and the M8 Corridor in Scotland;
- by disseminating good practice;
- by promoting better coordination between Whitehall departments;
- by rethinking the influence of Treasury on regeneration and strategic investments, particularly those which have a long-term benefit stream.

Reform of challenge funding

Although there are some advantages in forcing the pace of change, challenge funding creates illogical competition between deprived areas. Failure to secure funding reinforces cynicism about participation. It can also mean that, as regeneration of selected areas fosters bending of main programmes, other areas fall further into deprivation. A new approach would begin with need and establish national funding priorities on a rational and defensible basis, with responsibility for central funding delegated to the Government Offices for the Regions (GORs) working with other regional partners to develop vision and strategy. Progress and outcomes could be overseen by a 'good practice unit' within the Audit Commission or the Department of Environment, Transport and the Regions (DETR). This would be a national source of practical knowledge on urban regeneration and a means of translating good practice from one area to the next. For Scotland, the role could be taken on by the Accounts Commission.

Recommendation 2: Better integration at the regional level

Whatever the outcome of deliberations on Regional Development Agencies (RDAs), it would be a mistake to allow a simplistic competition for inward investment to dictate the long-term pattern of regional development, even in areas desperate for jobs. A comprehensive approach is required, which integrates inward investment with regional vision for human resource development, land use, transport, competitiveness and urban regeneration objectives linked to education and training. There should be 'regional vision statements' with a 25-year perspective. These should not be vague or ineffectual, but link Vision, Strategy and Operational Policies (the VSOP approach) in a clear framework. The regional vision statement would represent the broadest perspective in an *integrated hierarchy of development guidance*, including:

- integrated regional planning and transport guidance (20-year perspective), to provide the contextual framework;
- structure or unitary development plans (15 years);
- city development strategies, to encompass city-wide regeneration strategy (10-15 years), and key objectives from neighbourhood plans;
- neighbourhood vision statements (10 years), with local plans and service quality agreements.

The English regions

To achieve integration, it makes sense for the GORs, working closely with the relevant regional forum for local government and civil society, to coordinate the activities of RDAs to maximum benefit. In the regions studied, there has been good progress towards establishing a coherent regional framework for sustainability and regeneration. The promotion of new business and inward investment is one aspect of a broader framework of sustainable development, which works to maximise economic, social and environmental benefits simultaneously, and achieve lasting regeneration.

Policy coordination and planning by GORs has some way to go to underpin regeneration. First, there is as yet little common purpose, strategy or timetabling between regeneration initiatives funded from Single Regeneration Budget (SRB), European Programme and mainstream programmes. This mirrors the failure to integrate UK regional and structure planning with management of regional programmes supported by Structural Funds. Second, there remain gaps in the administrative framework of GORs. Health, social services, education and land reclamation are outside the organisational framework. The Treasury could have regional representatives in the GORs – to foster understanding of the effects of public expenditure regulations on urban development and regeneration.

The Scottish city-regions

With the 1996 local government reorganisation, a shift to unitary local government abolished regional government. Although there is a good overall inward investment, for Scotland's city-regions there is no longer any regional perspective, outside of weak, voluntary structure planning arrangements between local authorities and sometimes illogical competition between local enterprise companies (LECs) in the same metropolitan area. There is no equivalent to Regional Planning Guidance (RPG), and no forum for regional discussion such as the North West Partnership and similar bodies in England. This situation is undermining regeneration, particularly in Glasgow. There is disjuncture between where jobs are created and where they are needed, and little opportunity for coordinating transport between the two. A Scottish Parliament will need to re-establish a level of regional coordination to regain the more strategic approach now emerging for the English regions.

Recommendation 3: City-wide, integrated urban development strategies

City Pride and Programme for Partnership have initiated city-wide partnership and strategy – a key step to sustainable regeneration. Areas of innovation are documented, including:

- sophisticated partnership between Birmingham Council, the Chamber of Commerce and other stakeholders, and including a major role for the voluntary sector and for young people;
- fast-track decision making on regeneration by Manchester City Council, with specialist sub-committees, strong executive leadership and innovation in Neighbourhood Strategy Initiatives;
- partnerships between Glasgow City Council, community-based housing associations and private builders (using Scottish Homes' Grants) to diversify council estates as a step to fostering sustainable neighbourhoods;
- a new city strategy in Edinburgh, and innovative approaches to joint ventures and use of a wholly-owned private company as a regeneration agency.

This innovation, while inspiring, will not be enough to achieve sustainable regeneration. The main challenges to local governance are:

- coordination of policy, based on strategic information, at the centre;
- integration of service delivery at the area level;
- devolution of opportunity for visioning and community planning and encouragement of self-responsibility in the neighbourhood.

The report recommends that the next step for cities is *integrated urban development strategies*, encompassing physical, economic and social development, urban regeneration and Agenda 21. This is needed to provide an overall strategic approach, coordinating local government's line departments and agencies such as health, the police and so on. The example of Copenhagen is reported.

The report then distinguishes between *area*-level service coordination – a function of local government – and *neighbourhood* visioning – an opportunity for direct citizen interaction with local government and other stakeholders.

Recommendation 4: A call for neighbourhood visioning

Community participation remains one of the biggest challenges to sustainable regeneration.

Temporary participation exercises, such as Planning for Real, are valuable, but cannot be representative or democratic, nor do they allow communities to regularly influence mainstream programmes or strategic issues. Beyond temporary participation, there is a 'chaotic' patchwork of statutory and informal "consultation, when the real decisions have already been taken". To counter this, local governments have an interest in decentralisation, but less positive experience.

To foster genuine participation, and side-step the plethora of inefficient, token consultations, a streamlined, one-stop participation process for each neighbourhood is proposed. This recognises that local people, in and out of regeneration areas, need the opportunity for less intensive, less wearing but lifelong participation which assesses neighbourhood prospects holistically rather than in the compartmentalised boxes of administration. Children also need to participate because they are full of good ideas, and because today's student is tomorrow's young adult.

A neighbourhood visioning process, on a voluntary basis, would give local people the opportunity to establish a sense of purpose for local development and priorities for action by stakeholders including community groups. The focus would be on future direction and how different policy areas, and citizens and professionals, interact to move towards the sustainable neighbourhood, as well as providing local input to the city strategy. A major advantage is that residents would not be dependent on institutional stakeholders providing the chance for participation, but would know that they could avail themselves of the opportunity to participate, *as a right of citizenship*.

1

Urban regeneration in Britain – past and future

In 1999, 30 years will have passed since Britain's first urban regeneration areas were designated. These were the General Improvement Areas set up under the 1969 Housing Act. In the absence of major changes in the nation's approach to regeneration, the record of this past 30 years may be a guide to the next.

The record is mixed. On the positive side, city centres have been revitalised and civic pride rekindled in cities such as Birmingham, Manchester and Glasgow. Economic and physical regeneration has taken place in some former industrial areas, particularly around features such as docks, canals and Victorian warehouses. There have been some solid achievements in estate regeneration, particularly by local government working in partnership with community-based organisations, housing associations and private builders. Many towns and cities have inspiring examples of regeneration.

But we have been unable to generate sustainable solutions to other pressing challenges. In many ways, we appear to be *managing* deprivation rather than *resolving* the problem. Male unemployment in some neighbourhoods is still over 40%, bringing a host of social problems for disadvantaged households. These affect the future of children – who will be adults in 10 or 15 years. There is too much damp, cold housing – with dramatic health impacts, including 'winter deaths' of older people. The decline of the traditional manufacturing base in industrial cities continues to haunt us with vacant buildings and derelict, contaminated land covering up to 15% of our urban land area.

Although there is progress, it does not seem sufficient to complete the task. The steady shift of economic and social activity, and thus people, out of the cities makes urban regeneration more difficult. Industrial location policy, with the New Towns policy and the 'weak' planning years of the 1980s all fostered decentralisation of employment, housing and retailing. This reduced the locational advantage of cities and towns in favour of automobile-dependent, greenfield locations, which are poorly served by public transport and thus out of bounds to households without cars. For example, during the last 15 years a third of all the nation's retail sales have shifted from our high streets and local shopping precincts to out-of-town malls and large shed-type buildings. This has been at the very time when there has been a substantial net shift of public resources away from urban areas, making it more difficult for local authorities to redress the impacts of these policies.

There are disincentives to investment in urban regeneration areas. In spite of Planning Policy Guidance (PPG), out-of-town locations continue to be more profitable for developers of business parks, houses and shops than the thousands of hectares of derelict land in inner cities. This means urban regeneration is working against the flow of the market – an uphill battle requiring seemingly endless subsidy. The key point is that brownfield development is intrinsically more costly than greenfield, and the limited financial incentives available to the private sector do not fully compensate it. In the absence of a more generous structure of incentives, a greenfield development tax, or firm principled land use control which eliminates greenfield development as an option, we cannot expect developers to build with enthusiasm on contaminated land in decayed inner cities.

Temporary initiatives versus the 'long haul' in urban management

Perhaps the biggest challenge is that, while we have become better at property-led regeneration, whether of houses or canal-side industrial premises and pubs, we have not managed to solve the problem of disadvantaged households stuck in the social and economic deprivation caused by long-term unemployment.

These problems continue in spite of an enormous input of financial and human resources to urban regeneration, and a large number of short-term policy initiatives. Since 1969, these have included the Housing Action Areas, Community Development Projects, Educational Priority Areas, Urban Development Corporations (UDCs), Priority Estate Projects, City Action Teams, Estate Action, Urban Priority Areas, Action for Cities, Inner City Task Forces, City Grants, Housing Action Trusts, Urban Programme, City Challenge, SRB, Priority Partnership Areas (PPAs) and others.

With a few exceptions, many of these initiatives have had to be applied again and again to the same estates and neighbourhoods (Fordham, 1995). Because of an over-reliance on short-term initiatives, policy making is too often 'reinventing the wheel'. Compounding the problem, new challenges are surfacing out of recent initiatives. Housing association estates and low-cost owner-occupied estates are slipping into patterns of decline once confined to the council sector (Page, 1993). Council estates 'regenerated' 10 years ago are ripe for demolition (Glasgow City Council announced in November 1997 that 872 houses in Central Drumchapel, renovated in the late 1980s, are to be demolished. Three hundred are currently vacant). Home ownership by families with low, vulnerable incomes, encouraged by Right-to-Buy, is now linked to rising household poverty.

Failure to achieve sustainability may derive in part from a misassumption that deep-seated urban problems can be resolved by temporary or 'catalyst' initiatives, such as listed above. These can be useful to focus resources and energies, but they are clearly *not sufficient* for sustainable regeneration. Indeed, the energies that go into them can divert attention from some real needs. For example:

- to make steady, incremental improvements in long-term housing and urban management policies and processes;
- to change local organisational culture to support broadened participation, and to encourage leadership and innovation;
- to improve the symbiotic relationship between the top-down urban policy framework and bottom-up local initiatives which generate real, on-the-ground outcomes.

The past, therefore, is not a very good guide to what we might do to make regeneration sustainable. This is mainly because of *failures of integration*: failure to integrate physical regeneration with social and economic development; failure to link policy streams, such as industrial location, transport and training; failure to link regional, city and local initiatives in a coherent framework; failure to link necessary partners in a common effort; and failure to devise genuinely participative mechanisms for strategy and implementation.

To achieve better integration, a shift in policy and practice is necessary. In particular, it cannot simply be an issue of more new policies or initiatives, and we cannot rely on the expectation of more resources, which will always be tight. Although well-financed initiatives can achieve excellent outcomes, managerial and organisational resources are important where finances are limited, which is always the case when regeneration challenges are analysed at the city-wide level. In this case, what needs to be done is to make better use of existing resources, human and financial, for urban management. Over a long time this could amount to a considerable achievement for sustainable regeneration.

Integration unlocked by organisational innovation

The premise of this research project is that enhanced integration is a hidden resource that can be unlocked by organisational innovation. The research suggests that three types of integration are important:

- *Temporal integration* means that short-term regeneration projects and initiatives of 5-10 years are carried out within a framework of long-term vision on the future of cities, and a medium-term, 15- to 20-year development strategy.

- *Horizontal integration* means better linkage between central and local government, business interests, the voluntary sector and local communities; and better integration of strategy in different policy streams in a unifying framework.
- *Vertical integration* means that regional policy and planning guidance positively support city-level and neighbourhood initiatives. In turn, the learning generated at the 'front line' of regeneration should systematically inform higher levels of policy in a virtuous, repetitive cycle of strategy–implementation–feedback. This is the opposite of inventing a new urban policy every three years or so.

This integration is achieved, not by dictate of a minister or a chief executive but by organisational change and changing organisational culture. Is this radical? The Prime Minister does not think so: "The key to modernising local government is for councils to change the way they govern and organise themselves" (*Guardian*, 3 November 1997).

Organisational innovation, doing things in new ways, can be an important tool of regeneration. But innovation needs to be carefully thought out and built on existing constructive practice. Sometimes the problem in Britain is not lack of local initiative or good example, but too much 'chopping and changing' in response to short-term policy initiatives and funding opportunities, dictated by political expedience. This precludes a steady 'learning-by-doing' in the long haul of urban management. Despite this constraint, and given the complexity of the task, what we *are* doing is still the best means for learning about how to do better.

The research examined, in a questioning but constructive way, how strategic, city-wide urban regeneration is carried out in Birmingham, Manchester, Glasgow and Edinburgh, and how the process might be improved. In addition to field studies, the report is also based on a long-standing research programme on sustainable development, and the organisational frameworks which might bring about its achievement (Carley, 1995a; Carley and Christie, 1992; Carley and Spapens, 1998; Scottish Homes, 1995). An important aspect of this organisational perspective is to assess the potential for integration between regional, city-wide and neighbourhood initiatives and to link regeneration to the agendas of regional planning, the emergence of Regional Development Agencies (RDAs) at one end of the spatial scale, and decentralisation programmes within local government at the other.

In addition to the study of city-wide approaches to regeneration, there was also analysis of the link between strategic regeneration and estate action for four neighbourhoods in each of the cities: North Glasgow; Craigmillar, a peripheral estate in Edinburgh; the inner-city areas of Cheetham and Broughton in Manchester; and Aston Newtown in Birmingham. The lessons from these neighbourhood initiatives are discussed in the Appendix.

The concept of sustainability applied to regeneration

An assumption of the research is that regeneration efforts will continue to underachieve unless there is a pronounced shift of perspective to reflect the longer-term nature of the regeneration task. The concept of sustainable development provides a framework for both integration and this long-term view. Although deriving originally from environmental concerns, the concept now defines, first, beneficial interaction between economy, environment and social development and, second, intergenerational equity, that is, ensuring that whatever we do now leaves future generations better off.

Three aspects of sustainable development are relevant. First, there is growing awareness that poverty, social alienation and urban dereliction are incompatible with sustainable development. Among other things, this has given rise to analysis intended to develop long-term policies to promote the generation of employment, and to define minimum acceptable standards of quality of life consistent with a sound urban ecology, which extend to all income levels of society (Spangenberg et al, 1994). Figure 1 shows how these elements interact to give rise to sustainable development.

Figure 1: A model of sustainable development

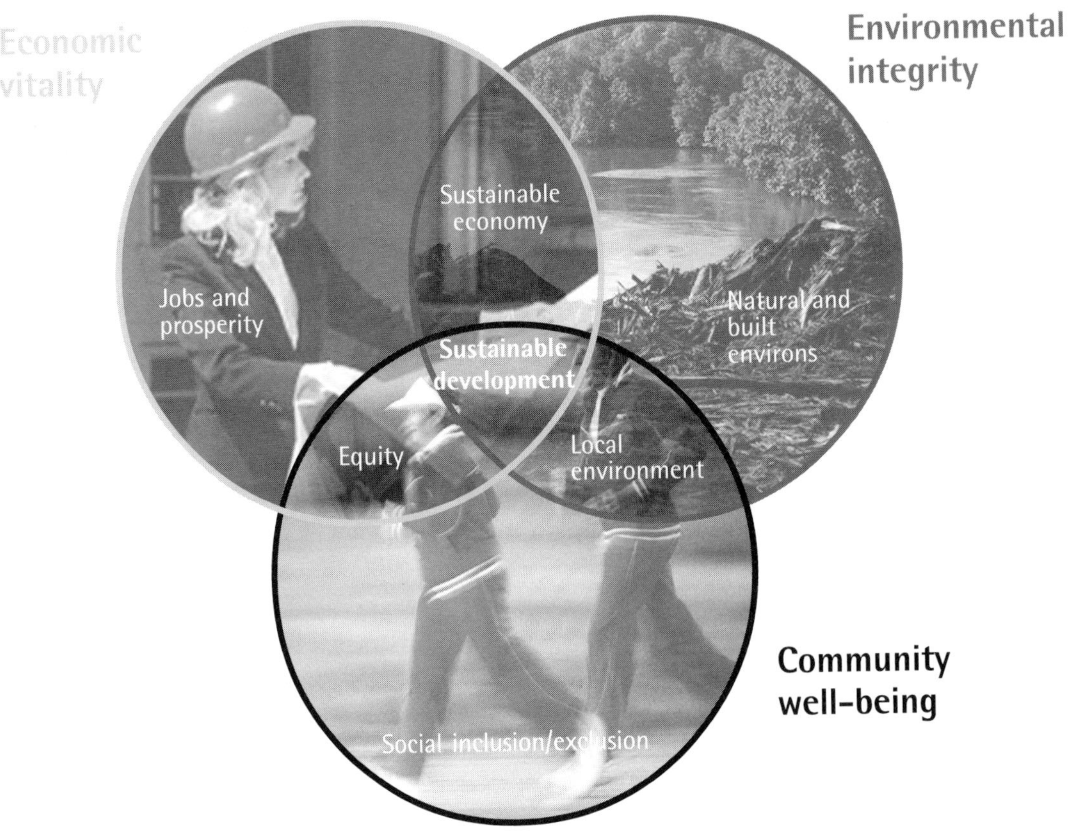

Source: Forward Scotland

Second, linked to this is recognition that a sustainable urban society is defined in part by a judicious combination of private consumption and availability of high quality public goods which contribute to a sense of community. These include good education and schools to ensure for the future, civic amenities, a high quality city centre, good libraries, high quality parks, public transport, a good walking or cycling environment, and one safe for children, elderly people and other vulnerable members of society. The achievement of the best mix requires a sophisticated interaction between public, private and voluntary sectors. The renewed interest in the joys of urban living in Britain is in part an understanding that community life and urban amenities can be as valuable to quality of life as private consumption – a key point for cities which may contain the greatest concentrations of need but also major potential for community interaction.

Third, there is an emerging focus on the processes of governance, management and democratic participation, which are necessary to achieve a sustainable society. For example, Carley and Christie define sustainable development as:

> A continuing, participative process of management and mediation among economic, social and environmental needs which results in positive socio-economic change, and which does not undermine the social and ecological systems upon which healthy communities and societies are dependent. (Carley and Christie, 1992)

In this perspective, organisational innovation is at the heart of the task of sustainable development. Following from this, broad criteria for defining sustainable urban regeneration emerge. It:

- gives robust, *long-term* solutions, of benefit to the next generation while being cost-effective for the current generation;
- implies steady, *strategic* processes of urban development which can weather unforeseen

intervening variables, such as are derived from the global economy;

- generates *positive reinforcement* (or multiplier benefits) in development or investment sectors (housing, employment, training, retailing, transport, education, etc);
- leads consistently towards a physical, economic and social *reintegration* of hitherto disadvantaged estates or neighbourhoods into the broader townscape;
- fosters continuous *innovation*, which implies learning-by-doing or adaptive management, with systematic monitoring and adjustment of strategy.

These longer-term processes, which unfold both within local government, and in linking local government to other important partners such as central government, regional administration, the community or the private sector, suggest a need for basic, *organisational prerequisites* for sustainable urban regeneration. This research is intended to explore these organisational prerequisites:

- to enhance our understanding of their importance and potential contribution to regeneration efforts;
- to understand the political, organisational and knowledge constraints which inhibit their achievement;
- to identify constructive good practice which can suggest ways forward to improve regeneration practice.

Questions addressed by the research

In this exploration, more than 100 key informants in the four case study cities and elsewhere were asked four broad questions:

- What separates us as a nation from sustainable urban development and regeneration? (That is, what is the agenda of sustainability for our cities?)

Key definitions

National sustainable development: coordinated improvement in the economic and social life of the nation, balanced in urban and rural areas, with reductions in social inequality, pollution and resource consumption and without curtailing, and preferably improving, the prospects of coming generations. The objectives are set out in *Sustainable development: The UK strategy* (Her Majesty's Government, 1994), with national dialogue supported by the UK Round Table on Sustainable Development. Internationally, strategies are coordinated by the United Nations' Commission for Sustainable Development.

Sustainable urban development: improvement in quality of life and participation in decision making on issues affecting city-regions and local neighbourhoods, including efficient use of urban space, maximised opportunity for economic and social development for all citizens, minimised social cost of transport and reduced resource consumption and pollution (for a discussion see Roseland, 1997 and Haughton, 1997).

Sustainable urban regeneration: management and participation processes and investments, directed at disadvantaged areas and households, giving long-lasting improvements in the prospects of residents and full integration with society. Initiatives are democratically determined, accord with residents' needs and aspirations, and likely to benefit their children and grandchildren.

Sustainable neighbourhoods: lively, local, mixed-use settlements which maximise quality of life and social interaction and minimise negative effects whether social or environmental, thus benefiting both local residents and society at large.

Agenda 21: a global programme on sustainable development initiated by the 1992 United Nations Conference on Environment and Development. It emphasises national strategies to support local action, and the need to improve the social, economic and environmental quality of cities and towns, and the living and working environments of all people, especially the poor.

- What are the main organisational constraints on sustainable regeneration, and how can we 'reorganise' ourselves to get on the road to sustainability?
- What can we learn, particularly in terms of areas of innovation, from existing efforts in our big cities?
- What recommendations should follow from this analysis?

Each question is addressed in the subsequent chapters. Chapter 2 looks at the challenge of regeneration, Chapter 3 proposes eight 'organisational prerequisites' for achieving sustainability, Chapter 4 looks at the four case studies and Chapters 5 and 6 make recommendations based on the field work.

The unique contribution of this research is in its focus on organisational aspects of regeneration in a city-wide strategic framework. The research intends to raise fundamental questions about objectives and processes of urban management in Britain, and provide constructive suggestions for going forward towards a more robust achievement of regeneration objectives.

2

The challenge of sustainable urban regeneration

The idea of *sustainable* regeneration is important because, as a society, we have enormous, if unrealised, expectations of our urban regeneration programmes. We expect them to address: the problems caused by global economic restructuring, such as deindustrialisation, and a national deconcentration of people and jobs out of traditional cities; the revitalisation of cities, industry and derelict and contaminated land; and poverty and unemployment, long-standing failures of education and training systems, lack of adult basic skills, crime and vandalism, family dysfunction, housing disrepair, and so on.

Most regeneration programmes with a *human* rather than a *buildings* focus, also need to be participative, so that local people have a stake in the solution rather than being part of the problem. But this means addressing 'democratic deficit', a term which describes our declining faith in formal systems of governance, and the endemic cynicism and apathy which characterises many deprived estates, where so many previous initiatives have failed to deliver on their promises.

The extent to which regeneration programmes on their own can deal with this range of problems should be questioned, but the list suggests key dimensions of the agenda of regeneration. The intention in this chapter is not to attempt a comprehensive agenda but to demonstrate the range and the seriousness of the task and to suggest where organisational innovation should be directed.

Increasing numbers of poor households

Poverty is the key constraint on sustainable regeneration. Unfortunately, during the 1980s more British households became poor. The number in poverty rose by half between 1979 and 1991 to 14.6% of the population. This high incidence of poverty accounts for Britain's low ranking on the United Nations' Human Development Index, at 16th of developed countries in 1996, and 12th of the European countries (UN Development Programme, 1996). In terms of GDP per head, Britain is one of the four poorest countries in the European Union, and second only to Portugal in the high percentage of the population living in poverty (Mullaney, 1997). There is growing evidence that inequality in itself, aside from its impact on households, increases social, crime and health problems in societies.

Given the extent of poverty, the term 'social exclusion' has real resonance in Britain where the 20% of the population living in the poorest circumstances may have children with low birth weights, an indicator commonly associated with poor, developing countries, and premature death rates twice that of Britain's well-off. There is evidence of the intergenerational impacts of unemployment and dysfunction in families, with the social development of children as young as three to four years blighted by the financial crises of their parents, and the limitations on experience brought about by poverty (Watt, 1995). The rate of children living in poverty is a predictor of the incidence of low birth weight and, later in childhood, low GCSE achievements, which decrease employability. Given that

Britain is 23rd of the 25 Organization for Economic Co-operation and Development (OECD) nations in percentage investment of GDP in education, it is unlikely that the educational system will make up for the in-built disadvantage faced by these children (OECD, 1997).

Aside from low benefit rates, unemployment is at the root of much poverty. This is a key challenge in most regeneration areas. On the Alexandra Park Estate in Manchester, for example, male unemployment is 47% and youth unemployment 42% (Manchester City Council, 1996). Research shows that the long-term unemployed in Britain are more likely to be unable to afford the basic necessities of life, and to be in serious debt, than similar households in Germany or Sweden (Clasen et al, 1997).

A main challenge for regeneration is to link wealth creation, education and training and the provision of employment. With the exception of some good intermediate labour market projects, such as those initiated by the Wise Group, too few regeneration projects have employment creation at their heart. As a result, our learning-by-doing in this vital area is weak, undermined by government policy of the 1980s and early 1990s. This has led to a fragmentation of provision (eg, creation of Training and Enterprise Councils [TECs], incorporation of further education colleges) based on a simplistic market model of competing agencies, which has made integration more difficult.

Spatial concentration of poor households

During the 1980s, as the numbers of poor increased, poor households also tended to become more spatially concentrated or 'residualised' on run-down estates. So, although the poor can be found almost everywhere, pockets of acute disadvantage are tightly clustered in inner-city wards and peripheral estates. Three million people live on the worst estates, where only half the adults may be employed. The interplay of elements of multiple deprivation make regeneration all the more difficult – something known for 30 years, but difficult to get to grips with.

The employment prospects of the residents of these estates have been substantially reduced because the jobs have either disappeared or moved away. Deindustrialisation, such as the decline of the metal working industry in Birmingham, or shipbuilding on the Clyde, resulted in large areas of inner cities being decimated of jobs. Birmingham, for example, lost 25% of its manual jobs between 1981 and 1991; Glasgow lost 44% of its manufacturing jobs during the same period. Growth in service employment in these cities offset less than 10% of these losses. This means that the less economically-able, living on estates characterised by a high proportion of immobile tenants, unable to move to higher-priced zones in the city and dependent on expensive, poor quality public transport, are no longer linked to the locations of employment.

Residualisation is most apparent in social housing. In Glasgow, for example, the council is the landlord to three quarters of the city's unemployed and two thirds of its lone parent households. Eighty-five percent of Glasgow's council tenants are in receipt of Housing Benefit. One half of the children in Glasgow live on the peripheral estates. Increasing rents in the social sector mean that a mortgage is often cheaper than social rent without Housing Benefit. Those who can buy do so, causing a decline in the social mix of tenants. At the same time, the economically empowered have moved on from the worst estates – positive mobility and residualisation are two sides of the same coin. Residualisation reinforces the stigmatisation which is the common lot of estates, households and jobseekers, who are turned away by prospective employers at the very mention of their area of residence.

In a disturbing turn of events, residualisation appears to be worsening the growing challenge of problem families. Every housing department, and many councillors interviewed in the course of this research mentioned problem families and the difficulty of addressing the issue in a local climate of fear and intimidation. In the worst cases, near anarchy can result. One of these situations arose during the course of the study on the Barlornock Estate in Glasgow. The estate, renovated seven years ago and given an award at the time by the Royal Institute of Architects in Scotland, is now ready for demolition. Young vandals and their adult collaborators have ravaged the estate, making it a no-go area for the police, and causing a mass exodus of long-standing tenants, including the local councillor. The Housing Committee decided in 1997 that the battle was lost and demolition the only solution – perhaps begging the question of whether the problem will shift to another nearby neighbourhood.

Are these sink estates to be permanently places for the poor households in our society, the long-term unemployed and elderly people who cannot get away? Will they get worse? Given 30 years of regeneration, the situation of these estates is a sharp reminder of the failure of regeneration. One lesson is that it is unlikely that the problems can be resolved at the estate level. It is right, therefore, to also address these issues at a national and city-wide level.

Poor quality housing

The condition of the nation's housing stock is a key aspect of physical sustainability. This is both because of the health and social effects of damp and disrepair, and because the energy inefficiency of the nation's housing makes it, with motor vehicle emissions, a main contributor to global warming. Household heating and transport account for 50% of the UK's energy use (National Consumer Council, 1997).

Analysis of the Scottish House Condition Survey and its English counterpart reveal that, although substantial numbers of houses are brought up to a comprehensive standard of repair each year, a *more or less equal number* decline in quality at the same time, leaving an overall task of unchanging magnitude. For example, Birmingham's *City Pride prospectus* (1995) reports that, in that city alone, 47,720 homes in the private sector are unfit for habitation, and 212 council tower blocks are structurally unfit, demolition being the only feasible option for at least 100.

Fifty per cent of British homes do not meet minimum energy standards, and 15% of the housing stock is grossly inefficient. The English House Condition Survey notes that elderly and disabled people are concentrated in the worst performing dwellings, with over half of England's pensioners unable to maintain minimum heating of 18°c within their homes. In Scotland, around a quarter of all houses suffer dampness, affecting 30% of Scottish children (*Scotland on Sunday*, 30 November 1997).

Around 6 million Britons, more than 10% of the population, are classified as 'fuel poor'. Poor housing quality has major knock-on effects in terms of hospitalisation rates of elderly people, and so on. It impinges not only on the health of children but on their ability to do homework and to prepare for life.

Every winter as many as 30,000 elderly people in Britain die from the cold – a situation unheard of in countries with far harsher climates such as Canada or Sweden ('Cold comfort for winter', *Guardian*, 16 October 1997). Many sub-standard homes are in the inner cities. For example, 37% of Birmingham's homes are without central heating. Even in prosperous Edinburgh, 17,939 council homes (that is, 50% of the total stock) suffer condensation and dampness. Forty per cent of these houses have no central heating. Children also suffer from life-long, damp-induced illnesses, such as asthma.

The refurbishment of the nation's housing stock is a major issue – it is hard to imagine that households living in damp, cold housing are in the best position to meet the challenges of education and employment in a global economy. But the investment required to raise the UK housing stock to the thermal equivalents of our northern European neighbours is massive – in the order of £26 billion, according to the Energy Report. Current policies, such as small amounts of additional money for heat, although well-meaning, are just skirting around the edge of the problem and must be seen against a background of declining national investment in social housing – down 50% since 1980 (National Housing Federation, 1997).

Urban–rural balance and the future of cities: sustainable land use

The loss of industry in the inner city coincided with, and was related to, loss of the urban working population as they moved to the new suburban estates and industrial–business parks in greenfield locations. This reflects a long-term decline in Britain's urban population – down 1.25 million between 1981 and 1994 – in favour of semi-rural locations. Manchester, for example, has suffered *both* 25% loss of population and jobs, although in many cases those who lost their jobs were not the ones moving on. This shift is reinforcing a socioeconomic divide which is progressively leaving urban areas worse off than the non-metropolitan hinterland – residualisation at a regional level. Against this tide, even highly visible urban regeneration efforts, such as London Docklands, have little impact (ESRC, 1996).

Population and employment shift is creating major development pressure in hitherto rural areas, fuelling traffic congestion and air pollution, and leaving a legacy of derelict land in cities. Richard Rogers, in his maiden speech to the House of Lords on 20 May 1997, argued that if the amount of floor space of vacant buildings was included in the figure for derelict land, the total amount of unused urban space would be 15% of the national total.

The process of land dereliction is far from over. For example, in Glasgow vacant land is being created at twice the rate of its clear-up, as firms shift to motorway-side business parks, to reduce shipping costs and attract skilled, car-borne employees prepared to drive 30 miles or more to work. Yet mixed in with derelict land are valuable on-going businesses which must be nurtured if they are not to close or move to greenfield sites inaccessible to local households. At the same time, big sites for big manufacturers must be made available, because they in turn support a broad range of small and medium size enterprises as suppliers. Businesses will migrate away from the cities if there are not the purpose-built buildings and sites suitable for the high-technology, clean production, required for electronic components such as semi-conductors. The situation is complicated by the fact that there is no coherent national policy for derelict land, and funding regimes, insufficient to a problem which the market cannot solve, are overly focused on short-term outcomes.

The situation has created a disjuncture between housing-based regeneration in the cities and the creation of new employment out-of-town. For example, residents of Glasgow's Easterhouse, one of the most deprived of the city's peripheral estates, have been unable to share in the employment benefits of one of Scotland's most massive new industrial developments which is five miles away in Lanarkshire and virtually inaccessible by public transport (or even bicycle). This is reflected by the fact that of the 1,500 applicants for the first jobs on offer, only eight applicants were from Easterhouse.

The real costs of greenfield development

A related problem is a failure to assess the true range of costs and benefits in the brownfield–greenfield development equation. On the revenue side, loss of business rates handicaps the regeneration options of councils. On the supply side, loss of the inner-city population raises the unit cost of basic services, and the cost to the nation of then replicating these at suburban locations. For example, around one fifth of Glasgow's primary schools are seriously under capacity and need to be closed. Forty per cent of places in secondary schools are currently surplus to requirements – even though the number of secondary schools has declined from 55 to 38 since 1981 (Glasgow City Council, 1997). At one secondary school in the Gorbals regeneration area there are 283 pupils in a building designed for 1,400. These underutilised schools continue to incur fixed costs such as those for heating and janitorial services, but cannot offer the range of courses and facilities needed by students, many already from disadvantaged households.

School closures are politically contentious, because people know that schools play a vital role in maintaining local identity and both child and adult social networks. In Edinburgh's Muirhouse Estate, for example, keeping local schools open is the first priority of residents. Of course, students from households without cars are not in a good position to travel long distances to schools not well served by public transport, thus reducing further their opportunities and increasing social polarisation.

Under current arrangements, greenfield development tends to be cheaper and at lower market risk. But as with many complex issues, the market doesn't take into account the full range of costs. The issues are summarised in Table 1.

Table 1: The real costs of land development

Cost of brownfield development to the nation	Cost of greenfield development to the nation
Cost of land decontamination and improvement or rebuilding of outdated infrastructure to new build standards	Cost of building new roads, schools, libraries, health services and other infrastructure in the suburbs
	Economic and social costs of declining school rolls and underinvestment in inner-city schools; loss of client base for inner-city health services, libraries, etc; foreclosing of options for inner-city residents and students
	Health costs of air pollution and global warming if development is car dependent
	Loss of prime agricultural land and rural tranquillity

3

Organisational prerequisites for sustainable regeneration

Sustainable regeneration comes from a positive relationship between the regeneration *strategy* process, that is, deciding what to do, and the *organisational framework*, or how to do it. The organisational framework fosters partnership of key stakeholders, including community participants, to debate and refine the strategy, and generates commitment to coordination of policy, funding and action. The remainder of this report is about this organisational dimension.

The research began with a hypothesis of a set of organisational prerequisites for sustainable regeneration, to be tested in the field. The logic of these is discussed in this chapter, expanded as a result of the fieldwork. The next chapter looks at the four case studies. The final two chapters make recommendations based on the fieldwork.

First prerequisite: Shift to a long-term perspective

Most of the key players interviewed in the research singled out a primary constraint on sustainable regeneration: our failure as a nation to enable a long-term perspective on the future of cities and their hinterlands. This has two aspects: a failure to develop vision on which to build consensus and guide policy, and an assumption that regeneration can be accomplished quickly, giving rise to 'short termism' in policy and funding.

Our failure to envision the kinds of cities and towns to bequeath to coming generations was flagged by many key players as apparent in the lack of coherent urban policy and in a patchy, uncoordinated urban investment framework, whether in transport, social housing or land reclamation. Lack of vision reveals itself in an unclarity about whether cities are valuable national resources, to be lovingly maintained, or an outdated, uneconomic form of settlement to be superseded by suburban land use on American lines. Lack of vision is also evidenced by unclarity about the relationship of the urban to the rural during this period of shift of population and jobs out of the cities.

The problem is worsened by a preference for quick, funding-driven solutions to deep-seated challenges. These affect local regeneration partnerships which gear up with great fanfare and lots of hard work only to disappear a few years later. Opportunities for incremental learning-by-doing are thus lost. These could be a crucial resource to see through regeneration over what might need to be a 20-year frame of action.

Short termism has conditioned people to think of regeneration as separate from mainstream tasks and funding. Too often, even under improved current initiatives such as SRBs or PPAs, or the Scottish New Housing Partnerships, regeneration is characterised by a desperate rush to secure funding in competition with other local authorities, and then begin spending the money rapidly in year one, lest the opportunity slip away. Although a short deadline can force the pace of action, unless it is within a clear policy framework, it can preclude a steady approach which might generate better long-term outcomes. It can also put irrational pressure on mainstream budgets and community initiatives when funding ends before tasks are accomplished.

Players in regeneration from all walks of life want a longer-term framework. Private investors from industry, property development and house building were almost unanimous in wanting clear, long-term goals and plans from the public sector for investment on training and education, and for physical infrastructure, especially for transport and land reclamation. This, they argue, would help develop a skilled and internationally competitive workforce. It would create conditions of confidence to encourage investment in inner cities.

The Local Government Association, in its *Regeneration: The new commitment* has flagged the disbenefits of short-term 'annuality' in local authority budgeting, and the emerging benefits of the longer-term framework encouraged by SRB. Local government officials and politicians argue that a longer perspective, and funding mechanisms, are essential to the visions and objectives they have for their cities. Local community representatives want to participate in neighbourhood regeneration processes which give lasting improvements, not only for themselves, but for their children – not a seemingly endless round of temporary initiatives.

Regeneration partnerships are based on human relationships, which grow and cement over time by a process of mutual learning about problems and opportunities. This learning is vital because there are no off-the-shelf solutions, from this country or any other, to the challenges of socioeconomic regeneration. Rather, successful strategies are fashioned locally and represent the 'art of the possible'. Short termism means chopping and changing – wasting the valuable human resources invested in building workable partnerships.

On the positive side, City Pride and the Programme for Partnership in Scotland, whatever their faults, have nurtured a metropolitan, strategic approach – the first, key step to sustainable regeneration. Birmingham's City Pride, for example, includes a board of stakeholders and a small secretariat jointly resourced by the City Council, TEC and the Chamber of Commerce to drive forward the regeneration agenda. It is important to support and learn from these partnerships. A positive trend to the strategic is reinforced by the city-wide, thematic elements of funding within SRBs and PPAs.

Second prerequisite: Linking the top-down and the bottom-up

Local regeneration projects and initiatives under Agenda 21 were found in the research to provide good examples of community-based or bottom-up initiatives (see, for example, Dwelly, 1996). But too often these have been undermined by inconsistency in the top-down policy framework. At the national level, the requirement for a long-term approach of incremental learning sits uneasily with the needs of ministers, changing hats frequently in the recent past, to be seen 'ribbon-cutting' bright new initiatives. In the city, top-down departmentalism of officers and councillors may find little reward in supporting community initiatives, compared with the pull of interdepartmental rivalry over budgets, or the lure of ruling group politics.

Because regeneration is difficult, a more sophisticated interaction is needed between bottom-up knowledge of what does and does not work, and the enabling policy framework. In this view, at the national level, a ministerial 'U-turn' on policy might be a good thing if it represented *learning* from present initiatives and past mistakes. One of the biggest challenges is to enable the lessons of failure to be incorporated into the next rounds of policy, without threatening professional stature or career in central or local government. By the same token, a successful programme might remain in place for one, or even two, decades, surviving changes in government.

This approach implies regular and honest monitoring based on clear objectives (discussed later) and a kind of subsidiarity in policy and practice which reinforces the links between central policy, city regeneration strategy and neighbourhood action. The designation of the first round of Welfare to Work's New Deal initiatives as 'Pathfinders' could represent this kind of learning – based on the recognition there are no easy or 'gimmicky' answers to difficult policy challenges, but that we need to learn, step-by-step, what does and does not work to improve the next round of policy. The proposed Employment Zones could be a real 'laboratory' of national policy on training and education. Hopefully the learning generated can be incorporated quickly into extension and improvement of the initiative even while it is unfolding.

At the city level, the research suggests that the main challenges to local governance on regeneration and sustainability are:

- *coordination of policy*, based on strategic information, at the centre, or city hall;
- *integration of service delivery* at the area level;
- *devolution of opportunity* for visioning and community planning and encouragement of self-responsibility in the neighbourhood.

The research suggests that one of the most powerful ways of linking city-wide strategy and local action is by seeing regeneration as an opportunity for *mutual learning* among local government officers, key stakeholders and community representatives. In cities such as Birmingham and Manchester, senior local government officers and politicians are getting involved directly in neighbourhood initiatives, thus fostering the learning environment necessary to inform city strategy, as well expressing commitment to action in the neighbourhood. In Edinburgh, 'area managers' are providing a bridge between central policy and local neighbourhood concerns, and working to integrate service delivery.

Finally, policy and planning processes – if they are open, participative and encompass the technical and professional requirements of governance within a broader 'layperson-friendly' consideration of quality of life issues – can also be processes of mutual learning which link top-down and bottom-up. Chapters 5 and 6 make recommendations for linking regional, city-level and local planning processes. This suggests a third prerequisite.

Third prerequisite: Estate and city in a regional framework

A key to improved integration is to link regional, city-wide and local initiatives in a systematic development framework, recognising that guidance and decisions at the level of the region can have profound impacts on the viability of local regeneration. After a long hiatus in regional planning, many respondents noted with approval that we seem to be moving in this more systematic direction. Without it, city competes with city for inward investment, replicating regional 'bidding wars', some of which serve only to shift employment from one locale to another. For example, long-standing employers in Manchester's SRB regeneration areas of Cheetham and Broughton are in danger of being lured away to greenfield sites, which are able to offer a tempting array of incentives.

Similarly, a large shopping mall can draw shoppers away from a local high street or precinct, undermining economic viability and employment in local neighbourhoods, accessible without a car. Boarded up shops are commonplace following this 'retail revolution' (for a discussion, see Carley, 1996). In Edinburgh, for example, Safeway is attempting to close their popular store within the urban regeneration area of Wester Hailes in favour of two massive new stores on the city's ring road, and despite £17m of urban regeneration funding to Wester Hailes' retail plaza. Car-less (or better, car-free) households will thus be substantially disadvantaged.

For neighbouring local authorities, all of which may have suffered deindustrialisation, there is a temptation for each to go for inward development at all costs – even if it doesn't represent the best option for the region. Incentives for inward industrial location can undermine urban regeneration unless in a coordinated framework. For example, in Scotland there is intense competition between competing LECs, and little doubt that Glasgow is losing out to the surrounding Enterprise Zones and New Towns in the inward investment sweepstakes. For example, grant payment thorough Regional Selective Assistance is reported to be lower on per capita basis in Glasgow than in surrounding districts (*The Herald*, 19 May 1995).

This is not to argue that industry requiring big, motorway-side factory sites not available in inner cities should not go to neighbouring areas, but only that the employment and other benefits of subsidised inward investment should be maximised at the regional level and within cities. Decisions should also strongly reflect the principles of sustainable land use and transport. The research suggests that regional integration of land use, transport, urban regeneration, and economic development is a key future task, building on the achievements of PPG 13 and recent planning research. This is discussed in Chapter 5.

Fourth prerequisite: Linking physical to social and economic regeneration

Too often regeneration projects, begun with the best intentions, end up being organised around the requirements of property development rather than addressing the difficult task of tackling the social and economic exclusion of disadvantaged households. This failure to tackle long-term unemployment is partly a legacy of the notion that the 'trickle down' of economic benefits to the poor will resolve the problem, but also due to the very intractability of those problems, at least on the worst estates. There was widespread agreement among key informants that trickle down does not work.

When regeneration is allowed to be property-led, contracting regimes then impose their own logic on investment and hiring, with a gradual slide away from commitment to local benefit. Key informants noted that the common requirement to spend public funds quickly, to achieve early visual results and boost investor confidence to bring in private funds (called 'front-ending'), often pushes the development process too fast to link it to the requisite employment strategy, and the skills assessment, training and adult basic education which needs to go with it. When new employers do hire, there is no motivation to hire locally and, until recently, little means for public agencies to ensure local employment benefit. The end result is that local people are excluded from the job positions created, or they will only have access to the lowest paid service jobs, such as cleaning. Chapter 5 proposes that a local employment strategy should be embedded in every regeneration project.

In the long term, education is the key to employment, because in future there will simply not be jobs for the uneducated, unskilled. Nationally, the demand for labour has substantially shifted in favour of people with education as shown by the fact that manual wages are steadily declining as a proportion of non-manual wages, down from 76% to 64% since 1980.

There is an organisational dimension, insofar as a local authority's traditional committee structures, and inter- and intradepartmental divisions, sometimes preclude the coordinated effort which can link physical regeneration with employment and other social strategies. A switch away from traditional departmentally-based committee structures to thematic committee structures can help bridge the gap, as does Manchester's Social and Urban Regeneration Sub-Committee.

Fifth prerequisite: Community involvement in regeneration partnerships

At the regeneration project or programme level, there are many effective partnerships between local government and business. Top-down funding regimes empower institutional or corporate stakeholders who are easily represented in partnerships by a few paid professionals, skilled at meetings, who can forge ahead with regeneration strategy. More challenging is genuine partnership with the community, which implies enhancing the ability of communities to participate in the development and implementation of regeneration strategy and more long-term community governance which needs to follow.

Temporary participation exercises, such as Planning for Real, Community Planning Weekends, and so on, are valuable, particularly for initiating participation processes, for neighbourhood design initiatives and for local confidence building. But they cannot be expected to be representative or democratic, nor do they allow communities to influence mainstream programmes or important strategic issues, such as the location of new shopping or industry. Beyond temporary participation, there is a patchwork of statutory and informal consultation – described by an interviewee as "chaotic" – with as many as 15 local government departments with different boundaries and management structures, not to mention health boards, transport executives, police authorities, and so on.

> "The partners with money play the benevolent uncle and we are the poor relations." (community representative).

In spite of widespread commitment to community participation, there is concern expressed by many local people that too much is superficial and token, consisting of "consultation, when all the real decisions have already been taken". The following concerns about participation were identified during the course of this research:

- representatives of institutional stakeholders are often perceived as paternalistic by community members;
- the need to overcome cynicism about participation, which pervades estates with a history of unsuccessful regeneration, and which means that there is apathy about new initiatives;
- the need to involve the community at the beginning of the process in establishing development priorities for their neighbourhood, particularly to address key issues of economic deprivation by employment and training initiatives;
- the need to foster community capacity to play a meaningful role in regeneration partnerships, and the development of strategy;
- control of the consultation process – the 'doling out' of information to the community in fragments in a series of tedious public meetings, precluding the community taking an holistic view; local people are sometimes afraid to speak up at meetings because officials 'hoard' information to reinforce their sense of superiority;
- participation ought to imply a sharing of power but politicians and officers are ambivalent – the rhetoric is right but there is seldom the will for genuine devolution;
- the effect of population movement which sees the economically successful depart from problem estates;
- the need to create opportunities for all community members to participate, balanced against the need to select, in a manner acceptable to the community, a small number of representatives who will sit on partnership boards;
- concern that a few key activists dominate participation processes, without representing the community, in part related to the onerous time commitments required; the risk of 'burn-out' from too much participation in a short time;
- the need to reconcile the role of elected members with that of community representatives;
- the multiplicity of policy units and administrative boundaries which makes understanding the holistic task difficult if not impossible, and appears an administrative convenience based on tradition rather than on service to the community;
- the risk that competition for funding among cash-strapped community groups can undermine cooperation between them;
- the need to create opportunities for long-term, less intensive participation which puts local people at the forefront of regeneration rather than only responding to the interests of institutional stakeholders and short-term funding mechanisms.

To address this broad range of issues simultaneously implies rethinking participation processes and strengthening *longer-term* organisational mechanisms for community involvement as full, rather than token, partners in regeneration. Overall there may need to be better opportunities for citizen participation in local democracy, reviews of local service priorities and decentralised delivery, as well as enabled self-management initiatives, such as community development trusts. The statutory planning process may offer potential for regular participation as yet almost wholly untapped. This 'rethink' is set out in Chapter 5.

> "All the bits and pieces that make up the total puzzle of peoples' lives are provided for by different departments and agencies, with different perspectives and organisational culture and different ways of interacting. The only thing in common is the annual funding round." (official from Manchester)

Sixth prerequisite: Leadership and strategic vision at the city level

To complement participation, the research found a strong requirement for leadership and strategic vision at the city level, leading to consensus around strategy. Although leadership cannot be measured, many informants thought that it was fundamental to success. It ensures that organisational culture, in the local authority and other institutional stakeholders, values partnership and community participation, rather than just paying it lip-service. Commitment at senior levels legitimates working relationships at the officer level. Leadership can emanate from within local government at chief executive and leader level, or by combined leadership initiatives between public and private sectors (which have nurtured successful regeneration in Manchester and Birmingham) (Carley, 1991). Leadership is almost always required to drive forward partnership initiatives, and build confidence to secure maximum investment levels.

To realise strategic regeneration, local authorities need a corporate approach which bridges interdepartmental rivalries and provides the framework in which more specialised expertise (eg, housing) can make an optimum contribution. Mainstream departmental funding may need to be 'bent' towards regeneration objectives, while meeting statutory responsibilities. Leadership, whether firm and formal or informal and consensual, coordinates the policy and actions of powerful line departments in local government with different policy streams, funding mechanisms and organisational cultures. The interactions between these affect people and neighbourhoods holistically but can be unrelated one to another.

The research found that it is not unusual for a local authority to have a regeneration strategy, an economic development strategy, a housing strategy, an anti-poverty strategy, an environment strategy, a unitary plan, a transport plan and a decentralisation strategy, among others. (In Scotland, the production of a decentralisation strategy is a statutory requirement.) Most of these are linked to a powerful chief officer in a high-spending line department and to a committee chair. However, passenger transport executives, health authorities, and so on, also have separate forward plans. Unless all these strategies are coordinated to a common purpose it is unlikely that maximum benefit will derive from public expenditure, and local people will remain in ignorance or be confused about the intentions of the council. This will be more important as councils move away from direct service delivery toward a strategic and coordinating role.

For policy integration in the neighbourhood, the local councillor should play an enabling role, which is particularly important where there is a diversity of interest groups or ethnic minority groups. However, some councillors identify more closely with the committee they convene, and find it difficult to take the holistic or constituency view. The traditional committee system is described by a former, long-time council leader interviewed in the research as "a comfortable imprisonment, not without its modest financial rewards".

One complaint of local residents is that some councillors can be disdainful of community participation, which they perceive as threatening their authority, or they may be more concerned with political in-fighting within the ruling party group than local issues. This is not to say that there are not many councillors who devote themselves to improving their city and local area. But the system does not, as yet, encourage or reward this local identification.

Finally, the research suggests a strong link between the seemingly diverse agendas of:

- promoting high quality leadership in local government, particularly to develop corporate vision and integration between policy areas;
- rethinking the role of elected members to give more stature to local representation and to promote sophisticated leadership in local communities;
- reforming local government in terms of devolution, but also changing organisational culture to value devolution and decentralisation;
- new, long-term means of community participation in regeneration and other aspects of local decision making, such as Agenda 21 (Hambleton, 1996; McNulty, 1996; Stewart, 1996).

The solution to the challenge of participation could arise from some clear thinking around the conjunction of these initiatives. Suggestions are given in Chapter 5.

Seventh prerequisite: Clear objectives for the success of regeneration are essential for monitoring

The research found that regeneration initiatives do not always have clear, stated vision of the long-term goal. This can lead to 'fuzzy' objectives on which to base short-term action plans and guide investment in housing and other sectors, and undermines attempts to monitor achievement (McGregor et al, 1992; Carley, 1995b). Yet monitoring, and incremental adjustment of strategy, is a key to 'adaptive management' for sustainability.

One problem is that we may, with the best of intentions, over-focus on solving idiosyncratic problems of disadvantaged estates, when the real objective must be the reintegration of those estates in the townscape so, in a sense, they 'disappear' into a more typical fine-grain urban fabric. In this conception, average, healthy neighbourhoods, rather than disadvantaged estates, may be a better guide to the objectives of regeneration. These objectives can be derived by empirical analysis which will suggest *physical, economic and social parameters* of sustainable regeneration. For example, lively urban neighbourhoods of medium density usually offer a range of house sizes and tenancy types. The diversity of choice represented is a characteristic we may want to develop and encourage throughout the city. Combining regeneration with notions of sustainable development gives rise to the idea of sustainable neighbourhoods or urban villages, examined again in Chapter 6.

However, it is important to note that reintegration is not just a physical concept. A major factor distinguishing advantaged households from disadvantaged households is the degree of control over the household's economic and social environment, and future options. Increasing control through community participation is therefore as important as empirical evidence on what constitutes sustainability. Analysis can inform local decisions, so they are better, more sustainable decisions and so that local development contributes to, rather than detracts from, sustainability at the city level.

Eighth prerequisite: Enhanced organising around social housing

Given the backlog of housing repair documented in the previous chapter, social housing and urban regeneration will be linked for many decades to come on a variety of issues: refurbishment, energy efficiency and heating, tenure diversification, and with regard to the role of tenant management in fostering participation. There is also a long history of social housing funders, such as Scottish Homes, working with community-based housing associations in nurturing regeneration processes.

If physical regeneration takes place, but national welfare policy and local housing allocations continue to concentrate disadvantaged families and unemployed single people on 'sink' estates, while encouraging the economically active to leave those estates, regeneration is unsustainable. This indicates a need for pro-active, transparent housing allocation policies which meet both housing and regeneration objectives, and are derived within the context of a full inventory of available social housing, including numbers, condition and likely future of stock of the city-region. This can be difficult because housing allocation policies serve statutory and multifunctional service objectives. There is also a political dimension to housing policy which can ensure a constituent base for some elected members, and can therefore serve ideological ends. At the same time, however, the research found considerable evidence of local authority innovation in the way that it is thinking about housing need and opportunities for its contribution to city development, whatever the tenure or ownership. Glasgow, for example, uses Scottish Homes' National House Condition Survey to assess need and opportunity across the city, as a guide to policy, and to support initiatives by community-based housing associations. The housing department is also concerned with the needs of social housing tenants and has played a key role in urban regeneration at the city-wide and local levels.

From an organisational point of view, the research finds that we are embarking on a period of major change and opportunity in social housing. Elements identified in the research include:

- a shift in the role of local authorities in social housing, and in their willingness to take a holistic view of all housing need and opportunity whatever the tenure, and cooperate with other providers and managers;
- continued large-scale voluntary transfers;
- growing acceptability of tenure diversification as a tool of regeneration (but with insufficient understanding of its implications);

- expansion of the range of Registered Social Landlords, to include financial and investment institutions;
- separation of development and management functions in social housing, to allow specialised organisations to engage in either area;
- renewed interest in the potential of community-based housing associations in Scotland and housing and regeneration community associations in England;
- in Scotland, New Housing Partnerships are used as a catalyst for integration of housing and regeneration;
- new options for joint working among social housing providers, including local government, in development, joint stock management and waiting lists, and joint repairs.

There is also preliminary evidence that the recent change in government has increased the confidence of local authorities to work with the private sector in social housing provision. To take advantage of this period of change means linking social housing investment plans to strategic regeneration objectives to ensure:

- that investments are made in a way as to maximise their economic, social and environmental benefits;
- that new and refurbished housing is viable within its city-wide context and doesn't become difficult-to-let for environmental and contextual reasons;
- that there is no risk of oversupply of social housing, as is occurring in some northern English cities, putting developments in competition with one another for the same tenants;
- that attention is also directed to the condition of declining, older private housing stock in cities.

Innovation Box 1: Housing options appraisal in Muirhouse, Edinburgh

A housing options appraisal group was set up in the Muirhouse neighbourhood of the North Edinburgh Area Regeneration (NEAR) Initiative at a time when the City Council and Scottish Homes were facing severe reductions in capital allocations. These affected the ability of the regeneration project to deliver the housing strategy agreed with residents after a successful community planning process. Alternative funding methods had to be sought and the group was established in order to involve key tenant, community and institutional stakeholders.

The group decided that a holistic, informed approach was required. A series of briefing sessions were organised covering: housing, shopping, leisure, environment, economic development, education and one on the political framework of decision making. For housing, for example, a comprehensive briefing pack was prepared covering local housing stock, housing associations and options for stock transfers and joint ventures.

The aims of the group were then identified as being: to bring a systematic approach to decision making on housing investment; to achieve an objective appraisal of options; and to ensure better cooperation of all stakeholders. The process consists of a number of steps carried out under the guidance of an independent facilitator:

- establishing residents' priorities, and those of other stakeholders;
- identifying potential resources from all sources;
- identifying physical, social, political and financial constraints;
- agreeing a vision statement, objectives and critical success factors;
- evaluating options against critical success factors;
- linking to other strategies;
- identifying the preferred option and agreeing a wider consultation process with the full community.

The critical success factors identified include: a five-year time-scale for achievement; integrated housing development which meets needs of current and future residents including affordability, energy efficiency and barrier-free design; ability to sustain other infrastructure, including schools and shops; ability to incorporate environmental improvements including traffic calming and play areas; locally accountable management; and incorporation of a local employment and training scheme.

For Muirhouse, the strength of the process is that it produced a redevelopment plan for the area which was more radical than anything previously envisaged. A constraint on the process was that, due to yet further capital cuts, problems arose with implementation. The fact that residents did not 'own' the means of resource delivery undermined confidence in the common vision. The group, which continues to meet monthly, has now recommended the introduction of devolved area-based budgeting by both the council and Scottish Homes, to give an assured five years' of funding. This would support the creditability of the process and engender private sector confidence in public sector intentions, thus promoting opportunities for leverage of private sector funding. On the positive side, the detailed planning by the options appraisal group has meant that Muirhouse has been able to respond promptly to the Scottish Office's unexpected 1998 New Housing Partnership funding programme.

4

Strategic regeneration in four cities

Birmingham, Manchester and Glasgow play important roles as regional capitals in the national settlement pattern. As such, their health and vitality is important to all of us. They also have a typical range of problems, such as multiple deprivation and derelict land stemming from deindustrialisation, restructuring of the labour market and population decline. Edinburgh is more prosperous, with an expanding population and a good flow of inward investment. Nevertheless, the residents of its peripheral estates suffer multiple deprivation, in some cases unresolved after 25 years of urban regeneration activity.

Case studies in England and Scotland enabled instructive comparison of differing organisational frameworks for strategic regeneration. For England, GORs had recently been established to provide for coordination of national policy and regional planning for mainly unitary authorities. These have been paralleled by the rise of regional organisations of local government officials, and those of civil society, such as the North West Regional Forum. With the proposed RDAs, this is a potentially strong organisational framework for regional development and regeneration, especially if the RDAs use their economic expertise to further a broader programme of sustainable development and quality of life.

At the same time, Scotland was shifting to unitary local government, having abolished its nine Regional Governments as part of the 1996 local government reorganisation. For Scotland, there is no longer any regional government or administration, outside of weak, voluntary structure planning arrangements between local authorities and competition between LECs for inward investment. This brings Scotland in 1998 to a similar position to England in 1986, after the abolition of the Metropolitan Counties. The loss of this regional dimension appears to be undermining regeneration in Glasgow. The organisational framework for each country, and the city-wide approach are discussed in this chapter.

Organisational framework for England

Integration at the regional level

A major step has been the establishment of the GORs, responsible since 1994 for implementation of national policies on employment, trade and industry, environment and land use and transport. GORs currently oversee expenditure of around £5 billion per year and provide a mechanism for linking central policy to local initiative in regeneration, and for coordinating policy streams to link physical with human resource development.

For example, the GOR for the North West oversees expenditure of around £655m per year. It has 282 employees seconded from the Department of Trade and Industry, Department of Education and Employment and the DETR. These staff are 'reallocated' from their previous departmental focus to thematic groups which reflect the development requirements of the region: competitiveness, skill and enterprise, infrastructure and planning, and regeneration. As a result of this allocation there is a broad range of skills in each thematic group. In addition, the director of each thematic group also has special coordinating responsibility for a sub-regional area. The director for regeneration, for example, is responsible for initiatives relating to Greater Manchester.

Where appropriate, GORs encourage local authorities to work together on regeneration, which may not happen spontaneously. The GOR is responsible for implementation of Structural Fund assistance on behalf of central government departments, and works with local authorities to secure government and European funding. The GORs, in their three years of existence, have already provided a bridge between central and local governance. Various means of fostering regional coordination, such as RPG and regional competitiveness strategies, are the first steps to promoting regional development for long-term benefit.

However, policy coordination and strategic planning by GORs working with partner regional organisations has some way to go to realise its true potential. The *skeleton* framework has emerged, but there is not enough flesh on the bones. From an urban regeneration perspective, there are three immediate constraints. First, the previous government shied away from allowing GORs to produce a regional framework document specifically on urban regeneration, leaving a key element of coordination missing, both in terms of a document and the process of interaction which must give rise to its production and regular revision.

Second, there is as yet little common purpose, strategy or timetabling between regeneration initiatives funded from the three main sources: the SRB, the European Programme and mainstream programmes. This mirrors the parallel failure to integrate UK regional and structure planning with management of regional programmes supported by Structural Funds (Roberts, 1997). With the advent of a new round of European Structural Funding in the year 2000, this is required. Third, there remain gaps in the administrative framework of GORs. For example, health, social services, education and land reclamation are outside the organisational framework. It was also suggested during interviews that the Treasury should have regional representatives in the GORs to foster a more practical understanding of the implications of public expenditure regulations on urban development and regeneration.

A framework of regional consultation

From an organisational perspective, the potential of the emerging consultation framework in the English regions is wholly positive. The GORs have consultative counterpart organisations of two sorts: first, those of representatives of local governments and second, those representing broader civil society. For example, the GOR in Birmingham works with the West Midlands Regional Forum, representing seven metropolitan districts and four shire counties. The Regional Forum itself has a small permanent secretariat.

For Manchester, the North West Regional Association is the consortium of local authorities from Greater Manchester, Merseyside and the surrounding region. Their 1994 'Greener Growth' proposals initiated and informed the RPG process for the region, underpinned by their Regional Transport Strategy and Regional Environmental Action Framework. The result is an emerging dialogue between central and local government around key strategic regional issues.

In 1994 key decision makers from public, private, voluntary, education, cooperative and trade union sectors formed the North West Partnership to link civil society with government and provide a platform for influencing regional development. One responsibility it sets itself is to prepare and update a Regional Economic Strategy, in association with the GOR and North West Regional Association. The current Strategy, looking ahead to the year 2004, is focused on key areas for progress including innovation in telematics and the knowledge base of the region, access to seed capital by small and medium sized enterprises, a stronger European profile for the region, and advances in the financial, professional and tourism sectors of the economy. The North West Partnership provides the GOR with a strong representative partner for consultation and analysis over key issues, including the preparation of the RPG.

An emerging role for Regional Planning Guidance

These documents, and the consultative process for their preparation, provide a coherent, if currently superficial, overview of regional development options and a formal context for SRB expenditure, land use in terms of structure and unitary development plans, transport plans and for some energy matters. The West Midlands Regional Forum and the North West Regional Association both cooperate with their respective GOR on preparation of regional guidance. A good example is the RPG for the West Midlands (RPG11), which identifies current key tasks as to promote urban regeneration, competitiveness and sustainability, the latter through integrated sustainable transport and Green Belt preservation.

The RPG are described by a senior GOR official as "well begun but not yet sufficiently robust". Given political will, they could evolve into a consensual expression of vision for the region and a sophisticated development framework linking spatial decisions to competitiveness and regeneration, as well as guiding difficult decisions on the location of employment, retail expansion, and housing, all of which influence the market for urban locations and thus regeneration prospects. One option is for a 20-year perspective in RPG, revised every five years, giving an "overall vision on intergenerational decisions". There is also potential to integrate energy and transport and incorporate Agenda 21 concerns at the regional level, including PPG13 on settlement patterns related to transport emissions.

Whether RPG broadens its focus to encompass economic and social development or some other policy framework, such as a visioning process, evolves to encompass RPG, it is appropriate that the role of the GORs should expand and mature. In addition to the benefits of regional vision and coordination of economic development to underpin regeneration, there are emerging issues beyond the capacities of individual local authorities which will have to be coordinated by GORs. The need to manage urban air quality across local authority boundaries is one example. ("The Committee on the Medical Effects of Air Pollutants reports that air pollution hastens the death of 24,000 persons every year, including 10,500 from the effects of diesel engine exhausts and 12,500 related to excess low level ozone related to road transport", *Financial Times*, 15 January 1998.) Here the benefits of integration are obvious. For example, volume house builders prefer greenfield over brownfield sites but these often can only be reached by automobile commuting, a main contributor to global warming. This points to the need for the strategic framework to balance the cost of land decontamination, and the urban regeneration benefits, against the intergenerational health costs of increases in CO_2 emissions caused by low density suburban settlement patterns. Although we are some way from this level of analysis, it will be necessary to achieve sustainable urban development.

Urban regeneration policy

City Pride in Manchester, Birmingham and London was initiated in late 1993 at the invitation of the Secretary of State for the Environment for partner agencies in those cities to come together to take a 10-year perspective on regeneration. The City Pride Initiatives can be credited with fostering genuine multi-stakeholder partnerships to provide coordination to underpin specific initiatives. The approach has since been extended to an additional seven cities. In conjunction with City Pride, the establishment of the SRB in April 1994 brought together 20 hitherto separate regeneration programmes from five central government departments with new funding under a Challenge Fund initiative. Projects may be thematic or have an area focus, but must be developed within a partnership framework with clear lines of authority among major stakeholders.

Birmingham

Spatially, the city is the biggest unitary local authority in England, with one million of the region's five million population. The industrial sector still provides around 25% of the city's employment, but over 253,000 jobs have disappeared since 1961, with 29,000 disappearing between 1991 and 1995. In recognition, full Development Area Status has been granted by the Department of Trade and Industry. Constraints on the economy identified by City Pride include: low levels of capital investment in manufacturing compared to the national average, resulting in low uptake of advanced manufacturing and distribution processes; the lure of greenfield sites elsewhere in the region to existing and inward industries; the danger to city centre retail function of out-of-town shopping; and deurbanisation and social polarisation (Birmingham City Pride, 1995). Unemployment affects 21% of households, and a quarter of the city's children. Around half of households have no car, making good public transport vital to their well-being.

Innovation Box 2: City Pride in Birmingham

Birmingham has a long history of regeneration partnership between the City Council and the Chamber of Commerce. City Pride continues that tradition. Its main board is chaired by a senior businessman; the Chamber provides offices and expenses to the City Pride secretariat, while the Council and the TEC provide staff seconded to the Secretariat. City Pride represents a common vision, with both Leader and Deputy Leader of the Council joining business and community representatives on the board. There is a management group which meets monthly and acts as an executive to the board. It consists of representatives of five core partner organisations: the Council, the Chamber of Commerce, the TEC, the Voluntary Services Council and Birmingham 2000, which fosters economic development and city centre regeneration.

There is also an innovative City Pride youth board representing 16-25-year-olds, which has three seats on the main board and its own funded programme of work. The youth board's current activities are focusing on issues of homelessness among young people, crime and Birmingham's status as a European city.

In spite of these economic constraints, there are developments of real vitality. The city centre has been transformed on a pedestrianised European model. Among many high profile projects, £100m has been invested in the Brindley Place complex giving rise to the National Sea Life Centre, art galleries, shops, a hotel, and four new office blocks. A £300m project for the Bull Ring is just one of other privately funded projects which will pump about £1 billion into the city centre during the next few years. A measure of Birmingham's success is that it has attracted the 1998 G7 Conference. Although some observers debate the relevance of the city centre initiative to inner-city residents, it is hard to imagine that any city-wide initiative could be built on the back of a run-down, depressed urban centre (for an alternative view see Loftman and Neven, 1994). On the fringe of the city, in the Green Belt, a large semi-conductor plant at Peddimore is proposed on a 140-acre site, giving 2,500 jobs. The decision comes after a fierce debate between pro-development and Green Belt protection advocates.

City Pride originally proposed an action plan of 41 projects. This caused some confusion, however, as a number of those projects were in existence or had been developed independently of City Pride, which was never intended to be a project management agency (Clarke and Prior, 1996). To clear up the confusion, City Pride more clearly defined its role as three-fold:

- to provide a coordinated strategic framework for all regeneration projects and proposals seeking national and European funding;
- to endorse initiatives which contribute to the City Pride vision, and to assist them to secure funding;
- to monitor initiatives for annual reporting purposes, but not to intervene in their operation.

Within the first role, City Pride establishes key strategic aims. Those set out in the 1996/97 programme included: matching workforce skills to employment opportunities, and promoting community involvement in regeneration and establishing an integrated transport strategy. Key sectors of activity are monitored and reported annually. Partnership has also given rise to organisational innovation. For example, the forward economic strategy has shifted from being prepared by the City Council 'with consultation' to a fully joint City Council–TEC–Chamber of Commerce initiative (Birmingham City Council, 1997).

Greater Manchester

The North West has 25% of all derelict land in England, a portion of which has been contaminated by chemical and industrial processes. Greater Manchester has an unemployment rate of around 11%, but Manchester City's is 18%, with youth unemployment at 28% and 31% for ethnic minority males. The scale of the task of regeneration is indicated by the fact that, of the city's 33 wards, 20 are within the top 10% of most deprived areas in England (City Pride, 1997).

At the heart of the conurbation, Manchester City's population has declined, from 662,000 in 1961 to 431,000 in 1994 while the population of the urban region remains at around 2.6 million persons, spread across 10 local authorities. This necessitates more cross-boundary initiatives than in the other three case studies. Four local authorities are partners in City Pride including Salford, Trafford and Tameside. SRB Round 3 includes further partnership between Salford and Bolton. This continues a history of inter-authority cooperation. In 1989 for example, Manchester, Salford and Trafford initiated the Integrated Development Operation which oversaw £120m of the European Regional Development and European Structural funding for regeneration. Greater Manchester, like Glasgow, is eligible for funds under Objective 2 of Structural Funds Regulations.

The city is engaged in a comprehensive redevelopment of its centre. One reason for this is the IRA bomb which damaged 350 businesses in June 1996. The City's response was the establishment of the Manchester City Task Force under the determined leadership of the Deputy Chief Executive. In the 20 months since the bomb, £413m of investment has been committed to rebuilding and enhancing the city centre in line with parameters set out in an international design competition. The work has made substantial progress, and a new range of retailers have been attracted.

Among other notable developments is the completed new Bridgewater Hall – home of the Halle Orchestra – and the nearby Castlefield development initiative which includes new housing, hotels, restaurants and shops. The renewed prosperity of the city centre reinforces regeneration in nearby inner-city areas such as Hulme and Ancoats. Other notable achievements include a funded £120m new Commonwealth stadium, for the 2002 Commonwealth Games, with 2,500 new jobs predicted in associated retail and leisure development, and the extension of Manchester's pioneering Metrolink tram system to encompass urban regeneration areas and the airport.

City Pride

The first City Pride prospectus for Greater Manchester was prepared in 1994, with a strategic vision to the year 2005, focusing on the city's future as a European regional capital in competition with such cities as Barcelona, Frankfurt and Bordeaux as a place in which to invest and live. Within this context, SRB integrates area and city-wide initiatives. The latest City Pride prospectus identifies four key themes:

Innovation Box 3: Council decision making in Manchester

In order to support and facilitate implementation of the comprehensive regeneration of Hulme, Manchester City Council took the then unprecedented step of establishing an area sub-committee vested with all the Council's powers in relation to this City Challenge area, and with full delegated powers to fast-track decisions without reference to the full Council or other committees. The Hulme Sub-Committee was chaired by the Leader of the Council and members included the Deputy Leader, local Ward councillors and Chairs of the main Council service committees. Three seats were allocated to opposition parties to ensure cross-party support. A past Director of Hulme Regeneration Limited, since moved on to another city, described the Council's approach as "remarkable in its vision and its corporate ability to deliver".

The need for rapid, supportive decision making in regeneration areas on issues such as planning, land disposals or site assembly has to be balanced against the need for consistent policies across the city as whole, and against the requirement for full accountability in the use of public funds. As the number of regeneration areas in the city has multiplied, the Council has established an Urban and Social Strategy Sub-Committee which provides similar fast-track decision making for all regeneration initiatives, but which also ensures coordination between them and extends ownership of the projects to major service committees. These arrangements are supported at a political level within the officer structure by the Deputy Chief Executive and Assistant Chief Executive who chair, manage and coordinate all regeneration initiatives from within the Chief Executive's department.

- sustainable communities;
- international competitiveness and local benefit;
- Manchester and the North West as a regional centre in Europe;
- Manchester's 2002 Commonwealth Games as a catalyst to community benefit (City Pride, 1997).

The Sustainable Communities Initiative in particular represents "a fundamental shift of emphasis":

> People, and particularly young people and children, will be at the centre of the new thrust. The Partners believe the need is clear and the time is right to take radical steps; to identify and address in a holistic fashion those critical factors that are needed to equip and engage all individuals in the City Pride area.
>
> This will not easily be achieved, there will be a need to question, re-direct and re-orientate main programmes and better coordination and delivery across boundaries and between institutions will be vital. The challenge will involve ... breaking down of unnecessary barriers between departments of local authorities, between public agencies and with government departments and their replacement by a shared strategy and direction. (City Pride, 1997)

A five-fold approach is intended: a social strategy group of key stakeholders, priority areas for action-learning, involvement of young people in assessment of their own needs, community plans and social impact analysis of plans, projects and investments.

Manchester also makes good use of public–private sector joint venture companies to oversee regeneration. North Manchester Regeneration Limited represents a formal partnership between the Council and Bellway Urban Renewal Limited, just as the successful Hulme Regeneration Limited represented a joint venture with Amec plc. In each case, community representatives and local business interests are included on the joint venture board.

To target more specifically the urban regeneration requirements of Manchester's many ethnic minority groups, comprising around 13% of the population, SRB initiatives for 1997-2004 are being taken forward in the context of the establishment of the Progress Trust. This is an independent limited company founded by the Manchester Council for Community Relations, the TEC, the Chamber of Commerce and the Council, and overseen by a board of 24 "who command the respect and confidence of black and ethnic minority communities" (Progress Trust, 1996).

Organisational framework for Scotland

The main vehicle for strategic urban regeneration is the Programme for Partnership, which synthesises resources and the lessons of the Urban Programme and the *New life for urban Scotland* White Paper. This shifted the focus of central government from the inner cities to the peripheral estates. These huge 1950s and 1960s estates have all the dramatic problems of deprivation, but are located on the fringes of the big cities, adjacent to Green Belt farmland, often complete with grazing cows. The practical outcome of *New life* was the urban partnerships on peripheral estates in Edinburgh, Glasgow, Paisley and Dundee.

While the massive infusion of funding and attention to these four estates have produced results in physical regeneration, these have not always been matched by corresponding socioeconomic improvements, or by the effective empowerment of local communities. The latter situation, it is argued, is a result of the lack of parity of community partners in terms of resources and influence (McCarthy, 1997).

The Urban Programme had previously been characterised by a mainly piecemeal series of uncoordinated initiatives, with little evidence of systematic achievement or value for money. The Programme for Partnership attempts to redress this failing (The Scottish Office, 1995). It requires city-wide, multiagency partnerships and strategies to provide a targeted framework for individual regeneration projects. There are area-specific, 10-year regeneration programmes (with funding in three-year blocks) in PPAs. Funding is also available for regeneration programmes, to run for five years. These are either scaled-down PPAs in areas of less severe deprivation, or thematic elements of a city-wide strategy, for which local authorities can bid for Block Grant allocations of Urban Programme funding. The commitment of partners to joint working is a condition of funding.

The PPAs are the main focus of the initiative. Twenty-nine PPAs were proposed by Scottish local authorities, and 12 were selected for funding in 1996 with 11 additional regeneration programmes. Total expenditure is around £60m. The PPAs range in size of population from 5,300 people in Aberdeen to 37,500 in Greater Easterhouse in Glasgow.

Although the PPA process is prominent in discussions of Scottish regeneration, it consumes only about one quarter of overall Urban Programme funding allocations. Although it is too early to assess the impact of the PPA approach, there is early evidence that its emphasis on a city-wide strategy is likely to encourage sustainable regeneration.

Strategic planning in Scotland

The research finds that for Edinburgh and especially Glasgow, loss of regional governance, such as that of Strathclyde Region, without any replacement agency such as a GOR, is a major constraint on regeneration. The overall problem is that, although there were good reasons for initiating local government reorganisation in 1992, it did not follow, ipso facto, that universal application of single-tier governance in 1996 was the optimum solution. This leaves the Scottish Office, with spatial responsibilities from the Borders to the Outer Hebrides, as the only 'overseeing' agency for 'competing' local authorities.

The implication for urban regeneration is competition for inward investment of industry and retailing between areas within the same metropolitan region, and no planning framework for ensuring inward investment benefits the unemployed or for assessing the benefits of brownfield reclamation. The Glasgow Regeneration Alliance (GRA), for example, warns starkly of "severe competition for economic investment from nearby Enterprise Zones" and that "greenfield developments for new private housing beyond the city continue to attract population from Glasgow".

In England a series of cross-local authority partnership arrangements for urban regeneration have arisen on the ashes of metropolitan government. No metropolitan (or regional) mechanisms exist for Glasgow or Edinburgh. This is a key concern of many people active in urban regeneration. Practitioners speak of the loss of inter-authority linkage, strategic focus, regional information systems and the networking contacts which buttress regeneration efforts. There is no equivalent territorial planning guidance to the RPGs, other than National Planning Policy Guidance Notes (the equivalent of PPGs for England) which cover the entire country and cannot therefore provide guidance on specific regional issues. Finally, the failure to provide a framework for development integration at the regional level will undermine efforts at sustainable development in Scotland.

> "For Glasgow, there is a desperate need to reinstate a metropolitan perspective. Labour market areas, travel-to-work areas and the housing market are all wider than the city. Without coordination, urban regeneration is an uphill struggle. For every thousand houses built on a greenfield site outwith Glasgow another school in the inner city closes."
>
> "Local government reorganisation [in Scotland] followed 1980s thinking that single-tier local authorities should compete like little businesses, without recognising the need to create a greater good." (officials from Glasgow)

Statutory decentralisation strategies

An area of innovation brought about by local government reorganisation under the 1994 Local Government Scotland Act is the duty placed on councils to prepare draft decentralisation schemes by mid-1997. These have now been tabled and are described below.

Glasgow

Glasgow suffered severely from deindustrialisation and deconcentration. Eleven per cent of its land base, 1,710 hectares, is vacant, with half of that contaminated. Continued out-migration of population, now at

624,000, leaves it at half its high. Population loss, and changing family structure, means 16 primary and five secondary schools should be closed, much to parents' distress. The average vacancy rate in Glasgow schools is 40%, raising the cost of education per child in a local authority desperately strapped for funding. City officials argue that the three New Towns and Enterprise Zones which surround the city, offering rate-free premises, undermine its economic development. They also feel that the city's boundaries have been gerrymandered for political purposes, cutting the city off from prime ratepayers in its well-off suburbs such as Bearsden.

There are still 102,569 homes in the council sector, representing around 46% of the city's total housing stock. Overall unemployment is 8.5% and male unemployment in the city is 12.4%. Unemployment of young males on peripheral estates is around 40-60%. Glasgow has the lowest car ownership of any local authority in Britain; in 1991 two thirds of households had no car. When peripheral estates like Castlemilk were built people commuted to Clydeside, but the jobs have moved elsewhere and transport links either do not exist or are expensive.

The economic regeneration of the city as a whole is a fundamental task. Like the two English cities, this is being tackled with vigour. The city centre has been transformed with extensive pedestrianisation, a new modern art gallery, a lively renovated warehouse district called the Merchant City, and a funded, £71m science centre on the south bank of the Clyde. Glasgow's previous designation as European City of Culture, has been followed by the 1999 designation as UK City of Architecture and Design. Outside the city centre, the Council is working in partnership with community-based housing associations and private developers to reinvigorate council estates.

The Glasgow Regeneration Alliance

The idea of GRA was floated in the 1991 Housing Plan. Its launch in 1993 reflected the joint recognition of the City Council, Glasgow Development Agency (the LEC) and Scottish Homes that area-based regeneration was having the unintended effect of displacing problems from one neighbourhood to the next. A city-wide strategy was necessary to counteract this, linked to eight priority areas for more specific action and encompassing 40% of the city's population. By 1994, the GRA had already produced a sophisticated analysis of the linkages between housing, transport and employment for the cities regeneration areas (GRA et al, 1994). Glasgow's city-wide regeneration strategy is backed up by its unitary plan, *Glasgow – planning for development*, which puts the eight priority areas in a overall physical context.

Innovation Box 4: First steps to sustainable neighbourhoods in Glasgow – mixed tenure developments in regeneration areas

Glasgow has a solid history of urban regeneration partnership with community-based housing associations (CBHAs) and house builders. The CBHAs are local development organisations catering for residents of particular neighbourhoods, usually managing around 1,000-1,500 units of stock. In the late 1980s, CBHAs branched out from tenemental refurbishment and new build to develop more sophisticated regeneration programmes, including job creation, community development and environmental improvement (Carley, 1990).

Glasgow Council has long been committed to using tenure diversification as a tool to help single tenure council estates evolve with resident participation into mixed tenure neighbourhoods. Partnership between Glasgow Council, CBHAs and private builders provides the organisational framework, with Scottish Homes funding by HAG for CBHA development and GRO Grant. GRO Grant is an innovative funding mechanism for providing housing for owner-occupation in urban regeneration neighbourhoods where unsubsidised private housing would be unprofitable. For example, at Royston Hill a run-down council estate has evolved into a high quality, mixed-tenure neighbourhood of a 1,000 flats and houses for rent by the Council and three CBHAs, and for sale by Wimpeys. Building types are varied with high-rise and tenemental flats and semi-detached houses. There is no outward sign to distinguish the different tenure options.

Other city-wide initiatives include the successful Glasgow Works to help the long-term unemployed into the labour market, the Regeneration Fund to loan money to small businesses in poor neighbourhoods, and the Seed Capital Fund to assist start-up small and medium sized enterprises (GRA, undated).

Programme for Partnership is reported to have had a beneficial influence on the GRA by encouraging better communication between the ostensible partners and by broadening of the Partnership at board and executive levels. For example, both Directors of Social Work and Education are now members of the Officer Group. However, decision making in the GRA is reported to be slowed by the need for council representatives to refer back decisions to committee. One of the more successful initiatives, the Industrial Land and Property Policy, took two years to fashion on a consensual basis but other policy initiatives are said to be delayed or 'stalled'.

Finally, in keeping with the requirement to produce a decentralisation strategy, Glasgow proposes to maintain its current system of 11 decentralised committees consisting of elected members and community representatives selected by a formal election process. Unlike Edinburgh's strategy, there is no mention of linkage to urban regeneration, and there appears to be no commitment as yet to linking local committees to forward planning, policy or monitoring processes.

Edinburgh

Compared to the other three cities in this study, Edinburgh is has a strong range of advantages. The city-wide unemployment rate is 4.6%, compared to a Scottish national rate of 6.6%. The current generation of residents have inherited a dramatic site, a wealth of historic buildings and a Georgian 'New Town' as the inner city which is a UNESCO World Heritage Site. Only 10% of the city's population live in deprived areas, compared to 40% in Glasgow. The worst peripheral estates have overall unemployment rates of around 17%, although male unemployment ranges up to 27% on the partnership estate of Wester Hailes. The city's very strengths in finance and high technology do not generate low-skilled jobs.

The Capital City Partnership

Perhaps because of general prosperity, city-wide regeneration partnership came later than in other cities. But in 1995, spurred by a looming requirement of Programme for Partnership for partnership and regeneration strategy, the Capital City Partnership (CCP) was initiated. Its partners first came together in a future-oriented 'scenario-building exercise' linking key stakeholders and sponsored by Scottish Homes. This was to initiate a steadily growing interest in visioning in the city. The CCP is committed to strategic, thematic approaches to regeneration to supersede sectoral or departmentalised approaches.

The members of the CCP include seven departments from the Council, community representatives of regeneration partnerships, Scottish Homes, the Health Board and the LEC. For the City Council, urban regeneration is overseen by a small Strategic Policy Department. The CCP Steering Group is chaired by the Director of Strategic Policy. One constraint within the running of the CCP has been the size of the Steering Group. This was constituted large to include all main representatives of key community groups, but the result is an unwieldy size group of 35 persons. A streamlined executive is proposed.

Edinburgh was a successful bidder for two PPAs. It is linking urban regeneration initiatives to its decentralisation strategy by designating Community Planning Areas (CPAs) which link regeneration areas to economic growth areas, to focus emphasis on employment creation and transport to jobs issues. Integrated strategy development and service planning for these CPAs are intended (City of Edinburgh Council, 1997).

Areas of innovation in Edinburgh outside the regeneration framework, but relevant to it, include the integration, as a result of local government reorganisation, of the city's planning, transport and economic development functions in one 'super department' called City Development. This department is, in turn, taking forward implementation of the Council's decentralisation strategy in its mandated areas. This involves the city being divided into five areas for the development of vision, city management and community involvement in what are called Agenda for Action Programmes, under the management of the Head of Local Area Services, and with the assistance of Area Coordinating Teams, made up of councillors and representatives of key departments. Agenda for Action documents, based on consultation with community groups, range from expression of longer-term vision to detailed, three-year budgeting proposals in a single slim document.

Other CPAs are intended outside of regeneration areas. Portobello, for example, is a pilot CPA in which the local community will participate in the preparation of a land use plan, an education

A failure of integration? Economic development in Glasgow and North Lanarkshire

Lanarkshire, adjacent to Glasgow, is the largest LEC area in Scotland with two New Towns and an Enterprise Zone. Although it has its share of urban regeneration areas, such as Ravenscraig, its unemployment rate is about 25% less than Glasgow's.

The LEC has been highly successful in luring new inward investment, some say at the expense of Glasgow, which has its own LEC. For example, one senior Glasgow official says his city is:

> "... surrounded by a sea of Enterprise Zones [which] actively poach companies with promises of nil rates for 10 years and major capital investment in greenfield sites".

But other officials argue that Glasgow will never have the large, clean sites needed to attract huge new single floor factories, like that of Chunghwa. This Taiwanese electronics giant is building a £260m picture tube factory in the Lanarkshire Enterprise Zone. This will be completed in 1999 and employ 1,500 people, with a further 1,800 jobs in spin-off industries. As noted, virtually none of these jobs are going to residents of Glasgow's nearby, seriously deprived Easterhouse Estate – five miles away by direct motorway. There is no public transport from one to the other, because buses still follow the old routes to Glasgow city centre – the other direction.

Certainly no one can begrudge the LEC its success in attracting the factory to Scotland. But the underlying issue is whether social benefits have been maximised, given the public investment. The real problem is lack of integration between urban regeneration in Glasgow and economic development in neighbouring areas. The integration should have come about in at least three ways. First, it should be clear to all that the site is the best place in the metropolitan region for the factory, because the analysis had been done beforehand in the preparation of RPG, which integrated regeneration, land use and economic development objectives. There is no such integration or guidance. Second, when planning for the factory started around five years ago, adult basic education and training in Easterhouse should have geared up to get the jobs. There was no such linkage. Finally, two years ago thought should have been given to new transport links and, if necessary, whether the cost of transport subsidy would be less than the employment benefits to disadvantaged households. No such forward planning took place and opportunities for employment are pretty much confined to car owners.

The main problem is that there is no agency with a regional perspective to ask the right strategic questions. The issue will become more pressing as Lanarkshire has announced its intention to create another New Town on a 1,125-acre site with a proposed 3,400 new houses, a technology park and 1.5 million square feet of industrial, retail and leisure space.

It is hard to envisage how sustainable development can be achieved in Scotland's metropolitan regions in the absence of a regional framework, as is emerging in England based on the GORs' regional guidance prepared in association with the government's counterpart assemblies from business and civil society. This regional dimension of consultation, integration and strategy is an important organisational prerequisite for sustainable economic development. Finally, following the melt-down of the Asian economies, and delay and cancellation of proposed new plant in Scotland, people are questioning the cost per job and the wisdom of over-reliance investment from overseas firms as the main vehicle of economic regeneration.

plan, a social services plan, a local Agenda 21 plan and so on, brought together as the community plan. Portobello, as a waterfront community, then integrates into the city's waterfront strategy, as does the NEAR regeneration area. As part of the Portobello initiative, a series of community focus workshops have developed priorities for the neighbourhood under the Agenda for Action banner. Following from this, the next stage is to assess established departmental policies against neighbourhood priorities.

Edinburgh is moving toward an overall corporate framework. While the *City strategy* currently covers only a three-year period, the City Development Department's Strategy, *Edinburgh's way ahead*, covers the period to the year 2010, for key planning, transport and economic development issues. However, this doesn't integrate other issues such as education, urban regeneration, social exclusion and so on. This extended integration of strategy remains part of a forward agenda, which also includes better integration of the activities of different departments involved in regeneration, such as strategic policy, housing and city development. These issues are being tackled in a major corporate review by the Council's Leader, reported in the discussion document *Edinburgh 2000: Preparing the council for the new millennium*.

Innovation Box 5: New ways of tackling regeneration in Edinburgh

Edinburgh's main means of regeneration has been the Council-led partnerships, such as the successful NEAR. However, for the south Edinburgh peripheral estate area of Craigmillar, the Council is considering the use of a regeneration company overseen on a joint venture basis. This is likely to be established as a guarantee company with charitable status, with formal community representation on the board. This approach is in line with a current review, initiated by the Leader of the Council, of the appropriate role of the Council in the 21st century, and innovative but cost-effective options for delivering services to residents by new organisational arrangements.

The charitable company would guide the regeneration effort by deciding strategy and monitoring progress and impact. Implementation would be carried out by a separate trading company, which could, in turn, make use of the skills and abilities of the Council's arms-length Edinburgh Development and Investment Group (EDI). The precise means is yet to be agreed, but the trading company could enter into joint ventures with appropriate parties, including community groups, for social and economic regeneration, industrial and land development, retail refurbishment, housing stock transfer and so on.

The EDI Group was set up in 1988 and is wholly owned by the City Council. It operates as a private company and, having undertaken a number of successful property development schemes for the Council, is now broadening out into regeneration to secure social and economic benefits from development activity. The EDI's Board is made up solely of a cross-party group of councillors.

Companies like EDI can combine a robust private-sector approach to economic development with social objectives, in a legal framework of public accountability. For example, proceeds of EDI's past success in retail development have recently been recycled into regeneration funding in the North Edinburgh area.

In the Craigmillar case, the guarantee company eventually might be wound up, and could transfer its assets to a development trust, the trustees of which would be drawn in part from the local community. Details such as this are still under consideration. But the fact that the Council, community representatives and other stakeholders are considering innovative organisational options is a marker of what is needed for achieving rapid progress in regeneration and to generate local economic and social benefit from physical development.

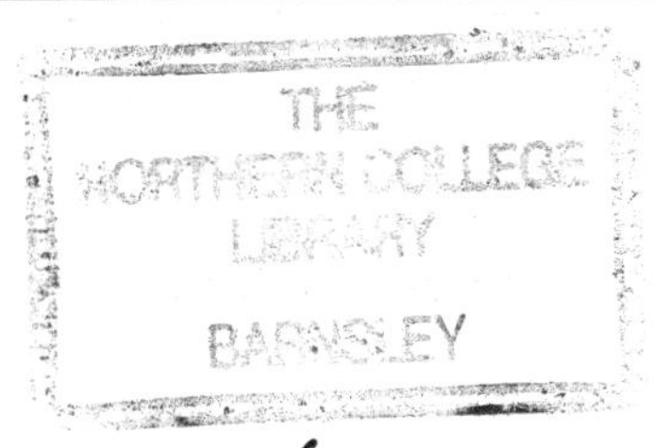

5

Urban policy, regional development and city strategy – key recommendations

National action towards sustainable regeneration

Urban regeneration is about the future of our cities. We can go down an American road of cities divided by social inequality, crime and no-go areas, of poverty and ill-health of third world magnitude, capped by an 'escape to the suburbs' settlement pattern where excess car use gives the world's highest per capita CO_2 emissions contributing to global warming. Or we can go down a European road of relative equality with prosperity, of only modest poverty and reasonable benefit levels, of high quality, energy efficient housing and settlement patterns based on reliable public transport. Of course, these are exaggerated pictures. But the main point is that the future of our cities is matter of national vision and political will rather than random circumstance or market working.

For urban regeneration, there are three challenges. The first is the need to address socioeconomic regeneration for the worst off estates and households, and especially long-term unemployment. The main solution must lie with education and training, with educational attainment at the heart of sustainable regeneration. Considering coming generations, the current situation is that many inner-city schools in areas of multiple deprivation produce few qualified school leavers. In Glasgow, for example, three inner-city secondary schools produced not a single person with the bare minimum university entrance requirement in 1996 ('Stop making excuses for Scottish schools', *Scotland on Sunday*, 30 November 1997). The reasons for this state of affairs are complex but the implications are not – recurring cycles of household deprivation. Also, what was described by a TEC executive as "year-on-year erosion of funding to address long-term unemployment" may mean these problems will not be resolved for this generation. Yet it is hard to conceive of the social alienation which will be engendered if the coming teenage generations on residualised estates have only a lifetime of unemployment and boredom to look forward to.

A related constraint is a mismatch of skills between the unemployed and labour market requirements, and lack of coherence in central funding for training and vocational education. Despite unemployment, all of the cities studied noted industry's difficulties in recruiting qualified staff. On the training side, a problem is that further and higher education is funded according to enrolment levels, which fosters "competition between colleges for gross numbers of students with little concern for outcomes". TECs, on the other hand, are funded in terms of vocational achievement, but funding has been eroded. A related issue is a continuing failure for more than a decade to provide for consistent school leaver and adult careers guidance, giving coverage which ranges from "hit or miss to non-existent".

In terms of overall effort, more powerful programmes may be fashioned around integrated economic development and regeneration regionally and city-wide, combined with next round Structural Funding under Objective 2 ('urban areas in difficulty') and Objective 3 ('education and training') for qualifying areas. Employment creation with training may also be strengthened by the use of revenues from ecological taxation. A precedent is the availability of a portion of the landfill tax for Welfare to Work programmes, but other forms of eco-taxation could follow a likely trend to shift the tax burden off low paid jobs onto pollution and resource consumption. The European Union sees urban regeneration as a key area where environmental and employment policies can be combined, such as in training the unemployed in land decontamination skills. The Intermediate Labour Market approaches of the Wise Group (Heatwise, Landwise, Treewise, etc) and similar programmes could be well placed to link these areas.

Second, urban regeneration requires firm commitment to sustainable land use patterns and integrated transport of the kind called for by the Royal Commission on Environmental Pollution (1994). The previous chapter argued the case for integration in the regions. It is also important to recognise that the number of non-car owning households in the case study cities ranges from half to two thirds. These majority car-free households should no longer be perceived as lagging behind wealthier households in the acquisition of material goods, but should be rewarded as being at the forefront of sustainable lifestyles with high quality public transport and a pleasant and safe pedestrian environment. The forthcoming White Paper should consider the importance of public transport to households in urban regeneration areas.

> "The property market will respond positively to firm guidance on land use – if it applies equally to all firms."
> (property developer and urban regeneration specialist)

Third, and within this context, local initiatives on derelict and contaminated land need to be underpinned by clear policy and funding, both the carrot of subsidy and the stick of firm land use planning, intended to bring all derelict land and building back into productive use. The government's stated intention of housing 60% of the additional 4.4 million households for England on brownfield sites can only be achieved with a major diversion of resources into land decontamination, particularly as less expensive sites are used up. To keep costs down, a high level of efficiency is needed. A key agency for each country should be designated as technical experts and policy and funding coordinators for land reclamation, for example, English Partnerships, and Scottish Homes or Scottish Enterprise. The Town and Country Planning Association suggests regional land agencies working under RDAs.

Challenge funding

Although the advent of the SRB for England is a step in the right direction in terms of coordinating central funding, there are concerns. The most pointed is that challenge funding underpins some good initiatives, but "it is a patchy, irrational approach to urban regeneration, without regard to need or priority". Challenge funding is a double-edged sword. At best, it sharpens strategy preparation, speeds development of partnership and generates quick achievements on the ground, while mainstream programmes may just loaf along. On the other hand, it can encourage chasing money for money's sake; and the bidding process uses substantial human resources. Because funding is 'top-sliced' off existing budgets, it hides real budget cuts and is therefore a reallocation of resources away from some local authorities and neighbourhoods to others. For example, the PPA programme in Scotland represents an overall reduction in funding and has been criticised for an arbitrary allocation of funds, bearing little relationship to either social need or bid quality (Capital City Partnership, unpublished notes; Turok and Hopkins, 1997).

Failure to secure challenge funding further disheartens disadvantaged neighbourhoods. In Birmingham, for example, one community has 'lost' SRB bids twice, despite much community participation in bid preparation. This creates illogical competition between deprived areas and reinforces cynicism about participation. It also can mean that, as the regeneration of selected areas encourages bending of main programmes, unselected areas fall further into the mire of multiple deprivation.

A revised approach would begin with need and establish national funding priorities on a rational and defensible basis with delegated responsibility for central funding to the GORs. Progress and outcomes of projects could overseen by a 'regeneration good practice unit' within the Audit Commission or the DETR. This would provide a national repository of learning-by-doing on urban regeneration, a means of translating good practice from one area to the next, and ensure that we retain a capacity to take account of performance in the way resources are used. For Scotland, the role could be taken on by the Accounts Commission, which has the remit to take an overview of the activities of Scottish local authorities. An alternative might be Scottish Homes, which has a long history of engagement in partnership regeneration.

Regional vision and guidance as the foundation of sustainable regeneration

It would be a mistake to continue to allow a simplistic competition for inward investment on greenfield sites at all costs to dictate the longer-term pattern of regional development, even in areas desperate for jobs. A more comprehensive approach is required, which integrates inward investment with regional vision for sustainable development, including for human resources, land use, transport and the role of the city in the region, a competitiveness strategy and objectives for urban regeneration linked to education and training as well as physical redevelopment.

Whatever the future of RDAs, and the regional agenda under a Scottish Parliament, there should be a commitment to the preparation of long-term 'regional vision statements' with a 25-year perspective on the future of the city-region. These should not be vague or 'airy-fairy', which discredits the process, but link Vision, Strategy and Operational Policies (the VSOP approach) in a framework beginning with clearly-stated core values. The highly-integrated, long-term sustainable development strategy for the cities and countryside of the Randstad in The Netherlands provides a good example. In the

Innovation Box 6: Planning sustainable development for the Randstad

For The Netherlands, a National Environmental Policy Plan (NEPP) integrates the National Spatial Policy Plan, concerned with density and quality of life in city and countryside, and the relationship between them, with the National Transport and Traffic Plan (Dekker, 1994; Ministry of Housing and Spatial Planning and Environment, 1994; Wintle and Reeve, 1994). The purpose of NEPP is to develop far-reaching sustainable development strategy across policy fields – economic development, transport, land use, environment and tax policy – and to link public bodies with business and consumers, in short-, medium- and long-term assessment of the direction of the country. Where development conflicts arise, for example, between industry and residential areas, participative negotiation/mediation is provided for. Within this context, there is concentration of jobs and housing in 13 larger urban-core regions to simultaneously promote economic development and public transport and discourage private vehicle use. There is formal agreement between national, provincial and local governments covering long-term targets and policy instruments.

For the Randstad urban region there is an integrated 'growth pole' development strategy, covering historic core cities, new settlements, the national airport area (Schipol), Euro seaport, the largest in the world (in Rotterdam), and the multinational headquarters area (outside Amsterdam). Regional transport and land use planning provides the framework for municipal development, and no central funding is available to any level of government unless an integrated strategy is agreed. Land use control insists on development at public transport nodes, with a bias towards urban concentration. There are high levels of environmental quality and public transport built into all housing developments, restriction of car parking space at commercial locations according to a regional parking plan, large investments in public transport and fiscal and price measures to discourage car use, such as hypothecation of car parking revenue to sustainable transport modes, including bicycle paths and bridges. This accounts for the fact that nationally 37% of all journeys are by bicycle, rising to over 50% in many cities. There are quantified environmental targets, for example, reduction of vehicle emissions by 2010: NOx by 75%; CO_2 by 10%; and a reduction in car usage of 20% with shift to public transport and bicycle.

Quantitative targets are set out for improving quality of life, with 'carrot and stick' policies to achieve integrated objectives. Responsibilities and interrelationships between spatial levels, and between government, business and voluntary action are also specified, as is monitoring, with a commitment to alter 'carrots' or 'sticks' if development objectives are not achieved. The situation in The Netherlands is far from perfect, but inspiring in terms of integration.

Randstad, for example, public transport links must be in place before land development goes ahead so housing and jobs are linked together in a common framework, which also balances the needs of cities against rural areas and hinterland economic development.

Regional vision statements must be based on widespread consultation processes led by regional assemblies, whether elected or appointed. If regional forums work closely with GORs (extended to include partners such as RDAs, English Partnerships, TECs and Departments for Health and Education) a cost-effective regional framework begins to emerge. Within this context, regional regeneration statements, based on consensus among regional partners, should be prepared by the GOR, which set out:

- regeneration objectives for a 10-year period;
- linkage of regeneration activity to other development policy areas, such as economic development, competitiveness, training and transport;
- a rational framework for expenditure of central government resources in the region in the light of the above two points.

Integrated hierarchy of development guidance

The regional vision statement would represent the broadest perspective in an integrated hierarchy of development guidance including:

- RPG (20-year perspective), integrating settlement, economic development, transport, energy conservation and urban regeneration strategy, and to provide the contextual framework:
- Structure or Unitary Development Plans (15 years);
- City Development Strategies (10-15 years), described in the next section, to encompass city-wide regeneration strategy (10 years), such as called for in the Local Government Association's *The new commitment*, and key objectives from neighbourhood plans;
- neighbourhood vision statements, as proposed in Chapter 6 (10 years), with local plans and service quality agreements. These can build on the community plans currently being promoted in England.

All can be revised on an efficient five-year cycle – recognising, as the Dutch framework explicitly does, that the *process* of visioning, planning and implementing is more important than the documents, plans or statements which periodically summarise the process.

City-wide integration for strategic urban regeneration

At the city level, there is a strong case for a unifying strategic development framework which integrates mainstream policies within local government with urban regeneration, economic development, reduction of social exclusion, environmental action and so on. Sustainable development requires integration and, if the city does not take the lead in integrating economic, social and physical development in its own territory, which agency would?

A strategic development framework

A director of housing describes the challenge:

> "We are coping with the problems, but where is the vision of what the city might be...? To work toward a genuine common agenda is an essential, long-term process."

The strategic development framework fuses vision of where the city wants to go with a more practical outline of how it intends to get there. It must be practical rather than just 'good intentions', or the process will be discredited. There must be strong commitment of the leader and the chief executive, and heads of other stakeholder agencies, to give clarity on vision and objectives, better coordination of policy and practice, and a more tangible basis for partnership. Edinburgh's *City strategy*, which begins the process of integrating seven more specific strategies, including urban regeneration, is a good first step in this direction. The *City strategy* describes itself:

> "It sets out the culture and values which the Council will pursue ... it describes the Council's key priorities and the ways they are related to city-wide objectives. It is more than a single document ... It is a process of setting objectives, action planning, monitoring and review."

The initial emphasis is on laying out the policy streams in a single document, in a short time frame. It can be expected to become more sophisticated over time. This kind of integrated strategy development is a learned process, it does not happen overnight. In Edinburgh, preliminary processes, like a scenario-building exercise initiated by Scottish Homes prior to development of a city-wide urban regeneration strategy, contribute to the steady building of vision. European cities such as Copenhagen, Barcelona and Vienna offer excellent examples of integrated urban development processes, represented in print by single volume urban development statements, combining long-term vision and short-term next steps.

Local authorities are recognising the importance of an organisational culture which fosters policy coordination. It cannot be imposed top-down but involves the Chief Executive's office exerting subtle leadership and encouragement towards coordinated effort. Officials stress that policy coordination develops gradually over time. It is a learned art which can be undermined by quick dashes to secure and spend regeneration challenge funding in frenzied bursts of activity.

One challenge is to change organisational culture so that corporate working is rewarded. As councils move away from direct service provision they will be defining new roles in strategic information and policy coordination. Currently most large cities, such as Birmingham and Edinburgh, have small central units or departments for policy integration – Birmingham's Policy Division of the Chief Executive's Office, or Edinburgh's Strategic Policy Department. An enhanced role is likely to emerge for these units to focus on strategic, cross-boundary and cross-department issues, and to force the pace of strategic urban development and integration.

A unified approach may need to surmount a typically uneasy relationship between the urban regeneration function of Chief Executive's departments and the powerful line departments for key aspects of regeneration such as housing, economic development or planning. However,

Innovation Box 7: Urban development strategy for Copenhagen

The Municipal Plan for Copenhagen, despite a pedestrian name, provides a model vision and integration. It begins at the level of Europe, with a consideration of Europe's 'metropolitan settlement' and transport pattern, and Denmark's European role and industrial profile. This provides the context for discussion of the national/ regional roles of the capital city and development initiatives which affect it. The Plan then sets out main 'planning themes' or development principles including (as in The Netherlands) a commitment to urban development around public transport nodes, recognition of its landscape as a 'city by the sea' and a commitment to sustainable urban development. It states that urban renewal "should not only create better housing, but reduce the distance between homes and places of work". To this end, "offices and industrial buildings can be reserved for companies particularly likely to provide workplaces for people of the local neighbourhood."

The Plan then sets out the objectives for short- and long-term development of the municipality, its urban structure, transport patterns and intended relationships between different spatial and functional areas. This includes energy and water supply, waste and sewage treatment, combined heat and power and pollution management, including from traffic. It then considers the 15 districts which make up the city, their relationship to the whole and movement patterns among them. The Plan concludes with the development objectives for each of the districts and the framework for local planning in the districts. The numbers of residents which take an active interest in local planning processes is much greater than in Britain.

Planning for Copenhagen is within the regional framework of Greater Copenhagen Council, which oversees land use, transport, environment, water and hospitals for 1.7 million people. Eighty per cent of the land administered by the Council is within designated rural zones. Under the Council, which has 37 members elected at the lower tiers of government, is the Regional Planning Council and the Metropolitan Public Transport Authority. The latter provides a fully integrated transport system of 234 bus and 16 rail lines, with coordinated scheduling and joint ticketing throughout the region.

with regard to the organisation of local government administration, there was no evidence to arise from the research to suggest that one particular arrangement was more efficient in this regard than another. Indeed, even in the most 'modern' local government arrangement, in the sense that key departments had been combined into 'super departments', it is possible to find difficulties of integration between the sections of combined departments. It is likely that the leadership of chief executive and officers, and commitment to integration, is much more important than a particular organisational arrangement.

Similarly, with regard to regeneration partnerships, the quality of the partnership depended less on the organisation (joint venture, limited company, public sector led, etc) than on, first, the inclusion of key stakeholders and their commitment to the partnership and its broad objectives, and second, the extent to which the operations of the partnership were integrated and compatible with mainstream policy and operations of local government, the LEC and so on. The extent to which the second is true is, of course, also dependent on the first.

Finally, it is important to stress that moving towards the kind of overall coherent urban development framework described here is not something that happens overnight – it is a gradual, learned and participatory process. Council officers, employees, councillors and interested lay people should all play a role in working towards better governance. Not everything will be got right the first time, but if the learning is incorporated in a gradual process of reform, building on existing strengths, then in 10 years a major overall of local government processes is entirely possible – and without the disruption of overnight, wholesale reform. The Local Government Association and the Convention of Scottish Local Authorities can play a key role in disseminating good practice.

Integrating job creation and physical regeneration

For many households, employment is the key to satisfactory participation in society. This report has stressed, therefore, that in future the creation of employment opportunity should be a fundamental plank of regeneration strategy, rather than a 'bolt-on'. So far, practice seldom fulfils this requirement and a high unemployment rate is the most difficult variable to influence in the regeneration strategy.

A local employment creation strategy

There is no one answer to the challenge of creating employment. The best response is to embed employment in the city-wide strategy from the outset, and to pace regeneration investments to the strategy. Particularly now that many cities have made significant achievements in physical regeneration in city centres, Urban Development Corporation areas and elsewhere, the time is right to refocus on job creation and enhancement of the economy of the inner city. The current government's commitment to Welfare to Work and New Deal, and its practical expression of such aspects as 'Gateways' (an intensive period of counselling, advice and guidance at the onset of involvement), an Employment Option, an Education and Training Option and the Environmental Task Force and Voluntary Sector Options all offer major potential to integrate regeneration with employment and training. Although the initiative was new at the time of this writing, already regeneration initiatives were responding positively to the opportunities.

A dedicated job creation strategy or employment initiative is likely to constitute, at least, a 10-year programme, but even looking ahead 20 years would not be unreasonable. The main emphasis must be on the long-term unemployed, out of work for 18 months or more, the young unemployed and students who are at risk of unemployment if their educational attainment levels and/or vocational skills are incompatible with labour market requirements. Employability skills, that is training to hold a job, is also vital. Close linkages between key agencies, including further and higher education institutes, the Employment Service, the Careers Service and LECs/TECs is a key to success.

There are three approaches to reducing unemployment in disadvantaged neighbourhoods: creation of local employment close by (increasing demand for labour, such as by intermediate labour schemes); training local residents to secure access to the wider urban economy (enhancing labour supply and people-to-jobs links); and provision of alternative employment in the social or voluntary sector. Recent research found no clear evidence for the efficacy of any particular approach (see Turok, 1996).

Transport and social exclusion

However, there is evidence that while better-off jobseekers will travel far and wide (up to 50 miles by car) to find better employment conditions, the long-term unemployed in car-less (or car-free) households have a search area often no more than three to four miles from home, and even that limited range depends on the cost of public transport (Webster, 1994). This has been called 'travel poverty' in recognition that being able to get to interviews, training or jobs is central to normal life, not a minor factor (Root, 1998). This reinforces that issues of unemployment and social exclusion should be part of 'integrated' approaches to transport.

Toward a multifaceted employment strategy

Finally, there is evidence that, without local employment creation, training and related supply-side measures may simply redistribute jobs among persons in employment or to the short-term unemployed, who bring many advantages to the job search. Given that there is no one answer, a multifaceted strategy is required. Table 2 sets out an initial list of the elements of a strategy.

There is evidence that most successful training schemes are those with strong links to local employers. The mix of employers attracted into the area will certainly influence the range of local employment benefits, and this should be subject to early assessment. A first step in regeneration strategy, therefore, is to ensure that inward investments meet 'win-win' criteria in terms of sectors that are likely to be economically strong in the future, and have a broad range of labour requirements, such as information and communications; environmental services; cultural and recreational facilities and so on (Commission of the European Communities, 1995).

Finally, it is worth noting that community representatives are emphatic that on-the-job training or the equivalent of 'apprenticeships' are important, and that companies must be given incentives to establish such training programmes. Unemployed people are disparaging about "training for training's sake" which they see as wasting money to little benefit. Research backs up their perception that training not linked to employment is of little value to the long-term unemployed (Turok, 1996).

Table 2: Elements of city-wide employment strategy

Function	Organisational implication
Overall coordination An employment initiative at the heart of regeneration Bending of main programmes to job creation	A single lead agency in each area should be designated to champion the unemployed, and one person (where 'the buck stops') to take overall responsibility for job creation benefits from development, and to ensure this objective is a key aspect of the development strategy. Otherwise the dictates of property-led development may prevail
Partnership of key stakeholders	All stakeholding agencies committed to employment creation should participate
Economic diversification key aspect of city-wide strategy	Under the leadership of local authority in partnership with key stakeholders
Retention of existing employers essential Promotion of new business appropriate to emerging market needs	Business support services, assistance to new businesses, market intelligence on company base – within the partnership context – can be delegated to a specialist agency
Inward investment packages	Must include employment creation commitments
Database on resident skills and incoming employer requirements	The prime responsibility of the formal development agency, but can be delegated
Career guidance, outreach, counselling, job clubs, and other confidence building work with the long-term unemployed	Building on the experience of active organisations
Adult basic education for literacy, numeracy and employability skills	The further and higher education sector should play a key role, within the context of lifelong education
Training for work and employability, and generating local social and environmental benefit, through intermediate labour market approaches Alternative employment in the community and voluntary sector	Extension and further learning from Wise Group-type initiatives* Guidance towards paid and unpaid work in the community and voluntary sector
Targets on employment Monitoring and evaluation	Regular reporting on achievements (or lack of) in getting and keeping the long-term unemployed in work essential, with commitment to understand and improve on insufficient progress Yearly evaluation of progress by a neutral outsider

*Note: * for an assessment of the Wise Group see McGregor et al (1997).*

6

A call for neighbourhood visioning

For urban regeneration, community participation represents a major challenge, given that initiatives may need to carry on for 10 to 20 years for difficult estates. With temporary participation exercises, it is often impossible to secure sustained interest. Community activists will come and go, and cannot represent residents in a fully democratic fashion, or substitute for formal governance. Over this length of time, community development to encourage participation becomes a major project in itself with sustainable regeneration indistinguishable from good urban governance.

Nor is participation something to be confined to urban regeneration areas. There are many policy areas where all residents could wish to have input to decision making: transport, housing, education, recreation and so on. Agenda 21 calls for full and lasting decentralised participation. As regeneration objectives are accomplished, residents should still have the opportunity, although not the obligation, to participate in the decisions which shape the future of their neighbourhood. Sustainability requires consensus, which is built on participation.

In local government, there is considerable interest in decentralisation, but less positive experience. All four case studies have pilot decentralisation programmes underway, and all have a long history of failed decentralisation initiatives, lapsed from lack of interest or because they were too expensive. In some cases there is confusion over the difference between managerial and physical decentralisation, and devolution or political decentralisation. Experience has shown that physical decentralisation to area offices, although sometimes worthwhile, can be expensive, causing the unit cost of service delivery to rise. Nor is the creation of area offices the same thing as devolving any real control.

Residents complain there is too much consultation, but not enough participation. Some councils argue that the complexity of council services requires a complexity of consultation mechanisms, but the argument seems biased to maintaining traditional professional control. There is no evidence that token participation reduces cynicism about local democracy. At the same time, current initiatives could be the inspiration for broader decentralisation.

A key question is not whether, or how much, to decentralise but are services delivered efficiently *and* democratically? If not, is it necessary to recast the balance between the council and its citizens? In the 21st century it is unlikely that older, top-down urban management will give rise to skilled, empowered, confident citizens. In this ‘city of the future’, residents and administrators will work together, in a cost-effective manner, to achieve strategic objectives, ensure quality of life and tackle difficult challenges of sustainability based on consensus. By recasting the balance, democracy and service delivery could benefit, and enhance the position of the city in the global marketplace. Four things are important:

- real political commitment at national and municipal levels is essential; the Scottish statutory requirement for a decentralisation strategy to be prepared by every local authority is a first step;
- systematic experiments in decentralisation, in and out of regeneration areas, are necessary, recognising that participation is a

learning process in which the way of deciding is as important as the decisions;

- these attempts must be monitored, with the participation of residents, so that learning can be applied to the next round of programmes;
- the objective has to be statutory decentralisation which enshrines citizens' rights to participation in key aspects of municipal affairs over their lifetime, and which represents a cultural change in favour of decentralisation on the part of all stakeholders.

Opportunity for neighbourhood visioning

To overcome the many constraints on genuine participation, and to side-step the plethora of inefficient consultations stemming from a myriad of departments and agencies, a streamlined, one-stop participation process for each neighbourhood is proposed. This recognises that, in addition to the often intensive participation required at the height of regeneration (which can be one-stop), local people need the opportunity for less intensive, less wearing, but *lifelong* participation which assesses neighbourhood prospects holistically rather than in the compartmentalised boxes of administration. This is important so that the achievements of regeneration are carried forward, but neighbourhood visioning can also provide a democratic framework for regeneration. And not only adults are involved – children too need the opportunity to participate because they have many good ideas, and the primary school student of today is the young adult of tomorrow.

> "A defining characteristic of disadvantaged areas is the residents' feeling that they can take no part in the decisions which affect their lives, including the availability of work, the quality of housing and the environment, and the standards of education and social facilities in their areas." (from a city-wide regeneration strategy, 1996)

Innovation Box 8: Neighbourhood Strategies Initiative in Manchester

This initiative had its origins in an analysis of housing demand in the city which revealed that, notwithstanding high levels of housing need, demand for council housing in certain neighbourhoods with severe social and economic problems was very low or non-existent. The City Council recognised that this housing issue in these 'non-sustaining' neighbourhoods could not be addressed in isolation, but needed to be considered alongside a range of other matters, in particular problems of unemployment, poverty and educational attainment.

The City Council therefore established a Working Party of Members which has initiated a comprehensive and multiagency approach to the problems of three pilot Neighbourhood Strategy areas in the City. The Neighbourhood Strategies Initiative brings together representatives of Council departments, police, probation service, local tenants' associations and a range of other interests. The strands of work in these initiatives include:

- further survey and research into problems in these areas and the existing level and pattern of public and voluntary sector provision in each;
- a multiagency approach to the specific problem of widespread social disruption and environmental degradation caused by a small number of severely anti-social families within the neighbourhoods;
- improved coordination among key service managers in the main Council service departments to improve delivery of council services and its impact on local areas;
- initiatives to promote communication, information and best practice across regeneration areas in the city.

In all cases, the intention is not to design new spending programmes but rather to bend mainstream funds and to coordinate departmental and voluntary sector processes to achieve neighbourhood regeneration objectives.

"One of the partners in this strategy is supposed to be the community. How can we have any influence if we are not informed? ... the 'vision' seeks a partnership between 'all agencies'. Maybe this is part of the problem – we are not an agency but we are those most affected by the policies." (comment on the strategy by the city's Tenants' Federation)

A neighbourhood visioning process, on a voluntary basis, would give local people the opportunity to establish a sense of purpose for local development and priorities for action by stakeholders including community groups. The focus would be on future direction and how different policy areas interact to move towards the sustainable neighbourhood, as well as providing local input to the city strategy. A major advantage in regeneration areas is that residents would not be dependent on institutional stakeholders providing the chance for participation, but would know that they could avail themselves of the opportunity to participate, *as a right of citizenship*.

Of course, not only residents but local business owners, managers and employees would also participate. This would redress the common situation where small businesses feel cut off from local authority decisions. In Birmingham, for example, the Chamber of Commerce reports that three quarters of small firms feel they are not consulted (*Chamberlink*, December 1996-January 1997). It goes without saying that local schools and voluntary organisations would also be welcome – the process would be inclusive of anyone with enthusiasm.

The output would be a broad vision for the future of the neighbourhood. Sometimes this would be easy to achieve, sometimes there could be a lot of argument. But the process should unlock real community interest and a common agenda may well emerge from the fray. This would not be a substitute for the usual service or land use planning, but would guide it.

Neighbourhood visioning as learning network

Neighbourhood visioning fits well with emerging concepts of linked top-down and bottom-up *learning networks*, which work in a less hierarchical, more egalitarian manner, thus fulfilling an organisational prerequisite set out in Chapter 3 (Stokes and Knight, 1997). It could result in contractual relationships with service providers, which set out rights and responsibilities on both sides. This could extend to service commitments which could be monitored, thereby enhancing the ability of residents to assess, and insist on, quality public services. In this way, neighbourhood visioning encourages bringing resource allocation and service decisions closer to people, enabling them to have a greater say in service delivery. Local approaches can develop, encouraging innovation, fulfilling the intentions of the government's Best Value Initiative.

Neighbourhood visioning also fits in well with the expressed desire of many local councillors to spend more time representing the interests of their wards and their constituents (Young and Rao, 1994 – reports on a survey of 1,682 councillors). For example, John Stewart notes that "in working with community forums, councillors are developing new ways of expressing their role in community governance" (Stewart, 1996, p 43). The idea of neighbourhood visioning also fits well with initiatives emerging in the case study cities, such as Local Involvement – Local Action in Birmingham, Manchester's Neighbourhood Strategies Initiative, or Edinburgh's Community Focus Workshops; elsewhere, such as local service partnerships as piloted in Coventry and Burnley, community visioning in the 'Choices for Bristol' project and, perhaps, the Community Planning initiative suggested for England by Government (Burton, 1997; Gregory, 1998).

Neighbourhood visioning should be fun, stimulating and challenging. It need not be labour intensive or expensive, need not involve any new organisations or neighbourhood offices, and would fit within attempts to devise practical, inexpensive means of decentralisation. Compared to overall municipal budgets, however constrained, the cost would be small. But it would require some resourcing in terms of local officials working with the community to understand the practicalities and constraints of urban development – a process of mutual learning. The vision could be revised every four or five years, and people could be involved all their lives if they so wished. Local people would then be 'ahead of the game' in decision making, rather than tagging along behind the institutional players. Funding mechanisms could be matched to long-term objectives, rather than dictating the nature and pace of participation.

Information technology for neighbourhood visioning

Neighbourhood visioning fits well with the growing use of information technology (IT) as a means of involving citizens. At the moment most people in the neighbourhood (and many professionals) cannot always grasp the language, the intention or the implications for them and their neighbours of local authority strategies and plans, research reports and large, integrated urban regeneration programmes. IT (say, using a neighbourhood website) offers real potential for overcoming this for three reasons:

- information 'richness' can boast confidence and abilities in a host of areas, from employment search to participation in developing regeneration strategy;
- school-age children and coming generations are, and will be, highly skilled at making use of IT, in intuitive ways which their parents never will be; IT will be an integral part of lifelong learning;
- websites, with hyper-links connecting different sites and levels of information, could enable information about the neighbourhood to be organised and accessed in a gradual learning manner, beginning with simple, child- and lay person-friendly information and graduating towards professional information, and beginning in the local neighbourhood but graduating towards information which links the neighbourhood to the wider world.

The use of IT is already underway. For example, Edinburgh's CAPINFO (Capital Information) system is a database for the general population accessed on closed network of 51 terminals, most located in public libraries, community centres and schools. Others can be found in a sports centre, a shopping mall and a multi-screen cinema. The numbers of terminals will expand, and the Council's decentralisation strategy looks forward to website and cable television access. Currently the communication is on the model council>citizen, but in future interactive links are possible such as: council–citizen, citizen–citizen and neighbourhood–neighbourhood, and so on.

In urban regeneration areas, many local schools have spare space. Neighbourhood visioning/IT centres could be established, thereby involving local children and their parents, and any interested members of the community. This is happening on Edinburgh's Craigmillar regeneration area where the Craigmillar Community Information Service links together 30 community organisations and the local library in a bulletin board service and provides free internet facilities, used extensively by many members of the community, including a group of 'cybergrans', who have established their own website (http://www.ccis.org.uk/users/bigkids). The Craigmillar Community Information Service does outreach training in IT access for the community, and expects its bulletin board service and website services to merge in two to three years. As IT systems become widespread and interactive, and move into homes themselves, there is real potential to foster information flows in both directions around neighbourhood visioning.

Box 9 shows a schematic diagram of a neighbourhood website which works at a number of levels. First, generic information on sustainable neighbourhood and city development could be linked to regularly-updated information and plans on the local neighbourhood. This could range in sophistication from simple, primary school-friendly oriented information to full, sophisticated adult information.

Second, hyper-links can be made to city-wide and regional information, for example, to show the relationship of local shopping to city and regional shopping in terms of floorspace, turnover and future plans; or local housing management schemes compared to other schemes in the city. Finally, another range of hyper-links can link this area-specific information to broader information on good practice and 'how-to' information from all over Britain and the world. For example, local organisations might want to tap into other websites on broad-based organising, Welfare to Work or other employment creation schemes, local environment action programmes, etc. The global network International Centre for Local Environmental Initiatives is just one source of information on exciting innovation at neighbourhood and city level. Digital urban design technology is also emerging which allows anyone at a terminal to range spatially over their neighbourhood, from a satellite image of the whole city to a zoom in on individual buildings and streets, to assess what is, and visions of what might be.

Potential integration of neighbourhood visioning and planning

Although local plans have a narrow, statutory focus at present, there is scope for unlocking planning processes to encompass the goals of neighbourhood visioning, economic development and employment issues and Agenda 21, and to reinforce long-term urban regeneration initiatives. For example, rather than involvement in planning being confined to *occasional* objections to proposals on statutory matters, people could be *regularly* involved in a whole variety of issues such as housing condition, tenure diversification and sites for new build; development of parks and recreation facilities; promoting the vitality of local shops; identifying sites for business and industry; considering transport proposals; and any other relevant issue with spatial implications.

In this way, the local plan would embody local vision, within the context of Unitary and Structure Plans. Local people would participate in a process of mutual learning with the planners about the future, the role of their neighbourhood in the city-region, and about the planning process itself. This kind of participative process implies that people are involved from the beginning in the development of planning objectives and development criteria, and in working up plans, rather than being presented with a fait accompli, as is too often the case.

However, there are constraints to be overcome. Currently local planning processes are slow and cumbersome: trying to anticipate planning appeals in advance and therefore very technical in orientation. This is a requirement which cannot be swept away, but it is possible to meet these technical requirements within a broader

Innovation Box 9: Diagram of interactive website for neighbourhood visioning

Spatial level of information	Child-friendly information	Layperson-friendly information	Professional information	Hyperlinks to other websites
National	+	+	+	=
Regional	+	+	+	=
City	+	+	+	=
Neighbourhood	+	+	+	=

Innovation Box 10: Local Involvement – Local Action in Birmingham

Birmingham City Council has embarked on a major initiative aimed at devolving power to the Council's 39 wards. This is to enable local people to become more directly involved in influencing Council decision making, development and service planning and delivery. Each ward in the city, with three councillors per ward, now has a ward sub-committee intended to reflect and respond to local issues. Each ward is being encouraged to set up a ward advisory board, composed principally of local residents. Their role is to foster the creation of a ward development plan, which is an analysis of local needs and a strategy for meeting them, and to advise the ward sub-committee on the implications of decisions in light of the development plan.

To assist this process, every ward has been allocated £50,000 to address immediate priorities. A senior Council manager is also designated as Lead Officer for the ward, giving a single point of focus for residents interacting with the Council over ward issues. Local Involvement – Local Action is said by Council decision makers to be having a substantial bottom-up impact on decision making and service planning.

framework. Second, combining planning and visioning would require a new kind of professionalism in planning with commitment to working with the community rather than dictating from a position of professional superiority. Of course, many planners active in urban regeneration already work in this way, described as "giving voice to communities and seeing a role for professionals as *on tap, rather than on top*" (Ward, 1995).

Neighbourhoods, communities and boundaries

Exactly what a neighbourhood is, or is not, is not defined here because it is obvious in one way, and a local issue in another. Clearly within cities there are 'areas' or 'districts' (sometimes served by area offices, as by Glasgow's housing department). Those areas are in turn made up of a series of neighbourhoods, not necessarily with official boundaries, but clearly legible to most of their residents. Neighbourhood visioning can proceed on the basis of perceived boundaries, which can be adjusted over time as part of the learning process.

Neither have we tackled the meaning of 'community' except to note that we are all members of multiple communities, some spatial – local, regional, national and so on – and some functional. There is much interesting thinking just now about the role of community in modern life, and a the relationship of the local to the global. An advantage of neighbourhood visioning is that it can foster local community at a time of globalisation of production, consumption and information.

However, the issue of service boundaries is important, because neighbourhoods are cross-cut with administrative boundaries reflecting the interests of service providers. The temptation is to say that each service is professionally unique and boundaries sacrosanct. But the service inefficiencies, in terms of failures of integration, that arise from uncoordinated boundaries may be costly in the long run. For Scottish urban regeneration PPAs for example, there is evidence that local authorities are encountering serious difficulty in monitoring and evaluating outcomes because of the mismatch between boundaries of relevant administrative units, such as school catchments and wards (Pawson et al, 1997). The indicators most seriously affected are those relating to employment and training, and to educational attainment – perhaps the most important indicators of achievement in urban regeneration.

This lack of 'coterminosity' in boundaries need not be a barrier to neighbourhood visioning however. Regeneration areas have lived with the problem for a long time. A general principle may be that coterminous boundaries for different services are more efficient, because they aid both service integration and participation. But starting with a neighbourhood definition generally accepted by local people, developing information around that definition as nearly as possible, while also moving gradually towards coterminous boundaries (or sub-boundaries), over some years, is a reasonable tactic.

Neighbourhood visioning: a national pilot project on the local authority in the 21st century

An initial step at the national level would be a pilot programme of neighbourhood visioning in a variety of local authorities. These could be in two stages over five years. The first stage would fund around 25 local authorities to mount pilot projects, half in regeneration areas and half in other neighbourhoods. These could include a variety of salient elements: voluntary involvement of local councillors in a key role, professional advice to community groups on strategic and organisational issues, use of IT, linkage of vision and statutory planning, boundary coordination, linkage of visioning and Agenda 21, and so on.

The pilot projects would only be useful if there was keen commitment in each local authority from the leader and the chief executive, which could nurture commitment from line departments and agency officers. Organisational culture would need to shift towards acceptance of this type of devolution, but also to acceptance of experimentation and mutual learning between residents, officers and councillors. During the rounds of experimentation, systematic monitoring would be required, with residents as well as researchers involved in the assessment. After the first stage, the lessons could be consolidated and a second round begun on the foundation of that knowledge.

Neighbourhood visioning – in a nutshell

This is intended to paint a picture of what might be, but not what ought to be. The purpose of the whole proposal is to trigger discussion and debate at national and local levels. The ideal format and focus of neighbourhood visioning will be decided by local government and local community groups in each city and town. This would be enabled by central government and might well include, as already exist in Scotland, statutory requirements for city-wide decentralisation strategy, beginning with pilot areas and gradually covering the city, on a learning-by-doing basis.

Focus of activity

- Broad vision on the development of the neighbourhood over, say, the next 10 years.
- Integration of that vision with statutory planning processes, driving toward consensus between residents and planning professionals, so much of the vision is found in the local plan and, where it cannot be, residents understand the larger issues at work.
- More specific priorities for institutional stakeholder action over, say, the next three to five years, including local government departments, LECs/TECs, the education authority and so on; defined as a neighbourhood strategy agreement, local service partnership, or similar.
- Priorities for resident action over a similar period, either organisational (form Neighbourhood Watch, street associations, football coaching group, etc) or action-oriented (maintain estate environment and/or nearby open space), either funded or on a voluntary basis.

How does it start?

- Local community groups, business and retail organisations form into partnership and request designation as neighbourhood visioning group from local authority; local authority in turn designates a rota of professionals to advise the process. Community development workers could be a special advisor to neighbourhoods on:
- *Capacity building and techniques* which could include community conferences, future search, open space techniques, scenario building, community planning weekends, or (plain old-fashioned) meetings.

Advantages of neighbourhood visioning

- Locally-based, one-stop issue assessment on a holistic perception of community needs rather than departmental or agency basis.
- Provides an agenda for action around key issues identified by the community.
- Influences policy at the outset of decision processes rather than token participation after decisions are made.
- Provides a valuable, tangible focus for mutual learning about practicalities and opportunities for urban development between residents and professionals.
- Empowers local community groups and the voluntary sector with strategic information.
- Provides a role in monitoring the quality of service delivery, including in regeneration areas, employment and other strategies.
- Provides guidance for coordination of catalyst funding in urban regeneration areas.
- Provides guidance for bending of main programmes.
- Enhances democracy by linking residents and local councillors around a common agenda, which the councillor takes forward in city level deliberation.
- Enhances the opportunities for local partnerships, for example, residents with retailers and local business community.
- Provides an organisational dimension to the sustainable urban village concept.

Towards the sustainable neighbourhood

Finally, Britain's urban neighbourhoods, disadvantaged or not, need to shift towards sustainable, mixed-use modes of living and working. These emphasise quality of life in terms of public and urban amenities and reduce the need for motorised transport by good public transport and a high quality walking and cycling environment. Higher-density living is an appropriate option, as research has demonstrated that densely settled urban areas are more economic in terms of energy consumption than smaller towns or rural areas, but also because higher densities support more variety in local services, commercial and the public sector (Newman and Kenworthy, 1989; Ecotec, 1993).

The basic design of the sustainable neighbourhood is a mix of housing types with shops, places of work, community facilities and recreation, all within walking or biking distance. The design guide produced for Hulme's regeneration, later replicated at the city level, is a model for the application of these principles (Hulme Regeration Limited, 1994). The Sustainable Urban Neighbourhood Initiative, based in Hulme's Homes for Change cooperative demonstration project, monitors and promotes sustainable neighbourhoods. The project itself is of 74 flats with workspaces and community facilities, developed in partnership with the Guinness Trust (Newsletter, *Sun Dial – The Sustainable Neighbourhood*, available from 41 Old Birley Street, Hulme, Manchester, M15 5RF).

Sustainable neighbourhoods will include fine grain, mixed land uses with both flexible tenure and mixed tenure housing. Flexible tenure, applicable for housing association property, allows households to 'staircase' up through part to full ownership of their houses, or to reduce their equity stake in their home down to the point of full rental if economic circumstances require. Mixed tenure estates combine full ownership and rented tenures. The advantage of mixed tenures is that more householders are likely to be in work, reducing the ghettoisation of unemployed claimants of housing benefit (Joseph Rowntree Foundation, 1996).

From an organisational point of view, sustainable neighbourhoods or urban villages are already the result of visioning and cannot be realised without keen partnership at local level between institutional stakeholders and local communities. Urban regeneration projects are providing real-life laboratories for exciting variations on this theme. The vision of a Sustainable Ancoats in Manchester's Eastside Regeneration Area is one example. Bordesley Village in the Birmingham Heartland's Regeneration Area is another. Both combine the key elements of strategy and participation. Bordesley is attracting back residents who had moved out and has a strong Neighbourhood Forum which meets regularly to put forward the concerns and ideas of the local community. In Edinburgh, the Council has joined the Urban Villages Forum and sees the concept of holistic urban villages as a guide to development in both local planning and urban regeneration.

Conclusion

The core themes of this research have been sustainability, vision, strategy, integration and participation. It is about a revival in our cities, a regeneration, but also about extending the benefits of this revival to all residents so that no one is excluded. If cities are more desirable places to live, pressure is reduced on our precious and diminishing rural areas. Leadership, determination and imagination are required, from both institutional stakeholders and from communities of all sort. The research has argued that organisational innovation can unlock real benefits to the process, particularly integration of bottom-up with the top-down and all the points in-between.

The purpose has been to better understand how we can shift to a virtuous cycle of regeneration rather than tolerating recurring, intergenerational multiple deprivation. The main priorities for sustainable urban regeneration are straightforward:

- to eliminate substandard and energy inefficient housing;
- to secure major achievements in the educational qualification of coming generations;

- to increase employment opportunities for all households;
- to build healthy, sustainable neighbourhoods, in the context of sustainable cities and regions;
- to provide opportunities for genuine, lifelong participation in sustainable development.

References

Birmingham City Council (1996) *Economic development strategy for Birmingham, 1996-99*, Birmingham: Birmingham City Council.

Birmingham City Pride (1995) *Moving forward together: Birmingham's City Pride prospectus*, Birmingham: Birmingham City Pride.

Burton, P. (1997) *Community visioning: An evaluation of the 'Choices for Bristol' project*, Bristol: The Policy Press.

Carley, M. (1990) *Housing and neighbourhood renewal: New urban challenge*, London: Policy Studies Institute.

Carley, M. (1991) 'Business in urban regeneration partnerships: a case study in Birmingham', *Local Economy*, vol 6, no 2, pp 100-15.

Carley, M. (1995a) 'The bigger picture: organising for sustainable urban regeneration', *Town and Country Planning*, vol 64, no 9, pp 236-40.

Carley, M. (1995b) *Using information for sustainable urban regeneration*, Innovation Report 4, Edinburgh: Scottish Homes.

Carley, M. (1996) *Sustainable transport and retail vitality*, Edinburgh: Scottish Historic Burghs Association/Donaldsons.

Carley, M. and Christie, I. (1992) *Managing sustainable development*, London: Earthscan/ Kogan Page.

Carley, M. and Spapens, P. (1998) *Sharing the world: Sustainable living and global equity in the 21st century*, London: Earthscan/Kogan Page.

City of Edinburgh Council (1997) *Scheme of decentralisation*, Edinburgh: City of Edinburgh Council.

City Pride (199?) *Employment, enterprise and training SRB 95-96*, Manchester: City Pride.

City Pride (1997) *Prospectus*, Draft for consultation, Manchester: City Pride.

Clarke, M. and Prior, D. (1996) 'City Pride in Birmingham – an experiment in urban policy and governance', unpublished paper.

Clasen, J., Gould, A. and Vincent, J. (1997) *Long-term unemployment and the threat of social exclusion*, Bristol: The Policy Press.

Commission of the European Communities (1995) *A European strategy for encouraging local development and employment initiatives*, Com 95: 273, Brussels: Commission of the European Communities.

Dekker, A. (1994) 'Dutch environmental policy: the 1994 balance', in *Proceedings of the 22nd Summer Annual Meeting*, PTRC.

Dwelly, T. (1996) *Living in the future: 24 sustainable development ideas from the UK*, York: Joseph Rowntree Foundation.

Economic and Social Research Council (ESRC) (1996) *Annual report*, ESRC.

Ecotec (1993) *Reducing transport emissions through planning*, London: HMSO.

Fordham, G. (1995) *Made to last: Creating sustainable neighbourhood and estate regeneration*, York: Joseph Rowntree Foundation.

Glasgow City Council (1997) *Business plan for education in Glasgow*, Glasgow: Education Department, Glasgow City Council.

Glasgow Regeneration Alliance (GRA) (nd) *Shaping the future: A commitment to area regeneration*, Glasgow: GRA.

GRA Roads and Transport Working Group and Webster, D. (1994) *Housing, transport and employment in Glasgow*, Glasgow: GRA.

Gregory, S. (1998) *Transforming local services: Partnership in action*, PEP Report, York: York Publishing Services.

Hambleton, R. (1996) *Leadership in local government*, Bristol: Faculty of the Built Environment, University of the West of England.

Haughton, G. (1997) 'Developing sustainable urban development models', *Cities*, vol 14, no 4.

Her Majesty's Government (1994) *Sustainable development: The UK strategy*, Cmnd 2426, London: HMSO.

Hulme Regeneration Limited (1994) *A guide to development: Hulme, Manchester*, Manchester: Hulme Regeration Limited.

Joseph Rowntree Foundation (1996) *Mixed and flexible tenure in practice: A briefing note*, York: Joseph Rowntree Foundation.

Kirk, K. and Carley, M. (1998 forthcoming) *Strategic urban regeneration: The view from the bottom up*, Research Paper Series, Edinburgh: School of Planning and Housing, Heriot-Watt University.

Loftman, P. and Neven, B. (1994) 'Prestige project developments: economic renaissance or economic myth? A case study of Birmingham', *Local Economy*, vol 8, no 4, pp 307-25.

McCarthy, J. (1997) 'Empowerment or exclusion', *Town and Country Planning*, January.

McGregor, A. et al (1992) *A review and critical evaluation of strategic approaches to urban regeneration*, Research Report 22, Edinburgh: Scottish Homes.

McGregor, A. et al (1997) *Bridging the jobs gap: An evaluation of the Wise Group and the intermediate labour market*, Glasgow: Training and Employment Research Unit, University of Glasgow.

McNulty, D. (1996) *The future of public policy in Scotland in the context of local government reorganisation*, Caledonian Papers, Glasgow: Glasgow Caledonian University.

Manchester City Council (1996) *Moss Side Initiative phase II delivery plan*, Manchester: Resource Procurement Group, Manchester City Council.

Ministry of Housing, Spatial Planning and the Environment (1994) *National environmental policy plan 2* (English summary), The Hague: Ministry of Housing, Spatial Planning and the Environment.

Mullaney, A. (1997) 'Auditing equity', *Town and Country Planning*, vol 66, no 6, June, pp 162-3.

National Consumer Council (1997) *A consumer blueprint for a greener world*, London: National Consumer Council.

National Housing Federation (1997) *Housing for a competitive economy*, London: National Housing Federation.

Newman, P. and Kenworthy, J. (1989) *Cities and automobile dependence*, Aldershot: Gower Technical.

Organisation for Economic Cooperation and Development (OECD) (1997) *OECD education database*, Paris: OECD.

Page, D. (1993) *Building for communities: A study of new housing association estates*, York: Joseph Rowntree Foundation.

Pawson, H. and Lancaster, S. (1997) 'Research to establish baseline data for PPAs', Interim report to the Scottish Office, Edinburgh: School of Planning and Housing, Heriot-Watt University, unpublished.

Progress Trust (1996) *Progress Trust: SRB challenge fund bid 1997-2004*.

Roberts, P. (1997) 'Regional planning and the RDAs: welcome first steps', *Town and Country Planning*, September.

Rogers, Lord Richard (1997) Maiden speech to the House of Lords, 20 May.

Root, A. (1998) 'Poverty – home alone', *Transport Retort*, vol 21.

Roseland, M. (1997) 'Dimensions of the eco-city', *Cities*, vol 14, no 4.

Royal Commission on Environmental Pollution (1994) *Eighteenth report: Transport and the environment*, London: HMSO.

Scottish Homes (1995) *A community participation strategy for urban regeneration*, Edinburgh: Scottish Homes.

Scottish Office, The (1995) *Programme for partnership*, Edinburgh: The Scottish Office.

Spangenberg, J. (ed) (1994) *Towards sustainable Europe: The study*, Wuppertal: The Wuppertal Institute.

Stewart, J. (1996) *Reviewing structures and processes for councillors*, Birmingham: School of Public Policy, University of Birmingham.

Stokes, P. and Knight, B. (1997) *Organising a civil society*, Birmingham: Foundation for Civil Society.

Turok, I. (1996) 'Work within and outside of the labour market', Theme Paper 5, York: Area Regeneration Subcommittee, Joseph Rowntree Foundation.

Turok, I. and Hopkins, N. (1997) *Picking winners or passing the buck?*, Glasgow: Department of Urban Studies, University of Glasgow.

United Nations' Development Programme (1996) *Human development report 1996*, Oxford: Oxford University Press.

Ward, C. (1995) quoting Tony Gibson, in *Town and Country Planning*, vol 64, no 9, September.

Watt, G. (1995) 'Health and wellbeing in an ecological city', in *Urban regeneration, health and livelihoods in Glasgow*, Report of OECD Seminar.

Webster, D. (1994) *Home and workplace in the Glasgow conurbation: Summary paper*, Glasgow: Glasgow City Housing Department.

Wintle, M. and Reeve, R. (eds) (1994) *Rhetoric and reality in environmental policy*, Studies in Green Research, Aldershot: Avebury.

Young, K. and Rao, N. (1994) *Coming to terms with change? The local government councillor in 1993*, London: LGC Communications.

Appendix: The estate and strategic regeneration – the view from the bottom up

> "Every time we go into this exercise it is as though it is new. In spite of the community development work done, we always seem to be starting at the beginning." (Glasgow City councillor)

> "The whole process is a messy business. We are probably too close to City Challenge to see where the missed opportunities were.... A lot of people will continue to reinvent the wheel. Until you get real community involvement it will never be sustainable." (community worker, Birmingham)

During the course of the research, it was decided to take the opportunity to extend the project from the city-wide perspective to include some analysis of strategic regeneration from the view of community representatives active in estate or neighbourhood initiatives in the four cities. It was also decided to focus on areas where regeneration was recently initiated or in progress, and which had not been the object of much study. The areas selected were Newtown, South Aston, Birmingham; Cheetham–Broughton, a cross-boundary initiative in Manchester and Salford; North Glasgow; and Craigmillar in Edinburgh.

This analysis has informed the main report. However, because this was outside the terms of reference of the original project, and thus running to a slightly different schedule, the main output of this analysis will be published separately (Kirk and Carley, 1998 forthcoming). The publication will give full details of the case studies. Here we summarise some preliminary conclusions.

Research findings

Starting point – auditing scope and extent of existing community activity

The situation prior to the introduction of a regeneration initiative can influence its success in terms of efforts to involve the community. The nature and scope of existing community activity, the legacy of previous initiatives and the historic relationship between residents and the agencies all have an impact. Familiarity with the history of the community and past attempts at participation is a building block of future development work.

There are advantages to building on existing structures, but it is also important to build in a mechanism for the inclusion of other interests as an initiative gains momentum – some residents move on, new residents move in, new groups are formed, and so on. Where participation structures do not exist and those involved are starting from scratch, community initiatives may have to overcome a distrust of authority and a legacy of failed initiative.

A community audit is a good start to a process of understanding. For Cheetham and Broughton in Manchester for example, this was supplemented by a survey of community groups' needs and priorities. However, it is important to stress that the benefits will be lost if the findings of such a needs survey are not incorporated into the main regeneration strategy.

Defining boundaries – recognising the 'real' geography of communities

The extent to which a designated regeneration area recognises the geography of people and communities, and follows natural boundaries, can be important to successfully integrating community interests. For example, the large Glasgow North Priority Regeneration Area (70,000 residents) has been defined by need and Priority Partnership funding arrangements. However, it is made up of a number of separate communities, each with its own district identity and with little interaction between. The need to link these communities in a common agenda is a hurdle to coordination at a strategic level. However, a strategic approach can also be constrained by the targeting of deprivation on too small a scale. This can mean neighbouring communities with equally serious problems being treated differently, resulting in marginalisation and local resentment.

The benefits of commitment to the wider strategic area also need to be balanced against the practicalities of dilution of resources. There is no easy answer to the question of how to define the boundaries of targeted regeneration areas. However, as noted in the main report, it has to be a matter of learning by doing, that is consolidating knowledge of workable neighbourhood and area boundaries from one year to the next for the purposes of municipal governance and community initiative.

Identifying who speaks for the community

The case studies demonstrate that on setting up an initiative, identifying who speaks for the community can be problematic and have major implications on the success of initiative in terms of credibility in the eyes of councillors, officials and the wider community. Each area studied is dealing with this issue in a different way, but the need for some kind of mechanism for ensuring 'representativeness' has been central to all.

Careful thinking from the outset on the role of proposed structures is crucial to integrating community views. There is too often an assumption that "if you involve the community in some way, everything will be OK". Often community structures are set up for the benefit of the regeneration initiative, but without reflecting communities' needs. Similarly, because such structures may be in themselves top-down, they are unlikely to continue beyond the life of the initiative.

Evidence from the case studies suggests the need to guard against community structures being used as a vehicle in local power struggles. As one person put it, once people see the object of the exercise as capturing the structure, it then becomes unsuitable for delivering anything. In the Manchester and Birmingham case studies, an additional consideration focused on the extent to which it is appropriate to pursue a spatially-defined, neighbourhood approach where residents' loyalties are strongly defined by religion or ethnicity. In these circumstances, barriers are difficult to break down and, sometimes, those involved do not want them broken down, being keen to preserve their sense of community. How policy makers handle these kind of difficult and delicate issues can have major implications for the success of a regeneration initiative. One lesson is that as soon as there is a problem of this sort, it should be tackled head on rather than being allowed to drift. It also suggests that participants should not be afraid of abandoning organisational arrangements which are not working.

Involvement in a strategic visioning process

An important factor for the community is the extent to which the regeneration plan reflects community interests. Institutional stakeholders often have priorities which do not coincide with those of the community. In particular, emphasis on physical development and flagship projects can be at odds with more 'invisible needs' such as provision for childcare, young people, elderly and small-scale social facilities. As noted in the main report, a fundamental problem is where physical regeneration fails to address chronic unemployment.

Sometimes, in a not unreasonable haste to take advantage of funding opportunities, the regeneration strategy becomes officer driven, with little input from community. The need to respond to tight deadlines and the amount of information needed for bidding makes it difficult for communities without established participation structures to organise around a bidding process. Many local people spoken to during the course of this analysis felt that it would be a 'real boon' if the tightness of deadlines for producing regeneration funding proposals could be eased to allow more time for real community involvement at this crucial initial stage of regeneration. This is a good argument for neighbourhood visioning – even where regeneration initiatives are not yet intended.

Beyond local area regeneration strategy, a second stage of strategic thinking is for community organisations to participate more fully in forums which set the city-wide strategy. Here, where the opportunity presents itself, residents can develop their abilities to participate. For example, community representatives attending the city-wide Capital City Partnership in Edinburgh find meetings useful in developing consensus between regeneration areas at opposite ends of the city which used to feel in competition with each other for scarce resources, and in positive learning from each other's experience.

> "If you are going to get consensus, you need to start on that basis and not draw in the community later down the road. The community is keen to achieve joint understanding on the issues and what they entail, to identify priorities for action, appropriate responses and how and when they be brought forward. The main thing is that we can't be part of seeking solutions if residents aren't equal partners in the 'seeking' process." (community worker, Salford)

On partnership and capacity building

A key to the quality of community involvement is the extent to which partnership structures allow access to decision making. The dynamics of partnership, and the extent to which the community is recognised as an equal partner, impacts on whether community priorities are taken on board. Officers sometimes assume strategic plans are beyond the comprehension of the community. Residents, however, argue that confusion arises over the way strategic plans are put across using complex professional concepts and language rather than any failure on their part to grasp the underlying issues.

The resources dedicated to setting up community structures and building human resource capability to engage in strategic thinking should match the scale of the task involved, especially if other barriers are significant. The development of strategic skills as part of training programmes for community activists can help. A positive feature of Manchester's approach has been an emphasis early in the life of SRB on the need for a capacity-building strategy.

The need for adequate time to develop capacity was also emphasised. In one area, residents noted that by the time residents became organised the three-year initiative was virtually over. More appropriate timescales should involve anything from at least 4 to 20 years. Putting in place resources such as development workers *prior* to commencement of an initiative could be of real benefit.

A particular problem is for community organisations to have the structure, financial systems and technical writing/language abilities to go to funders and prepare lengthy bids. The benefits of developing the infrastructure of the community and voluntary sector were highlighted in this regard. Respondents point particularly to problems associated with accessing European Social Funding. Although the programme aims to reach the most disadvantaged groups, its highly bureaucratic application process often defeats community bids. Cooperation between community groups and another institutional partner can help overcome this.

Leadership and strategic vision – the role of councillors

As ward representative and a link to wider council policy and expenditure, councillors have a critical role to play in the support of community priorities. Communities that have a good relationship with their councillor benefit considerably in terms of access to officers and wider decision-making processes. In a number of the case study areas, it was local councillors who had taken the initiative in promoting the establishment of a vehicle to give voice to resident views.

Community-led resource allocation

Each of the case study areas had experimented with either involving community representatives in spending decisions or with providing a budget which they could then allocate to local initiatives in line with community priorities. In Scotland, this is by way of formal community involvement in Urban Programme decisions. At best, when funding for projects connects directly with a community's strategic objectives, this can lead to a surge of community activity directly related to local priorities. However, although welcome, the need to respond fairly to numerous competing but worthy funding applications in a time of budget constraints, and to juggle grants to maintain employment in community projects, can severely cut into the time needed to develop a strategic approach. Effective monitoring to ensure accountability in the use of public money is also important for the credibility of the process.

> "I'd rather we got the foundations of a pilot right. To start small and work through trial and error and to know if it is sustainable – that's the key." (officer, Manchester)

Funding mechanisms and the need for a long-term perspective

The short-term nature of community funding, the uncertainty associated with the Urban Programme and the need to secure match funding undermine community groups' ability to plan ahead and work consistently towards vital community objectives. The need for long-term strategies to tackle problems such as unemployment run counter to the notion that community-led approaches should be short term in budget commitment.

Many respondents emphasised that somehow we need to move away from this project mentality and provide core funding for essential community development services. Similarly, the chance for newly established organisations and organisations working in new fields to experiment and make mistakes and not be punished for taking risks was highlighted.

> "How many times can you put a new spin on it, tart it up, give it another coat of gloss? Why can't we just say we are looking for funding because it works. But it looks like we will all have to do this, go to the dressing up box. But maybe, if enough people say that basic services are needed." (community worker, Birmingham)